QUALITATIVE RESEARCHING
WITH TEXT,
IMAGE AND SOUND

QUALITATIVE RESEARCHING WITH TEXT, IMAGE AND SOUND

A Practical Handbook

Edited by
Martin W. Bauer and George Gaskell

SAGE Publications
London • Thousand Oaks • New Delhi

SAGE Publications Ltd
6 Bonhill Street
London EC2A 4PU

SAGE Publications Inc
2455 Teller Road
Thousand Oaks, California 91320

SAGE Publications India Pvt Ltd
32, M-Block Market
Greater Kailash – I
New Delhi 110 048

British Library Cataloguing in Publication data

A catalogue record for this book
is available from the British Library

ISBN 0 7619 6480 0
ISBN 0 7619 6481 9 (pbk)

Library of Congress catalog card record available

Typeset by Photoprint, Torquay, Devon
Printed in Great Britain by The Cromwell Press Ltd,
Trowbridge, Wiltshire

Contents

List of Contributors

Bas Aarts is Reader in Modern English Language and Director of the Survey of English Usage at University College London. His main research interest is present-day English syntax. His publications include *Small Clauses in English: The Nonverbal Types* (1992, Mouton de Gruyter), *The Verb in Contemporary English: Theory and Description* (1995, edited with C.F. Meyer, Cambridge University Press) and *English Syntax and Argumentation* (1997, Macmillan).

Nicolas C. Allum is a Research Officer at the Methodology Insitute, London School of Economics and Political Science. He is currently investigating public perceptions of biotechnology with George Gaskell and Martin Bauer. His doctoral research focuses on risk perception, trust and moral reasoning in respect to controversial technologies. Other interests are voting behaviour, computer-assisted textual analysis, and philosophies of science and probability. Recent publications include 'Worlds Apart? The Reception of Genetically Modified Foods in Europe and the US', *Science*, July 16 1999; and 'A Social Representations Approach to the Analysis of Three Textual Corpora using ALCESTE', MSc thesis, LSE, 1998.

Martin W. Bauer read Psychology and History at the University of Bern, and has a PhD from the London School of Economics. He is Lecturer in Social Psychology and Research Methodology at the LSE and Research Fellow at the Science Museum, London. He researches science and technology in public perceptions and media reportage, and the functions of resistance in organisational and societal transformation. Recent publications include 'Towards a Paradigm for Research on Social Representations', *Journal for the Theory of Social Behaviour*, (vol. 29, 1999), 'The Medicalisation of Science News – from the Rocket-Scalpel to the Gene-Meteorite Complex', *Social Science Information* (vol. 37, 1998); *Resistance to New Technology: Nuclear power, Information Technology, Biotechnology* (1997, Cambridge University Press).

Robert Boyce teaches International History at the London School of Economics where he specialises in the politics of international economic relations. Among his recent publications are studies of the interwar economic crisis, central bank relations, the development of high-speed communications, the economic origins of the Second World War, the British beverage industry inside Europe, and French monetary policy.

Uwe Flick is a sociologist and psychologist and Professor for Empirical Nursing Research at the Alice-Salomon University of Applied Sciences, Berlin, Germany, and Privatdozent in Psychology at the Technical University of Berlin, Germany. Research interests include everyday knowledge, social representations, qualitative methodology, individual and public health and technological change in everyday life. Recent publications include *An Introduction to Qualitative Research* (1999, Sage) and *Psychology of the Social* (edited with U. Flick, 1998, Cambridge University Press).

Gerhard Faßnacht is Privatdozent at the Department of Psychology, University of Bern, Switzerland. His research interests include personality (in particular social development), human ethology, observation, diagnostics, research methodology and philosophy of science. Recent publications include *Systematische Verhaltensbeobachtung* (3rd fully revised edition, 1995, Reinhardt); and *Theory and Practice of Observing Behaviour* (1982, Academic Press).

George Gaskell is Professor of Social Psychology and Director of the Methodology Institute at the London School of Economics. He lectures in the areas of research design, surveys and questionnaires, qualitative inquiry, attitudes and social representations and economic psychology. Recent research projects include cognitive aspects of survey methodology and an international comparative study of public perceptions of modern biotechnology. He is editor of *Societal Psychology* (1990, Sage) with H. Himmelweit, and *Biotechnology in the Public Sphere* (1998, Science Museum Press) with John Durant and Martin Bauer.

Rosalind Gill is a social psychologist who lectures in Gender Theory at the LSE. She is an expert in media and new technologies and is author of *The Gender-Technology Relation* (with Keith Grint, 1995, Taylor & Francis) and *Gender and the Media: Representations, Audiences and Cultural Politics* (2000, Polity Press).

Sandra Jovchelovitch is a Lecturer in Social Psychology at the London School of Economics and Political Sciences. She has worked extensively with local communities and publishes widely in the field of social representations. Her current research is on how transformations in public spheres shape the production and rationality of social representations.

Udo Kelle is a Lecturer in Social Research Methods at the University of Vechta. His main research interests cover the fields of methodology of quantitative and qualitative research, decision theory and sociology of the life course. Currently he works on concepts to integrate qualitative and quantitative methods in social research. He is the editor of *Computer-aided Qualitative Data Analysis: Methods, Theory and Practice* (1995, Sage).

Nicole Kronberger is a Master of Psychology, University of Vienna. Her research focus is on social psychological issues of morality, public understanding of science and qualitative analysis. Recent publications include *Schwarzes Loch, Geistige Lähmung und Dornröschenschlaf: Ein Metaphernanalytischer Beitrag zur Erfassung von Alltagsvorstellungen von Depression* (*Black Hole, Mental Paralysis and Deep Sleep: a Metaphor Analysis of Lay Conceptions of Depression*) and *Psychotherapie und Sozialwissenschaft* (1999) 1 (2), 85–104.

Joan Leach is a Lecturer in Science Communication at the Imperial College of Science, Technology & Medicine. She received her Arts Baccalaureate in English Literature and Science Baccalaureate in Biology from the University of Illinois at Urbana-Champaign. She received her Master in Communication and her PhD as an Andrew Mellon Doctoral Fellow in the Rhetoric of Science from the University of Pittsburgh. She is editor of the quarterly journal *Social Epistemology*, and has published on discourse ethics, the history of the role of communicators in science and medicine, and the representations of science in the media during the BSE crisis. She teaches an undergraduate course on Science Communication and lectures on the MSc course in Science Communication at Imperial College.

Miltos Liakopoulos completed his PhD at the London School of Economics on the controversy over GM food in Britain. His research is on public attitudes to biotechnology and media coverage of biotechnology.

Peter Loizos had a first career as a documentary film-maker before turning to social anthropology, which he has taught at the LSE since 1969. He is the author or co-editor of *The Greek Gift: Politics in a Cypriot Village*; *The Heart Grown Bitter: A Chronicle of Cypriot War Refugees*; *Gender and Kinship in Modern Greece* (with E. Papataxiarchis); *Choosing Research Methods: Data Collection for Development Workers* (with Bryan Pratt); *Innovation in Ethnographic Film: From Innocence to Self-consciousness*; *Conceiving Persons: Ethnographies of Procreation* (with P. Heady), and over 50 papers, reports, chapters and articles on a range of themes, including property transfer and class; political development and patronage; ethnic conflict; participation in DFID development projects (Nepal, and Nigeria), refugee adaptation to destitution, and refugee social capital conservation; and issues in television film representation.

Greg Myers is a Senior Lecturer in Linguistics and Modern English Language at Lancaster University, where he teaches on the programme in Culture, Media and Communications. His most recent book is *Ad Worlds: Brands, Media, Audiences* (1999, Arnold), and he is working on the dynamics of opinion in focus groups. The work in his chapter was supported in part by a grant from the Economic and Social Research Council (UK).

Gemma Penn gained her PhD in 1998 from the Department of Social Psychology at the LSE, where she also lectured for two years. She is currently working as a freelance social research and statistics consultant. Her research interests include advertising and sales promotion, the social psychology of health, with a particular emphasis on smoking and medicalisation and on patient satisfaction with service provision.

Diana Rose was educated at Aberdeen and London Universities and holds a PhD from the latter. She has written widely on sociolinguistics, qualitative methods, social represenations, analyses of television and mental health. She has lectured in social psychology and women's studies and is currently senior researcher at the User-Focused Monitoring team at The Sainsbury Centre for Mental Health in London. Diana Rose is a survivor of the mental health system.

Wolfgang Wagner is Professor at the Department of Social and Economic Psychology, University of Linz, Austria. His research interests span everyday cultural and social thinking, social representation theory, distributed and shared cognition, group processes, and problems of transfer and applications of theory in professional practice. His many publications include *Alltagsdiskurs: die Theorie Sozialer Repräsentationen* (*Everyday discourse: The Theory of Social Representations* (1994), Göttingen: Hogrefe).

Introduction

Martin W. Bauer and George Gaskell

This book has a history of some five years. It started in the Methodology Institute of the London School of Economics, established to provide research students with a broad training in quantitative and qualitative research methods. We were responsible for the development of courses and support for qualitative research. At that time increasing numbers of students and researchers were happily engaged in qualitative studies, and publishers even more happily supplied an increasing number of books which fuelled a strange war of words between quantitative and qualitative methods. The idea that these are mutually exclusive approaches within social inquiry has a long history, objectified in the very useful series of green and blue volumes produced by Sage.

In our endeavours we have tried to avoid three popular stances. First, we are reluctant to equate qualitative research with the knowledge interest of 'empowerment' or 'giving voice to the oppressed'. Though these may be laudable enthusiasms, in the context of much qualitative research practice they are at best naive and possibly misguided. Secondly, we consider the range of data available to social research to go beyond words elicited in interviews. From the beginning we have included other forms of text as well as images and sound materials in our consideration of sources of data. Thirdly, we consider the epistemological battles between qualitative and quantitative researchers, between a variety of ingroups and outgroups, as polemical, verbose and unproductive. Hence we focused our effort on clarifying procedures, public accountability and good practice in empirical inquiries. This philosophy, which one could broadly identify as 'social constructivist', informed our search for like-minded contributors to this book. Some of the authors are from the LSE and have contributed to the methodology teaching programme for several years. We found other distinguished practitioners who accepted the invitation to contribute to what might be termed the 'LSE approach' to qualitative research: to focus on procedures and good practice, and to avoid epistemological obfuscations.

After an introduction to the key issues of quantity, quality and knowledge interests, the book is structured into four parts.

Part I covers different ways of collecting data, and different types of data: text, image and sound materials. The main argument here is that corpus construction is the principle that allows for systematic collection of data without following a statistical sampling rationale. Part II introduces eight different analytic approaches covering again text, image and sound materials. Each approach introduces its specific nomenclature, is briefly contextualized, provides an example, and explicates the procedures step-by-step followed by a discussion of what constitutes good practice.

Part III introduces two types of computer support for data analysis – indexing and coding, otherwise known as CAQDAS, and KWIC co-occurrence analysis – as examples of the considerable movement in software development in this area. Part IV addresses problems of interpretations from the point of view of the historian who seeks to understand actors in the past, but whose problems are similar to those of the social researcher. Eleven fallacies of interpretation give an indication of what can go wrong in any attempt to interpret the situated 'other'. Finally, we propose our recommendations about quality criteria for qualitative research. We outline six criteria that are different from but functionally equivalent, in terms of public accountability, to the traditional criteria of representative sampling, reliability and validity. Criteria for the assessment of qualitative research are unavoidable, but different ones apply to define good practice.

We express our gratitude to colleagues in the Institute and students on the MSc Social Research Methods course for their encouragement and constructive criticism as this volume took shape, and thank Jane Gregory for her assiduous editing of the manuscript.

1

Quality, Quantity and Knowledge Interests: Avoiding Confusions

Martin W. Bauer, George Gaskell and Nicholas C. Allum

KEYWORDS

data analysis
data elicitation
the ideal research situation
knowledge interests

the law of instrument
mode and medium of representation
research design

Imagine a football match. Two opposing players run after the ball, and suddenly one of them falls to the ground, rolling over several times. Half the spectators whistle and shout, and the other half are relieved that the potential danger is over.

We may analyse this competitive social situation in the following terms. First, there are the actors: the football players, 11 on each side, highly trained, skilled and coordinated in their roles for the purpose of winning the match; and the officials, namely the referee and the linesmen. This is the 'field of action'.

Then we have the spectators. Most of the spectators are loyal supporters of one or other of the teams. Very few do not identify with either of the teams. However, there may be one or two spectators who are new to football, and are just curious. The terraces of the spectators are the 'field of naive observation' − naive in the sense that the spectators are basically enjoying events on the pitch, and are almost a part of the game itself, which they may experience almost as if they were players. Through their loyalty to one of the teams, they think and feel with a partisan perspective. When one of the players falls, this is interpreted by his supporters as indicating foul play, while for the opposing fans it is a self-inflicted and theatrical stumble.

Finally, there is the position from which we describe the situation as we do here. We are curious about the tribal nature of the event, of the field of action, and of the spectators under observation. Ideally this description requires a detached analysis of the situation, with no direct involvement with either team. Our indirect involvement may be in football in general – its present problems and its future. This we call the 'field of systematic observation'. From this position, we may be able to assemble three forms of evidence: what is going on on the field, the reactions of the spectators, and the institution of football as a branch of sport, show business or commerce. Avoiding direct involvement requires precautions: (a) a trained awareness of the consequences that arise from personal involvement; and (b) a commitment to assessing one's observations methodically and in public.

Such observations with different degrees of detachment are the problematic of social research. By analogy we can readily extend this 'ideal type' analysis of what we call a 'complete research situation' (Cranach et al., 1982: 50) to other social activities, such as voting, working, shopping and making music, to mention just a few. We can study the field of action, and ask what the events are in the field (the object of study); we may subjectively experience each event – what is happening, how it feels, and what are the motives for it. This naive observation is analogous to the perspective of the actors as self-observers. Finally, we focus on the subject – object relation that arises from the comparison of the actor perspective and the observer perspective within a larger context, and ask how events relate to people's experience of them.

Adequate coverage of social events requires a multitude of methods and data: methodological pluralism arises as a methodological necessity. Recording the action field requires (a) the systematic observation of events; inferring the meanings of these events from the (self-) observations of the actors and spectators requires (b) techniques of interviewing; and interpreting the material traces that are left behind by the actors and the spectators requires (c) systematic analysis.

Research design: data elicitation, reduction and analysis

It is useful to distinguish four methodological dimensions in social research. These dimensions describe the research process in terms of combinations of elements across all four dimensions. First, there is the research design according to the strategic principles of research, such as the sample survey, participant observation, case studies, experiments and quasi-experiments. Secondly, there are the data elicitation methods, such as interviewing, observation and the collection of documents. Thirdly, there are the data analytic procedures, such as content analysis, rhetorical analysis, discourse analysis and statistics. And finally, knowledge interests refer to Habermas's classification into control, consensus building and emancipation of the subjects of study. The four dimensions are elaborated in Table 1.1.

Much methodological confusion and many false claims arise from the confounding of the qualitative/quantitative distinction of data eliciting and

Table 1.1 *The four dimensions of the research process*

Design principles	Data elicitation	Data analysis	Knowledge interests
Case study	Individual interviewing	*Formal*	
Comparative study	Questionnaire	Statistical modelling	
Sample survey	Focus groups	Structuralist analysis	Control and prediction
Panel survey	Film		Consensus building
Experiment	Audiovisual recordings	*Informal*	Emancipation and
Participant	Systematic observation	Content analysis	empowerment
observation	Collection of documents	Coding	
Ethnography	Recording of sounds	Indexing	
		Semiotical analysis	
		Rhetorical analysis	
		Discourse analysis	

analysis with principles of research design and knowledge interests. It is quite possible to conceive an experimental design accommodating in-depth interviewing to elicit data. Equally, a case-study design may incorporate a survey questionnaire together with observational techniques, for example to study a business corporation in trouble. A large-scale survey of an ethnic minority group may include open questions for qualitative analysis, and the results may serve the emancipatory interests of the minority group. Or we can think of a random survey of a population, collecting data through focus group interviews. However, as the last example shows, certain combinations of design principles and data eliciting methods occur less frequently because of their resource implications. We contend that all four dimensions should be viewed as relatively independent choices in the research process, and the choice of qualitative or quantitative is primarily a decision of data eliciting and analysis methods, and only secondarily one of research design or knowledge interests.

While our examples have included survey research, in this volume we deal mainly with data eliciting and analysis procedures within the practice of qualitative research, that is, non-numerical research.

Modes and mediums of representation: types of data

Two distinctions about data may be helpful in this book. The world as we know and experience it, that is, the represented world and not the world in itself, is constituted in communication processes (Berger and Luckmann, 1979; Luckmann, 1995). Social research therefore rests on social data – data about the social world – which are the outcome of, and are realized in, communication processes.

In this book we distinguish two modes of social data: informal and formal communication. Furthermore, we distinguish three media out of which data can be constructed: text, image and sound materials (see Table 1.2). Informal communication has few explicit rules: people can talk, draw or sing in any way they like. That there are few explicit rules does not mean that rules do not exist, and it may be that the very focus of social research is

Table 1.2   *Modes and media*

Medium/mode	Informal	Formal
Text	Interviews	Newspapers Radio programmes
Image	Children's drawings Telephone drawings	Pictures Photographs
Sound	Spontaneous singing Soundscapes	Musical scripts Sound rituals
'Biased', 'false' or staged accounts	Strategic noise	False claims to representation

to uncover the hidden order of the informal world of everyday life (see Myers, Chapter 11 in this volume, on conversation analysis). In social research we are interested in how people spontaneously express themselves and talk about what is important to them, and how they think about their actions and those of others. Informal data are constructed less according to the rules of competence such as govern text writing, painting or musical composition, and more on the spur of the moment, or under the influence of the researcher. The problem arises that the interviewees tell what they think the researcher would like to hear. We need to recognize false accounts, which may say more about the researcher and the research process than about the researched.

On the other hand, there are acts of communication that are highly formal in the sense that competence requires specialist knowledge. People need to be trained to write articles for a newspaper, to generate pictures for an advertisement, or to produce an arrangement for a brass band or a symphony orchestra. A competent person has mastered the rules of the trade, sometimes in order to break them productively, which is called innovation. Formal communication follows the rules of the trade. The fact that the researcher uses the resulting traces, such as a newspaper article, for social research is unlikely to influence the act of communication: it makes no difference to what the journalist wrote. In this sense data based on traces are unobtrusive. However, a second-order problem arises in that the communicators may claim to represent a social group that, in reality, they do not represent. The social scientist must recognize these false claims of representation.

Formal data reconstruct the ways in which social reality is represented by a social group. A newspaper represents the world for a group of people in an accepted way, otherwise people would not buy it. In this context the newspaper becomes an indicator of their worldview. The same may be true for pictures that people consider interesting and desirable, or music that is appreciated as beautiful. What a person reads, looks at, or listens to places them in a certain category, and may indicate what the person may do in the future. Categorizing the present and at times predicting future trajectories is the quest of all social research. In this book we focus almost exclusively on the former issue: the categorization problem.

The philosophy of this book assumes that there is no 'one best way' of doing social research: there is no good reason for us all to become 'pollsters' (people who conduct opinion polls), nor should we all become 'focusers' (people who conduct focus groups). The purpose of this book is to overcome the 'law of instrument' (Duncker, 1935), according to which a little boy who only knows a hammer considers that everything is in need of a pounding. By analogy, neither the survey questionnaire nor the focus group is the royal road for social research. This route can, however, be found through an adequate awareness of different methods, an appreciation of their strengths and weaknesses, and an understanding of their use for different social situations, types of data and research problems.

We have now established that social reality can be represented in informal or formal ways of communicating, and that the medium of communication can be texts, images or sound materials. In social research we may want to consider all of these as relevant in some way or another. This is what we hope to clarify.

Qualitative versus quantitative research

There has been a lot of discussion about the differences between quantitative and qualitative research. Quantitative research deals with numbers, uses statistical models to explain the data, and is considered 'hard' research. The best-known prototype is opinion-poll research. By contrast, qualitative research avoids numbers, deals with 'interpreting' social realities, and is considered 'soft' research. The best-known prototype is probably the depth interview. These differences are displayed in Table 1.3. Much effort has been invested in juxtaposing quantitative and qualitative research as competing paradigms of social research, to the extent that people have built careers in one or the other, often polemicizing on the superiority of hard over soft or soft over hard research. Publishers have been quick to spot a market and have established book series and journals with the effect of perpetuating this distinction.

It is fair to say that much quantitative social research is centred around the social survey and the questionnaire, supported by SPSS and SAS as standard statistical software packages. This has set the standards of methodological training at universities, so that the term 'methodology' has come to mean 'statistics' in many fields of social science. In parallel, a large

Table 1.3 *Differences between quantitative and qualitative research*

| | Strategy | |
	Quantitative	Qualitative
Data	Numbers	Texts
Analysis	Statistics	Interpretation
Prototype	Opinion polling	Depth interviewing
Quality	Hard	Soft

business sector has developed, offering quantitative social research for a multitude of purposes. But recent enthusiasm for qualitative research has successfully challenged the simple equation of social research and quantitative methodology; and a space has reopened for a less dogmatic view of methodological matters – an attitude that was common among the pioneers of social research (see, for example, Lazarsfeld, 1968).

In our own efforts, both in research and in teaching social research methods, we are trying to find a way of bridging the fruitless polemic between two seemingly competing traditions of social research. We pursue this objective on the basis of a number of assumptions, which are as follows.

No quantification without qualification

The measurement of social facts hinges on categorizing the social world. Social activities need to be distinguished before any frequency or percentage can be attributed to any distinction. One needs to have a notion of qualitative distinctions between social categories before one can measure how many people belong to one or the other category. If one wants to know the colour distribution in a field of flowers, one first needs to establish the set of colours that are in the field; then one can start counting the flowers of a particular colour. The same is true for social facts.

No statistical analysis without interpretation

We think it odd to assume that qualitative research has a monopoly on interpretation, with the parallel assumption that quantitative research reaches its conclusions quasi-automatically. We ourselves have not conducted any numerical research without facing problems of interpretation. The data do not speak for themselves, even if they are highly processed with sophisticated statistical models. In fact, the more complex the model, the more difficult is the interpretation of the results. Claiming the 'hermeneutic circle' of interpretation, according to which better understanding comes from knowing more about the field of research, is for qualitative researchers a rhetorical move, but one that is rather specious. What the discussion on qualitative research has achieved is to demystify statistical sophistication as the sole route to significant results. The prestige attached to numerical data has such persuasive power that in some contexts poor data quality is masked, and compensated for, by numerical sophistication. However, statistics as a rhetorical device does get around the problem of 'garbage in, garbage out'. In our view, it is the great achievement of the discussion on qualitative methods that it has refocused attention in research and training away from analysis and towards the issues of data quality and data collection.

It seems that the distinction between numerical and non-numerical research is often confused with another distinction, namely that between formalization and non-formalization of research (see Table 1.4). The polemic

Table 1.4 *The formalization and non-formalization of research*

	Quantitative	Qualitative
No formalization	Descriptive frequencies	Citations, descriptions, anecdotes
Formalization	Statistical modelling, e.g. an introduction book	Graph-theoretical modelling, e.g. Abell (1987)

around these types of research is often conflated with the problem of formalism, and based on the methodological socialization of the researcher. Formalism involves abstractions from the concrete context of research, thus introducing a distance between the observation and the data. In a sense, formalism is a general-purpose abstraction available for treating many kinds of data providing certain conditions are satisfied, such as independence of measures, equal variance and so on. The abstract nature of formalism involves such specialization that it can lead to a total disinterest in the social reality represented by the data. It is often this 'emotional detachment' that is resented by researchers of other persuasions, rather than the numbers themselves. However, as we will show below, this is to do with a particular research method, but can be more fruitfully considered in the larger context of knowledge interests. Numerical research has a large repertoire of statistical formalisms at its disposal, while the equivalent repertoire in qualitative research is still rather underdeveloped – despite the fact that its oft-invoked ancestor, structuralism, was rather keen on formalisms (see, for example, Abell, 1987).

Methodological pluralism within the research process: beyond the law of instrument

An unfortunate consequence of the focus in research training on numerical data has been a premature closure on the data collection phase in the research process. With many people competent in handling numerical data, the data collection process is quickly reduced to the industrial routines of questionnaire design and survey sampling, as if this were the only way to conduct social research. Without doubt, much has been achieved in refining these procedures over the years, and the survey's status as the most important social research method is justified because of this. However, nothing justifies its status as the sole instrument of social research. Here we are in danger of succumbing to the 'law of instrument': give a boy a hammer and all things in the world need pounding.

What is needed is a more holistic view of the process of social research, to include defining and revising a problem, conceptualizing it, collecting data, analysing data and writing up the results. Within this process, different methodologies have different contributions to make. We need a clearer notion of the functional strengths and weaknesses of different strands of methods, and of different methods within any one strand.

Time ordering

One way of describing the functionality of different methods is to order them in a design time-line. Traditionally, qualitative research was considered only at the exploratory stage of the research process (pre-design), to explore qualitative distinctions in order to develop measurements, or to get a 'feel' for the research field. More recent formulations consider qualitative research as equally relevant after the survey, to guide the analysis of the survey data, or to support its interpretation with more fine-grained observations (post-design). More extensive designs consider two parallel streams of research, either simultaneously or in oscillating sequences (parallel design; before-and-after design). Finally, qualitative research can now be considered to be a self-contained research strategy without any functional connection to survey or other quantitative research (stand-alone). Qualitative research is seen as an autonomous research endeavour in the context of a research programme with a series of different projects.

The stand-alone function of qualitative research has a weakness that we try to address with this book. While it is possible to consider numerical and non-numerical research as autonomous endeavours, the problem with qualitative research is that it is a 'didactic nightmare'. Compared with the numerical research tradition founded on sampling, the questionnaire and statistical analysis, qualitative researchers, and those who want to become qualitative researchers, find very little procedural clarity and guidance in the literature. Although this is slowly changing as the critical mass of like-minded researchers grows, much of the literature is still preoccupied with demarcating the legitimate territory of this autonomous methodological path. This legitimizing rhetoric has led to an epistemological hypertrophy, producing definitions of positions and counter-positions in a competitive field with more obscurantism and jargon than clarity, and ultimately has been of very little help when it comes to knowing what to do when doing qualitative research. Up to now we have much support for 'feeling good' in the face of traditional critique, but little critical self-observation.

Independent discourse of 'standards of good practice'

The didactic and practical advantage of numerical research is its procedural clarity and its developed discourse on quality in the research process. A quality discourse serves various functions in research: (a) to establish a basis for self-criticism, (b) to demarcate good from bad practice by serving as standards of peer review, (c) to gain credibility in the context of publicly accountable research, and (d) to serve as a didactic tool in the training of students. Rather than imitating quantitative research to the letter, qualitative research needs to develop *functional equivalents*. In order to strengthen the autonomy and credibility of qualitative research, we need clear procedures and standards to identify good and bad practice, both by examples and by abstract criteria. This book makes a contribution in this direction.

Rhetorical elements of social research

Historically, science and rhetoric have had an uneasy relationship. Rhetoric was regarded by scientific pioneers as a form of verbal embellishment that needed to be avoided if one was to reach the truth of the matter: consider the motto of the Royal Society of London, *nullius in verba*. This scientific ideal of the description and explanation of nature without recourse to rhetorical means is increasingly challenged by the realist view of what is going on in communication among scientists and between scientists and other sections of the public (Gross, 1990). The 'ought' of science is clouding the 'is' of science. An essential element of scientific activity is 'communicating', and communicating involves persuading listeners that some things are the case and others are not. Persuasion leads us into the traditional sphere of rhetoric as the 'art of persuasion'. Hence, we consider social scientific research as a form of rhetoric with particular means and rules of engagement.

Rhetorical analysis postulates the 'three musketeers' of persuasion: logos, pathos and ethos (see Leach, Chapter 12 in this volume). Logos refers to the logic of pure argument, and the kinds of arguments used. Pathos refers to the kinds of appeal and concession made to the audience, taking into account the social psychology of emotions. Ethos involves the implicit and explicit references made to the status of the speaker, which establish his or her legitimacy and credibility for saying what is being said. We would therefore assume that any presentation of research results is a mixture of the three basic elements of persuasion, as researchers want to convince their peers, politicians, funding sources, or even their subjects of study of the truth-value and significance of their findings. In the context of communicating research results, the scientific ideal of a rhetoric of pure argumentative rationality, without pathos or ethos, is an illusion.

This perspective has several useful implications for our problem of qualitative research. First, we feel free to consider social research methodology as the rhetorical means by which the social sciences can strengthen their particular form of persuasion. The historical rise and trajectory of this form of rhetoric in the public sphere of modern society are historical and sociological problems in themselves. Secondly, we are liberated from the epistemological obfuscation that burdens discussions of methods, and we can concentrate on developing credible communications within the rules of the game of science. Thirdly, we can treat quantitative and qualitative research equally in these terms. Fourthly, rhetoric is developed in the context of public speaking and writing, which reminds us that method and procedure constitute a form of public accountability for research, which must be lived up to. And finally, the scientific ideal is not lost but is preserved in a collective motivation to build and to maintain the particular form of scientific persuasion – that is, to maintain a rhetoric that we bias towards logos by reducing the ethos and pathos in communication. The rules of method and procedures for gaining and presenting evidence in public protect us from over-reliance on authority (ethos), and from mere pandering to the audience – from telling them what they want to hear (pathos). Serving neither authority nor audience remains a key value of any research that deserves the label. This is only relevant in contrast to other forms of rhetoric in public life, which differ in their mixture of logos, ethos and pathos. The worlds of politics, art and literature, the media and the law courts encourage and cultivate forms of persuasions that are different from the form used in science. Note that 'different from science' does not mean 'irrelevant': news-making, legal judgment and gossiping are important forms of communication, however much they differ in their mixture of logos, pathos and ethos from what would normally be considered scientific communication.

So we consider methods and procedures of gathering and presenting evidence as essential for social scientific research. They define the particular rhetorical bias that demarcates the scientific from other public activities, and they place research squarely within the public sphere and subject it to the demands of accountability. Methods and procedures are the scientific way of being publicly accountable for evidence. However, we have to assume a public sphere that is free to allow the uncensored pursuit of evidence, which is not to be taken for granted (Habermas, 1989).

Knowledge interests and methods

> Quantitative and qualitative methods are more than just differences between research strategies and data collection procedures. These approaches represent fundamentally different epistemological frameworks for conceptualizing the nature of knowing, social reality, and procedures for comprehending these phenomena. (Filstead, 1979: 45)

This assertion typifies the view that quantitative and qualitative orientations to social research represent profoundly different epistemological positions. They are, in this conception, mutually exclusive modes of social enquiry. But a further claim that is often made concerns the critical, radical or emancipatory significance entailed by the researcher's choice of method. Qualitative research is often seen as a way of 'empowering' or 'giving voice' to people, rather than treating them as objects whose behaviour is to be quantified and statistically modelled. This dichotomy is unhelpful, as we have already seen.

An alternative way of thinking about the objectives of social research and their relation to methodology is to consider the philosophy of Jürgen Habermas presented in *Knowledge and Human Interests* (1987). Habermas identifies three 'knowledge interests' that must be understood in order to make sense of the practice of social science and its consequences in society. But he points out that it is not the intentional and conscious epistemological orientations of scientists that provide the key to this understanding. Instead, he conceives of knowledge interests as 'anthropologically deep-seated' traditions (Habermas, 1974: 8). The knowledge-constitutive interests to which Habermas refers are, in fact, the 'conditions which are necessary in order that subjects capable of speech and action may have experience which can lay a claim to objectivity' (1974: 9). In making this clear, we dispose of the idea that interests, in Habermas's sense, can be 'served' by any particular methodological approach; instead, they exist as necessary conditions for the possibility of research practice in the first place, independent of which particular methods are employed:

That we disavow reflection *is* positivism. (1987: vii)

In *Knowledge and Human Interests*, Habermas wants to reconstruct the 'prehistory' of positivism to show how epistemology, as a critique of knowledge, has been progressively undermined. Since Kant, Habermas argues, 'one makes one's way over abandoned stages of reflection' (1987: vii). Since the ascendancy of positivism, philosophy can no longer comprehend science; for it is science itself that constitutes the only form of knowledge that positivism admits as critique. The Kantian enquiry into the conditions of possible knowledge has been replaced by a philosophy of science that 'restricts itself to the pseudo-normative regulation of established research' (1987: 4), such as Popper's falsificationism. Habermas attempts to rehabilitate an epistemological dimension within the philosophy of science, 'critical self-reflection', through which science can become capable of (non-scientistic) self-understanding. And in so doing, Habermas argues, science, and particularly social science, is able to reveal the conditions that might prohibit critical and emancipatory research practice.

We can now turn to the specific typology of interests that Habermas employs. Through an interpretation of Marx, Peirce, Gadamer and Dilthey, Habermas identifies three knowledge-constitutive interests that lie at the base of the 'empirical-analytic', the 'historical-hermeneutic' and the 'critical' sciences. The empirical-analytic sciences have as their basis an interest in technical control. The perpetual struggle for control over the natural world necessary for the reproduction of ourselves as human beings leads us to formulate rules that guide our purposive-rational action. In other words, the rational imperative for the acquisition of scientific knowledge has always been to gain control over the material conditions in which we find ourselves, and thereby to increase our physical and spiritual health and security. Because our interest in nature is primarily to control its conditions, 'this system of action binds, with transcendental necessity, our knowledge of nature to the interest in possible technical control over natural processes' (McCarthy, 1978: 62). The empirical-analytic sciences aim to produce nomological knowledge. Prediction and explanation, therefore, have a relationship of symmetry. Empirically supported universal laws are combined with a set of initial conditions, resulting in a set of (predictable) covariances of observable events. This is a model that can be recognized in much quantitative social research.

The historical-hermeneutic sciences, argues Habermas, arise through a practical interest in the establishment of consensus. For science (and, indeed, any other social practice) to take place, it is imperative that there is reliable intersubjective understanding established in the practice of ordinary language. Hermeneutic understanding (*Verstehen*) aims to restore broken channels of communication. This takes place in two dimensions: the first is in the link between one's own life experience and the tradition to which one belongs; and the second is in the sphere of communication between different individuals, groups and traditions. The failure of communication is a perpetual and ubiquitous feature of the social world, and constitutes an obvious social problem. The concern to re-establish mutual understanding is also, therefore, a perpetual and ubiquitous one. The historical-hermeneutic sciences arose via a genealogy of practices in public affairs – in politics, and in the organization of communities and of labour for production – where individual life and social organization are impossible without some stability of intersubjective meaning. These, then, are the conditions that necessitate the development of the cultural or social sciences. Habermas contrasts the aim of the empirical-analytic sciences with the cultural sciences (*Geisteswissenschaften*):

> The first aims at replacing rules of behaviour that have failed in reality with tested technical rules, whereas the second aims at interpreting expressions of life that cannot be understood and that block the mutuality of behavioural expectations. (1987: 175)

The cultural scientist needs to learn to speak the language that he or she interprets, but must necessarily approach such interpretation from a specific historical point. And, in so doing, it is impossible to avoid taking into account the totality of interpretation that has already taken place: the researcher enters into what could be termed the 'hermeneutic circle'. The point towards which all this leads, for Habermas, is the establishment of consensus between actors. This consensus is necessarily fluid and dynamic, as it is reached through an interpretation that has evolved, and continues to evolve, historically. This consensual orientation for apprehending social reality constitutes the 'practical interest' of the hermeneutic sciences – whose (unstated) aim is to establish the common norms that render social activity possible.

At this point, one can clearly see how the quantitative/qualitative gap could be characterized as one that separates techniques of 'control' on the one hand and 'understanding' on the other. But this does not, in fact, confront the stronger claim often made for qualitative research that it is intrinsically a more critical and potentially emancipatory form of research. An important objective for the qualitative researcher is to be able to see 'through the eyes of those being studied' (Bryman, 1988: 61). This type of approach contends that it is necessary to understand the interpretations that social actors have of the world, because it is these that motivate the behaviour that creates the social world itself. While this is certainly true, it does not follow that the outcome is necessarily a critical piece of work. In fact, one can imagine a situation where such 'understanding' as is generated serves as a basis for the establishment of mechanisms for social control.

A successful critique is one that explains the phenomena under investigation more successfully than previously accepted theories. And in so doing, it must challenge assumptions that hitherto have been uncritically accepted. We run the risk, with the phenomenological, social constructionist or whatever particular qualitative approach, of replacing our own assumptions uncritically with those of our informants. In this way, via a sort of 'empiricism by proxy', qualitative research may repeat the errors more commonly thought of as being associated with unreflective positivism.

At this point Habermas is, again, helpful. The emancipatory interests of what Habermas (1987: 310) calls the 'critical' sciences do not exclude an empirical-analytic mode of enquiry: but equally they go much further than hermeneutic understanding. Habermas's thesis is that emancipatory interests provide the framework for going beyond nomological knowledge and *Verstehen*, and allow us to 'determine when theoretical statements grasp invariant regularities of social action as such and when they express ideologically frozen relations of dependence that can in principle be transformed' (1987: 310). It is through a self-reflective process that the critical sciences can come to identify constraining structures of power that, unreflectively, appear as 'natural', but are in fact the result of 'systematically distorted communication and thinly legitimized repression' (1987: 371).

Habermas sees the period of the Enlightenment as a golden age of 'critical' science, from astronomy to philosophy. But what distinguishes this period is not simply that it marked the beginning of 'the scientific method', but that the application of reason, as embodied in the method, was *inherently* emancipatory because of the challenge it posed to the legitimacy of the Church and of the existing social hierarchy. Habermas's claim is therefore that reason (what we commonly understand now as rationalism) itself inheres in an emancipatory knowledge interest, and that the application of reason is fundamentally a critical enterprise. One should not attempt to understand this position as a normative prescription to be taken up by 'radical' social scientists, though; rather, it is a way of conceptualizing how and why good science, of whatever variety, can be a liberating activity for humankind.

Zygmunt Bauman, writing alongside Habermas in the critical theory tradition, has a practical suggestion for the operationalization of a critical research approach – 'authentication':

> The emancipatory potential of knowledge is put to the test – and, indeed, may be actualised – only with the beginning of dialogue, when the objects of theoretical statements turn into active partners in the incipient process of authentication. (1976: 106)

The authentication of a critical theory, in this view, can only be achieved by the acceptance of its account by those who constitute its objects. For example, qualitative research that involves the feeding back of findings to the participants in the study may achieve just such a result. Of course, the limits of this approach are reached when the objects of research are those

occupying powerful or elite positions already – such as politicians, managers and professionals. In such cases, the informants might have vested
interests to protect and might, accordingly, seek to misrepresent their real
views on the critical interpretations made by researchers.

But criticism need not be exclusively the domain of the qualitative
approach. Victorian studies of poverty, such as Rowntree's *Poverty: a Study
of Town Life* (1902), achieved critical status, we would argue, by uncovering
the extent of poverty on a quantitative scale:

> the labouring class receive upon the average about 25 per cent less food than has
> been proved by scientific experts to be necessary for the maintenance of physical
> efficiency. (1902: 303)

> That in this land of abounding wealth, during a time of perhaps unexampled
> prosperity, probably more than one-fourth of the population are living in poverty,
> is a fact which may well cause great searchings of heart. (1902: 304)

Rowntree's quantitative work consisted in simple descriptive statistics; but
they conferred power on his ability to expose undiscovered conditions of
poverty and deprivation. Numerical representations of data frequently
achieve attention within media discourse; they are rhetorical devices. And
this constitutes a way in which social theorizing, to quote Bauman's phrase,
'departs from the theorist's writing desk and sails into the open waters of
popular reflection' (1976: 107).

It seems clear, then, that one also needs to consider the reception of
research findings by their intended (or perhaps unintended) audience as
part of the 'complete research situation'. The findings of focus group
research on alcohol consumption, for example, have a varying significance
depending on whether they are published in the popular press as part of a
public health campaign aimed at helping alcoholics, or used to inform the
marketing strategy of a major brewery. In this case, the reception of
findings, by whom and for what purpose, is the crucial point. The recent
controversy surrounding the US Census 2000 is an example where the
statisticians, who were pushing for the use of a sophisticated multi-stage
sampling methodology, wished to rectify the undercounting of ethnic
minorities inherent in the constitutionally enshrined method of 'complete
enumeration' (Wright, 1998). The political storm that followed is a case
where widespread public reflection on important social issues has been
precipitated by the perceived implications of a classical quantitative
research methodology.

The implication, then, of Habermas's typology of knowledge interests is
that we can consider the critical potential of different research methodologies, *sui generis*, to be unimportant in relation to the discussions presented in the following chapters. The willingness of researchers to challenge
their own assumptions and subsequent interpretations according to the
data, combined with the way in which the results are received and by

whom, are greatly more significant factors for the possibility of emancipatory work than is the choice of technique employed.

References

Abell, P. (1987) *The Syntax of Social Life*. Oxford: Clarendon.

Bauman, Z. (1976) *Towards a Critical Sociology: an Essay on Common Sense and Emancipation*. London: Routledge.

Berger, P. and Luckmann, T. (1979) *The Social Construction of Reality* (1968). Harmondsworth: Peregrine.

Bryman, A. (1988) *Quantity and Quality in Social Research*. London: Unwin Hyman.

Cranach, M. von (1982) 'The psychological study of goal-directed action', in M. von Cranach and R. Harré (eds), *The Analysis of Action*. Cambridge: CUP. pp. 35–73.

Cranach, M. von, Kalbermatten, U., Indermuhle, K. and Gugler, B. (1982) *Goal Directed Action*. Cambridge and London: Academic Press.

Duncker, P. (1935) *Zur Psychologie des produktiven Denkens*. Berlin: Springer.

Filstead, W.J. (1979) 'Qualitative methods: a needed perspective in evaluation research', in T.D. Cook and C.S. Reichardt (eds), *Qualitative and Quantitative Methods in Evaluation Research*. Beverly Hills, CA: Sage.

Gross, A.G. (1990) *The Rhetoric of Science*. Cambridge, MA: Harvard University Press.

Habermas, J. (1974) *Theory and Practice*. London: Heinemann.

Habermas, J. (1987) *Knowledge and Human Interests*. Cambridge: Polity.

Habermas, J. (1989) *The Transformation of the Public Sphere*. Cambridge: Polity (German original 1962, Luchterhand).

Lazarsfeld, P.F. (1968) 'An episode in the history of social research: a memoir', in D. Fleming and B. Bailyn (eds), *The Intellectual Migration: Europe and America 1930–1960*. Cambridge, MA: HUP. pp. 170–337.

Luckmann, T. (1995) 'Der kommunikative Aufbau der sozialen Welt und die Sozialwissenschaften', *Annali di Sociologia*, 11: 45–71.

McCarthy, T. (1978) *The Critical Theory of Jurgen Habermas*. Cambridge: Polity.

Rowntree, B.S. (1902) *Poverty: a Study of Town Life*. London: Macmillan.

Wright, T. (1998) 'Sampling and Census 2000: the concepts', *American Scientist*, May.

Part I

Constructing a Research Corpus

2

Corpus Construction: a Principle for Qualitative Data Collection

Martin W. Bauer and Bas Aarts

KEYWORDS

corpus
corpus-theoretical paradox
homogeneity
population
relevance
representations (internal variety)
representative sample

sampling bias (non-coverage, response rate)
sampling frame
sampling strategy
saturation
strata and functions (external variety)
synchronicity

All empirical social research selects evidence to make a point, and needs to justify the selection that is the basis of exploration, description, demonstration, proof or disproof of a particular claim. The most elaborate guideline for selecting evidence in the social sciences is *statistical random sampling* (see Kish, 1965). The proficiency of representative sampling is uncontested. However, in many areas of textual and qualitative research, representative sampling does not apply. How do we select people for focus group research? Do we really want to represent a population in four or five focus group discussions? Unfortunately, to date this issue has been given little attention. In practice, researchers often try to fit the sampling rationale that seems misguided, like the choice of a false analogy. In this chapter we propose 'corpus construction' as an alternative principle for data collection. We use strong definitions for our basic terms: 'sampling' means statistical random sampling; 'corpus construction' means systematic selection to some alternative rationale, which will be explored below. Sampling and corpus construction are two different selection procedures. Like representative sampling, we steer the middle way between enumeration of a population and convenient selection. Unsystematic selection violates the principle of public accountability of research; however, corpus construction maintains the efficiency that is gained from selecting some material to characterize the whole. In this sense, corpus construction and representative sampling are functionally equivalent, although they are structurally different. With this use of language, we come to a positive formulation for qualitative selection, rather than defining it as a deficient form of sampling. In short, we contend that corpus construction typifies unknown attributes, while statistical random sampling describes the distribution of already known attributes in social space. Both rationales need to be distinguished carefully, to avoid confusions about, and false inferences from, qualitative research.

We develop this argument in three steps. First, we briefly review the key concepts of representative sampling, and allude to problems arising from unknowable populations. Secondly, we demonstrate corpus construction in the field in which it developed: linguistics. Thirdly, we abstract rules from this practice as guidelines for data selection in qualitative social research.

Representative sampling in social research

The act of taking stock of a population has a long history: governments have wanted to know what sort of inhabitants they govern in order to guide policy. The short history of random sampling began in the late nineteenth century in an atmosphere of conflicting opinions among researchers: some believed in complete enumeration, some in sampling, and others in single case studies. Only an unholy alliance between case-study researchers and random samplers could end the dominance of the total enumerators (O'Muircheartaigh, 1997).

Sampling secures efficiency in research by providing a rationale for studying only parts of a population without losing information – be that a population of objects, animals, human individuals, events, actions, situations, groups or organizations. How can the study of a part give a reliable picture of the whole? The key to this puzzle is *representativeness*. The sample represents the population if the distribution of some criterion is identical in the population and in the sample. Population parameters are estimated from observed sample estimates. The larger the sample, the smaller is the error margin of these estimates, while the sampling process itself may bring additional errors. In principle, there is a need to prove that the sampling criteria and the focal variables actually correlate. However, in practice, one often assumes that if the sample represents the population on a number of criteria, then it will also represent the population in those criteria in which one happens to be interested: The researcher may interview 2000 British people, carefully selected by age, sex and social class, and she will be confident in characterizing the nation's opinions on, say, genetically modified foods, with a known margin of error. This is achieved by following the rationale of sampling, which brings enormous savings in time and effort.

Sampling refers to a set of techniques for achieving representativeness. The key requirement is the sampling frame that operationalizes a population. It is a concrete list of units that are considered for selection. Every list entry represents only one member of the population, and every entry has an equal probability of being selected. A sampling frame may consist of telephone numbers, addresses and postal codes, electoral lists or lists of companies. For example, the list of students taking exams at a university is a sampling frame for the student population of that particular year. The quality of sampling frame is measured by its non-coverage. Most intensional definitions of the population are wider than its operationalization in an available list: for example, a nation's population includes its prisoners and mentally ill people, although the electoral list will exclude them. Telephone numbers create non-coverage, as some households may have no telephone while others have several. Non-coverage is the first bias of sampling.

A sampling frame is a precondition for the application of a sampling strategy. By generating 100 random numbers between 1 and 5000, and by selecting the items from the list that correspond to these 100 random numbers, a simple random sample of 100 out of 5000 is created. Take as a more elaborate example a multi-stage sample for a study into opinions on genetically modified food. The researcher may select a sample of 50 postal areas stratified by socio-economic characteristics, such as average income and urban or rural living. The assumption is that income and urban or rural living will influence opinions. In the second step, he randomly selects, in each of the 50 areas, 40 households from the postal area code, in which finally the field interviewer will talk to the one household member over 15 years of age whose birthday is nearest to the date of the interview. We have a quota sample if, at the last stage, the units are selected not randomly, but by giving the field interviewer some quota to find: the quota could be 20 women and 20 men, because we know that men and women are about equally distributed in the population.

Of the selected 2000 interviewees, some will not be reachable. This non-response introduces a second sampling bias. In the case of random sampling we will know how many were not approachable; but in the case of quota sampling we do not know, which makes the quota version a non-random and, for many researchers, a dubious procedure. Representative sampling reaches the best possible description of the population, despite observing only a part of it. However, it hinges on the availability of a sampling frame, a list or a combination of lists of members of the population, or knowledge of the distribution of key features in the population. Without lists or known distributions, the procedure cannot be used.

Let us consider some cases where the assumption even of a population is problematic. Some discussions of representativeness have argued for three dimensions: individuals, actions and situations (see, for example, Jahoda et al., 1951). Individuals act in situations, and, to generalize results of research to individuals acting in situations, all three dimensions need to be controlled. However, sampling focuses on individuals, not least as this is achieved most successfully. Neither for actions nor for situations are routine attempts at sampling made. Very few human actions (working, shopping, voting, playing, thinking, deciding) have been the focus of intense psychological study which has led to generalizations about human action without a basis in sampling. Equally, no attempts are made to sample situations in which people act. Why not? Neither actions nor situations seem to have a definable population. We would have to study *unknown populations*. Voting, working and shopping are important activities; however, it remains unclear how far their structure and function represent all human activity. Most social scientists regard results that are consistent across a few different situations as replicated and therefore robust. In doing so, they stick to induction for actors, but violate induction for actions and situations; sampling is applied neither for actions nor for situations (Dawes, 1997). Social science seems to rest happily with this contradictory practice.

Consider cases of *unknowable populations*. A prize of several thousand pounds was recently offered at a public lecture for anyone who came up with a sampling frame for human conversations and interactions. The speaker was confident that no-one would be able to meet the challenge. Consider the content of speech, the concatenation of words from a finite vocabulary according to a grammar. At any time the number of possible sentences is infinite, because the combinatorial space of words is an infinite resource. Speech, conversations and human interactions are open systems, with words and movements as the elements and an infinite set of possible sequences. For open systems, the population is unknowable in principle. Its elements can at best be typified, but not listed.

The rationale of representative sampling is useful for much social research, but it does not fit all research situations. There is a danger that we unduly extend the procedures of representative sampling to studies in which it may be inappropriate. We criticize certain forms of data collection as deviations from the 'probabilistic standard'. However, even in the empire of chance, the 'law of small numbers' rules. Humans tend (except statisticians, of course) to overestimate the representativeness of everyday observations (Tversky and Kahnemann, 1974; Gigerenzer et al., 1989: 219ff). The moral is clear: pay more attention to sampling. However, our efforts may be misguided: the quest for representativeness may be channelling scarce resources towards strategies of selection that are inappropriate for the problem at hand.

The notion of 'corpus'

Now we will explore what the linguist offers in constructing his corpus. Language is an open system. One cannot expect a list of all sentences from which to select randomly. The linguistics community has recently rejected a motion that language corpora be representative of language use (Johansson, 1995: 246).

The word 'corpus' (Latin; plural 'corpora') simply means 'body'. In the historical sciences it refers to a collection of texts. It may be defined as 'a body of complete collection of writings or the like; the whole body of literature on any subject . . . several works of the same nature, collected and bound together' (*Oxford English Dictionary*, 1989); or as 'a collection of texts, especially if complete and self-contained' (McArthur, 1992). Examples, mainly collected during the nineteenth century, are the Corpus Doctrinae, a body of theological treatises of German ecclesiastical history; the Corpus Inscriptorum Semiticorum, a complete collection of ancient Jewish texts at the French Academy; or the Corpus Inscriptorum Graecorum of ancient Greek texts at the Berlin Academy. These collections tend to be *complete* and *thematically unified*, and to serve *research*.

Another definition of a corpus is 'a finite collection of materials, which is determined in advance by the analyst, with (inevitable) arbitrariness, and on which he is going to work' (Barthes, 1967: 96). Barthes, in analysing texts, images, music and other materials as signifiers of social life, extends the notion of corpus from text to any material. In his booklet on the principles of semiology he relegates considerations of selection to a few pages. Selection seems less important than analysis, but is not to be separated from it. Arbitrariness is less a matter of convenience, and more inevitable in principle. The materials ought to be homogeneous, so do not mix text and images in the same corpus. A good analysis stays within the corpus and accounts for all variation that is contained within it. In summary, while older meanings of 'text corpus' imply the complete collection of texts according to some common theme, more recent meanings stress the purposive nature of selection, and not only of texts but also of any material with symbolic functions. This selection is inevitably arbitrary to some degree: comprehensive analysis has priority over scrutiny of selection. Corpus linguistics, however, offers a more systematic discussion.

What are language corpora?

Corpora in the linguistic sense are collections of language data for the purposes of various types of language research. The term is tied to developments in computer studies of language (Johansson, 1995; Biber et al., 1998). A linguistic corpus is 'written or spoken material upon which linguistic analysis is based' (*Oxford English Dictionary*, 1989), or 'texts, utterances, or other specimens considered more or less representative of a language and usually stored as an electronic database' (McArthur, 1992). The corpora are structured along a number of parameters such as channel (spoken or written, written to be spoken, etc.), domain (art, domestic, religious, education, etc.), function (persuade, express, inform, etc.). Combinations of these subcategories may form a *hierarchical typology of registers*, as we will see. The earliest language corpora were usually of the written kind, and collected manually.

Once constructed, corpora can be used as databases for linguistic research. When the first corpora were constructed, data retrieval also had to take place by hand. So, for example, a researcher who was interested in working on verbs of perception in English (verbs like 'see', 'hear', etc.), would have to go through the corpus manually in order to find these verbs. Later corpora were computerized: the first was the Brown Corpus, constructed in the 1960s at Brown University in Providence, Rhode Island. Nowadays all corpora are computerized and allow automatic searches.

The early computerized corpora emerged at an interesting point in the history of linguistics, namely the beginning of the Chomskyan era. Chomsky's book *Syntactic Structures* (1957) is the seminal publication in this period. Chomsky claimed that all humans are endowed with an innate language capacity, which he labelled 'universal grammar'. Ever since the beginnings of Chomskyan linguistics there has been an emphasis on how linguists can go about constructing abstract representations of each and every speaker's knowledge of language. Because the theory is all about abstract representations, this field of linguistics is characterized by a move away from empiricism, and by a reliance on the internal knowledge of language that we have as native speakers. Chomsky made a distinction between what he called *competence*, which is the innate knowledge that speakers have of language, and *performance*, the way that they make use of their innate knowledge. More recently he has introduced the term 'I-language' (internalized language) and 'E-language' (externalized language). Chomsky's theory is a competence theory (a theory of I-language) and not a performance theory (a theory of E-language). In the Chomskyan model, any particular language constitutes an epiphenomenon, with the term 'language' now reserved to mean I-language.

Early followers of Chomsky very much railed against empirically oriented linguistics. Nelson Francis, the compiler of the Brown Corpus, was asked at a conference by Robert Lees, one of Chomsky's followers, what he was working on. Francis replied that he was compiling a corpus of American written and spoken English. This was met with exasperation by Lees who held that this was a complete and utter waste of time. Lees's view, and that of many Chomskyans at the time, was that one only needs to reflect for a moment in order to come up with one's own examples of particular linguistic phenomena in English. Chomskyan linguists have always insisted that the only interesting data for language study are introspective data, that is, data that are made up on the basis of one's native-speaker knowledge of a language. The aversion to real data has persisted to this day. Chomsky, when he was recently asked by one of us what he thought of modern corpus linguistics, simply replied 'it doesn't exist'. The collection of data in a corpus is regarded by Chomsky as being on a par with butterfly collecting.

Corpus linguists in turn claim that corpora can be useful for linguists who are not native speakers, and may contain examples that are hard to think of, because they are rare. They feel that linguistics should concern itself with real language data, that is, performance data, and not with made-up, artificial competence data. Of course, the question of what kind of data to use was not the only bone of contention. Corpus linguists are, on the whole, inductivists, while Chomskyans are deductivists. The dispute, then, is also a methodological one.

What is corpus linguistics, and how can corpora be used in linguistic research?

The field of linguistics is vast, and includes subdisciplines such as psycho-linguistics, neurolinguistics, forensic linguistics, socio-linguistics, formal or theoretical linguistics, semantics and so on. People now also speak of 'corpus linguistics'. One might wonder whether corpus linguistics is to be regarded on a par with the other branches of linguistics. Strictly speaking, corpus linguistics is not really a branch of linguistics in itself: it is a linguistic methodology that might be used in all branches of linguistics. So, for example, a syntactician might turn to a corpus to study particular grammatical structures, while a socio-linguist might want to study tele-phone conversations in a corpus to see whether people speak differently on the phone from the way they do in face-to-face situations. In fact, with this use in mind, some corpora contain not merely one but various categories of phone conversations: for example, conversations between people of the same social status, and between people of different social status. Another use that socio-linguists have made of corpora is to study the differences between the ways in which men and women speak (see, for example, Tannen, 1992a; 1992b; Coates, 1996). Linguists or socio-linguists who are interested in the phenomenon of 'handwritten notices', one of the categories found in the original Survey of English Usage Corpus at University College London, might have been amused by the following notice found on the door of a public lavatory at Euston station in London: 'Toilets out of order, please use platform 6.'

How do researchers go about using a corpus? And what do they search for? Obviously, this depends on their research goals. In any case, a computer program is needed that can make intelligent searches. The simplest kind of search is for a particular lexical item, say the word 'the'. Things become more complex if a search is made, say, for all the nouns in a corpus. To do this, the corpus needs to be parsed. In the early days, parsing was done by hand; now it is done automatically. The first stage of parsing is called tagging. During this process each and every word is given a word class label, such as noun, verb, adjective, etc. This can be done automati-cally by a computer program. The results are around 90 per cent accurate, and need to be corrected manually. The second stage of parsing involves analysing the corpus into grammatical constructions. For example, in a sentence such as 'The dog bit the postman', the program must analyse 'the dog' as the subject of the sentence, and 'the postman' as the direct object.

Again, the automatic parsing has to be corrected manually. Once parsing is complete, queries can be formulated. For this a search program is needed. For example, the search program can be instructed to find all the direct objects following the verb 'see'. Researchers at University College London have developed a tagger, a parser and also a search program. The search program is called the ICE Corpus Utility Program, or ICECUP for short.

An example of a corpus: the International Corpus of English

As an example of a corpus, Figure 2.1 shows the text categories in the International Corpus of English (ICE), developed in the English Department at University College London. ICE is international in the sense that identically constructed corpora have been set up, or are in the process of being set up, in some 20 English-speaking countries, among them the USA, Canada, Australia, New Zealand, Kenya and Nigeria. This corpus was designed to contain both spoken and written material, and both the spoken and written categories are further subdivided. The ICE-GB corpus of British English is now complete, and is available on CD-ROM; the other national corpora are still under construction. (See www.ucl.ac.uk/english-usage).

The different corpora in the ICE project are being constructed in order to allow researchers to study particular aspects of the English language in different varieties of English. Identical construction of the different national corpora is being implemented so as to allow meaningful statistical comparisons between the varieties of English. To give an example, somebody who is interested in comparing the use of verbs of perception in Australian English with their use in British English would be able to use the ICE-GB and ICE-Australia corpora for her research.

How are language corpora constructed?

One would have thought that corpus linguists would have concerned themselves from the early days with the issue of how to construct corpora, and with related issues such as statistical representativeness. Surprisingly, this is not so. Fairly fundamental papers dealing with this issue were published as recently as the early 1990s (Atkins et al., 1992; Biber, 1993). The rationale for corpus construction developed autonomously from solving practical problems. Statistical sampling had little influence on the development of corpus linguistics; indeed, the merits of a statistical rationale for language corpora are contested. A motion that 'language corpora should be based on statistical representation' was voted down at a meeting of linguists in Oxford some years ago. Standard approaches to statistical sampling are hardly applicable to building a language corpus (Atkins et al., 1992: 4).

Issues of corpus construction that are discussed are as follows. Which categories of speech and writing should be included? How big should the samples be for each category of writing or speech, in terms of number of words? How large should the corpus be in terms of number of words? It is

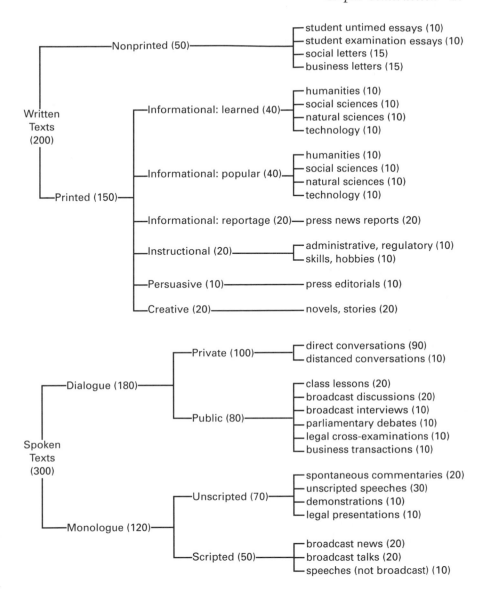

Figure 2.1 *An outline of the ICE map*

commonly accepted that corpus size is a less relevant consideration, while representativeness deserves more attention.

Corpus linguists recognize two important dimensions of representativeness in corpus design (Biber, 1993: 243). First, a corpus should include 'the range of linguistic distributions in a language' (1993: 243) – for example, a comprehensive range of grammatical constructions. What exactly constitutes 'the range of linguistic distributions' is something that is hard to determine *a priori*, but one could say that this locution refers to the sum

total of the empirically established and diachronically accumulated knowledge that working grammarians have of a particular language – in other
words, the material that most linguists would agree should be covered by a
wide-ranging grammar of English, such as Quirk et al. (1985). This internal
variation of language is called type or dialect variation.

Secondly, a corpus should include a sufficient range of text in the target
population, where target population is taken to mean a bounded, that is
rigidly defined, collection of textual material from different contexts. These
variations are also called registers, genres or functions, and differ according
to situational and thematic variables. This necessitates careful thought. The
choice of target population depends on one's research aims: a linguist who
is interested in language development will construct a corpus in a different
way from someone who wants to study, say, dialectal variation (see Aston
and Burnard, 1998: 23). The classification of registers or functions of speech
that may bear internal variation is a matter of linguistic intimation and
intuition: the question arises of how one decides whether or not the target
population is sufficiently diverse. Atkins et al. (1992: 7) note that the range
of text types to choose from is open-ended as well as culturally specific. For
example, one could imagine that someone constructing a corpus representative of a society in which religion plays a pivotal part may want to include
sermons, while in other corpora this category may be of much less interest.
In the end the decisions as to which text types to include and which to
exclude in a corpus are arbitrary.

Large, general-purpose corpora differ in the taxonomy of texts they
include, and this variety reflects their different objectives. The Brown
Corpus defined the target population for written material as all English
texts printed and published in the USA in 1961. It included 15 text genres
with subgenres. An example of a text genre would be 'learned science', and
a subgenre of this could be 'natural sciences'. Another example of a text
genre could be 'newspaper language', with 'sports commentary' as a
possible subgenre. Samples were chosen from a list of all the items in the
Brown University Library and Providence Athenaeum that were published
in 1961. The Survey of English Usage Corpus at University College London,
which dates from roughly the same period as the Brown Corpus, had
educated spoken and written adult English as its target population (see
Figure 2.1).

Also, as far as corpora that are aimed to represent a particular language
as a whole are concerned, it should be clear that for linguistic research a
corpus constructed proportionally, that is following a random sampling
rationale on the basis of all language use, would not be suitable. Such a
corpus would consist predominantly of spoken language, because an
estimated 90 per cent of all language produced is conversation (Biber, 1993:
247). Rather, linguists require a range of samples of language use that are
sufficiently diverse, and contain the full range of grammatical structures.
So, in addition to samples of conversation, there should be samples of
material that is not produced in great quantities, such as highly technical
scientific language (see Figure 2.1). Linguistic corpus construction is highly

overselective of certain functions of speech and genres of text, because of their significance in revealing specific type variety. Linguists consider the rare event, while representative sampling would suggest ignoring it.

The corpus-theoretical paradox

In corpus design, the genres and functions of text and speech are set up on what seem to be intuitive grounds. Josef Schmied, a German corpus linguist, has called this a 'corpus-theoretical paradox':

> On the one hand, a corpus is more representative of language use in a community if its subdivisions reflect all the variables that determine language variation in that community; on the other hand, we need results from a representative corpus in order to determine these variables empirically. (1996: 192)

In order to remedy such problems, corpus design is regarded by Biber as a cyclical process (see Figure 2.2), as one cannot determine *a priori* what a representative corpus looks like. In other words, the construction of successive corpora with a particular focus should lead to something like an industry standard for the 'balanced corpus'. For Atkins et al. (1992), a balanced corpus is finely tuned on the basis of multiple user feedback, so that a manageable small-scale model of the linguistic material emerges. Balancing means that successive corrections are implemented to compensate the biases that are being identified. A cyclical process will give due recognition to two rules of corpus construction. Biber observes that external variation precedes awareness of internal variation, and so corpus construction has to start from different contexts (rule 1). According to Atkins et al., the aim is to maximize internal dialect variety through the extension of the functions, registers or genres that are being considered (rule 2). A corpus is balanced when additional efforts add little dialect variance. The problem is to determine those external variations that add significantly to internal type variety.

A future standard of corpus construction may include documentation of cyclical improvements, working towards a standard taxonomy of texts and speech situations, and conventions to mark the selected token texts and speech examples with standard codes. Transparency will not change the inevitable arbitrariness in the selection, but it brings it to light so that we might avoid false claims and suggest further improvements (Atkins et al., 1992).

Figure 2.2   *Corpus design as a cyclical process (Biber, 1993: 256)*

Corpora in the social sciences

The question now arises of what we might learn from linguists in thinking about how to select data for qualitative research. 'Corpus' is not a technical term that is widely used in the methodology of the social sciences. With qualitative research gaining critical mass, the selection of interviews, textual and other materials requires a more systematic treatment comparable to that of survey research.

One may distinguish general-purpose corpora from topical corpora. A *general-purpose corpus* is designed with a broad range of research questions in mind, and serves as a resource in the widest sense. Most large-scale linguistic corpora constitute such projects. Judged by the effort involved, these corpora are resources comparable to the 10-year census or the annual labour force survey conducted in many countries.

Archival collections constitute general-purpose corpora for research. We may think of the many national libraries that contain complete collections of newspapers and magazines published in that country, as hard copy and/ or on microfiche. The British Newspaper Library in London stores every daily and weekly newspaper printed in the British Isles since the early nineteenth century. In recent years, on-line services have emerged that provide complete collections of newsprint on a daily basis, such as FT-Profile or Reuters, or with a regular update on CD-ROM directly from the newspaper publishers. Many of these sources are nearly complete and are listed, and so lend themselves to representative, even strict random, sampling. Classical content analysis profits from these developments.

A *topical corpus* is designed for a narrowly defined research purpose; it may become a general research resource for secondary analysis. Most text- or interview-based social science research is of this kind. An example of a topical corpus is Ulm Textbank (Mergenthaler and Kaechele, 1988). The collection includes verbatim transcripts of over 8000 sessions of psychotherapy, from over 1000 patients and around 70 therapists, from Germany, Austria, Sweden, Switzerland and the USA. It was conceived as a tool for psychotherapy research, for studying the dynamics of interaction and experience. While the largest part of the material is psychoanalytically oriented, not all of the recordings are. Psychotherapy is a particular form of human interaction that happens worldwide, and in this corpus representativeness is not the principle of data selection: such a rationale would have to consider urban world centres of psychotherapeutic activities such as New York, Zurich, Vienna and Buenos Aires as locations of sampling. By contrast, the criteria that guided the selection are therapeutic orientation (register 1), diagnosis of the patient (register 2), the success of the treatment (register 3) and a minimum length of 300 to 500 hours (register 4). The selection aims at balancing different registers to enable comparative research. It does not aim to be representative, either by the real-life distribution of success and failure, or across the 600 different therapy schools, but aims to have sufficient examples across 34 text types relating to therapeutic interactions. The focus of analysis is the verbal activity, the expressions of various forms of emotionality during the course of therapy. The purpose is to relate particular initial diagnosis and subsequent patterns of verbal dynamics to the outcomes of therapy. The corpus is designed to maximize internal variety of verbal dynamics during sessions across the external registers of the therapist's orientation, diagnosis, therapy outcome and length of treatment (Mergenthaler, 1996).

How to construct a corpus in the social sciences

Linguists and qualitative researchers face the corpus-theoretical paradox. They set out to study the varieties in the themes, opinions, attitudes, stereotypes, worldviews, behaviours and practices of social life. However, as these varieties are as yet unknown, and therefore also their distribution, the researchers cannot sample according to a representativeness rationale. But paradoxes often resolve when we consider time. Linguists suggest a stepwise procedure:

(a) to select preliminarily
(b) to analyse this variety
(c) to extend the corpus of data until no additional variety can be detected.

In other words, they conceive the corpus as a system that grows. This is the first lesson for qualitative selection:

Rule 1 Proceed stepwise: select; analyse; select again.

Relevance, homogeneity, synchronicity

Barthes's (1967: 95ff) suggestions for corpus design may be helpful for qualitative selection: relevance, homogeneity, synchronicity. First, materials must be theoretically relevant, and should be collected from *one point of view* only. Materials in a corpus have only one thematic focus, only one particular theme. For example, a study of science and technology news requires a corpus of news items that refer to science and technology and that excludes all other news items. It is a different problem from determining the proportion of science news among all news: this would require a representative sample of all news. Trivial as this criterion may be, it serves as a reminder to be focused and selective.

Secondly, materials in a corpus must be *as homogeneous as possible*. This refers to the material substance of data. Textual materials should not be mixed with images, nor should communications media be mixed; transcripts of individual interviews should not be grouped with transcripts of focus group interviews. Images, texts and individual and focus group interviews may address parts of the same research project; however, they must be separated into different corpora for comparison.

Thirdly, a corpus is a cross-section of history. Most materials have a natural cycle of stability and change. The materials to be studied should be chosen from within one natural cycle: they must be *synchronous*. The normal cycle of change will define the time interval within which a corpus of relevant and homogeneous materials should be selected. For example, family patterns are likely to be stable over one or two generations; clothing fashions change on a yearly cycle; newspaper and television editorial policy may have a cycle of a few years; opinion has a short cycle of days or weeks. For corpus construction, several materials within one cycle are preferable to one type of material over several cycles of change. Changes across cycles are studied by comparing two corpora, not within one single corpus.

Saturation

A procedure to overcome the corpus-theoretical paradox is depicted in Figure 2.3. The social space is unfolded in two dimensions: strata or functions, and representations. The horizontal dimension comprises the *social strata*, *functions* and *categories* that are known and are almost part of common sense: sex, age, occupational activity, urban/rural, income level, religion and so on. These are the variables by which social researchers usually segment the population; they are external to the actual phenomenon in question. Qualitative researchers' main interest is in typifying the varieties of representations of people in their life world. The ways in which people relate to objects in their life world, their subject–object relation, is observed with concepts such as opinions, attitudes, feelings, accounts, stereotypes, beliefs, identities, ideologies, discourse, worldviews, habits and practices. This is the second or vertical dimension of our scheme. This variety is unknown, and worth investigating. Representations are particular subject–object relations tied to a social milieu. The qualitative researcher wants to understand different social milieus in social space by typifying social strata and functions, or combinations thereof, together with particular representations. Social milieus occupy a social space and may have a

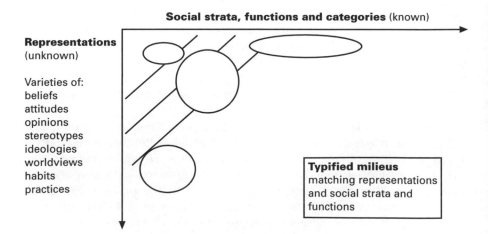

Figure 2.3   *The two dimensions of social space: strata and representations*

project of common interest and investment that underpins their particular representations. External and internal variety, strata and representations may correlate, but need not. There are old social milieus and new ones emerging in a dynamic society. It requires sociological imagination and historical intimation to recognize new social milieus and to identify the traditional milieus that make a difference for the representation of a new issue in society (Bauer and Gaskell, 1999).

To select interviewees or documents for qualitative research, we choose people and sources according to external criteria: social strata, functions and categories. For example we may invite interviewees for a focus group study on moral issues of human cloning by sex, age and education. However, the focus of research is not the difference between the sexes or the age groups, but the variety of moral issues and their argumentative structure. In other words, qualitative research tends to maximize the variety of the unknown phenomenon, in this case the moral issues of cloning. This is different from sample survey research: there, the opinions and attitudes are *a priori* framed in the questions and compared across known strata of people. For example, research will report the differences in opinions according to levels of education, sex or age. Following these considerations we formulate three further rules:

Rule 2   In qualitative research, strata and function variety precedes variety of representations.

Rule 3   Characterizing variety of representations has priority over anchoring them in existing categories of people.

Rule 4   Maximize the variety of representations by extending the range of strata/functions considered.

An implication of these rules may be that certain strata are deliberately overselected, so that a particular group that offers complex views may be given an overproportional attention in the research. If, for example, in focus group discussions on human cloning, women show much greater concern and diversity of views, one would not hesitate to explore different strata and functions among women only – for example, with or without children, religious background, etc. One would ignore the fact that the corpus contained more women-talk than men-talk. However, to avoid false conclusions, any judgement about the distribution of opinions should be avoided. Only representative sampling of opinions allows us to describe conclusively the distribution of opinions. In this sense corpus construction helps typifying unknown representations, while by contrast representative sampling describes the distribution of already known representations in society. Both rationales need to be distinguished with care in order to avoid confusion and false conclusions.

In order to overcome the initial paradox of corpus construction, research starts with the external strata and functions (rule 2). In focus group research, one may consider age groups or educational strata following an initial hunch about what would make a difference for representations of an issue. However, researchers are well advised not to rely on their hunches alone when they segment social space. They need to maintain an open mind for further strata and functional distinctions that may not be obvious in the first instance. They may start with sex, age and education, but may have to consider ethnicity, religion and urban/rural divisions in order to identify and maximize variety in people's representations of an issue. Here the law of diminishing returns may apply: adding further strata may make only a small difference with regard to additional representations. When this occurs, the corpus is saturated. Rule 1 stipulates that selection for qualitative research is a cyclical process, and a cyclical process requires a stopping criterion, otherwise a research project has no end. *Saturation* is the stopping criterion: one searches for different representations only until the inclusion of new strata no longer adds anything new. We assume that representational variety is limited in time and social space. To detect additional variety adds disproportionately to the costs of research; thus the researcher decides to stop studying additional strata. The dangers of this criterion are local maxima: it may be that talking to another regular in the local pub does not add any new facet of opinion; however, going to a very different neighbourhood or going out of town might well do so. Researchers live in a life world; and they have to ask themselves whether the variety they have detected covers their locale or wider ground.

Size of corpus

Little can be said about the size of corpora for qualitative research. One needs to consider the effort involved in data collection and analysis, the number of representations one would like to characterize, and some minimal and maximal requirements, for example in automatic text analysis, as criteria for the size of a corpus.

Most limitations come from the effort that is required to run a large number of focus groups or in-depth interviews, or to collect documents. The time available to conduct these interviews, and to analyse them, will be the first constraint on corpus size. Qualitative research involving large amounts of material has been rightly identified as an 'attractive nuisance' (Miles, 1979). Researchers easily collect more interesting material than they can effectively handle within the time of a project. This leads to the usual complaint that the project ends without the materials having been analysed in any depth. This results in the creation of 'data dungeons': materials collected but never really analysed. A considered assessment of the time required for selection and analysis procedures will increase the realism of many researchers.

The more representations that the researcher expects on a particular issue, the more different strata and functions of people or materials need to be explored, and the larger the corpus. The researcher will have to decide to study one or many representations in detail. Equally, if automatic textual analysis is considered, including the application of statistical procedures, this may require a minimum number of words in a corpus to reach reliable results. For example, ALCESTE (see Kronberger and Wagner, Chapter 17 in this volume) will require a text with a minimum of 10,000 words. Such procedures may also put an upper limit on the corpus size, beyond which the procedures either do not work or take a very long time to run.

Towards basic standards of corpus construction and reportage

As in corpus linguistics, one may renounce any hopes for a fully representative general-purpose corpus on a topic. A multitude of topical corpora may emerge from a flourishing practice of qualitative research. The problem arises of how to make these materials comparable and accessible for secondary analysis. A way forward in this direction is the development of guidelines for corpus construction and reporting. Survey research has developed elaborate standards of reporting representative sampling procedures, and analogous standards may be necessary for qualitative research. These may include:

- a description of the substance of materials involved: text, images, sounds, etc.
- a characterization of the research topic, e.g. moral issues of human cloning
- a report on the modalities of the stepwise extension of the open corpus
- the social strata, functions and categories that were used at entry
- the social strata, functions and categories that were added later
- evidence for saturation
- the timing of the cycles of data collection
- the place of data collection.

Indeed, the ESRC Data Archive at Essex University (Heaton, 1998; or ESRC at http://www.essex.ac.uk/qualidat/) is already undertaking to build an archive for qualitative research for which standards of reportage are required, and which protects the privacy of the informants – an issue that is very sensitive in qualitative research.

STEPS IN CONSTRUCTING A CORPUS

1 Decide on the topic area, and consider the four rules of corpus construction:

> *Rule 1* Proceed stepwise: select; analyse; select again.
>
> *Rule 2* In qualitative research, strata and function variety precedes variety of representations.
>
> *Rule 3* Characterizing variety of representations has priority over anchoring them in existing categories of people.
>
> *Rule 4* Maximize the variety of representations by extending the range of strata/functions considered.

2   Consider a two-dimensional social space: strata and functions; and representations of the topic. List as many social strata and functions as possible.
3   Explore representations of the topic, with one or two strata or functions to start with.
4   Decide on whether these strata are likely to exhaust the variety of representations, or whether additional strata or social functions need to be explored.
5   Extend the corpus accordingly. Check whether you have achieved a saturated variety. Which strata are left unconsidered?
6   Conduct the final analysis and revise the social space in the light of the findings, and report your findings; or follow a cyclical procedure by returning to step 4.

References

Aston, G. and Burnard, L. (1998) *The BNC Handbook: Exploring the British National Corpus with Sara*. Edinburgh: Edinburgh University Press.

Atkins, S., Clear, J. and Ostler, N. (1992) 'Corpus design criteria', *Literary and Linguistic Computing*, 7: 1–16.

Barthes, R. (1967) *Elements of Semiology*. New York: Hill and Wang, The Noonday Press [translation from French original, 1964].

Bauer, M.W. and Gaskell, G. (1999) 'Towards a paradigm for research on social representations', *Journal for the Theory of Social Behaviour*, 29(2): 163–86.

Biber, D. (1993) 'Representativeness in corpus design', *Literary and Linguistic Computing*, 8(4): 243–57.

Biber, D., Conrad, S. and Reppen, R. (1998) *Corpus Linguistics: Investigating Language Structure and Use*. Cambridge: Cambridge University Press.

Chomsky, N. (1957) *Syntactic Structures*. The Hague: Mouton.

Coates, J. (1996) *Women Talk*. Oxford: Blackwell.

Dawes, R. (1997) 'Qualitative consistency masquerading as quantitative fit'. Paper presented at the 10th International Congress of Logic, Methodology and Philosophy of Science, Florence, Italy, August 1995.

Gigerenzer, G., Swijtink, S., Porter, T., Daston, L., Beatty, J. and Krueger, L. (1989) *The Empire of Chance: How Probability Changed Science and Everyday Life*. Cambridge: Cambridge University Press.

Heaton, J. (1998) 'Secondary analysis of qualitative data', *Social Research Update*, issue 22 (autumn), Sociology at Surrey, University of Surrey.

Jahoda, M., Deutsch, M. and Cook, S.W. (1951) *Research Methods in Social Relations*, Vols 1 and 2. New York: Dryden.

Johansson, S. (1995) 'ICAME – Quo vadis? Reflections on the use of computer corpora in linguistics', *Computers and the Humanities*, 28: 243–52.

Kish, L. (1965) *Survey Sampling*. New York: Wiley.

McArthur, T. (1992) *The Oxford Companion to the English Language*. Oxford: Oxford University Press.

Mergenthaler, E. (1996) 'Computer-assisted content analysis', in *Text Analysis and Computers*. Mannheim: ZUMA Nachrichten Spezial. pp. 3–32.

Mergenthaler, E. and Kaechele, H. (1988) 'The Ulm Textbank management system: a tool for psychotherapy research', in H. Dahl, H. Kaechele and H. Thomae (eds), *Psychoanalytic Process Research Strategies*. Berlin: Springer.

Miles, M.B. (1979) 'Qualitative data as an attractive nuisance: the problem of analysis', *Administrative Science Quarterly*, 24: 590–601.

O'Muircheartaigh, C. (1997) 'Measurement error in surveys: a historical perspective', in L. Lynberg, P.P. Biemer, M. Collins, E. deLeeuw, C. Dippo, N. Scharz and D. Trewin (eds), *Survey Measurement and Process Quality*. New York: Wiley. pp. 1–25.

Quirk, R., Greenbaum, S., Leech, G. and Svartvik, J. (1985) *A Comprehensive Grammar of the English Language*. London: Longman.

Schmied, J. (1996) 'Second-language corpora', in S. Greenbaum (ed.), *Comparing English Worldwide: the International Corpus of English*. Oxford: Clarendon. pp. 182–96.

Tannen, D. (1992a) *You Just Don't Understand: Men and Women in Conversation*. London: Virago.

Tannen, D. (1992b) *That's Not What I Meant! How Conversational Style Makes or Breaks your Relationships with Others*. London: Virago.

Tversky, A. and Kahnemann, D. (1974) 'Judgement under uncertainty: heuristics and biases', *Science*, 185: 1124–31.

3

Individual and Group Interviewing

George Gaskell

KEYWORDS

focus group interview   moderator
group dynamics   stimulus materials
individual depth interview   topic guide

This chapter is something of a personal reflection on 25 years of qualitative research, and draws on various training courses and lectures I have attended. It is an attempt to explicate the tacit knowledge that one develops over countless projects. While the conceptual discussions draw mainly from social psychological research, it is hoped that those from other social scientific persuasions will find the practical advice of value.

The objective of the chapter is to provide both a conceptual background and a practical guide to qualitative interviewing. Here, qualitative interviewing refers to interviews of a semi-structured type with a single respondent (the depth interview) or a group of respondents (the focus group). These forms of qualitative interviewing can be distinguished on the one hand from the highly structured survey interview, in which a predetermined series of questions is asked; and on the other hand from the less structured ongoing conversation of participant observation or ethnography, where the emphasis is more on absorbing the local knowledge and culture over a longer period than on asking questions within a relatively confined period.

In the empirical social sciences, qualitative interviewing is a widely used methodology for data collection. It is, as Robert Farr (1982) writes, 'essentially a technique or method for establishing or discovering that there are perspectives or viewpoints on events other than those of the person initiating the interview'.

The first point of departure is the assumption that the social world is not an unproblematic given: it is actively constructed by people in their everyday life, but not under conditions of their own making. It is assumed that these constructions form people's paramount reality, their life world. Using qualitative interviewing to map and understand the respondents' life world is the entry point for the social scientist, who then introduces interpretive frameworks to understand the actors' accounts in more conceptual or abstract terms, often in relation to other observations. Hence the qualitative interview provides the basic data for the development of an understanding of the relations between social actors and their situation. The objective is a fine-textured understanding of beliefs, attitudes, values and motivations in relation to the behaviours of people in particular social contexts.

Uses of qualitative interviewing

The understanding of the life worlds of respondents and specified social groupings is the *sine qua non* of qualitative interviewing. This may contribute to a number of different research endeavours. It may be an end in itself, providing a 'thick description' of a particular social milieu; it can be used as a basis for generating a framework for further research; it may provide empirical data to test expectations and hypotheses developed out of a particular theoretical perspective.

Beyond the broad objectives of description, conceptual development and the testing of concepts, qualitative interviewing may play a vital role in combination with other methods. For example, insights gained from qualitative interviewing may improve the quality of survey design and interpretation. In order to write appropriate questions it is necessary to appreciate both the concerns and the language of the target group. Equally, survey research often throws up results and surprises that need further exploration. Here the more in-depth understanding offered by qualitative interviewing may provide valuable contextual information to help to explain particular findings.

The versatility and value of qualitative interviewing is evidenced in its widespread use in many of the social scientific disciplines and in commercial social research in the areas of media audience research, public relations, marketing and advertising.

Preparation and planning

In this section some of the key aspects of individual and group interviewing are introduced. These cover preparation and planning, selecting respondents, and an introduction to individual and group interviewing techniques. It is assumed here that the researcher has either developed a theoretical or conceptual framework to guide the inquiry, and identified key concepts and issues to be addressed in the research, or decided to work within the framework of grounded theory (Glaser and Strauss, 1967). Following this choice, two key issues must be considered prior to any form of interviewing: what to ask (the specification of the topic guide) and whom to talk to (how to select the respondents).

The topic guide

The topic guide is a vital part of the research process and needs detailed attention. Behind the apparently natural and almost casual conversation seen in the successful interview is a well-prepared interviewer. If inappropriate questions are asked then not only is the respondent's time wasted but so is the researcher's. It is essential to put time and effort into the construction of the topic guide and it is likely to go through a number of drafts. Essentially it is designed to capture the aims and objectives of the research. It will be based on a combination of a critical reading of the appropriate literature, a reconnaisance of the field (which might include observations and/or some preliminary conversations with relevant people), discussions with experienced colleagues, and some creative thinking. Ideally the topic guide should cover one page. It is not an extensive series of specific questions, but rather a set of paragraph headings. It acts as a prompt to the interviewer, a security blanket when the mind goes blank in the middle of an interview, a signal that there is an agenda to follow, and (if a number of minutes is attached to each paragraph) a way of monitoring the progress over the period of the interview. A good topic guide will create an easy and comfortable framework for a discussion, providing a logical and plausible progression through the issues in focus. As the topic guide is drawn up it is a reminder to the researcher that questions about social scientific issues must be pitched in ordinary language using everyday terms adapted to the interviewee. Finally, it acts as a preliminary scheme for the analysis of the transcripts.

However the topic guide is, as the label suggests, a guide, and it should not be followed slavishly as if the success of the research depended on it. The interviewer must use his or her social scientific imagination to recognize when issues beyond prior planning and expectation arise in the discussion which may be important. When such an issue arises this may lead to a modification of the guide for subsequent interviews. Equally, as a series of interviews progresses some topics which were originally considered central in the design phase may turn out to be uninteresting, either for conceptual reasons or because respondents have little if anything to say about them. Finally, as the study progresses the interviewer may form some hypotheses, which can then be explored with a different form of questioning. Essentially, while the topic guide should be well prepared at the beginning of a study, it must be used with some flexibility. Importantly, any such changes should be fully documented with the rationale.

Selecting respondents

The term 'selecting' is used explicitly in preference to 'sampling'. This is because sampling inevitably carries connotations from surveys and opinion polls, where from a systematic statistical sample of the population, results may be generalized within specified confidence limits. In qualitative research the selection of respondents cannot follow the procedures of quantitative research for a number of reasons.

First, in the unlikely event of selecting a random probability sample of say 30 persons for a qualitative study, the range of error attached to a 50/50 split on any indicator would be in the region of plus or minus 20 per cent. So if 30 doctors were interviewed, and half said they would prescribe homeopathic medicines and the other half said they would not, one could confidently say that in the population of doctors between 30 and 70 per cent would prescribe homeopathic cures. With a non-probability sample the range of error might be doubled. Clearly, if one wanted to assess medical enthusiasm or the lack of it for homeopathy, other forms of social research would be better indicated, for example the survey. But often reports of qualitative research include numerical details or vague quantifiers such as 'more than half' concerning the distribution of opinions or experiences among the respondents, as if somehow such numbers lend weight to the interpretation and legitimate generalization to a wider population. This is to misconceive the purpose of qualitative research.

The real purpose of qualitative research is not counting opinions or people but rather exploring the range of opinions, the different representations of the issue. Given a particular social milieu, for example the medical profession, what one is interested in finding out is the variety of views on the issue in question, for example homeopathy, and crucially what underlies and justifies these different viewpoints. In order to be confident that the full range of views has been explored the researcher would need to interview different members of the social milieu. Not all doctors have the same views. But equally, it is generally the case that there are a relatively limited number of views or positions on a topic in a particular social milieu. Thus the researcher would need to consider how this social milieu might be segmented on the issue. There may be some survey data or recorded information to inform the selection of respondents, but this is not often the case. With no prior information to inform the selection of respondents a researcher might talk to some people in the medical profession and ask why they think there are differences regarding support for homeopathy, or he/she might assume that such factors as recency of training, gender, or the profile of the patients would be related to different practices. Whatever the criteria, the objective is to maximize the opportunity to understand the different positions taken by members of the social milieu (see Chapter 2 in this volume).

For other research questions the problem of the selection of respondents may be more complex, as the issue is of relevance to more than one social milieu. Take for example the introduction of genetically modified foods. This is a new technology that impinges on most, if not all, of the public. To understand the range of reactions to GM foods it would be necessary to define relevant milieus from which to make a selection. The default or traditional option is to use the standard socio-demographic variables, that is gender, age, social category and some geographic split, for example urban/rural. Let us assume that each of these indicators is classified as a dichotomy. This would give 16 cells to cover all possible combinations. On the assumption that for both individual and group interviews, at minimum, two interviews for each cell would be required, this would give 32 interviews.

This would be a major undertaking, too large for many studies. So the researcher makes a selection from the 16 cells, picking out combinations of socio-demographic characteristics which are likely to be of interest. All the characteristics are thereby included, but not all possible combinations of the characteristics.

An alternative way of thinking about segmentation is to use 'natural' rather than statistical or taxonomic groups. In natural groups people interact together; they may share a common past, or have a common future project. They may also read the same media and have broadly similar concerns and values. In this sense natural groups form a social milieu. Returning to the example of GM foods, instead of proceeding on the assumption that social and demographic characteristics will be diagnostic of differing views of the topic, the selection of respondents could be based on relevant natural groups or social milieus. Since GM foods have been discussed by environmentalists in terms of risks, by consumer groups in terms of safety issues particularly for children, by religious groups in terms of ethics, and by farmers in terms of both profits and threats to organic farming, these are candidate milieus. Thus interviews might be conducted with members of environmental organizations, mothers with children, people of different religious faiths and those involved in farming. Within these groupings it would be necessary to consider whether such characteristics as gender, age and education would be relevant or not. It is known for example that while males tend to be more accepting of new technologies than females, the relationship with age is not straightforward. Once again the researcher has to make some judgements about the trade-off between the benefits of researching certain segments and the costs of ignoring others. For such choices a social scientific imagination is essential. There are no right answers.

In summary, the objective of qualitative research is to sample the range of views. Unlike the sample survey where the probability sample can be applied in most research situations, there is no one method for selecting respondents for qualitative inquiries. Here, because the numbers of respondents are necessarily small, the researcher must use his or her social scientific imagination to inform the selection of respondents. While standard socio-demographic characteristics may be relevant and clearly are for consumer and political issues, it may be more efficient and productive to think in terms of the relevant social milieus for other issues in question. In some circumstances the research may follow a phased approach. Here the first phase may use a sample design based on all the available information prior to researching the topic. Having evaluated the data from this phase, a second phase may then focus on particular categories of respondent who seem to be particularly interesting. Finally, whatever the criteria of respondent selection, the procedures and choices should be detailed and justified in any report.

How many interviews are required?

In many respects this question invites the response, 'how long is a piece of string?', and in reality the answer is, 'it depends'. It depends on the nature of the topic, on the numbers of different milieus that are considered relevant and, of course, on the resources available. However there are some general considerations to guide the decision. A key point to bear in mind is that, all things being equal, more interviews do not necessarily imply better quality or more detailed understanding. There are two bases to this claim. First, there are a limited number of interpretations or versions of reality. While experiences may appear to be unique to the individual, the representations of such experiences do not arise in individual minds; in some measure they are the outcome of social processes. To this extent representations of an issue of common concern, or of people in a particular social milieu, are in part shared. This can be seen in a series of interviews. The first few are full of surprises. The differences between the accounts are striking and one sometimes wonders if there are any similarities. However, common themes begin to appear and progressively one feels increased confidence in the emerging understanding of the phenomenon. At some point a researcher realizes that no new surprises or insights are forthcoming. At this point of meaning saturation the researcher may depart from the topic guide to check his or her understanding, and if the appreciation of the phenomenon is corroborated it is a signal that it is time to stop.

Secondly, there is the issue of the size of the corpus to be analysed. The transcript of an interview may run to 15 pages; thus with 20 interviews there are some 300 pages in the corpus. In order to analyse a corpus of texts from interviews and to go beyond the superficial selection of a number of illustrative quotations, it is essential to almost live and dream the interviews – to be able to recall each setting and respondent, and the key themes of each interview. There is a loss of information in textual record and the interviewer must be able to bring to mind the emotional tone of the respondent and to recall why they asked a particular question. Accounts or comments which at first hearing appear to be inconsequential may suddenly come into focus as the contributions of different interviewees are compared and contrasted.

For these two reasons there is an upper limit to the number of interviews that it is necessary to conduct and possible to analyse. For the single researcher this is somewhere between 15 and 25 individual interviews and some six to eight focus group discussions. Of course the research may be phased: a first set of interviews, followed by analysis, and then a second set. Or there may be a combination of individual and group interviews. In such situations it may be desirable to conduct a greater number of interviews and to analyse the different components of the corpus separately, bringing them together at a later stage.

A cautionary note on qualitative interviewing

Becker and Geer (1957) argue that participant observation is 'the most complete form of the sociological datum'. As such it provides a benchmark against which to judge other methods, or as they put it, to 'know what orders of information escape us when we use other methods'. In comparison with the intensive fieldwork of participant observation, Becker and Geer see three limitations or shortcomings with the interview. Essentially these arise from the fact that the interviewer relies on the informant's account of actions that occurred elsewhere in space and time.

In this situation the interviewer may not fully understand the 'local language': the connotation of some ordinary terms may be quite different. Secondly, for a variety of reasons the informant may omit important detail. It may be that some things are just part of the taken for granted; others may be difficult to put into words or appear to the respondent to be impolite or insensitive. Thirdly, an informant may view situations through 'distorted lenses' and provide an account which is misleading and not open to checking or verification.

These limitations of the interview may lead the researcher to make invalid inferences about situations and events. With participant observation the researcher is open to a greater breadth and depth of information, is able to triangulate different impressions and observations, and is able to follow up emergent discrepancies in the course of the fieldwork.

Becker and Geer do not suggest that these potential limitations of the interview invalidate the method. They acknowledge that for reasons of practicality and economy the interview is a useful method. What they offer are issues for consideration to sensitize researchers to the problems and to act as a catalyst for better interviewing skills. Practically speaking the implications of Becker and Geer are threefold. First, the interviewer should not take anything for granted. Secondly, they should probe assiduously for more detail than the interviewee may offer as a first reply to a question. Finally, it is in the accumulation of insights from a set of interviews that one comes to understand the life worlds within a group of respondents.

Methodological choices: individual versus group interviewing

Having acknowledged Becker and Geer's warnings, we now address the key consideration of which type of interviewing methodology would be best suited to the inquiry, individual or group interviewing. There is a striking contrast in choice of methods between academic and commercial research. Generally speaking academic research uses the individual depth interview, while the commercial sector favours group interviewing. The different orientations may be justified on the grounds of tradition, or on pragmatic considerations. For example since commercial research is often time pressured it is much quicker to run a small number of focus group interviews than it is to interview the same number of people individually.

Of course there are many similarities between individual and group interviewing. In both types of interview the researcher does not lead the inquiry with a set of predetermined questions, as in a survey or questionnaire. While the broad content is structured by the research questions as these inform the topic guide, the idea is not to ask a set of standard questions or to expect the respondent to translate their thoughts into specified response categories. The questions are almost an invitation to the respondent to talk at length, in their own terms, and with time to reflect. Furthermore, unlike in the survey the researcher can obtain clarification and amplification of interesting points, with appropriate probing and targeted questioning.

But are there any conceptual grounds that might inform the choice of method? Any research interview is a social process, an interaction or cooperative venture, in which words are the main medium of exchange. It is not merely a one-way process of information passing from one (the interviewee) to another (the interviewer). Rather it is an interaction, an exchange of ideas and meanings, in which various realities and perceptions are explored and developed. To this extent both the respondent(s) and the interviewer are in different ways involved in the production of knowledge. When we deal with meanings and feelings about the world and about events there are different feasible realities depending on the situation and the nature of the interaction. Thus the interview is a joint venture, a sharing and negotiation of realities. In analysing the production of social knowledge or representations, Bauer and Gaskell (1999) argue that the minimal social system involved in representation is a dialogical triad: two persons (subject 1 and subject 2) who are concerned with an object (0) in relation to a project (P), along the time dimension. This triangle of mediation, extended in time (S–O–P–S), is the basic communication unit for the elaboration of meaning. Meaning is not an individual or a private affair, but is always influenced by the 'other', concrete or imagined.

With this in mind, consider the depth interview. It is a one-to-one conversation, a dyadic interaction. But it differs from ordinary conversations in a number of respects. It lasts for over an hour and is between two previously unacquainted people. There is an unusual role relationship. One person, the interviewer, is expected to ask the questions; the other, the interviewee, is expected to respond to them. The topic is the choice of the interviewer; the interviewee may or may not have given it serious consideration beforehand.

In this strange situation the interviewee may be rather self-conscious and perhaps a little hesitant and defensive. What role should they take in this conversation of unequals? Can they trust the interviewer, can they say what they really feel? Their initial inclination may be to follow the norms of everyday conversation, to limit answers to what is presumed to be relevant and informative (Grice, 1975), and to adopt positions on issues that match a particular self-image.

To counter these understandable tendencies and to encourage the interviewee to talk at length, to expand on aspects of their life and to be frank, the interviewer must put the interviewee at ease and establish a relationship of trust and confidence, so-called rapport. This is achieved by the interviewer's form of questions, by verbal and non-verbal reinforcement, and by being relaxed and unselfconscious. As the rapport develops, so is the interviewee more likely to be relaxed and expansive, to think and talk about things beyond the level of surface opinions, and less likely to offer normative rationalization. At the same time the interviewer is increasingly able to follow up issues with further questions and probes. To some degree the interviewer must adopt the role of a counsellor.

Essentially, in the successful depth interview the personal worldview of the interviewee is explored in detail. While such personal views reflect the residues or memories of past conversations, the interviewee has centre stage. It is their personal construction of the past. In the course of such an interview it is fascinating to hear a narrative under construction: some of the elements are well remembered, but details and interpretations are voiced which may even surprise the interviewee himself or herself. Perhaps it is only by talking that we know what we think.

Moving from the unique form of dyadic interaction of the depth interview to the group interview brings qualitative changes in the nature of the social situation. In the focus group the interviewer, often called the moderator, is a catalyst for social interaction (communication) between the participants. The objective of the focus group is to stimulate the participants to talk and to respond to each other, to compare experiences and impressions and to react to what other people in the group say. To this extent it is a more genuine social interaction than the depth interview. It is an example of the minimal social unit in operation, and as such the meanings or representations that emerge are more influenced by the social nature of the group interaction, rather than relying on the individual perspective, as in the depth interview.

The social processes in groups have been studied extensively in the literature on group dynamics. There are at least three progenitors of the focus group: the group therapy tradition of the Tavistock Institute (Bion, 1961), the evaluation of communication effectiveness (Merton and Kendall, 1946), and the group dynamics tradition in social psychology (Lewin, 1958).

Essentially research shows that the group, as distinct from a number of people in the same location, is more than the sum of the parts: it becomes an entity in itself. Processes occur in groups which are not seen in the dyadic interaction of the depth interview. The emergence of the group goes hand in hand with the development of a shared identity, that sense of common fate captured in the self-description 'we'. A group may subdivide into factions challenging each other's views and opinions. Group interaction may generate emotion, humour, spontaneity and creative insights. People in groups are more willing to entertain novel ideas, and to explore their implications. Groups have been found to take greater risks and to show attitude polarization – the movement to more extreme positions. Based on these insights the focus group is a more naturalistic and holistic setting in which the participants take account of the views of others in formulating their responses and commenting on their own and others' experiences.

Based on these considerations we can summarize the key features of the group interview:

1 A synergy emerges out of the social interaction: in other words, the group is more than the sum of its parts.
2 It is possible to observe the group process, the dynamics of attitude and opinion change and opinion leadership.
3 In a group there can be a level of emotional involvement which is seldom seen in one-to-one interviews.

Underlying the focus group are various theoretical frameworks about the process of group formation. For example, Tuckman (1965) identified four developmental stages. First, there is the *forming* stage in which there is confusion and uncertainty, the establishment of acquaintances and the beginnings of the establishment of a group identity. This is followed by the *storming* stage where there is conflict between group members and between the group as a whole and the leader. If this period of conflict is resolved the group becomes cohesive, the *norming* stage. With roles defined and the group established, the *performing* stage is reached in which the real work of value to the researcher is done. To this list Gordon and Langmaid (1988) add a final phase, that of *mourning*. Here, as the group session comes to a close and the tape recorder is off, there are semi-private discussions between group members themselves and between some of the group and the moderator. There are last things to be said, explanations for embarrassing admissions and more generally a re-entry to the real world. The moderator may wish that the tape was still recording as points of some significance may be raised. In such circumstances it is always a good idea to take notes after the participants have left the room.

The task of the moderator is to facilitate the group's progress towards the final stage, that of 'performing', which in the typical 90 minute group session may take between 15 and 45 minutes.

Having considered some conceptual issues underlying individual and group interviewing, we turn to the problem of deciding how to select between the two approaches. While many practitioners have well-articulated views on when and why they would use one or other approach, on this issue the research literature is rather equivocal (Morgan, 1996). There is no consensus as to when one method is likely to be more effective. Some suggest that groups are more creative, others not; some recommend individual interviews for sensitive topics, but other researchers have successfully explored sexual behaviours in focus groups. In all probability it depends on the nature of the research topic, on the research objectives, on the types of respondent, and to some extent on the skills and personal preferences of the researcher. There is insufficient methodological research to draw hard and fast conclusions. However, it is possible to make some general observations which may help researchers to consider the options and make an informed decision.

For the same number of respondents the focus group is more efficient. The group gives insights into the emerging consensus and the way people handle disagreements. In a group setting people may be creative; the reseacher/moderator can explore metaphors and imagery and use projective type stimuli. In the group situation the sharing and contrasting of experiences builds up a picture of common interests and concerns which, in part experienced by all, are seldom articulated by the single individual. The group is rather like a soap opera, a perspective on everyday life that is revealed only through watching the whole programme and not merely the contribution of a single actor.

But there are a number of disadvantages to focus groups which illustrate the advantages of the individual interview. First, the participants in focus groups tend to be somewhat self-selective. Not all those invited turn up and some target groups are difficult to recruit, e.g. ethnic minorities, the old and disabled, mothers with very young children. Similarly it is difficult, but not impossible, to recruit busy elite respondents to a group session. Such selection problems can be avoided with individual interviews, where the interview can be scheduled at a time and place convenient to the respondent. Secondly, it is not feasible to focus attention on a particular individual in a group discussion in the same way that can be achieved in a one-to-one interview. With the single respondent, far richer detail about personal experiences, decisions and action sequences can be elicited, with follow-up probe questions focusing on motivations in the context of detailed information about the particular circumstances of the person. What the interviewee says, and how the interview develops, can be related to other relevant characteristics of the individual in a way that is not possible within the discussion and subsequent analysis of a focus group.

In Table 3.1 the various advantages of individual and group interviewing are tentatively summarized. Given these differential strengths and limitations of focus groups and individual interviews, some researchers opt for a

Table 3.1   *A summary of the indication of depth and group interviews*

Individual interview	Group interview
Where the research objective is to:	
Explore the life world of the individual in depth	Orient the researcher to a field of inquiry and the local language
Do case studies with repeated interviews over time	Explore the range of attitudes, opinions and behaviours
Test an instrument or questionnaire (the cognitive interview)	Observe the processes of consensus and disagreement
	Add contextual detail to quantitative findings
When the topic concerns:	
Detailed individual experiences, choices and personal biographies	Issues of public interest or common concern, e.g. politics, the media, consumer behaviour, leisure, new technologies
Issues of particular sensitivity which may provoke anxiety	Issues and questions of a relatively unfamiliar or hypothetical nature
When the respondents are:	
Difficult to recruit, for example the elderly, mothers with young children, the ill	Not from such different backgrounds as to inhibit participation in the discussion of the topic
Elite or high-status respondents	
Children younger than about seven years	

mixture of the two methods within the same project: a multi-method approach that has some justification.

The practicalities of interviewing

The focus group interview

One might characterize the focus group as an approximation of Habermas's (1992) description of the ideal public sphere. It is a debate open and accessible to all; the issues at stake are common concerns; inequalities of status between participants are disregarded; and the debate is based on rational discussion. On this final characteristic the idea of 'rational' is not that of the logical and dispassionate. The debate is an exchange of views, ideas and experiences, however emotionally and illogically expressed, but without privileging particular individuals or positions.

The traditional focus group comprises six to eight previously unacquainted people, meeting in a comfortable setting for between one and two hours. The participants and the moderator sit in a circle so that there can be eye-to-eye contact between everyone. When people have sat down the moderator's first task is to introduce himself or herself, the topic and the idea of a group discussion.

To start this process the moderator asks each participant in turn to introduce themselves by name, and may add a request for some non-controversial personal information. Each contribution ends with the moderator saying 'thank you', using the person's first name. As this is done the moderator takes note of the names and positions in the room. As with the depth interview the moderator has a topic guide summarizing the questions and issues for discussion. The moderator actively encourages all the participants to talk and to respond to other group members' comments and observations. When person A says something the moderator may thank them, again using their name, and turn to person C, asking something such as, 'I was very interested in Bill's views on X, does that tally with your experience?' The objective is to progress from a moderator led discussion to one in which the participants react to each other.

But the moderator must be much more than a facilitator of the discussion. In the spirit of Becker and Geer's cautions, it is imperative that the moderator takes nothing for granted. Perhaps the most common probes following a comment are questions to the effect, 'what do you mean by that?' and 'why is that?'

Consider some examples. If an interesting word or phrase is introduced into the discussion, always ask, 'when you say X, what does it mean to you?' If a respondent makes a factual statement, the moderator might ask, 'and do you think that is a good or a bad thing?' Equally, if someone says that they don't like something, the moderator should probe, 'So you say you don't like X, why is that?' And each time one member of the group responds to a probe for further information, the moderator should turn to other members of the group and ask for their view. Of course it is not always necessary for the moderator to probe as other members of the group may spontaneously enter the discussion with comments and views.

Another useful approach is for the moderator to switch the group's perspective between the general and the particular. If a general statement is made the moderator might ask for an example of it, and follow this up with, 'is that a good example, can you think of others?' Conversely a discussion around a specific case might invite the intervention, 'is this typical, is this what generally happens?'

Moderators may use free association tasks, pictures, drawings, photographs and even drama as stimulus materials to promote ideas and discussion as a means of getting people to use their imagination and to develop ideas and themes.

Consider the following examples.

FREE ASSOCIATION   To find out how people frame an issue, that is the perspective they bring to it, and to understand the range of related concepts and ideas, free association can be revealing. The moderator might ask:

> There is a lot of talk about genetic engineering these days; when you think about the term 'genetic engineering', what words or phrases come to mind?

The question is posed to the group as a whole. Now of course, some of the group may be uncertain whether they know what the term means, but that does not matter. Invariably someone has an opinion and suggests some words, which leads on to a serial association task. Some will agree with others and provide a further illustration, others will take a different perspective. From the initial frames the moderator may guide the group towards a discussion of genetic engineering in general, or may ask where people have heard about it, or who they would trust to tell the truth about it. Thus a free association task may lead on to many different avenues of debate depending on the moderator's interests and those of the group.

PICTURE/ISSUE SORTING   The moderator may ask the group to look at eight to ten carefully selected examples of an issue depicted by words and phrases on cards or by pictures (photographs or cutouts from magazines). The cards or phrases are placed on a table or on the floor so that all the participants can see them. The moderator asks the group to sort the stimuli into two piles. Normally, the introduction of such a task is followed by a request for more information: 'on what basis should we sort them?' The moderator might say, 'well, on any characteristic that you feel is relevant'. Typically one or two participants will rise to the challenge and offer a suggestion; others will then ask for the justification for the scheme and this will lead to agreements, disagreements and modifications. As the group comes to an agreed categorization, the criteria of categorization are developed and explained. The moderator may ask for further clarification, and/ or ask whether there are any other ways in which the stimuli could be categorized. In this way, the set of stimuli become a catalyst for discussion around aspects of the issue.

Photo Sorts   Here a set of photographs of a broad range of people are shown to the group. They are asked, 'which of these people would . . .?', and after that, 'which of these people would not . . .?' And of course as choices are made the moderator asks, 'and why do you think that?' While such stereotypes provide insights into popular beliefs, they also act to open up broader issues related to the topic in question and will often elicit personal details and preferences which then can be contrasted and reflected on in the group.

Role Playing   For the more ambitious moderator, who enjoys theatre, the creation of a role play situation can be very revealing. Consider a study on doctor and patient relations. One might give two people the role of the doctor, with one being told that he/she is running late and is under time pressure, while the other is given no such information. Two other group participants are instructed to play the patient role. It is quite surprising how well people assume the roles and take their instructions seriously. The roles are enacted and the rest of the group (the audience) may comment, applaud or offer their experiences to illustrate the accuracy of the role enactment. Again, the behaviour and what is said by the role players is a source of insight in itself, but this also acts as a basis for a broader discussion on the issue in question.

Although the traditional focus group uses unacquainted people this is not a precondition. Indeed there are times when prior familiarity is an advantage. Studies of organizational cultures and of particular social groupings benefit from taking people who share a common social milieu. Here the moderator is likely to be an outsider and may use this to advantage. The moderator can take the position of the naive observer and ask for instructions or education on particular points. People enjoy the opportunity of taking on the teaching role and, as they individually and collectively explain their situation, some aspects of the self-evident and tacit knowledge are elaborated in a way that would be difficult to elicit from a set of questions.

The individual interview

The individual or depth interview is a conversation lasting normally for one to one and a half hours. Prior to the interview the researcher will have prepared a topic guide covering the key research issues and problems (see above). The interview starts with some introductory comments about the research, a word of thanks to the interviewee for agreeing to talk, and a request for permission to tape record the session. The interviewer should be open and relaxed about tape recording, which can be justified as an *aide-mémoire* or a helpful record of the conversation for later analysis. It also allows the interviewer to concentrate on what is said rather than the taking of notes. Always double check that the recorder is working properly before the interview and take care to press the correct buttons in the interview itself. To get the interview going it is helpful to start with some fairly straightforward, interesting and unthreatening questions. The interviewer should be attentive and interested in what the respondent says: encouragement in the form of eye contact, nods and other reinforcements should be given. Introduce the idea of a conversation by picking up a point and asking for some more detail. Some respondents take a little time to relax, but that is to be expected. As the interview progresses the interviewer needs to keep the research questions in mind, occasionally checking the topic guide, but the focus of attention should be on listening and understanding what has been said. It is important to give the respondent time to think, so pauses should not be filled with a further question.

SOME EXAMPLE QUESTIONS   Most of these can be followed up by probes.

Inviting descriptions:

> Could you tell me about the time you . . .?
>
> What comes to mind when you think of . . .?
>
> How would you describe . . . to someone who had not come across it before?

And taking things further:

> Can you tell me more about . . .?
>
> What makes you feel like that?
>
> And is that important to you? Why is that?

Eliciting contextual information:

> When did you first hear about X, where were you and who were you with?
>
> What did other people you were with say at the time?
>
> What was your immediate reaction?

Projective:

> What sort of a person do you think would like X?
>
> What sort of person would dislike X?

Testing your hypotheses:

> From what you say it seems that you think. . . I am right there?
>
> What would you think if such and such?

From specific to general and vice versa:

In your experience is X typical of things/people like that?

Can you give me a particular example of that?

Taking a naive position:

I am not very familiar with that, could you tell me a little more about it?

How would you describe that to someone who was new to the situation?

Final thoughts:

We have covered a lot of interesting issues, is there anything we have not covered?

Is there anything else you would like to tell me?

When closing the interview, try to end on a positive note. Thank the respondent and reassure them of confidentiality. Give the respondent time to 'come out' of the interview mode before leaving, they may wish to add some comments now that the tape recorder is switched off. Finally, explain how the information will be used and perhaps the progress of your research.

Analysis

In Part II of this volume various approaches to the analysis of a corpus of text are described. Each one comes from a different conceptual orientation, asks different questions of the text corpus and provides a different language for interpretation. All are based on a full text of the interview, so whatever analytic orientation is selected the first stage is to produce a good quality transcript. For the present purposes this transcription includes all the spoken words, but not the paralinguistic characteristics. If the transcript is not prepared by the researcher, he or she should check it against the original tape recording and edit accordingly.

The broad aim of the analysis is to look for meanings and understanding. What is actually said is the data, but the analysis should go beyond accepting this at face value. The quest is for common content themes and the functions of these themes. Some theoretical perspectives talk of core and peripheral representations, the former being those that are widespread within a social milieu.

In practical terms analysis and interpretation require time and effort and there is no one best method. Essentially, they involve the researcher immersing himself or herself in the text corpus. In the process of reading and rereading, the traditional techniques employed, usually with a pencil and other low-technology aids (colour highlighters), include: marking and highlighting, adding notes and comments to the text, cutting and pasting, the identification of concordance in the context of certain words, forms of graphical representation of issues, note cards and card sorts, and finally thematic analysis. In reading the transcripts, aspects of the interview beyond the words are recalled and the researcher almost relives the interview. This is an essential part of the process and it is why it is rather difficult to analyse interviews conducted by other people.

A useful procedure is to construct a matrix with the research aims and objectives set out in questions as the column headings, and what each respondent (group) said as the rows. This structures the data, bringing responses together in an accessible way. In a final column add notes and preliminary interpretations.

As the transcripts are read and reread, make notes of ideas that come to mind. Keep the aims and objectives of the research to the fore, look for patterns and connections, look for the larger picture that goes beyond the specific detail. Sometimes work quickly and imaginatively, at other times work methodically, carefully examining the sections of text related to particular topics. Look out for contradictions, for the way in which attitudes and opinions develop in the interviews, and for typical rationalizations.

The analysis is not a purely mechanical process. It hinges on creative insights, which may well occur when the researcher is talking to a friend or colleague, or in those moments of contemplation when driving, walking or taking a bath.

As the interpretation develops, return to the raw material, both transcript and tape recording. Sometimes a single comment will suddenly take on particular significance and suggest a new way of looking at the interviews; at other times the data may reinforce the emerging analysis. It is vital to check that any interpretation is rooted in the interviews themselves, so that when the analysis is written the corpus can be drawn upon to justify the conclusions.

Computer-assisted qualitative data analysis software (CAQDAS)

Recent software developments implement the traditional techniques of textual analysis in a user-friendly computer interface. Many of the elements of these software developments are derived from standard word processing (the cut-and-paste function, for example). But importantly the more advanced packages offer additional features, sometimes theoretically driven, which go beyond the mere manipulation of text towards facilitating interpretation. Commonly available functions include:

- *Memoing* Adding commentary to the process of analysis.
- *Coding, tagging, labelling* Identifying similar text units.
- *Retrieving* Finding units in the same category.
- *Linking* Text–text, code–text, memo–text, memo–code, code–code.
- *Boolean searching* Finding specified combinations of codes such as 'and', 'or' and 'not' relations.

- *Graphical interface* Representing the relations between codes and texts.
- *Comparisons between texts of different origins* Social categories, time series.

The main outputs from CAQDAS are as follows. First, coding, cutting and pasting produce printouts of all text passages which concern the same category, e.g. theme codes, contributor codes and formal features. This provides a summary of all relevant elements of a text pertaining to a particular code of interest. This form of output is an efficient way of representing the textual elements, so that the researcher can illustrate his or her interpretation with selected citations.

Graphical interfacing and/or cognitive mapping provide the opportunity to develop a graphical representation of the structure of relations between codes in the text. This may be hierarchical, using linked superordinate and subordinate categories, or it may involve different forms of linkage such as 'causal', 'associative', 'contradictory', other. The graphical representation of the text is the place where textual features and theoretical preconceptions meet in a formal and iterative procedure.

Most qualitative analysis software packages produce an optional output of code frequencies, which can be imported for further statistical analysis, e.g. into SPSS. This facility provides a link between the qualitative and quantitative approaches and affords the opportunity for such approaches as profiling, cross-tabulations and correspondence analysis. There are many interesting examples in the academic literature of complementary interpretations obtained with qualitative and numerical analysis. A feature of these software packages is that they open new options without closing old.

There are many such CAQDAS packages available. All take some time to master but the effort can be worthwhile, particularly with a medium to large text corpus. Two of the popular packages are NUD*IST, based on the 'grounded theory' of the symbolic interactionists; and ATLAS/ti, which is also compatible with grounded theory, but in addition offers a graphical interface function drawing on ideas from semantic memory theory. At a minimum CAQDAS will do what researchers have always done, but do it more systematically and more efficiently. Rather than having card systems and marker pens, the computer maintains the filing system, and allows for modifications and changes to the analysis with relatively little effort. A possible development of these new tools will be that standard procedures for handling textual data become commonplace and provide a framework within which to define basic quality standards and assessment for qualitative research.

However, a word of caution is necessary. It would be unfortunate to fall into the trap of the 'computer myth', the assumption that software packages will replace the skills and sensitivities of the researcher. Computers will not do the intuitive and creative work that is an essential part of qualitative analysis. At most they will support the process and provide a representation of the output of the analysis. Because the computer packages contain many features, they carry the danger that the researcher gets absorbed in the technology and loses sight of the text.

STEPS IN QUALITATIVE INTERVIEWING

Note that in actual research these steps are not in a linear sequence. The process of research is circular and reflexive. For example, after a few interviews both the topic guide and the selection of respondents may change. Equally, analysis is part of the ongoing process of research.

1 Prepare the topic guide.
2 Select the method of interviewing: individual, group or a combination of the two.
3 Design a strategy for the selection of respondents.
4 Conduct the interviews.
5 Transcribe the interviews.
6 Analyse the text corpus.

References

Bauer, M.W. and Gaskell, G. (1999) 'Towards a paradigm for research on social representations', *Journal for the Theory of Social Behaviour*, 29(2): 163–86.

Becker, H.S. and Geer, B. (1957) 'Participant observation and interviewing: a comparison', *Human Organisation*, 16(3): 28–32.

Bion, W.R. (1961) *Experiences in Groups*. London: Tavistock.

Farr, R.M. (1982) 'Interviewing: the social psychology of the interview', in F. Fransella (ed.), *Psychology for Occupational Therapists*. London: Macmillan.

Glaser, B.G. and Strauss, A.L. (1967) *The Discovery of Grounded Theory: Strategies for Qualitative Research*. New York: Aldine.

Gordon, W. and Langmaid, P. (1988) *Qualitative Market Research: a Practitioner's Guide*. Aldershot: Gower.

Grice, H.P. (1975) 'Logic and conversation', in P. Cole and J.L. Morgan (eds), *Syntax and Semantics: Speech Acts*, Vol. 3. New York: Academic Press. pp. 41–58.

Habermas, J. (1992) *The Structural Transformation of the Public Sphere: an Inquiry into a Category of Bourgeois Society*. Cambridge: Polity Press.

Lewin, K. (1958) 'Group decision and social change', in E.E. Maccoby, T.M. Newcomb and E.L. Hartley (eds), *Readings in Social Psychology*, 3rd edn. New York: Holt, Rinehart & Winston.

Merton, R. and Kendall, P. (1946) 'The focused interview', *American Journal of Sociology*, 1: 541–57.

Morgan, D.L. (1996) 'Focus groups', *Annual Review of Sociology*, 22: 129–52.

Tuckman, B. (1965) 'Developmental sequence in small groups', *Psychological Bulletin*, 63: 384–99.

4

Narrative Interviewing

Sandra Jovchelovitch and Martin W. Bauer

KEYWORDS

concluding talk	main narration
eigentheory	narrative
exmanent and immanent	narrative and representation
questions	narrative interview
indexical and non-indexical text	questioning phase
informant	self-generating schema
initial topic	trajectories; individual and collective

The study of narratives has gained a new momentum in recent years. This renewed interest in an old topic – concern with narratives and narrativity goes back to Aristotle's *Poetics* – is related to increasing awareness of the role story-telling plays in shaping social phenomena. In the wake of this new awareness, narratives have become a widespread research method in the social sciences. Discussion about narratives, however, goes far beyond their use as a method of inquiry. Narrative as a discursive form, narratives as history, and narratives as life stories and societal stories have been approached by cultural and literary theorists, linguists, philosophers of history, psychologists and anthropologists.

This chapter addresses the use of narratives in social inquiry by discussing some elements of narrative theory and introducing the narrative interview as a specific technique of data collection, in particular in the format systematized by Schütze (1977; 1983; 1992). In what follows we introduce conceptual issues related to narratives, and present the narrative interview as a method of data elicitation, discussing in detail the procedure, indication for its use and potential problems associated with this technique. We conclude with a discussion of the thorny epistemological problem of what, in fact, narratives tell us.

Conceptual issues

There is no human experience that cannot be expressed in the form of a narrative. As Roland Barthes pointed out:

> Narrative is present in myth, legend, fable, tale, novella, epic, history, tragedy, drama, comedy, mime, painting (think of Carpaccio's Saint Ursula), stained-glass windows, cinema, comics, news items, conversation. Moreover, under this almost infinite diversity of forms, narrative is present in every age, in every place, in every society; it begins with the very history of mankind and there nowhere is nor has been a people without narrative . . . Caring nothing for the division between good and bad literature, narrative is international, transhistorical, trans-cultural: it is simply there, like life itself. (1993: 251–2)

Indeed, narratives are infinite in their variety, and we find them everywhere. There seems to be in all forms of human life a need to tell; story-telling is an elementary form of human communication and, independently of stratified language performance, it is a universal competence. By telling, people recall what has happened, put experience into sequence, find possible explanations for it, and play with the chain of events that shapes individual and social life. Story-telling involves intentional states that alleviate, or at least make familiar, events and feelings that confront ordinary everyday life.

Communities, social groups and subcultures tell stories with words and meanings that are specific to their experience and way of life. The lexicon of a social group constitutes its perspective on the world, and it is assumed that narrations preserve particular perspectives in a more genuine form. Story-telling is a skill relatively independent of education and language competence; while the latter is unequally distributed in any population, the competence to tell stories is not, or at least is less so. An event can be rendered either in general terms or in indexical terms. Indexical means that reference is made to concrete events in place and time. Narrations are rich in indexical statements, (a) because they refer to personal experience, and (b) because they tend to be detailed with a focus on events and actions. The structure of a narration is similar to the structure of orientation for action: a context is given; the events are sequential and end at a particular point; the narration includes a kind of evaluation of the outcome. Situation, goal-setting, planning, and evaluation of outcomes are constituents of human goal-directed actions. The narration reconstructs actions and context in the most adequate way: it reveals place, time, motivation and the actor's symbolic system of orientations (Schütze, 1977; Bruner, 1990).

The act of telling a story is fairly simple. According to Ricoeur (1980), someone puts a number of actions and experiences into a sequence. These are the actions of a number of characters, and these characters act out situations that change. The changes bring to light elements of the situation and of the characters that were previously implicit. In doing so, they call for thinking, or for action, or for both. Story-telling comprises two dimensions: the chronological dimension, which refers to the narrative as a sequence of episodes, and the non-chronological, which involves the construction of a whole from successive events, or the configuration of a *plot*.

The plot is crucial to the constitution of a narrative structure. It is through the plot that individual units (or smaller stories within the big story) in the narrative acquire meaning. Therefore a narrative is not just a listing of events, but an attempt to link them both in time and in meaning. If we consider events in isolation they appear to us as simple propositions that describe independent happenings. But if they are composed into a story, the ways in which they are related allow for the meaning-production operation of the plot. It is the plot that gives coherence and meaning to the narrative, as well as providing the context in which we understand each of the events, actors, descriptions, goals, morals and relationships that usually form a story.

Plots operate through specific functions that serve to compose and configure various events into a narrative. First, it is the plot of a narrative that defines the temporal range that marks the beginning and end of a story. We know that human life, and the vast majority of social phenomena, flow without precise beginnings and ends. Yet in order to make sense of life's events and understand what is going on, it is important to demarcate beginnings and ends. Secondly, the plot provides criteria for the selection of events to be included in the narrative, for how these events are ordered into an unfolding sequence until the conclusion of the story, and for the clarification of the implicit meanings that events have as contributors to the narrative as a whole. Deciding what is to be told and what is not, and what should be told first, are operations related to the meaning that a plot gives to a narrative.

In this sense, narratives live beyond the sentences and events that form them; structurally, narratives share the characteristics of the sentence without ever being reducible to the simple sum of its sentences or forming events. In the same vein, meaning is not at the 'end' of the narrative; it permeates the whole story. Thus to understand the narrative is not merely to follow the chronological sequence of events that are unfolded by the story-teller: it is also to recognize its non-chronological dimension expressed by the functions and meanings of the plot.

The narrative interview

The narrative interview (henceforth, NI) envisages a setting that encourages and stimulates an interviewee (who in NI is called an 'informant') to tell a story about some significant event in their life and social context. The technique derives its label from the Latin word *narrare*, to report, to tell a story. In an unpublished manuscript, Schütze (1977) has suggested a systematization of this technique. Its basic idea is to reconstruct social events from the perspective of informants as directly as possible. To date, we have used narrative interviews to reconstruct informants' perspectives in two studies: first, to reconstruct actors' perspectives in a controversial software development project in a corporate context (Bauer, 1991; 1996; 1997); and secondly, to investigate representations of public life in Brazil (Jovchelovitch, 2000). Positive experiences encourage us to recommend the technique, and to make Schütze's systematization available in the English language with some elaboration.

This particular version of narrative interviewing has not been accessible in English, although writings about narratives abound in different versions. Most writings about 'narratives' have an analytic focus, stressing the structural characteristics and philosophical significance of narratives (Riesman, 1993; Barthes, 1993; Bruner, 1990; Mitchell, 1980; Johnson and Mandler, 1980; Kintsch and VanDijk, 1978; Propp, 1928). The strength of Schütze's suggestion is a systematic proposal for eliciting narratives for the purposes of social research. Schütze's manuscript of 1977 remains unpublished; it spread widely as grey literature and became the focus of a veritable method community in Germany during the 1980s. The original idea developed out of a research project on power structures in local communities.

Narrative as a self-generating schema: 'once upon a time'

Story-telling seems to follow universal rules that guide the process of story production. Schütze (1977) describes as the 'inherent demands of narration' (*Zugzwaenge des Erzaehlens*) what others have called 'story schema', 'narrative convention' or 'story grammar' (Johnson and Mandler, 1980; Kintsch and VanDijk, 1978; Labov, 1972). A schema structures a semi-autonomous process activated by a pre-determined situation. A narration is thus elicited on the basis of particular clues, and, once the informant has started, story-telling will sustain a flow of narration drawing on underlying tacit rules.

Story-telling follows a self-generating schema with three main characteristic as follows.

DETAILED TEXTURE   This refers to the need to give detailed information in order to account plausibly for the transition from one event to another. The narrator tends to give as much detail of events as is necessary to make the transition between them plausible. This is done taking the listener into account: the story has to be plausible for an audience, otherwise it is no story. The less the listener knows, the more detail will be given. Story-telling is close to events. It will account for time, place, motives, points of orientation, plans, strategies and abilities.

RELEVANCE FIXATION   The story-teller reports those features of the event that are relevant according to his or her perspective on the world. The account of events is necessarily selective. It unfolds around thematic centres that reflect what the narrator considers relevant. These themes represent his or her relevance structure.

CLOSING OF THE GESTALT   A core event mentioned in the narration has to be reported completely, with a beginning, a middle and an end. The end can be the present, if the actual events are not yet finished. This threefold structure of a closure makes the story flow, once it has started: the beginning tends towards the middle, and the middle tends towards the end.

Beyond the question–answer schema

The narrative interview is classified as a qualitative research method (Lamnek, 1989; Hatch and Wisniewski, 1995; Riesman, 1993; Flick, 1998). It is considered a form of unstructured, in-depth interview with specific features. Conceptually, the idea of narrative interviewing is motivated by a critique of the question–response schema of most interviews. In the question–response mode the interviewer is imposing structures in a three-fold sense: (a) by selecting the theme and the topics, (b) by ordering the questions and (c) by wording the questions in his or her language.

To elicit a less imposed and therefore more 'valid' rendering of the informant's perspective, the influence of the interviewer should be minimal, and the setting should be arranged to achieve this minimizing of the interviewer's influence. The rules of engagement of the NI restrict the interviewer. The NI goes further than any other interview method in avoiding pre-structuring the interview. It is the most notable attempt to go beyond the question–answer type of interview. It uses a specific type of everyday communication, namely story-telling and listening, to reach this objective.

The narration schema substitutes the question–answer schema that defines most interview situations. The underlying presupposition is that the perspective of the interviewee is best revealed in stories where the inform-ant is using his or her own spontaneous language in the narration of events. However, it would be naive to claim that the narration is without structure. A narrative is formally structured; as we pointed out above, narration follows a self-generating schema. Whoever tells a good story complies with the basic rules of story-telling. Here the paradox of narration arises: it is the constraints of the tacit rules that liberate the story-telling.

The technique is sensitive to two basic elements of interviewing, as pointed out by Farr (1982): it contrasts different perspectives, and takes seriously the idea that language, as the medium of exchange, is not neutral but constitutes a particular worldview. Appreciating difference in per-spectives, which can be either between interviewer and informant or between different informants, is central to the technique. The interviewer is advised to carefully avoid imposing any form of language not used by the informant during the interview.

The elicitation technique

The NI as an interview technique consists of a number of rules on: how to activate the story schema; how to elicit narrations from the informants; and how, once the narrative has started, to keep the narration going by

Table 4.1   *Basic phases of the narrative interview*

Phases	Rules
Preparation	Exploring the field Formulating exmanent questions
1 Initiation	Formulating initial topic for narration Using visual aids
2 Main narration	No interruptions Only non-verbal encouragement to continue story-telling Wait for the coda
3 Questioning phase	Only 'What happend then?' No opinion and attitude questions No arguing on contradictions No why-questions Exmanent into immanent questions
4 Concluding talk	Stop recording Why-questions allowed Memory protocol immediately after interview

mobilizing its self-generating schema. The story develops out of factual events, anticipated interest of the audience, and formal manipulations within the setting. The rules that follow are a mixture of Schütze's proposal and our own elaboration.

Table 4.1 summarizes the basic concept of the NI and its rules of procedure. The narrative interview is conducted over four phases: it starts with the initiation, moves through the narration and the questioning phase, and ends with the concluding talk phase. For each one of the phases, a number of rules are suggested. The function of these rules is not so much to encourage blind adherence, but to offer guidance and orientation for the interviewer in order to elicit rich narration on a topic of interest, and to avoid the pitfalls of the question–answer schema of interviewing. Following these rules is likely to lead to a non-threatening situation, and maintains the informant's willingness to tell a story about significant events.

Preparing the interview

Preparing for the NI takes time. A preliminary understanding of the main event is necessary both to make clear the gaps that the NI is to fill, and to achieve a cogent formulation of the *initial central topic* designed to trigger a self-sustainable narration. Primarily, the researcher needs to make themselves familiar with the field under study. This may involve making preliminary enquiries, reading documents and taking note of rumours and informal accounts of any particular event. Based on these preliminary inquiries, and on their own interests, the researcher draws up a list of 'exmanent' questions. Exmanent issues reflect the interests of the researcher and their formulations and language. From this, we distinguish 'immanent' issues: the themes, topics and accounts of events that appear during the narration by the informant. Exmanent and immanent issues may overlap totally, partially or not at all. The crucial point of the exercise is to *translate exmanent questions into immanent ones* by anchoring exmanent issues in the narration and by applying nothing but the informant's own language. In the course of the interview, the attention of the interviewer should be focused on the immanent issues, on making notes of the language used, and on preparing for further questions at the appropriate time.

Phase 1: initiation

The context of the investigation is explained in broad terms to the informant. He or she must be asked for permission to record the interview on tape. Recording is important to support a proper analysis later. Then the procedure of the NI is briefly explained to the informant: uninterrupted story-telling, questioning phase and so on. In the preparation phase for the NI, an initial topic of narration has been identified. It should be noted that the initial topic represents the interests of the interviewer. To support the introduction of the initial topic visual aids may be used. A time-line, schematically representing the beginning and the end of the event in question, is a possible example. The narrator in this case would face the task of segmenting the time between the beginning and the end of the story.

The introduction of the central topic of the NI should trigger the process of narration. Experience shows that in order to elicit a sustainable story, several rules may be used as guidelines to formulate the initial topic:

- The initial topic needs to be experiential to the informant. This will ensure his or her interest, and a narration rich in detail.
- The initial topic must be of personal *and* of social or communal significance.
- The informant's interest and investment in the topic should not be mentioned. This is to avoid taking positions and role playing from the very beginning.
- The topic shall be broad to allow the informant to develop a long story which, from an initial state of affairs, through past events, leads to the present situation.
- Avoid indexical formulations. Do not refer to dates, names or places. These should be introduced only by the informant as part of his or her relevance structure.

Phase 2: main narration

When the narration starts, it must not be interrupted until there is a clear coda, meaning that the interviewee pauses and signals the end of the story. During the narration, the interviewer abstains from any comment other than non-verbal signals of attentive listening and explicit encouragement to continue the narration. The interviewer may, however, take occasional notes for later questioning, if this does not interfere with the narration.

Restrict yourself to active listening, non-verbal or paralinguistic support and showing interest ('Hmm', 'yes', 'I see'). While listening, develop, in your mind or on paper, the questions for the next phase of the interview.

When the informant marks the coda at the end of the story, probe for anything else: 'is this all you want to tell me?' or 'is there anything else you want to say?'

Phase 3: questioning phase

As the narration comes to a 'natural' end, the interviewer opens the questioning phase. This is the moment when the attentive listening by the interviewer bears its fruits. The exmanent questions of the interviewer are translated into immanent questions using the language of the informant to complete the gaps in the story. The questioning phase should not start unless the interviewer has sufficiently probed the end of the main narrative. In the questioning phase, three basic rules apply:

- Do not ask why-questions; ask only questions concerning events like 'what happened before/after/then?' Do not directly ask about opinions, attitudes or causes as this invites justifications and rationalizations. Every narrative will include the latter; however, it is important not to probe them, but to see them occurring spontaneously.
- Ask only immanent questions, using only the words of the informant. Questions refer both to events mentioned in the story and to topics of the research project. Translate exmanent questions into immanent questions.
- To avoid a climate of cross-examination, do not point to contradictions in the narrative. This is again a precaution against probing rationalization beyond that which occurs spontaneously.

The questioning phase is meant to elicit new and additional material beyond the self-generating schema of the story. The interviewer asks for further 'concrete texture' and 'closing of the Gestalt' by staying within the rules.

Phases 1, 2 and 3 are recorded for verbatim transcription with the consent of the informants.

Phase 4: concluding talk

At the end of the interview, as the tape recorder is switched off, interesting discussions often develop in the form of small-talk. Talking in a relaxed mood after the 'show' often throws light on the more formal accounts given during the narration. This contextual information proves in many cases to be very important for the interpretation of the data, and it can be crucial for a contextual interpretation of the informants' accounts.

During this phase, the interviewer may use why-questions. This may be an entry point for the analysis later, when the theories and explanations that the story-tellers hold about themselves ('eigentheories') become a focus of analysis. Furthermore, in this last phase the interviewer may also be in a position to rate the level of (mis)trust they command in the eye of the informant, which is important information for the interpretation of the narration in its context.

In order not to miss this important information, it is advisable to have a notebook or a prepared form for summarizing the contents of the small-talk in a memory protocol immediately after the interview. If one organizes a series of NIs, it is worth planning for time between the interviews for writing up the small-talk and other impressions.

Strengths and weaknesses of the narrative interview

Researchers using the narrative interview have pointed to two main problems of the technique: (a) the uncontrollable expectations of the informants, which raise doubts about the strong claim of non-directivity of the NI, and (b) the often unrealistic role and rule requirements of its procedures.

Uncontrollable expectations in the interview

The interviewer aims to obtain a complete narration of events out of every interview, which expresses one specific perspective. They therefore pose as someone who knows nothing or very little about the story being told, and who has no particular interests related to it. Every participant, however, will make hypotheses about what the interviewer wants to hear and what they probably already know. Informants generally assume that the interviewer *does* know something about the story, and that they do not talk about what they know because they take it for granted. It is highly problematic to stage a 'pretend play' of naivety, especially over a series of interviews where the informant knows that he or she is not the first to be interviewed.

As noted above, every informant will make hypotheses about what the interviewer wants to hear. The interviewer must thus be sensitive to the fact that the story they obtain is to some degree *strategic communication*, that is, it is a purposeful account either to please the interviewer, or to make a particular point within a complex political context that may be at stake. It may be difficult, if not impossible, to obtain a narrative from a politician that is not a strategic communication. The informant might try to defend himself or herself in a conflict, or might put himself or herself in a positive light with regard to the events.

The interpretation of the NI must take into account such possible circumstances, which are unavoidable in the very situation of the interview. The narration in an NI is a function of the whole situation, and it has to be interpreted in the light of the situation of the study, the assumed strategy of the narrator and the expectations that the informant attributes to the interviewer. Independently of what the interviewer says, the informant may suspect a hidden agenda. Alternatively, the informant may trust the interviewer, not assume a hidden agenda, and render an authentic narrative of events, but may at the same time transform the interview into an arena to advance his or her perspective for purposes wider than the research agenda.

The texture of the narrative will depend to a large extent on the preknowledge that the informant attributes to the interviewer. To play ignorant may be an unrealistic role requirement on the interviewer. Each interview demands that the interviewer presents themselves as ignorant, while in fact, their actual knowledge is increasing from one interview to the next. The credibility of this pretence has limits, and the knowledge of the interviewer cannot be hidden for long.

Under these circumstances, Witzel (1982) is sceptical about the claim that the relevance structures of the informants are revealed by narration. Any conversation is guided by *expectations of expectations*. Even in cases where the interviewer abstains from framing questions and answers, the active informant will tell her story to please or to frustrate the interviewer, or to use the interviewer for purposes beyond the interviewer's control. In all cases, the informant's relevance structures may remain hidden. The narration reflects the interpretation of the interview situation. Strategic storytelling cannot be ruled out.

Unrealistic rules

The rules of the NI are formulated to guide the interviewer. They are set up to preserve the informant's willingness to narrate some controversial events and problems under study. The main question is whether these rules are as helpful as they are well intended. Again, Witzel (1982) doubts that the prescribed format of the 'initial topic' is, in fact, suitable for every informant. The interviewer presents themselves as if they knew nothing about the topic under study. Informants might perceive this attitude as a trick, and this perception will interfere with their cooperation.

The way the interviewer initiates the interview co-determines the quality of the narration. This puts too much focus on the beginning of the interview. The narration is likely to be an outcome of the way the interviewer comports him or herself. The initiation phase is difficult to standardize, and relies totally on the social skills of the interviewer. This sensitivity of the method to the initial moment may be a cause of anxiety and stress for the interviewer. This may pose a difficulty for applying the NI technique in a research project with several interviewers who have different levels of skill. Another point of criticism refers to the fact that the rules of the NI technique were developed in a specific field study, which dealt with local politics and biographical research. The rules express suggestions for coping with the problem of interaction in these specific studies, and might not work as intended in other circumstances. This is an empirical problem that must be studied by applying the NI in different circumstances. However, little methodological research beyond a description or a general critique of the technique has been conducted.

The rules of the narrative interview define an ideal-typical procedure which may only rarely be accomplished. They serve as a standard of aspiration. In practice, the NI often requires a compromise between narrative and questioning. The narratives reveal the diverse perspectives of the informants on events and on themselves, while standardized questions enable us to make direct comparisons across various interviews on the same issue. Furthermore, an interview may go through several sequences of narration and subsequent questioning. The iteration of narration and questioning may occasionally blur the boundaries between the NI and the semi-structured interview. As Hermanns (1991) argues, rather than a new form of interviewing, we have semi-structured interviewing enriched by narratives. The question then arises of whether the multiplication of labels for procedures of interviewing serves any purpose. Flick (1998) has taken this practical uncertainty as an opportunity to develop the 'episodic interview' (see Flick, Chapter 5 in this volume) which may be a more realistic form of interviewing with narrative elements than the NI in Schütze's pure sense.

Differential indication for the narrative interview

Narratives are particularly useful in the following cases:

- Projects investigating specific events, especially 'hot' issues, such as corporate mergers, a specific development project or local politics (Schütze, 1977).
- Projects where different 'voices' are at stake. Different social groups construct different stories, and the ways in which they differ are crucial to apprehend the full dynamics of events. Different perspectives may highlight a different axis as well as a different sequence in the chronological events. Furthermore, difference in perspectives may establish a different configuration in the selection of events to be included in the whole narrative.
- Projects combining life histories and socio-historical contexts. Personal stories are expressive of larger societal and historical contexts, and the narratives produced by individuals are also constitutive of specific socio-historical phenomena in which biographies are grounded. Narratives of war are classical in this regard, as are narratives of political exile and persecution (Schütze, 1992).

Although story-telling is a universal competence and narratives can be used whenever there is a story to be told, not every social situation is conducive to producing 'reliable' narration. A good and simple indicator is the duration or the absence of the main narrative in the research project. Very short interviews or an absence of narration may indicate failure of the method. Bauer (1996) conducted 25 narrative interviews relating to a controversial software development project. Of a total of 309 minutes of narration, the average narration was of about 12 minutes, with a range of between 1 and 60 minutes uninterrupted narration. This indicates that the narrative interview was not equally adequate for all informants. Indeed, the larger the distance between the informant and the centre of action, the thinner was the interview. Direct and immediate involvement in the core activities of the event being narrated seems to be an enhancing factor in the production of narratives. However, *ceteris paribus*, the absence of narratives can be very significant. This is the case, for example, when some particular groups or individuals refuse to produce a narration, and by doing so express a defined position in relation to events (Jovchelovitch, 2000).

It is also important to consider problems associated with the researcher's performance. There are cases in which the formulation of the initial topic is inadequate, and it fails to engage the story-teller. In such cases, a reassessment of the interviewer's performance according to the rules of the NI can help to rule out or rule in this source of failure.

Furthermore, there are social settings that can lead to either underproduction or overproduction of narratives (Bude, 1985; Rosenthal, 1991; Mitscherlich and Mitscherlich, 1977). We distinguish at least three situations that can lead to underproduction of narratives, that is, where there is no or little story-telling, irrespective of the richness of experience. First, people who have undergone trauma may not be in a position to verbalize these experiences. As much as narration can heal, it can also produce a renewal of the pain and anxiety associated with the experience it narrates. Here, trauma silences the story-teller. Secondly, there are communities that maintain a genuine culture of silence in which silence is highly regarded and preferred over talking. Here, the flow of narrative may be rather brief or even absent. Lastly, there may be situations where the interests of a group of people would militate against the production of stories. Here, silence is privileged because of a political decision not to tell anything. This may be a general strategy of defence, or it may be directly related to mistrust of the researcher.

In relation to overproduction of narration, the following situations should be considered. Neurotic anxieties can lead to compulsive story-telling, and mobilize vivid imagination with little bearing on real events or experience. This overproduction can serve mechanisms of defence, and avoid confrontation with the real issues at stake. Anthropologists have observed that some communities appoint story-tellers to tell the researcher what the community thinks the researcher wants or needs to hear. This involves at times the concoction of fantastic narratives, which disguise rather than reveal.

All such situations need to be carefully assessed by the researcher. Sometimes narration can trigger unexpected psychological responses that are not manageable by the research team. Here, as in all research situations, ethical considerations apply.

Analysing narrative interviews

The narrative interview is a technique for generating stories; it is open in regard to the analytical procedures that follow data collection. In what follows we briefly introduce three different procedures that can assist researchers in the analysis of stories collected through the narrative interview. These are: thematic analysis, Schütze's own proposal and structuralist analysis.

Transcription

The first step in the analysis of narratives is to reduce the data by transcribing the recorded interviews. The level of detail of the transcriptions depends on the aims of the study. How far transcription involves elements beyond the mere words used varies according to what is required for the research. Paralinguistic features, such as voice tone or pauses, are transcribed in order to study the rendering of stories not only by content but also by rhetorical form. Transcribing, boring as it is, is useful for getting a good grasp of the material, and as monotonous as the process of transcribing may be, it opens up a flow of ideas for interpreting the text. It is strongly recommended that researchers do at least some transcriptions themselves, as it is actually the first step of analysis. If the transcript is given to somebody else, especially in a commercial contract, care needs to be taken to ensure the quality of the transcription. Commercial transcription for marketing purposes is often well below the quality that is needed when the use of particular languages is an issue for analysis.

Schütze's proposal

Schütze (1977; 1983) proposes six steps for analysing narratives. The first is a detailed and high-quality transcription of the verbal material. The second step involves separating the text into indexical and non-indexical material. Indexical statements have a concrete reference to 'who did what, when, where and why', while non-indexical statements go beyond the events and express values, judgements and any other form of generalized 'life wisdom'. Non-indexical statements can be of two kinds: descriptive and argumentative. Descriptions refer to how events are felt and experienced, to the values and opinions attached to them, and to the usual and the ordinary. Argumentation refers to the legitimization of what is not taken for granted in the story, and to reflections in terms of general theories and concepts about the events. The third step makes use of all the indexical components of the text to analyse the ordering of events for each individual, the outcome of which Schütze calls 'trajectories'. In the fourth step, the non-indexical dimensions of the text are investigated as 'knowledge analysis'. Those opinions, concepts and general theories, reflections and separations between the usual and the unusual are the basis on which to reconstruct operative theories. These operative theories are then compared with elements of the narrative, as they represent the self-understanding of the informant. The fifth step comprises the clustering of, and comparison between, individual trajectories. This leads to the last step where, often through extreme case comparison, individual trajectories are put into context and similarities are established. This process allows for the recognition of collective trajectories.

Thematic analysis: constructing a coding frame

A stepwise procedure of qualitative text reduction is recommended (see, for example, Mayring, 1983). Text units are progressively reduced in two or three rounds of serial paraphrasing. First, whole passages or paragraphs are paraphrased into summary sentences. These sentences are further paraphrased into a few keywords. Both reductions operate with generalization and condensation of meaning. In practice the text is arranged in three columns: the first column contains the transcript, the second column contains the first reduction, and the third column only contains keywords.

Out of paraphrasing, a category system is developed with which all texts may ultimately be coded if so required. First, categories are developed for each NI, which are later collated into a coherent overall category system for all NIs in the project. A final category system can only be stabilized through iterating revisions. The final product constitutes an interpretation of the interviews, fusing relevance structures of the informants and of the interviewer. The fusion of the horizons of the researchers and the informants is reminiscent of hermeneutics.

The process of data reduction described above may lead to quantitative analysis in the sense of classical content analysis (see Bauer, Chapter 8 in this volume). Once the text is coded, the data can also be structured in terms of frequencies that tell who said what, who said different things and how often. Statistical analysis for categorical data can then be applied. Cluster analysis may provide types of narrative contents. Quantitative results can be extensively illustrated by citations from the original narrations. Narrative perspectives of the event or problem under study can be described and classified qualitatively and quantitatively. Analysing the content is one possible approach; another approach may be to classify formal elements of the story.

Structuralist analysis

A structuralist analysis of narratives focuses on formal elements of narratives. The analysis operates through a combinatorial system that includes two dimensions: one is formed by the repertoire of possible stories, of which any given story is a selection, and the other refers to the particular arrangements of the narrative elements. In the *paradigmatic* dimension we order all the possible elements that appear in the stories: events, protagonists, bystanders, situations, beginnings, endings, crises, moral conclusions; in the *syntagmatic* dimension these particular elements are arranged in a sequence that can be compared across the narratives and related to context variables. Any particular corpus of narratives will be mapped onto this two-dimensional structure.

Generally speaking, the analysis of narratives always involves the analysis of chronological and non-chronological aspects of the story. Narratives are a succession of events or episodes that comprise actors, actions, contexts and temporal locations. The narration of events and episodes displays a chronological ordering that allows for the interpretation of how time is used by story-tellers. The non-chronological aspects of a narrative correspond to explanations and reasons found behind the events, to the criteria involved in the selections made throughout the narrative, to the values and judgements attached to the narration and to all the operations of the plot. To understand a story is to capture not only how the unfolding of events is described, but also the network of relationships and meanings that give the narrative its structure as a whole. It is the function of the plot to link episodes into a coherent and meaningful story. It is vital, therefore, to identify the plot in the analysis of narratives.

Abell (1987; 1993) proposes a graph-theoretical representation to compare narratives. This includes the paraphrasing of accounts into units comprising contexts, actions, forbearances and outcomes. In a second step, graphs, linking actors, actions and outcomes in time, are constructed to represent and to formally compare particular courses of actions. Ultimately, the method constitutes a mathematical formalism for handling qualitative data, without recourse to statistics.

Narrative, reality, representation

There are a number of questions that can be asked about the relationship between narratives and reality, all of them related to the connections between discourse and the world beyond it. Shall we consider every narrative as a 'good' description of what is going on? Shall we accept every story-teller's account as a valid one in relation to what we are investigating? And what about narratives that are obviously detached from the reality of events? As Castoriadis (1975) once put it, while trying to describe the Eiffel Tower, people can say either 'this is the Eiffel Tower' or 'this is my granny'. As social researchers, we need to consider this difference.

This debate is not simple, and it involves many angles. We think it is important to refute some recent excesses that have overstated the autonomy of narrative, text and interpretation while undermining an objective world. Yet, we also think it is crucial to consider the expressive dimension of every piece of narration, irrespective of its reference to what happens to be the case. In fact, narratives themselves, even when producing distortion, are part of a world of facts; they are factual as narratives and so should be considered. Even fantastic narrations just happen to be the case. In order to respect both the expressive dimension of narratives (the representation of the story-teller) and the problem of reference to a world beyond themselves (the representation of the world), we suggest the separation of the research process into two moments, each attending to different demands. Consider the hypothetical case in which the Eiffel Tower is described as 'granny'. If an informant produces such a description, it is, from the point of view of social research, nevertheless the task of the interviewer to elicit the account and render it with fidelity (Blumenfeld-Jones, 1995). In this first moment the task of the social researcher is to listen to the narrative in a disinterested way and render it with as much detail and consideration as possible. In fact, high fidelity in the rendering of narratives is one of the quality indicators of the narrative interview. In this primary moment of the research process, the following statements apply:

- Narratives privilege the reality of what is *experienced* by story-tellers: the reality of a narrative refers to what is *real* to the story-teller.
- Narratives do not copy the reality of the world outside themselves: they propose particular representations/interpretations of the world.
- Narratives are not open to proof, and cannot simply be judged as true or false: they express the truth of a point of view, of a specific location in space and time.
- Narratives are always embedded in the socio-historical. The particular voice in a narrative can only be understood in relation to a larger context: no narrative can be formulated without such a system of referents.

This, however, is not the end of the story. The social researcher not only elicits and renders narratives with as much fidelity and respect as they can. In the second moment, the observer needs to consider the story of 'granny', on the one hand, and the materiality of the Eiffel Tower on the other. Here narratives and biographies need to be situated in relation to the functions they fulfil to the story-teller and in reference to a world beyond themselves. In this sense, for the social researcher – as a listener and an observer – a story is always two-sided. It both represents the individual (or a collective) and refers to the world beyond the individual. As much as we need sensitivity to the imaginations and distortions that configure any human narrative, we also need to pay attention to the materiality of a world of objects and others, which not rarely resist the construction of particular stories. As Eco (1992, 43) has noted in relation to the task of interpretation, 'if there is something to be interpreted, the interpretation must speak of something which must be found somewhere and, in some way, respected'. We believe the same is true in non-fictional narrative.

The almost obvious question that follows from this position refers to who establishes the truth, and how we know whether a story is loyal or distortive of events. The answer lies in the full task of the researcher, who tries both to render the narrative with utmost fidelity (in the first moment) and to organize additional information from different sources, to collate secondary material and to review literature or documentation about the event being investigated. Before we enter the field we need to be equipped with adequate materials to allow us to understand and make sense of the stories we gather.

STEPS TOWARDS A NARRATIVE INTERVIEW

1 Preparation.
2 Initiation: start recording, and present the initial topic.
3 Main narration: no questioning, only non-verbal encouragement.
4 Questioning phase: only immanent questions.
5 Concluding talk: stop recording and continue the conversation as it comes.
6 Construct a memory protocol of 'concluding talk'.

References

Abell, P. (1987) *The Syntax of Social Life: the Theory and Method of Comparative Narratives*. Oxford: Oxford University Press.

Abell, P. (1993) 'Some aspects of narrative method', *Journal of Mathematical Sociology*, 18: 93–134.

Barthes, R. (1993) *The Semiotic Challenge*. Oxford: Basil Blackwell.

Bauer, M. (1991) 'Resistance to change: a monitor of new technology', *Systems Practice*, 4 (3): 181–96.

Bauer, M. (1996) 'The narrative interview: comments on a technique of qualitative data collection', *Papers in Social Research Methods – Qualitative Series*, Vol. 1. London: London School of Economics, Methodology Institute.

Bauer, M. (1997) (ed.) *Resistance to New Technology: Nuclear Power, Information Technology, Biotechnology*, 2nd edn. Cambridge: Cambridge University Press.

Blumenfeld-Jones, D. (1995) 'Fidelity as a criterion for practising and evaluating narrative inquiry', in J.A. Hatch and R. Wisniewski (eds), *Life History and Narrative*. London: Falmer. pp. 25–36.

Bruner, J. (1990) *Acts of Meaning*. Cambridge, MA: Harvard University Press.

Bude, H. (1985) 'Der Sozialforscher als Narrationsanimateur. Kritische Anmerkungen zu einer erzaehltheoretischen Fundierung der interpretativen Sozialforschung', *Kolner Zeitschrift für Soziologie und Sozialpsychologie*, 37: 310–26.

Castoriadis, C. (1975) *L'Institution Imaginaire de la Société*. Paris: Éditions du Seuil.

Eco, U. (1992) *Interpretation and Overinterpretation*. Cambridge: Cambridge University Press.

Farr, R.M. (1982) 'Interviewing: the social psychology of the inter-view', in F. Fransella (ed.), *Psychology for Occupational Therapists*. London: Macmillan. pp. 151–70.

Flick, U. (1998) *An Introduction to Qualitative Research*. London: Sage.

Hatch, J.A. and Wisniewski, R. (1995) (eds) *Life History and Narrative*. London: Falmer.

Hermanns, H. (1991) 'Narrative interviews', in U. Flick, E. von Kardoff, H. Keupp, L. von Rosenstiel and S. Wolff (eds), *Handbuch Qualitative Sozialforschung*. Munchen: Psychologie Verlags Union. pp. 182–5.

Johnson, N. and Mandler, J.M. (1980) 'A tale of two structures: underlying and surface forms of stories', *Poetics*, 9: 51–86.

Jovchelovitch, S. (2000) *Representações Sociais e Espaço Público: A Construção Simbólica dos Espaços Públicos no Brasil*. Rio de Janeiro: Vozes.

Kintsch, W. and van Dijk, T.A. (1978) 'Toward a model of text comprehension and production', *Psychological Review*, 85: 363–94.

Labov, W. (1972) 'The transformation of experience in narrative syntax', in W. Labov (ed.), *Language in the Inner City: Studies in the Black and English Vernacular*. Philadelphia, PA: University of Pennsylvania Press. pp. 354–96.

Lamnek, S. (1989) *Qualitative Sozialforschung*, Vol. 2. Munich: Psychologie Verlags Union.

Mayring, Ph. (1983) *Qualitative Inhaltsanalyse: Grundlagen und Techniken*. Basel: Beltz.

Mitchell, W.J.T. (1980) *On Narrative*. Chicago, IL: University of Chicago Press.

Mitscherlich, A. and Mitscherlich, M. (1977) *Die Unfähigkeit zu Trauern*. Munich/ Zurich: Pieper.

Propp, V. (1928) *Morphology of Folktales*. Austin, TX: Austin University Press.

Ricoeur, P. (1980) 'The narrative function', in W.J.T. Mitchell (ed.), *On Narrative*. Chicago, IL: University of Chicago Press. pp. 167–85.

Riesman, C.K. (1993) *Narrative Analysis*. Newbury Park, CA: Sage.

Rosenthal, G. (1991) 'German war memories: narratability and the biographical and social functions of remembering', *Oral History*, 19: 34–41.

Schütze, F. (1977) 'Die Technik des narrativen interviews in Interaktionsfeldstudien – dargestellt an einem Projekt zur Erforschung von kommunalen Machtstrukturen'. Unpublished manuscript, University of Bielefeld, Department of Sociology.

Schütze, F. (1983) 'Narrative Repraesentation kollektiver Schicksalsbetroffenheit', in E. Laemmert (ed.), *Erzaehlforschung*. Stuttgart: J.B. Metzler. pp. 568–90.

Schütze, F. (1992) 'Pressure and guilt: war experiences of a young German soldier and their biographical implications', Parts 1 and 2, *International Sociology*, 7: 187–208, 347–67.

Witzel, A. (1982) *Verfahren der qualitativen Sozialforschung*. Frankfurt: Campus.

5

Episodic Interviewing

Uwe Flick

KEYWORDS

argumentation   narrative
biographical narrative   narrative interview
communicative validation   repisode
critical incident technique   semantic memory and knowledge
episode   subjective definition
episodic memory and knowledge

Qualitative research has been developed and is applied against a variety of theoretical backgrounds. One common feature of the different research traditions and methodological branches of qualitative research (among other common features: see Flick, 1998a) is that almost every method can be traced back to two roots: to a specific theoretical approach; and also to a specific issue for which the method was developed. The method presented in this chapter was developed in the context of a study on the social representation of technological change in everyday life (Flick, 1996). This issue can be characterized by several features that influenced the elaboration of the method. First, a social representation is a form of social knowledge, which means that it is shared by those who are members of a specific social group and that it is different from the knowledge shared in other social groups (Moscovici, 1988; see Flick, 1998b for an overview). Secondly, technological change has an impact on more or less every part of everyday life, and on the life of almost everyone, although the degree and time may vary in which new technologies are accepted and used. Thirdly, on the one hand change occurs in concrete situational contexts: somebody buys a personal computer and this has an impact on the way he or she writes from then on. On the other hand, such little changes sum over time to a more or less general change in some parts of everyday life: today's childhood is completely different from earlier childhoods because of various new technologies and their different impacts. These impacts sum to a more general impact that is independent of particular situations, and becomes part of knowledge in a broad sense.

To study this situation, a method had to be developed that was sensitive to concrete situational contexts in which small changes occur, and to the broad, general accumulation of such changes. The method should also facilitate comparisons among cases from different social groups.

Underlying concepts

Narrative psychology

The episodic interview is based on several theoretical assumptions that can be traced back into different fields of psychology. One of its roots is the discussion about using people's narratives for collecting social science data (see Flick, 1998a: Chapter 9; Polkinghorne, 1988; Riemann and Schütze, 1987; Riesmann, 1993). In this context, a narrative is characterized as follows:

> First the initial situation is outlined ('how everything started'), and then the events relevant to the narrative are selected from the whole host of experiences and presented as a coherent progression of events ('how things developed'), and finally the situation at the end of the development is presented ('what became'). (Hermanns, 1995: 183)

This discussion can be seen as embedded in a wider discussion in the social sciences about the narrative structure of knowledge and experience (Bruner, 1987; Ricoeur, 1984; Sarbin, 1986). One of its sources is James (1893), who held 'that all human thinking is essentially of two kinds – reasoning on the one hand and narrative, descriptive contemplative on the other'. This distinction has been taken up in discussions about a narrative psychology or narrative thinking in Sarbin (1986). Here, narratives are seen as:

> the primary form by which human experience is made meaningful. Narrative meaning is a cognitive process that organizes human experiences into temporally meaningful episodes. (Polkinghorne, 1988: 1)

In this context, it is taken into account that experience and life do not have a narrative structure *per se*. Rather, they are constructed in the form of a narrative:

> On reflecting on the incident, trying actively to understand it, you are constructing an account the structure of which is essentially narrative. (Robinson and Hawpe, 1986: 118)

Therefore, narrative thinking is seen as consisting 'of creating a fit between a situation and the story schema. Establishing a fit, that is, making a story out of experience' (1986: 111) and as the 'projection of story form onto some experience or event' (1986: 113). This reconstruction of experiences as narratives involves two kinds of processes of negotiation. Internal/ cognitive negotiation between experience and the story schema includes the use of prototypical narratives given in a culture. External negotiation with (potential) listeners means either that they are convinced by the story of the event, or that they reject or doubt it for the most part. The results of such processes are contextualized and socially shared forms of knowledge.

Episodic and semantic knowledge

A second background is the distinction between episodic and semantic memory (going back to Tulving, 1972), which has been taken up to distinguish episodic from semantic knowledge, for example in expert systems (see Strube, 1989). According to this discussion, episodic knowledge comprises knowledge that is linked to concrete circumstances (time, space, people, events, situations), whereas semantic knowledge is more abstract and generalized, and decontextualized from specific situations and events. The two types of knowledge are complementary parts of 'world knowledge':

> Episodic knowledge is part of the world knowledge, whose other part – corresponding to semantic memory – is the general (i.e. not concrete, situatively anchored) knowledge, e.g. conceptual knowledge, rule knowledge, knowledge of schemes of events. (1989: 13)

In order to make accessible both parts of knowledge for studying a concrete issue like technological change, an interview should meet specific criteria:

- It should combine invitations to recount concrete events (that are relevant to the issue under study) with more general questions aiming at more general answers (such as definitions, argumentation and so on) of topical relevance.
- It should mention concrete situations in which interviewees can be assumed to have had certain experiences.
- It should be open enough to allow the interviewee to select the episodes or situations he or she wants to recount, and also to decide which form of presentation he or she wants to give (for example, a narrative or a description). The point of reference should be the subjective relevance of the situation for the interviewee.

Figure 5.1 summarizes these relations on the level of knowledge and presentation.

Episodic interviewing: how to get things going

The episodic interview was created to put this conception into concrete terms. It may be outlined in nine phases, each of which is a step towards the goal of analysing the interviewee's everyday knowledge about a specific issue or domain in a way that allows us to compare the knowledge

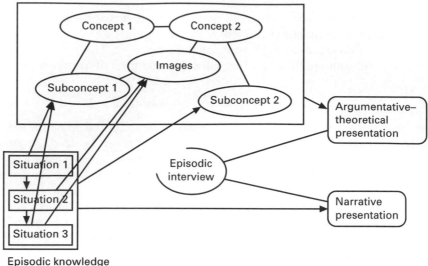

Figure 5.1   *Forms of knowledge and presentation in the episodic interview*

of interviewees from different social groups – that is, as a social representation. The examples given below come mainly from our study of people's understandings of technological change, but to illustrate the procedure beyond the context in which it was developed, some questions taken from a study on the social representation of health in different social groups are also used as examples.

Phase 1: preparation of the interview

The episodic interview is based on an interview guide in order to orient the interviewer to the topical domains for which narratives and answers are required. The interview guide may be developed from different sources: from the researcher's experience of the area under study, from theoretical accounts of this area, from other studies and their results, and from preparatory analyses of the area for relevant domains. In this step, it is important to develop a preliminary understanding of the area under study so that all relevant parts can be covered, questions can be formulated, and the guide can be left open enough to accommodate any new aspects that may emerge or be introduced by the interviewee.

In the technology study, the guide covered the following major areas of everyday life and technology (for more details, see below). The general first part of the interview focuses on the interviewee's 'technology biography' and the 'mechanization of his/her everyday life'. In the central part of the interview, the focus is on particular technologies – in this study, computers and television. Then, more general topics related to technological change are mentioned again: questions refer to consequences of technological change, to responsibility (for change and consequences), to trust, and to fears concerning technologies.

It has proved to be useful to examine the guide and the questions in one or two test interviews. If several interviewers are working on the same study, or if the interview is used in the context of research seminars with students, the interview training is a useful way of checking and learning the principle of the interview, the crucial questions, and the principle of situation narratives.

Phase 2: introducing the interview principle

The first part of the actual interview is the instruction of the interviewee. To make the interview work, it is important to explain the principle of the questions to the interviewee, and to familiarize him or her with this principle. The interview may be introduced by a sentence such as:

> In this interview, I will ask you repeatedly to recount situations in which you have had certain experiences with . . . (e.g. technology in general or specific technologies).

It is extremely important to take care over this introduction, and to check whether the interviewee has understood and accepted its message.

Phase 3: the interviewee's concept of the issue, and his/her biography in relation to it

To introduce the topic, the interviewee is first asked for their subjective definition of the issue in questions such as:

> What does 'technology' mean for you? What do you associate with the word 'technology'?

or

> What is 'health' for you? What is related to the word 'health' for you?

Then, the interviewee's path into the field under study is constructed by asking them to recall the first encounter they can remember with the issue under study:

> When you look back, what was your first experience with technology? Could you please tell me about it?

or:

> When you look back and remember, when did you first think about health? Could you please tell me about that?

In questions like these, the main principle of the episodic interview is applied: to ask the interviewee to remember a specific situation and to recount it. Which situation he or she remembers or selects in order to respond to this invitation is not fixed by the interviewer. This decision may be used in the later analysis, for example to compare the interviewee's degrees of proximity to the issue under study. The route through the interviewee's personal history with the issue is then pursued by asking for particularly important or meaningful relevant experiences:

> What was your most relevant experience or contact with technology? Could you please tell me about that situation?

or:

> What was your most significant experience of health? Could you please tell me about that situation?

Here again, it is the interviewee's subjective relevance that determines which technology and which situation he or she talks about. Whether an interviewee refers to keeping healthy or to a bout of more or less severe illness is his or her decision. Later these priorities go into the comparative analysis of the different cases. Especially in interviews where an indirect access to the issue (such as health) is chosen by the interviewee, a refocusing may be indicated. Then the interviewer should continue by asking:

> There are times when we feel more healthy than at other times. Could you please tell me about a situation in which you felt particularly healthy?

or:

> When does health become an issue for you? Could you please tell me about a situation of that kind?

Phase 4: the meaning of the issue for the interviewee's everyday life

The next part of the interview aims at clarifying the role of the issue in the interviewee's everyday life. In order to enter this realm, the interviewee is first asked to recount a day with reference to the issue:

> Could you please tell me how your day went yesterday, and where and when technology played a part in it?

or:

> Could you please recount how your day went yesterday, and when health played a role in it?

This kind of question aims at collecting narratives of a chain of relevant situations. Then those areas of everyday life that are regarded as relevant for analysing the issue are mentioned in greater detail. There the interviewer can choose one of several different strategies. In the technology study, we asked people whether they thought that technology had become more important in their lives these days:

> If you look at your life, do you have the impression that technologies today play a bigger role in it than they did before? Could you please recount a situation for me in which technology takes up more room than it did before?

Then the interviewees were asked various questions about areas of their everyday life that are free of technology, and areas that they wished were free of technology; and about areas where they wanted more or better technologies. They were also asked to describe situations to exemplify their answers for the interviewer.

In this study, areas such as the household, work and leisure were mentioned in sequence. For each of these areas a question like this was asked:

> If you look at your household, what role does technology play in it, and what has changed here? Could you please tell me about a situation that is an example of that?

In the health study, the domains to explore were 'everyday life and household' and 'work and leisure':

> If you think of food, what role does health play in this context for you? Please tell me about a typical situation.

or:

> Who in your household or family takes care of health? Please tell me about a typical situation.

These questions help the interviewee to reflect on the general meaning and relevance of the issue for different aspects of his or her everyday life.

Phase 5: focusing the central parts of the issue under study

The next part of the interview concentrates on the key aspect of the issue as defined by the actual research question of the study. In the technology example, the study focused not only on technology in general, but especially on computers and television as key technologies that have produced changes in everyday lives. Here again, the interviewee's subjective definition of each technology was mentioned first:

What do you associate today with the word 'computer'?
Which devices do you count as computers?

The interviewee's first encounter with each technology is the next step to mention for each technology:

> If you look back, what was your first encounter with a computer? Could you please recount that situation for me?

These questions are followed by several other questions focusing on the use of computers in different areas of everyday life. The same procedure follows for television:

> What do you associate with the word 'television' today?

> If you look back, what was your first encounter with television? Could you please recount that situation for me?

> What part does television play in your life today? Could you please recount a situation that makes this clear for me?

> How do you decide if and when to watch TV? Could you please recount a situation that makes this clear for me?

In the health study, the central focus was on the interviewee's dealing with prevention and intervention in questions as:

> Do you avoid situations that are risky for your health?
> Please recount a situation in which you avoided a danger to your health.

> What do you do if you don't feel well? Please recount a typical situation.

> What do you expect from your doctor with regard to your health? Please recount a typical situation.

This phase of the interview aims to elaborate the interviewee's personal relationship to its central issue. The questions just given as examples open the doors to the interviewee's personal experiences. A main task of the interviewer is to respond with deepening enquiries to the interviewee's answers and narratives in order to make the interview as substantial and deep as possible.

Phase 6: more general relevant topics

Finally, some more general topics are mentioned in the interview, in order to enlarge the scope further. Accordingly, the interviewee is asked for more abstract relations:

> In your opinion, who should be responsible for change due to technology? Who is able to take the responsibility or should take it?

or:

> In your opinion, who should be responsible for your health? Who is able to or should take responsibility?

A further aspect is the interviewee's fantasies concerning expected or feared changes:

> Which developments do you expect in the area of computers in the near future? Please imagine these developments, and describe for me a situation that shows them.

This part of the interview aims at elaborating the cross-situational framework knowledge that the interviewee has developed over time. As far as possible, the interviewer should try to link these general answers to the interviewee's more concrete and personal accounts given in earlier phases of the interview in order to make apparent any discrepancies and contradictions. Applications of this interview have demonstrated that in many cases discrepancies and contradictions can emerge between the more general argumentation in this phase and the personal experiences and practices that have been reported earlier.

Phase 7: evaluation and small-talk

The final part of the interview is devoted to its evaluation by the interviewee ('What was missing from the interview that could have given you an opportunity to mention your point of view?'; 'Was there anything bothering you during the interview?'). As in other interviews, it seems fruitful to add a period of small-talk to allow the interviewee to talk about relevant topics outside the explicit interview framework ('what I forgot to mention . . .'; 'What I actually wanted to say . . .'; 'My wife had a funny experience, I don't know if this fits in your study, but . . .').

Phase 8: documentation

In order to contextualize the narratives and answers received from the interviewee, a context protocol should be written immediately after the interview. It has proved helpful to use a prepared sheet as orientation for this purpose. Depending on the research question, it should include information about the interviewee (his or her family situation, profession, age, etc.) and about the interview (when, how long, who the interviewer was, etc.). Most important are the interviewer's impressions of the situation and the context of the interview, and of the interviewee in particular. Everything surprising and all that was said after the tape recording stopped should be noted (see Figure 5.2).

The interview should be tape recorded and transcribed in full and in detail. The degree of detailing and exactness needed depends on the kind of research question (see Flick, 1998a: Chapter 14).

```
┌─────────────────────────────────────────────────────────────────────┐
│ Contextual information about the interview and the interviewee        │
│                                                                       │
│ Date of the interview:              ..............................    │
│ Place of the interview:             ..............................    │
│ Duration of the interview:          ..............................    │
│ Interviewer:                        ..............................    │
│ Indicator for identifying the interviewee:  .....................     │
│ The interviewee's gender:           ..............................    │
│ Age of the interviewee:             ..............................    │
│ The interviewee's profession:       ..............................    │
│ Working in this profession since:   ..............................    │
│ Professional field:                 ..............................    │
│ Raised (countryside/city):          ..............................    │
│ Number of children:                 ..............................    │
│ Age of the children:                ..............................    │
│ Gender of the children:             ..............................    │
│ Peculiarities of the interview:                                       │
│     ...............................................................   │
│     ...............................................................   │
│     ...............................................................   │
│     ...............................................................   │
│     ...............................................................   │
└─────────────────────────────────────────────────────────────────────┘
```

Figure 5.2   *An example of a documentation sheet*

Phase 9: analysing episodic interviews

The coding procedures suggested by Strauss (1987), Strauss and Corbin (1990) or Flick (1998a, on thematic coding) can be used for analysing episodic interviews.

How long are episodic interviews?

Episodic interviewing itself (phases 2–7) takes around 60–90 minutes. This time varies according to the number of questions prepared, the interviewee's readiness to talk, and the skill of the interviewer in directing the interviewee towards detailing and comprehensiveness in his or her narratives.

Strengths and weaknesses of episodic interviews

The episodic interview method briefly presented here may be compared with other methods created with similar intentions. The comparisons are summarized in Table 5.1.

Table 5.1   *The episodic interview compared with alternative interview forms*

Criterion	Episodic interview	Critical incident technique	Focused interview	Narrative interview
Indication for using the interview	Everyday knowledge about certain objects or processes	Comparative studies of problematic situations	Evaluation of specific stimuli (films, texts, media)	Biographical processes
Openness to the interviewee's viewpoint by:	The selection of the situations to recount Giving room for narratives	Asking for detailed accounts of incidents	The criterion of specificity	Giving room for a comprehensive narrative
Structuration of the data collection by:	The interview guide Types of questions (for definitions and for narratives)	The focus of critical incidents The orientation on facts in the events	Giving a stimulus Structured questions Focusing feelings	Generative narrative question in the beginning
Technical problems	To make the interviewee accept the concept of the interview Explication of the principle Handling the interview guide	Reduction of the data to categorization of (many) incidents	Dilemma of combining the criteria	To maintain a narrative once begun by the interview Problems in directing the narrative to the issue Big masses of barely structured data
Limitations	The limitation on everyday knowledge	Restricted to problematic situations	The assumption to know objective features of the object in question	More case sensitive than ready for comparisons

The critical incident technique

The critical incident technique of Flanagan (1954) may be regarded as some kind of 'historical ancestor' of the episodic interview with regard to some common intentions. This method is mainly applied for analysing professional activities and demands. The concept of the 'critical incident' on which it is based is similar to the concept of episodes and situations in the episodic interview. Differences can be seen from the following characterization:

> The critical incident technique outlines procedures for collecting observed incidents having special significance and meeting systematically defined criteria. By an incident is meant any observable human activity that is sufficiently complete in itself to permit inferences and predictions to be made about the person performing the act. To be critical, an incident must occur in a situation where the purpose or intent of the act seems fairly clear to the observer and where its consequences are sufficiently definite to leave little doubt concerning its effects. (1954: 327)

This outline shows that the critical incident technique deals with clearly defined situations with regard to intentions and effects, which are analysed in order to draw conclusions and make assessments about the acting person. It is more the event, and less its situational context, that is in focus. Compared with this, the episodic interview allows the interviewee to decide which type of situation to mention in order to clarify a certain type of experience. Therefore, the episodic interview is more oriented towards obtaining narratives of different types of situations, rather than of situations that have been defined according to criteria fixed in advance. In an episodic interview, special attention is paid to the subjective meanings expressed in what is recounted, in order to find out the subjective and social relevance of the issue under study. The critical incident technique, on the other hand, is more interested in the facts in what is reported:

> it is clear that the critical incident technique is essentially a procedure for gathering certain important facts concerning behaviour in defined situations . . . The extent to which a reported observation can be accepted as a fact depends primarily on the objectivity of this observation . . . It is believed that a fair degree of success has been achieved in developing procedures that will be of assistance in gathering facts in a rather objective fashion with only a minimum of inferences and interpretations of a more subjective nature. (1954: 335)

Where the episodic interview aims at *contextualizing* experiences and events from the interviewee's point of view, the critical incident technique stresses instead a *decontextualization* of the factual content of the reported events. Accordingly, huge amounts of incidents are collected with this method (up to 2000 events in one study), which are classified and reduced afterwards. In the centre is

> the classification of the critical incidents . . . Once a classification system has been developed for any given type of critical incidents, a fairly satisfactory degree of objectivity can be achieved in placing the incidents in the defined categories. (1954: 335)

More recently Wilpert and Scharpf used the critical incident technique to analyse problems in the contact between German and Chinese managers:

> The interviews relied mainly on the Critical Incident Technique . . . whereby managers were asked to report particularly problematic incidents as detailed as possible. (1990: 645)

Here again, the factual events in the reports are more in focus than they are in the episodic interview. Furthermore, Flanagan's method is in general more restricted to a specific fragment of experience – particularly problematic events – which is justified in the research in which it is applied. The episodic interview is more open in this respect, because it focuses not only on problematic situations, but also on positive, surprising, satisfying, etc. situations: an issue like technological change does not necessarily have to be reduced to its problematic aspects. The episodic interview gives space to the interviewee's subjectivities and interpretations in the principle of situational narratives; it does not reduce and classify them immediately, but instead discovers the context of meaning in what is recounted.

The focused interview

The focused interview may be seen as a prototype of semi-structured interviews. Some of its principles and criteria for successful application (see Merton and Kendall, 1946) are also relevant for the episodic interview.

The criterion of *non-direction* was a guideline for the decision not to confront interviewees for reasons of a higher comparability and standardization with given situations, but instead to ask them to select and recount those situations that seem for them particularly relevant to a particular topic.

The criterion of *specificity* is put into concrete terms when the interviewee is asked to recount situations, and as far as possible situations in which he or she has had specific experiences. It is his or her decision whether and how far to take up the invitation to give a detailed narrative, and whether this criterion can be met in the interview. Merton and Kendall define their criterion as follows:

> Subjects' definition of the situation should find full and specific expression. (1946: 545)

The same is the case for the criterion of *range*: in episodic interviews no specific area of experience is defined for which one narrative is stimulated (as in the narrative interview of Schütze, for example: see below). Rather, the interviewee is asked for narratives of relevant situations coming from a variety of everyday areas. This comes closer to the criterion of Merton and Kendall, who postulate:

> The interview should maximize the range of evocative stimuli and responses reported by the subject. (1946: 545)

Finally, the episodic interview also tries to meet the fourth criterion of Merton and Kendall by focusing on situations:

> Depth and personal context: the interview should bring out the affective and value-laden implications of the subjects' responses, to determine whether the experience had central or peripheral significance. (1946: 545)

Again, the embedding of information to be collected in its context across narrative stimuli offers a way of meeting this criterion.

The narrative interview

The narrative interview was developed by the German sociologist Fritz Schütze (1977; see Riemann and Schütze, 1987; Bauer, 1996; Flick, 1998a: Chapter 9). Here, the following principle is applied:

> In the narrative interview, the informant is asked to present, in an extempore narrative, the history of an area of interest in which the interviewee participated . . . The interviewer's task is to make the informant tell the story of the area of interest in question as a consistent story of all relevant events from its beginning to its end. (Hermanns, 1995: 183)

After one 'generative narrative question' (Riemann and Schütze, 1987: 353), the interviewee is expected to recount in a long, extensive, extempore narrative his or her history with the issue under study – mostly his or her (professional or illness) biography. The interviewer's task is to refrain from any directive intervention once the narrative has started, until a clear signal (a coda) is given that the interviewee has arrived at the end of his story. Only then should the interviewer try to lead the interviewee back to aspects he or she has not yet narrated in full detail, and to try to make him or her take up these parts again and recount the missing details. Only in the very last part of the interview is the interviewer allowed to ask non-narrative questions. The quality of the data is assessed mainly by answering the question of whether and to what extent they are narrative data. Basic assumptions underlying the method are that the interviewee – once he or she has accepted the setting and has begun to narrate – will be driven not only to finish the story but also to tell true facts:

> In the narrative-retrospective edition of experiences, events in the life history (whether actions or natural phenomena) are reported on principle in the way they were experienced by the narrator as actor. (Schütze, 1976: 197)

This strength is attributed to narratives differently from other forms of interview. Narratives obtained with the narrative interview can be extremely long (up to 16 hours in some cases) and rather difficult to orient towards specific experiences and issues. This produces problems in the interpretation of data and in comparing data from different cases. Its strength is that it produces rather complex and comprehensive versions of the subjective views of interviewees. The episodic interview is more oriented towards small-scale situation-based narratives, and it is therefore easier to focus on the data collection. It refrains from claims for 'true' data and focuses instead on constructive and interpretive achievements by the interviewees. It does not give priority to one sort of data, as the narrative interview does with narrative data, but uses the advantages of different forms of data – episodic and semantic knowledge, and narrative and argumentative expressions.

Only answers? Good and bad use of episodic interviews

The episodic interview reveals its advantages over other methods especially when the interviewer receives many rich and detailed narratives. A bad application is one in which the interview generates only answers that name topics, rather than recounting narratives.

There are different types of situations that may characterize the response of the interviewee. The following examples illustrating these different types of situations are taken from the technology study mentioned above.

Types of situations in the episodic interview

The first and main type is the *episode*, that is a particular event or situation the interviewee remembers. In the following example, the interviewee recounts how he learnt to ride a bicycle:

> Well, I can remember, the day, when I learnt biking, my parents put me on the bicycle, one of these small children's bikes, sent me off, it was not that long, that I went by myself, my father gave me a push and let me off, and then I continued to ride until the parking lot ended and then I fell on my nose . . . I believe this is the first event I can remember.

A second type is *repisodes*, that is representations of repeated episodes (in the sense of Neisser, 1981): a situation that occurs repeatedly. One interviewee was asked for a situation that made clear the factors affecting his decisions to watch television, and he replied:

> Really the only time when television has a particular relevance for me is New Year's Day, because I am so struck, that I can do nothing else but watching TV, well I have been doing this for years, spending New Year's Day in front of the TV.

A third type is *historical situations*, referring to some specific event. One interviewee referred to Chernobyl when he was asked for his most relevant experience with technology:

> Probably, well the reactor catastrophe at Chernobyl, because that has intrigued rather decisively the lives of many people, that made it clear for me the first time, how much one is at the mercy of technologies.

Types of data in the episodic interview

Applications have shown that the episodic interview generates not only recollections of these different types of situations, but also the following different types of data (see Figure 5.3):

- *situation narratives* on different levels of concreteness
- *repisodes* as regularly occurring situations, no longer based on a clear local and temporal reference
- *examples*, which are abstracted from concrete situations, and metaphors, also ranging to clichés and stereotypes
- the subjective *definitions* (of technology or health) explicitly asked for
- linked to these, *argumentative-theoretical statements*, e.g. explanations of concepts and their relations.

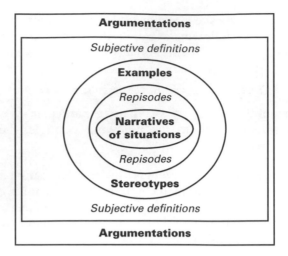

Figure 5.3   *Types of data in the episodic interview*

Quality indicators in episodic interviews

The quality of interviews cannot be judged simply by applying criteria such as reliability and validity in their traditional sense (for more detail see Flick, 1998a: Chapters 11 and 18). But some aspects of quality are closely linked to these criteria. The *reliability* of episodic interviews can be increased by the interview training mentioned above, and by a detailed analysis of the test interviews or the first interview. A second step towards greater reliability of the data obtained with the episodic interview is a detailed and careful documentation of the interview and of the context of what has been said and recounted. The third step is a careful transcription of the whole interview. *Validity* of the data may be increased by introducing a step of *communicative validation*, in which the interviewee is shown the data and/or interpretations resulting from his or her interview so that he or she may consent, reject or correct them. His or her consensus then is a criterion for the validity of the data. Finally, the episodic interview is in itself an attempt to put into concrete terms the idea of within-method *triangulation* (Denzin, 1989; see also Flick, 1992) by combining different approaches (of narrative and argumentative type) to the issue under study in order to raise the quality of data, interpretations and results.

STEPS IN EPISODIC INTERVIEWING

1   Prepare an interview guide based on a pre-analysis of the field under study. Run test interviews and interview training. Prepare a documentation sheet for the context of the interview. Does the interview guide cover the area under study? Did the interviewer(s) internalize the principle of the interview? Does the documentation sheet cover the information relevant for the research question?

2 Prepare a good introduction for the interviewee, and pay attention to its clarification to the interviewee. Did the interviewee understand and accept the principle of the interview?

3 Prepare questions for subjective definitions of relevant concepts. Prepare questions covering relevant steps in the interviewee's personal history with the issue or the field under study. Pay attention to any point where a deepening enquiry is needed. Do the questions touch relevant aspects of the subjective meanings for the interviewee? Are the questions oriented towards narratives of (relevant) situations? Did the interviewer enforce the narrative principle of the interview and ask additional questions to bring more depth into the interview?

4 Try to cover relevant areas of the interviewee's everyday life. Are questions heading for situation narratives? Are they open enough for the unexpected?

5 Try to get into the detail of the central parts of the issue under study. Try to increase the depth and richness of the interviewee's responses by additional enquiries. Has the interviewee gone into details and depth? Has the interviewer been sensitive for any extra depth on which to focus?

6 Try to avoid too general reasoning without any personal or situational reference in the interviewee's responses. Has the interviewer managed to lead the interviewee's responses back to the level of personal concerns?

7 Evaluation and small-talk: make room for some conversation, for critique and for additional aspects. Were additional aspects mentioned?

8 Use the documentation sheet, and make a good tape recording and a detailed transcription. Is all additional information (not on the tape) documented?

9 Choose an appropriate method for coding and interpreting the narratives and answers. Does the method take the quality of the data into account (e.g. the narrative structure of accounts)?

References

Bauer, M. (1996) 'The narrative interview – comments on a technique for qualitative data collection', in *Papers in Social Research Methods – Qualitative Series*, Vol. 1. London: London School of Economics, Methodology Institute.

Bruner, J. (1987) 'Life as narrative', *Social Research*, 54: 11–32.

Denzin, N.K. (1989) *The Research Act*, 3rd edn. Englewood Cliffs, NJ: Prentice-Hall.

Flanagan, J.C. (1954) 'The critical incident technique', *Psychological Bulletin*, 51: 327–58.

Flick, U. (1992) 'Triangulation revisited – strategy of or alternative to validation of qualitative data', *Journal for the Theory of Social Behaviour*, 22 (2): 175–97.

Flick, U. (1996) *Psychologie des technisierten Alltags – Soziale Konstruktion und Repräsentation technischen Wandels in verschiedenen kulturellen Kontexten.* Opladen: Westdeutscher.

Flick, U. (1998a) *An Introduction to Qualitative Research.* London: Sage.

Flick, U. (ed.) (1998b) *Psychology of the Social.* Cambridge: Cambridge University Press.

Hermanns, H. (1995) 'Narratives interview', in U. Flick, E. von Kardorff, H. Keupp, L. von Rosenstiel and S. Wolff (eds), *Handbuch Qualitative Sozialforschung.* Munich: Psychologie Verlags Union. pp. 182–5.

James, W. (1893) *The Principles of Psychology* (1950). New York: Dover.

Merton, R.K. and Kendall, P.L. (1946) 'The focused interview', *American Journal of Sociology,* 51: 541–57.

Moscovici, S. (1988) 'Notes towards a description of social representation', *European Journal of Social Psychology,* 22 (3): 211–50.

Neisser, U. (1981) 'John Dean's memory: a case study', *Cognition,* 9 (1): 1–22.

Polkinghorne, D. (1988) *Narrative Knowing and the Human Sciences.* Albany, NY: SUNY Press.

Ricoeur, P. (1984) *Time and Narrative,* Vol. 1. Chicago, IL: University of Chicago Press.

Riemann, G. and Schütze, F. (1987) 'Trajectory as a basic theoretical concept for analysing suffering and disorderly social processes', in D. Maines (ed.), *Social Organisation and Social Process – Essays in Honor of Anselm Strauss.* New York: Aldine de Gruyter. pp. 333–57.

Riesmann, C.K. (1993) *Narrative Analysis.* London: Sage.

Robinson, J.A. and Hawpe, L. (1986) 'Narrative thinking as a heuristic process', in T.R. Sarbin (ed.), *Narrative Psychology – the Storied Nature of Human Conduct.* New York: Praeger. pp. 111–84.

Sarbin, T.R. (ed.) (1986) *Narrative Psychology – the Storied Nature of Human Conduct.* New York: Praeger.

Schütze, F. (1976) 'Zur Hervorlockung und Analyse von Erzählungen thematisch relevanter Geschichten im Rahmen soziologischer Feldforschung', in Arbeitsgruppe Bielefelder Soziologen (eds), *Kommunikative Sozialforschung.* Munich: Fink. pp. 159–260.

Schütze, F. (1977) 'Die Technik des narrativen Interviews in Interaktionsfeldstudien, dargestellt an einem Projekt zur Erforschung von kommunalen Machtstrukturen'. Manuskript der Universität Bielefeld, Fakultät für Soziologie.

Strauss, A.L. (1987) *Qualitative Analysis for Social Scientists.* Cambridge: Cambridge University Press.

Strauss, A.L. and Corbin, J. (1990) *Basics of Qualitative Research.* London: Sage.

Strube, G. (1989) 'Episodisches Wissen', *Arbeitspapiere der GMD,* 385: 10–26.

Tulving, E. (1972) 'Episodic and semantic memory', in E. Tulving and W. Donaldson (eds), *Organization of Memory.* New York: Academic Press. pp. 381–403.

Wilpert, B. and Scharpf, S.Y. (1990) 'Intercultural management – joint ventures in the People's Republic of China', *International Journal of Psychology,* 25: 643–56.

6

Video, Film and Photographs as Research Documents

Peter Loizos

KEYWORDS

media as social facts
participatory video
perception, misperception,
    informed perception
representations
Scitexing

time codes
video evidence
video/photo feedback
visual data as indicators of collective
    psychological dispositions
visual records

This chapter is chiefly concerned with the use of photography and video as qualitative research methods. It assumes that you are neither familiar with using visual materials, nor committed on first principles to using them in any case. It also assumes that you might not have thought of these media as potentially helpful. It is not a 'how to do it' chapter, since there are cheap, readable technical manuals for this purpose. Nor is it about documentary film. It is more about openings for and applications of visual methods in the service of social research, and the limitations of these methods.

These approaches deserve a place in this volume for three reasons. The first is that the image, with or without accompanying sound recordings, offers restricted but powerful records of real – world, real – time actions and events. This is true whether it is photo chemically or electronically produced, and whether it is a single photograph or continuous moving images. The second reason is that although social research is typically in the service of complex theoretical and abstract questions, it can use as primary data visual information that need not be in the form either of written words or of numbers: analysis of the impact of traffic on urban planning, patterns of playground bullying, or election campaigns might all benefit from the use of visual data. The third reason is that the world we live in is increasingly influenced by communications media, whose outputs often depend on visual elements. Thus 'the visual' and 'the media' play big parts in social, political and economic life. They have become 'social facts', in Durkheim's phrase. They cannot be ignored.

But these records are not unproblematic, or above manipulation, and they are never more than representations or traces of more complex past actions. Because real – world events are three – dimensional, and the visual media are only two – dimensional, they are inevitably secondary, derived, reduced – scale simplifications of the realities that gave birth to them.

What do I mean, here, by 'visual'? Because most of us use our eyes to read, there is a trivial sense in which your reading this text could be called the use of a visual research method. In this chapter I will be concerned not with reading by itself, but with situations where images are supported either by written texts, as in the captions to photographs or paintings, or by the spoken words on sound – tracks of videos. Photographs and video sequences can also include written words, and often do: a good deal of what we know about the demography of classical Rome is based on the inscriptions on Roman tombstones (Hopkins, 1978). We would not normally include this as an example of 'the visual'. We would have to include the pioneering study by the social psychologist Siegfried Kracauer (1947) of the German cinema from 1918 to 1933, which argued that the films produced for and consumed by a nation allow privileged insight into 'deep psychological dispositions'. Kracauer pointed to themes and images that gave insight into ideas about fate and destiny, leaders and followers, humiliation, the healthy and diseased body, and much more. He included in the study an analysis of the Nazi propaganda film that was systematic and a model for subsequent film content analyses.

Figure 6.1   *A woman and five children*

Equally pioneering was the work of the social historian Aries (1962), who used paintings and etchings to suggest how, in pre-industrial Europe, conceptions of children and childhood differed markedly from those of more recent times. Aries showed how children were dressed in the same kinds of clothes as adults, how they were represented without the inno- cence that we now impute to young children, and how they participated in adult entertainment scenes, to support his otherwise text-based arguments. This must qualify as one of the most imaginative and influential early uses of visual evidence in social science research (see Figure 6.1 above).

Strengths and weaknesses of visual research materials

Before getting closer to specific uses, it is important to deal with several fallacies about visual records. One fallacy is implied by the phrase 'the camera cannot lie'. Humans, the agents who wield cameras, can and do lie: they fake paintings and forge wills and banknotes, and they can distort the evidential recording capacity of visual data just as readily as they can distort written words, but in specific ways. First, a photographic print can have information removed by 'airbrushing': in effect, painting something or someone out. And things can be misleadingly added, too: many photo- graphs of naked tribal people published in such 'realistic' photo magazines as *Picture Post* and *Life* in the 1940s had naked genitalia artificially 'clothed' or otherwise disguised, so they are misleading as historical sources. Composite doctored negatives can make two people appear to be sitting next to each other when in fact they have never met.

When manipulation is carried out electronically it is known to journalists and picture editors as 'Scitexing', after the leading technology, and it is frequently used to systematically alter the content of published photo- graphs (Winston, 1995). In a film or video, skilful editing can remove spoken words from a sentence, and visual reprocessing can remove essen- tial persons or features from a wider context. All these manipulations are hard for the untrained eye to detect, and 'Scitexing' is impossible to detect unless you can identify the original photograph, and be sure that it indeed is the original. The situation here may change, and new advances in technology may soon allow experts to be sure whether an image has been interfered with; but at this time, they apparently cannot. So, seeing should not be believing in any naive sense, and if something offered as visual evidence arouses your suspicions, it may need to be checked out – corroborated by further inquiry, witness testimony, and whatever other means are needed.

Manipulation of the visual image can be more subtle and covert, but distinctly ideological. Susan Moeller points out how a famous picture from the Korean War, the retreat of tired soldiers to a place called Changjin, by photojournalist David Duncan, had originally shown significant numbers of American dead, and had been important because it suggested some human cost to Americans of their commitments. Many years later, this image was used in an American 22 cent stamp, but without the dead bodies, thus commemorating American military tradition without the more disquieting reminders of heavy losses (Moeller, 1989: 447, n. 30). In the same book Moeller discusses how many other famous war photographs have come to stand for particular political perceptions of the conduct of wars (see also Lewinski, 1978).

A second common fallacy about photography is that it is simply and universally accessible to everyone in the same way – that it operates transculturally, and without regard for social contexts, in such a way that everyone will both see *and perceive* the same content in the same photograph. This is wrong for several reasons. First, we learn to see both the real world, and the rather special conventional reductions of it to flat two-dimensionality that occur in paintings, photographs and films (Gregory, 1966; Gombrich, 1960). People insulated from the global economy, who may be unused to photographs, or mirrors, have difficulty recognizing themselves, or their close relatives, in simple snapshots (Forge, 1966; Carpenter, 1976). Not only is 'learning' needed for very basic recognition, it is also involved differentially in perceiving significant detail: one observer, looking at a photograph, sees 'a motor car', a second one sees 'an elderly medium-sized family saloon', a third one sees 'a 1981 Ford Cortina with rally steering wheel and sports wheel-hubs'. The vehicle is the same real-world object to all three observers, but their perceptions, their ability to specify and describe it, and the meaning they give to it are different because of their individual biographies. Such perceptual variations complicate any naive objectivist account of the photograph as an unambiguous record. The information may be 'in' the photograph, but not everyone is equipped to recover it in full.

I will now consider several kinds of uses of photographic images with potential research applications. The first is the documentation of the specificity of historical change. Every still photograph, from the moment it has been taken, is a historical document. If you are interested in exploring or revealing the precise nature of change, then photographs taken at regular intervals from exactly the same place can be revelatory. Changes in urban neighbourhoods, landscapes or the contents of a room; the condition of a tree, a wall or a human body 'before' and 'after' a significant change; all these, when properly attested and witnessed, and logged for time, place and circumstance, can have powerful evidential or persuasive value. In a recent example, photography was used by Tiffen and colleagues to buttress an important argument about population densities, tree cover and the agricultural environment in a district of Kenya. Because they could use precisely labelled photographs (the time and place coordinates are given) from the British colonial period, compare them with pictures taken from virtually the same spot 45 years later, and correlate the photographs with social and economic indicators of various kinds, they were able to make an argument that challenges much conventional wisdom. In 1991, under conditions of higher local population density and more intensive cultivation, the local landscapes were in fact more thickly covered by trees than in 1937 (Tiffen and Mortimore, 1994; see also Vogt, 1974) (see Figures 6.2a and b).

Figure 6.2   *Two Kenyan landscape photos, taken in (a) 1937 and (b) 1991
(photos: (a) R.O. Barnes, 1937, photo 17, reproduced by permission of Kenya
National Archives; (b) M. Mortimore)*
Source: Courtesy of Dr. Mary Tiffen

Historical applications of photographs might recommend themselves in
other ways, too. Various kinds of oral history inquiries might be facilitated

if the researcher goes to an interview armed in advance with some relevant photographs. Suppose you were working on the history of a trade union, or a political party, and you had come across an earlier newspaper photograph of a mass meeting, an annual conference, or a celebration. The photograph, suitably enlarged, could act as a trigger to elicit memories of people an interviewee might otherwise not spontaneously recall, or access important 'passive' memories rather than the more 'active' ones.

Such elicitation methods could be used in micro-historical research as well: the 'family history' could be assisted by asking an interviewee to go through a family photo album with you, or to show you an old film of a wedding, a baptism or a birthday party. Images are resonant with sub-merged memories, and can help focus interviewees, free up their memories, and create a piece of shared 'business' in which the researcher and the interviewee can talk together, perhaps in a more relaxed manner than without such a stimulus.

A different kind of use of historical photographs might involve reading them for *implicit* cultural/historical information. In early 1993 Scandinavian Airlines (SAS) produced an annual report for the previous year, and distributed it to passengers. It was an interesting document that revealed more than its authors were aware of (see Figure 6.3). It showed, for example, its Board of Directors, and this photograph was of nine solid-looking corporation executives in dark suits. It also had pictures of cabin staff and pilots, but the only women to be seen were stewardesses. While it would be possibly misleading to read too much into a single document, without further knowledge of SAS's gender equality policies, that annual report at least provoked some thought. And 50 years ago, had such a document existed, it would have been considered unremarkable and unre-vealing by most of us. Indeed, the very idea that the document should be illustrated, and be available to passengers, is a recent development. But perhaps what is most surprising about the photograph is that its gender implications were apparently missed by the executives who approved the report. Thus, reading both the present visual records, and the 'absent' ones, is a possible research task. Who is missing from the photograph or painting, and why? The young? The old? The poor? The rich? Whites? Blacks? And what is implied by their absences?

This leads to a new question: what can be safely, or reasonably, inferred from a photograph? Casual inference is easy, but more secure inference is more demanding. Supposing we wished to infer something about gender attitudes and social change in Greece from the two photographs in Figure 6.4: would we be entitled to do so? Two photographs, with no further information about how they were taken, and how far they differ from or are like thousands of other photographs of Greek couples, can hardly be more than suggestive or impressionistic. If we inspected hundreds of engagement photographs and found recurring patterns, we might be entitled to think we were 'onto something' – but what, exactly? For a photograph may arise in one of at least these four ways:

Figure 6.3   *The SAS report shows nine suited middle-aged men, in banks of three*

1   The subjects can be caught off guard, behaving informally, by a photographer.
2   A group of subjects, hearing that there is to be a photograph taken, may position themselves in a way they consider to be appropriate.
3   A photographer may take the initiative to place subjects in a specific composition, and they may passively accept direction.
4   Some collusion or negotiation between photographer and subjects may take place.

Figure 6.4
Source: Photos by Cornelia Herzfeld

So, we would need to know how particular wedding photographs are produced. A little observation would soon reveal that photographers often take a lead, for their own professional and aesthetic reasons. But photographers are often of the same culture as those they photograph, and intend to please them. So, at one analytic level, what is revealed in a good-sized sample of wedding photographs may legitimately support a view of a culturally constructed understanding about what is 'appropriate'. In the 1960s in Cyprus, there was a fashion for newly engaged couples to have engagement photographs taken. These were often posed by professional photographers, and the couple were placed literally cheek-to-cheek, even though they had sometimes only known each other for a few hours. That pose might be read to suggest a transitional period between a more fully parentally arranged marriage system, and one in which young people were starting to acquire some powers of veto over persons they were to marry, whom they nevertheless first encountered by family-initiated meetings and at formal 'viewings'. But note that this reading is only reached on the basis of detailed historical knowledge of the time and place. It cannot be directly inferred from the pose in one or two photographs, unless, unusually, we have additional supporting information, as is the case in the photograph of a Ugandan family by A.F. Robertson (Figure 6.5). Here we are told that the composition of the photograph was arranged by the senior male (Robertson, 1978).

In a study of a Cypriot village, Sheena Crawford (1987) commented on the iconic resonances of photographs sent back by emigrant relatives. They showed 'good times' – wedding and baptism celebrations, and people dressed up, and well-appointed home interiors. They did not show workplace situations that might have hinted at long days worked in unglamorous conditions. The emphasis was on success, celebration, leisure, consumption and possessions. Toil, difficulty and failure were not represented. The interpretation requires reading both the presences and the absences in the visual record, and while some of the absences may be explained by 'opportunity cost' features (who carries a camera, when, where and why?), the homogeneity of the images recorded must carry semantic weight.

A study of what is and is not photographed can be suggestive. In contemporary Britain it is currently commonplace for weddings, birthdays and christenings to be photographed, and some wedding services are interrupted, or at least punctuated by, flash photography and video-making. But deaths and funerals are not normally photographed. Ordinary people do not see something to commemorate photographically, but it is by no means 'obvious' or 'common sense' that this should be the case. For members of the royal family, or other much-loved national celebrities (such as Winston Churchill), the funeral services and processions are thought to be fair game for visual commemoration. And there are peoples for whom the display of an ornate coffin, and the photography of a tomb, are acceptable for everyone.

Figure 6.5   *A Ugandan family: the composition was arranged by the senior male (Robertson, 1978)*
Source: Photos by A.F. Robertson

Video and film: some applications

Let us now turn to some uses of video and film in social research. I shall treat film and video as functionally the same, even though video recording is in many ways cheaper, simpler, and more flexible than 8 mm or 16 mm film used to be. In practice, for reasons of ease and cost, most researchers choose video rather than film, and 'low-band' video rather than the more expensive high-resolution professional 'high-band'. (In North America, the terms 'low-end' and 'high-end' are used for low-band and high-band.) We need again to distinguish between data initiated by a researcher, and visual information that already exists. We need also to distinguish between visual data that the researcher analyses unaided, and visual data serving to focus, or elicit, interviewees' comments.

Video has an obvious data recording function whenever some set of human actions is complex and difficult for a single observer to describe comprehensively while it unfolds. Any religious ritual or life-stage ceremonial (such as a wedding) might be a candidate, as might a dance performance, a classroom teaching hour, or a craft activity from making a shoe to cutting a diamond. There are no obvious limits to the range of human actions and narratives that might be recorded, using image and sound together, on video film. With mains electricity and low-fidelity thin videotape, you can record for up to four hours on a single camera without stopping. While recording, a time code can be registered on the image, so that every second, minute and hour is logged authoritatively. The researcher would then be faced with several tasks: systematic viewing of the research corpus; the creation of a notational system that was explicit about why certain actions or sequences of actions are to be categorized in a particular way; and finally the analytic 'processing' of the information captured.

Let us take a concrete example. Suppose the researcher is concerned to understand the dynamics of playground bullying, and has secured the consent of school authorities to make a confidential video record of a playground over a three-month period. Suppose the total time for all school breaks each day is two hours. Over three months, the study, using a single camera only, would generate 120 hours of records. The researcher will have to decide, either in advance on theoretical grounds, or during and after the recordings on empirical and interpretive grounds, what sorts of action will constitute 'bullying'. The analyst will then want to identify all the action sequences that might count as instances, and look for regularities. Are the perpetrators restricted to a small number of individuals, or is bullying a more general phenomenon? Are the victims a consistent and restricted set? Does any child ever lend their support to victims? Is bullying a group affair more often than an attack by a single individual? These and many other questions might be asked, and in principle answered, by the video records. But we are talking of many hours of viewing, notation, aggregation, reviewing, re-analysis and final synthesis. It would not be at all surprising if each hour of recorded data needed at least four hours of additional work. This could in principle be reduced by deciding to work with just a sample (5 or 10 per cent) of the materials. And it could also be reduced if the first major review of the material quickly revealed such gross and evident patterns that the more patient, fine-detail work would be redundant, and not cost-effective. Further empirical complications to the study could be added: comparisons between winter and summer patterns; social investigations of the backgrounds of bullies and victims; reported classroom behaviour; and so forth. There would be no reason to allow the visual data to limit or even dominate the study, even though at a particular stage it might have been the primary investigative tool. And it is quite possible that simply by sensitive interviewing of some key children, much the same information would be obtained quickly and more simply. The role of the visual record would be *evidential*, in the forensic sense, but it might not have been the primary generator of key concepts or insights.

This kind of example will raise ethical questions in the minds of civil libertarians. In general, most discipline-based professional associations produce ethical guidelines for the conduct of research, and these tend to treat the issue of surveillance without consent as an invasion of privacy, and to rule it as either unacceptable, or on the limits of acceptability. In medical research, there is usually a hospital ethics committee that has to balance patient interests against issues of wider public interest. The individual social researcher may be able to proceed without formal application to an ethics committee, under the normal provision that sensitive research information will remain restricted and confidential, and this is further reinforced by the UK Data Protection Act, which covers information stored in computers and word processors. But whereas with purely written information, the promise to conceal personal names may guarantee ethical protection against identification, the situation is more difficult with images. Small white electronic masks over the eyes may disguise a recorded face, but voices are more distinctive, and although they may be digitally scrambled, to listen to scrambled human voices for any length of time is quite frustrating.

However, there can still be situations that produce ethical dilemmas. In 1997 a British hospital team decided to use covert video recording to monitor the behaviour of children who were thought to be at risk, and who had shown previous evidence of bodily harm or severe failure to thrive. Evidence was obtained that some parents were apparently deliberately harming their children while the children were in hospital. This led to some public discussion, with some parents protesting that their privacy had been invaded; and it is not difficult to feel sympathy towards an innocent parent who feels 'under suspicion' and under surveillance. But it is clear what the medical defence must be: first, that the child has been admitted to hospital, and is under medical care, and the hospital has a statutory obligation to safeguard the child; secondly, that severely harming a child is a criminal offence, and may be directly or subsequently prevented by the video surveillance; thirdly, that the video record has evidential value.

But at this point we must stop to consider the quality and limitations of such a video record, and how a legal defence might call into question its evidential capacity. First, it is likely to be of low visual fidelity; secondly, the sound quality may vary between the clearly audible and the scarcely comprehensible; thirdly, camera angles may not always be optimum to show the most significant details of an action sequence; and lastly, because of the general reduction of subtlety in such a record, it might be open to real misinterpretation about readings of mood and intention, in addition to whatever problems of interpretation the actual three-dimensional human behaviour (as opposed to the low-fidelity record) might have led to. Add to these difficulties the likelihood that the camera observes from a fixed position, and we have a recipe for courtroom drama.

There is a different kind of research application for video recordings, in which the participation of the subject in analysis becomes important. Suppose, for example, that a piece of research were focused on the question of effective research supervision. With the agreement of both research student and supervisor, a series of recordings would be made of their meetings over a two-year period. Then, after each meeting, each person would be debriefed by the researcher, privately, and asked to comment in more detail about the strategic significance of advice given, help requested and so forth. Here, the video record would in effect be a rather 'friendly' set of field research notes, equally available to all three parties, and more efficient than the memories or verbatim notes of any of them. The feedback re-view situations would allow discussion in more depth, clarification, debate and dialogue, and a discussion of actions not taken and their implications. You can substitute for the supervisor–researcher pair any ongoing interactive situation in which there is an exchange of information, a training component and a negotiation.

Some practical and procedural issues

1 Log every roll of film, video cassette, sound tape or photo as you produce it. You need the fullest details of date, place and persons. You need to put an identifying label on each item, and keep a master list as an index. Protect your original sources, images and sounds by making extra copies. If you look like obtaining or generating a large quantity of material, whether in terms of individual images or minutes and hours recorded, you will have to think about storage, access and sampling problems. Do explore new computer-managed storage and retrieval systems, such as Avid, the new, fast way of editing video.
2 Using research images publicly raises issues of power, intrusion, owner-ship and privacy. Make sure your informants give you definite permis-sion to reproduce images about them. This applies equally to your use and possible publication of images they possess. Agreements should be in writing. Make sure, too, that you have informed them about your research intentions. For a thoughtful essay on the contract between a film-maker and a social researcher, see Asch (1988).
3 In video recording, it is relatively easy to get usable images, and relatively difficult to get good quality sound. Yet since the sense of what is going on often depends on researchers being able to hear clearly what was said, you need to pay at least as much attention to the quality of the sound record as to the quality of the picture. Get a good manual, such as Hale (1997); find out about types of microphones, and experiment with type and placement before doing anything important, until you really know what the problems are.
4 It is easy to get carried away by the idea of 'making a video', and to end up letting the technology, or the excitement, dominate the research. For

the social researcher, the images and the technology are a contributing means, not the end.

5   There is no reason to introduce video recording into a research situation unless it is the best or only way to record the data, and unless it is clearly imperative to record these data. Why this warning? Because the making of a video will inevitably distract your informants, at least until they get used to it, and it will probably influence people towards stating official positions. It takes a lot of time to get people to 'act naturally' in front of even a simple recording system.

6   Thousands of video recordings are made in community research settings, but many of them are probably never watched seriously, and may have the status of research and action 'fashion accessories' and have been a waste of time and money. No doubt, future historians will be grateful that these videos were made, but that was not the original point, or the point of this chapter.

STEPS IN ANALYSING VISUAL MATERIAL

1   Will the use of a visual record make an important improvement to my research output?
2   Do I have the recording skills (sound and picture) to carry out the recording myself?
3   Have I calculated the time needed to process the resulting body of visual data?
4   Have I designed a friendly logging/cataloguing system for managing, storing, retrieving and analysing the visual data?
5   How will I make explicit any classification decisions made, when I analyse 'grey areas' in my data? Will my criteria be transparent?
6   Have I adequately explained my intentions to the people who will be filmed, and have I their written consent? Is there a trade union or professional association involved which may need to be consulted? Will I be deemed intrusive? Or a 'management snooper'?
7   Will I have the copyright freedom to publish the resultant material? Have I obtained written permission from the owners of personal photographs, or videos?
8   Do I need to further inform myself about issues of image ownership and publication?

References

Aries, P. (1962) *Centuries of Childhood: A Social History of Family Life*. New York: Knopf.

Asch, T. (1988) 'Collaboration in ethnographic filmmaking: a personal view', in J.R. Rollwagen (ed.), *Anthropological Filmmaking*. New York: Harwood.

Carpenter, E. (1976) *Oh, What a Blow that Phantom Gave Me*. London: Paladin.

Crawford, S. (1987) 'Iconography, sacred and secular: visions of the family', in I. Hodder (ed.), *The Archaeology of Contextual Meanings*. Cambridge: Cambridge University Press. pp. 20–30.

Forge, A. (1966) 'Learning to see in New Guinea', in P. Mayer (ed.), *Socialization, the Approach from Social Anthropology*. London: Tavistock.

Gombrich, E. (1960) *Art and Illusion*. London: Phaidon.

Gregory, R. (1966) *Eye and Brain*. London: Weidenfeld and Nicolson.

Hale, N. (1997) *Making a Video: How to Produce and Present your own Film or Programme*. Oxford: How To Books.

Hopkins, K. (1978) *Conquerors and Slaves*. Cambridge: Cambridge University Press.

Kracauer, S. (1947) *From Caligari to Hitler*. Princeton: Princeton University Press.

Lewinski, J. (1978) *The Camera at War: a History of War Photography from 1848 to the Present Day*. London: W.H. Allen.

Moeller, S. (1989) *Shooting War: Photography and the American Experience of Combat*. New York: Basic Books.

Robertson, A.F. (1978) *Community of Strangers: a Journal of Discovery in Uganda*. London: Scolar.

Tiffen, M. and Mortimore, M. (with F. Gichuki) (1994) *More People, Less Erosion: Environmental Recovery in Kenya*. Chichester: Wiley.

Vogt, E.Z. (1974) *Aerial Photography in Anthropological Field Research*. Harvard, MA: Harvard University Press.

Winston, B. (1995) *Claiming the Real: the Documentary Film Revisited*. London: British Film Institute.

7

Bemetology: towards Continuous (Self-) Observation and Personality Assessment

Gerhard Faßnacht

KEYWORDS

aggregation	object
bemetology	predicator
cascade predication	predicator value
law and chance	resolution
monitoring behaviour or experience continuously	stationary and touring models

---

'Bemetology' is a neologism. It was condensed out of the expression 'behavioural meteorology', and was introduced to indicate that psychology might profit from collecting data like meteorology does.

Unlike other sciences, meteorology has installed hundreds of measurement devices all over the world, and they continuously gather data for weather forecasting. Psychologists have never seriously tried to monitor behaviour continuously to capture the fluctuations in their phenomena as meteorologists do. This is perhaps surprising: our topics are no less complex than those of meteorology, so that 'behavioural weather' can be predicted by a few interactions of situational factors with a few stable personality traits.

Although this proposition has been challenged on several grounds (Hartshorne and May, 1928; 1929; Hartshorne et al., 1930; Newcomb, 1929; Magnusson and Endler, 1977; Magnusson, 1981; Mischel, 1968; 1984), measurement in the sense of classical test theory is still the most practised procedure in psychology. Even when extended repetitions of behavioural measurements over time are needed, this is claimed to be within the framework of classical test theory. Aggregation over time is seen as a means of reducing errors of measurement and thereby augmenting reliability (Epstein, 1979; 1980; 1990). Thus the stability of traits is not discovered as naturally existing psychological laws, but instead it is postulated as residing behind the irregularities of the phenomenal surface. The problem of how the supposed laws, on the one hand, and the observed irregularities, on the other, come into being is left untouched.

Meteorology knows very well the basic laws of physics that merge dynamically into an unpredictable 'deterministic nonperiodic flow' (Lorenz, 1963); psychology, however, seems to be a long way from this state. There is no consensus on the basic laws of personality and psychology. So is there any other motive for psychology to follow in meteorology's methodological footsteps, besides an analogy and the argument of reducing errors of measurement?

Empirical laws and chance

How do empirical laws come into being? This question is seldom asked, and has not been clearly answered. There are no signs of agreement even on the simplest form a law can take – stability, like the specific weight of objects, or a supposed latent personality trait, both of which can be denoted as 'substance laws' (Campbell, 1921).

Although it is unable to give a proper answer to this question, psychology, like other sciences, is nevertheless striving for empirical laws, whether simple or complex. The assumed existence of hidden laws controlling psychological phenomena is an important cognitive motor in moving psychology forward as a science. Statements quantitatively expressed as hypotheses will be accepted eventually as empirical laws if they are resistant to falsification (Popper, 1959). This has become the ultimate credo and justification of experimental psychology.

Experimental strategy has however paradoxically been blamed for psychology's empirical as well as theoretical bewilderment; the fundamental question of whether empirical laws are constructs or whether they are independent, stable facts waiting to be discovered in a hidden corner of our phenomenal world (Hollis, 1994) has made no great impact on research strategy. This is not surprising, because how can experimental psychology doubt the existential prerequisite of its own being? In a strict sense, experimental psychology cannot be thought of without the general postulate that in nature there are laws at work.

Although psychology has been participating for some time in debates about chaos theory and dynamical systems (Vallacher and Nowak, 1994; Stewart, 1992), the question of how assumed psychological laws come into being is not satisfactorily explained by that approach. The chaotic point of view does not get along without laws, but instead sees them as an arbitrary starting point in a sort of circular process for explaining how order transforms into disorder, and vice versa.

But there is a another type of disorder: pure chance. Consequently, research on chaos has developed methods to distinguish chaotic disorder from pure chance (Grassberger and Procaccia, 1983). Chance can precede regularities just as well as chaotic disorder, but it does so differently. Throwing a regular dice will result in the long run in an equal frequency distribution of the six sides. That distribution can be forecast with high precision, although the result of a single toss is absolutely unpredictable. This process is far from being a chaotic one because there is no dynamic feedback or non-linearity involved: the single consecutive tosses are independent of each other. Theoretically, there is a simple 'substance law' that holds that for every side of the dice, $p = 1/6$. The corresponding empirical law emerges as an aggregation of a huge number of single-chance tosses which could be affected by any similar huge number of different influential factors. An empirical law prevails not in the detail but only in the whole result. This understanding can be stated in one phrase:

Empirical laws are aggregated chance.

This definition of natural law was advocated by the physicist Erwin Schrödinger in 1922 (Schrödinger, 1962), who had adopted it from the experimental physicist Franz Exner (1919). One of the most prominent physical examples is Boyle's law, which describes the relation between the volume, temperature and pressure in an ideal gas. While the motion and impulse of single molecules are random and therefore unpredictable, the behaviour of the whole body of gas follows strict rules and so is predictable with high precision.

Empirical laws and resolution

We can see from the example of Boyle's law that there can be irregular commotion on the micro-level but clear order on the macro-level. As Schrödinger puts it:

> Physical research . . . has clearly proved that – at least for the overwhelming majority of phenomena whose regularity and steadiness had led to the postulate of general causality – chance is the common root of the observed strict conformity to a natural law.
>   With every physical phenomenon – for which a conformity to a natural law can be observed – countless thousands, most often billions, of single atoms or molecules are involved . . . At least in a very big number of totally different cases we succeeded in explaining completely and entirely the observed law by combining the huge number of single molecular processes. Each molecular process may or may not have its own strict law – it need not be thought of as subscribing to the observed regularity of the mass phenomenon. On the contrary, that conformity to law is melted integrally into the averages of millions of single processes which (the averages) are the only accessible facts for us. These averages show their own pure statistical laws which would prevail even if the behaviour of each single molecular process were steered by tossing a dice, playing roulette or drawing from a box. (1962: 10, my translation)

From that impressive argument one may hypothesize that the degree of resolution into units that we apply to our phenomenal world plays an important role in whether we discover laws or not. With that in mind, it seems reasonable to take as a starting point the following three 'theses of specificity of resolution' (Faßnacht, 1995: 34ff):

1   The images of 'reality' are specific to the representational means (the instrument), and to the representational situation – that is, they are immediately correct within a local system of language.
2   At least some laws are specific to the resolution applied; that is, a certain grade of resolution in an area of interest leads to knowledge that is totally, partially, or not at all ordered.
3   Principally, the impossibility of an isomorphic transformation between different representational systems must be faced; that is, not all images of a presupposed equal area of 'reality' can be translated into each other.

Generally, the 'theses of specificity' emphasize the importance of resolution or its counterpart, fusion, for empirical knowledge about whatever areas of 'reality' are regarded by whatever means.

When it comes to evaluating psychological research according to resolutions applied, we find that researchers generally plunge more deeply into details by applying instruments that differentiate progressively into ever-finer quantitative and qualitative units of measurement. That seems to be the case for fields as diverse as early interaction research (Argyle and Dean, 1965), human ethology (McGrew, 1972; Schleidt, 1989), emotion (Ekman and Friesen, 1978) and social judgement (Vallacher and Nowak, 1994). Of course, there is no shortage of subtle resolution by itself. But given the hypothesis that the existence of empirical laws is a function partially of the units of scrutiny and measurement, the question of how finely we should resolve our topics can no longer be an innocent one.

Empirical laws and data

Psychology has long been thought of as different from the natural sciences in that its subjects do not obey natural laws (see, for example, Windelband, 1894). But are there laws in psychology? That question cannot be answered unless the meaning of the term 'law' is clarified.

Empirical laws

Methodologically, a law states that something is valid for all objects of a certain class. Formally, a law has the appearance of a generalized conditional, which can be expressed as:

For any x, if x is A then x is B.

Translating into ordinary language gives 'All A is B'. The feature of invariability or constancy, expressed in 'for any x', seems to hold for all types of laws (Nagel, 1961: 75ff).

This is unproblematic until x is specified concretely. Take x as 'human being', and it is doubtful whether any laws exist in psychology. So psychology has distinguished different classes of 'human beings', and established a 'differential psychology'. Unfortunately, that step does not lead to valid generalized conditionals, and so further distinctions are tried. As these too do not proceed to strict generalized conditionals, the process of ongoing differentiation inevitably ends up in a state of exhaustion: with a single-case x for which the statement 'for any x' no longer has any meaning. Of course, actual research stops long before that point is reached. Is there a way out of this problem, other than by stopping the process? To answer that question, another problem must be faced: as we are interested in empirical and not theoretical laws, we need to explain what might be understood by 'data'.

Data as cascade predication

Borrowing from critical language analysis (Kamlah and Lorenzen, 1973), we can start with the elementary predication:

object ← predicator

The term 'predicator' is understood as a designator and was introduced by Carnap (1956: 6) as a 'predicate expression(s), in a wide sense, including class expressions'. A predicator can never be a definitive description or a proper name for an entity, nor must it be mistaken for a grammatical part of a sentence (the predicate). Similarly, 'object', in the elementary scheme, has no material meaning as an entity that can be touched, felt or seen. Kamlah and Lorenzen put it thus:

> We understand 'object' as everything to which a predicator can be related or which can be referred to by a proper name or a deictic action (definitive description) in such a way that it is apprehensible by a partner in a dialogue. (1973: 42, my translation)

To represent a general scheme for psychological (process) data, the elementary predication has to take on a more complex form which I like to designate as 'cascade predication':

object ← predicator ← predicator value ← time value

Predicator values are assumed to vary quantitatively as well as qualitatively. The same holds for time values, although qualitative variation of time values is a less common notion. Values are said to vary quantitatively if they are expressed in terms of any system of numbers, irrespective of what the representational level of the scale is (ordinal, interval or ratio). Values are said to vary qualitatively if they are expressed in terms of different 'designative meaning' (Carnap, 1956: 6). Some examples of qualitative as well as quantitative variations are assembled in Table 7.1. With

Table 7.1 *Examples of qualitative and quantitative variations*

Qualitative data

Object	←	Predicator	←	Qualitative predicator value	←	Qualitative time value
London's air	←	temperature	←	icy	←	winter
London's air	←	temperature	←	lukewarm	←	summer evening
London's air	←	temperature	←	very hot	←	summer 1976
Peter	←	aggression	←	angry face	←	now
Peter	←	aggression	←	verbal	←	yesterday
Peter	←	aggression	←	physical	←	last Friday

Quantitative data

Object	←	Predicator	←	Quantitative predicator value	←	Quantitative time value
London's air	←	temperature	←	−30 °C	←	10.01.95
London's air	←	temperature	←	20 °C	←	12.07.97
London's air	←	temperature	←	36 °C	←	20.08.76
Peter	←	aggression	←	rating 1 of 3	←	9:30, 27.10.97
Peter	←	aggression	←	rating 2 of 3	←	9:34, 26.10.97
Peter	←	aggression	←	rating 3 of 3	←	24.10.97

these examples in mind, I propose that data are cascade predications – unique or singular statements with specific grades of resolution on four different levels. On all four levels of the cascade predication, different grades of resolution or fusion into units are conceivable:

1 On the level of objects we can either differentiate into Peter, Ralph, John, etc. or, vice versa, fuse them into 'boy'.
2 On the level of predicators, different units of behaviour and experience are distinguishable . . .
3 which on the value level can be related quantitatively or qualitatively to different predicator values . . .
4 which on the last level can be assigned qualitative or quantitative time values of different grades.

If we call a singular statement or a cascade predication an image of 'reality', then there are as many images of 'reality' as there are combinations of different grades that can be mastered by our instruments of resolution. Now, if we are interested in finding empirical laws, and if our hypothesis is true that the existence of an empirical law is specific to the resolution applied, we have to decide what combination of resolutions is best for finding those empirical laws.

Empirical laws and 'bemetology'

A common recommendation for finding laws is 'try some theories'. But that misses the point that theories are themselves formulated and framed within the context of a specific language. Such a theory in turn presupposes a certain combination of resolution on all four levels of the cascade predication. Of course, that view is primarily true for a theory that seeks to explain empirical facts. No doubt, such theories can be a strong lead in finding empirical laws. If – as happened in physics – at least some strict empirical laws have been found by common logical reasoning or even by chance, and if these laws have then been empirically proved, then theorizing by logical reasoning and consecutive hypothesis testing is much easier than if these laws had not been confirmed. However, this is by no means an argument for generalizing on an epistemological level that all scientific empirical approaches must follow these lines. Furthermore, this fact from the history of physics is no argument that theory-driven hypothesis testing is the only valid and credible method of doing research. Theorizing and hypothesis testing in that strict sense are reasonable if and only if the empirical areas aimed at are structured isomorphically with the rules of logic.

If logic is not at work, then there is no logical way to approach the problem. This is not to say that there is no logic at all. But we should take such a possibility into account, or we may miss the basic and most important fact: that the logical accessibility of our empirical world is only a special case of the more general one – its chance emergence.

When it happens in a science that no strict empirical laws are found either by logical reasoning or by chance, theoretical predictions – logical deductions – of further laws are difficult or even impossible. Imagine physics had started by doing research on elementary particles that resisted the conception of strict empirical laws (Lindley, 1993): physics would probably be in no better shape than psychology is today.

Now, by analogy, we can speculate whether psychology's frustration in achieving strict empirical laws emanates from inadequate combinations of resolutions. As in particle physics, the phenomena psychologists scrutinize are ruled by chance. So far, there is no difference between physics and psychology: both are confronted with chance processes that cannot be predicted. But why do we find strict empirical laws in physics and not in psychology?

If the Exner–Schrödinger concept of a natural law is correct, then the answer is clear: as natural laws are the result of a fusion or aggregation of millions or even billions of naturally occurring events, the simple fact that in actual psychic functioning no events of such a huge number exist explains why psychology has not yet found any strict empirical laws, and probably never will. The key point is: no mass events, no laws.

While human beings may be better off not running like automatons, psychology as a science could nevertheless look for regularities in the sense of general laws. What 'general' means in that context depends upon the class of objects to which the 'all' is attached. Automatically, 'all' is applied to those things that are assumed to be equal. From an ethical point of view, that is held for 'human beings'. Although differential psychology has implicitly challenged this view, the methodological step of dividing 'all human beings' into subclasses has not proved useful.

If there should be any strict psychological laws that are valid for all human beings or for all members of any subclass, these laws are likely to be very special. First, they will be true with a superficial generality ('all human beings can learn or be conditioned'), and be no more informative than analytical statements such as 'all physical objects are extended'. Secondly, if there are any general laws, they would be valid in tiny empirical fields that are not seen as being particularly important for solving everyday life problems ('pupils dilate during sexual excitement'). But when it comes to socially relevant facts, laws are much less solid, as is true for the development of sex segregation in preschoolers (LaFrenière et al., 1984) or for the greater aggressiveness of males compared with females (Eagly, 1987; Eaton and Enns, 1986). Although this last phenomenon has been observed in nearly all societies, inferential statistics are employed to prove it. Galileo did not need inferential statistics to prove the law of gravity.

Psychology will probably never reach a Newtonian state of a solid system of natural laws. Nevertheless, it behaves as if that were possible: hypotheses are tested as if they are laws. If variance is not totally explained, as is usually the case, additional but as yet unknown factors are presumed to be responsible. Anything that cannot ultimately be explained by any means, however, is called error variance. This methodological approach is a long way from comprehending natural laws as an aggregation of a huge mass of naturally occurring chance events. On the contrary, aggregation is understood as a methodological trick of filtering out laws lying beneath an irregular phenomenological cover, instead of as a way of constituting them.

If we seriously take laws as a result of an aggregational constitution – brought about either naturally or artificially – then we must envisage a different methodological approach to naturally occurring events, and different theoretical interpretations of them. The following methodical and meta-theoretical canon adopts this view, and can be seen as the conceptual background of 'bemetology':

1   The being of a natural law is a fused or, say, aggregated case of immense natural mass phenomena that are fundamentally driven by chance.
2   Being driven by chance does not necessarily imply indeterminacy. A single totally unpredictable natural event could nonetheless be determined by local as well as proximal factors. Determinism in that sense is compatible with chance in the sense of unpredictability, and must not be equated with predeterminism.
3   There are naturally occurring and artificially generated events. Free fall and the motion of gas molecules and atomic particles are naturally occurring objects or events. If, for the sake of research, these events are isolated, they retain their character as natural rather than artificial events. Otherwise the topic under scrutiny changes. For psychology

that is more difficult to achieve than it is for classical physics. The examples of free fall that Galileo scrutinized at Pisa were as natural as an apple falling from a tree. However, artificially generated events do not occur in nature. They are constructed or induced by the researcher: for example, the answer to a personality questionnaire or to an item of an intelligence test. Both types of events – natural and artificial – can be aggregated into empirical laws. But if one is interested in natural empirical laws, data for aggregation must be natural too. That is what bemetology aims for.

4   Aggregation can act at all levels of the cascade predication: at the levels of objects, predicators, predicator values and time values. Also, at the level of predicator values and time values, quantitative as well as qualitative aggregation is possible.

5   Just as there are two types of data, so there are two types of aggregation: one is accomplished by nature itself, and the other – the artificial type – is accomplished by the researcher's aggregational methods. Both may lead to empirical laws. Combined with the two types of data, four different cases can be imagined:

(a)   Natural aggregation of natural data leads to natural laws, as in Boyle's law.
(b)   Natural aggregation of artificial data seems to be impossible.
(c)   Artificial aggregation of natural data is what meteorology accomplishes, for example, by computing mean temperature over months (aggregation over time) to test whether there is a regular or law-like trend in the warming up of the atmosphere. This approach leads to quasi-natural laws.
(d)   Artificial aggregation of artificial data leads to artificial laws, such as the stability of intelligence measured by tests of intelligence.

6   Empirical laws are specific to the combination of different types of resolution – quantitative or qualitative – and to different grades of resolution. As a counter-process to aggregation, resolution opens a set of data, in turn a view of 'reality', which is possibly governed by chance.

7   Because, unlike in physics, an individual's actual psychic functioning is not affected, as far as we know, by huge masses of simultaneously co-acting events, we seldom find empirical laws that are valid for single individuals. In other words: the absence of natural aggregation of masses of simultaneously occurring natural events at an individual level explains why psychology lacks strict natural laws. To approximate at least these natural laws, artificial aggregation of naturally occurring events is mandatory. That is what bemetology proposes to do.

8   Most regularities found in psychology are the result of an aggregation of individuals at the object level of the cascade predication. Consequently, these regularities are valid at first only for an aggregate of individuals, and not for a single individual.

9 If natural empirical laws – natural regularities – are sought for single individuals, aggregation is not allowed at the object level but must come into play at all other levels of the cascade predication: at the levels, of natural predicators, natural predicator values, or time values.

10 To determine natural empirical laws that are valid for individuals, intra-individual aggregation over time is probably the most important strategy.

11 There is no *a priori* distinguished doctrine as to which combination of either resolution or aggregation yields the most regular results, that is the best empirical laws.

12 Consequently, instead of theory-driven hypothesis testing that relies on logic, intuitive aggregational manipulation of large quantities of naturally produced data is absolutely crucial. This may be accomplished by combining different grades and different types of resolution with the help of computers and efficient software. Such an 'artistic' approach is possible only because we can use computers.

13 Ultimately, there is no guarantee that aggregation leads necessarily to empirical laws.

The essence of these points is a bemetological model for data acquisition that will apply the following pattern of resolution:

- At the level of objects: observe a single object – one person, one dyad, one interacting group of persons or even one situation.
- At the level of predicators: observe one naturally occurring behaviour of that single object.
- At the level of predicator values: observe relatively few qualitative values of that behaviour.
- At the level of time: observe continuously during continuous blocks of time, repeatedly over long periods of time.

Because this approach enables artificial aggregation over time of naturally occurring behaviour values, it is aiming at quasi-natural laws. If, as in the above outline, no additional information is considered, the resulting law will be a substance law. In accordance with the theses of specificity, the resulting laws – if any are found – will only be valid for the specific combination of types and grades of resolutions applied. That is, the result will be valid at first only for the single object under scrutiny. Further, the result will be valid only for the whole aggregated block of time. If, in addition, predicator values are aggregated, again the result is only valid for that pattern of resolution.

The minimal model for bemetological data acquisition as outlined above is similar to that used by observational sciences like astronomy and meteorology, which do not manipulate their objects: the continous monitoring of the cosmic background radiation, and of the temperature, humidity and pressure of our atmosphere, are examples of that model. The predominant model in psychology, however, aggregates at the level of objects:

few data of many individuals are aggregated into group means. According to the specificity theses, this produces results that are valid in a strict sense for object aggregates, rather than for individuals as objects. This impedes the transfer of scientific results into practice, because psychology is often more interested in individuals than in aggregates of them.

Consequences for research on personality

Classically, intelligence and personality are conceived of as a bundle of agencies working in the dark to produce personal achievements or personal behaviour. A dynamical theory such as psychoanalytic theory will see those agencies as self-active psychic entities, whereas a methodological theory, like a trait theory, sees them as latent dimensions on which a person can be characterized quantitatively. These quantitative scores are seen as constants representing individual faculties or qualities that help or hinder the person in solving problems or in behaving in a certain way. The latter view is said to be the leading one, at least in psychology. In particular, the dimensional concept often regards such agencies as units of homogeneous simplicity, in contrast with units of diversity that are in themselves heterogeneous (Faßnacht, 1982: 66; 1995: 115).

When one is measuring these latent traits, an actual personality or achievement score is constituted of two parts: its true value and its error value. Traditionally, the true value is understood as being constant, and thus characteristic of a person. The existence of a constant of an object can be said to be an empirical law of substance for that object. The error component, however, is said to be governed by chance. Now, that is different from what has been elaborated above as the bemetological point of view. According to bemetology, the controlling force of a natural law is not enrolled backstage, but is the concerted macroscopic result of an aggregational process of different single-chance events. It is not only error variance, but also true variance that is ruled by chance. Everything that contributes to or even hinders an achievement or a behaviour is seen to be a 'true' supplement. If many contributing events are at work, or if many of them are aggregated artificially over time, the contour of an empirical law may probably, but not necessarily, emerge. In other words, the concept of error variance as exclusively nourished by a lot of different chance events, and, vice versa, the concept of true variance built up of a few monolithic crystalline pure entities, should be revised.

Let us take intelligence as an extreme example. By and large, intelligence is conceived of as a bundle of quantifiable latent features that change little over time, but are disguised by disturbing factors. That is quite different from a bemetological view: intelligence would be measured on the basis of naturally occurring events, and IQ would be the result of a naturally occurring aggregation. The conventional measure of IQ is an artificial aggregation of artificial events. In our terminology, the statement 'intelligence is stable' is an artificial empirical law.

When it was first conceptualized, intelligence was conceived as a two-factor phenomenon comprising a general factor g and test-specific factors s. Consecutive theoretical and methodical developments have brought into consideration additional aspects like verbal comprehension, logical reasoning, spatial ability and so on. These are still regarded as being dimensional quantities contributing to a whole true enduring value of intelligence. If variations of intelligence scores are encountered, they are interpreted as an ephemeral influence of fatigue, or perhaps a momentary lack of concentration or motivation. But in life, where 'intelligent' behaviour and 'intelligent' achievements are requested, factors like concentration, motivation, fatigue or even situational influences are important. To cope with these problems and to reduce error variance one step further, these factors themselves are normally taken into account by integrating them as dimensional quantities too.

From a methodological point of view, such an approach is correct. However, it runs the risk that the quantitative dimensions as such – although attached to comprehensible words – lack any real meaning. What is their ontological status? Is there in everybody a real, albeit hidden, object that we call 'intelligence'? Without doubt such intelligence dimensions are constructions that are – often paradoxically enough – presupposed to 'exist' as quantitative essentials in a 'real' world. To say these are dispositions only moves the problem to the analogous question of the ontological status of dispositions. Are such dispositions quantitative objects – continuous dimensions – or are they qualitative objects: an organized body of discrete events, cognitions, feelings, behaviours and physiological and neurological structures as well as chemical substances, each with a clear intension and a finite extension?

Considerations like these provoke the crucial question: how can we know whether psychological 'reality' is better understood as continuous rather than discrete? There seem to be two tiny but important advantages of the discrete over the continuous view. First, the discrete view relies on concrete single psychic facts like a motive, a feeling, a cognition or a behaviour. Although the contours of these units are often fuzzy, they can be really experienced or observed. Secondly, a discrete view is amenable to quantification. On the other hand, if we start with dimensions we often miss concrete designative meanings. Dimensions earn their keep as obscure agencies that are said to have a facilitating or inhibiting function. The price we pay for that silent service is an insurmountable duplicity of our world: laws are ruling behind the scenes while on stage the turbulent show of particulars goes on.

What is comprehensible are concrete single events. And for that reason, at least for my part, I prefer the discrete view. This view is also compatible with the bemetological view, which explains natural as well as artificial laws – not, like the traditional view, as an extraction but as an aggregation or fusion of single concrete events.

Two examples of a bemetological approach to personality

I think there are good reasons for assuming that the concepts of intelligence or personality as measured by tests or questionnaires are scientifically reasonable, and that it is possible to define such general notions on the basis of concrete naturally occurring events. So we should try it, even though it will be a difficult and far-reaching programme that will stay descriptive for most of the time.

The biggest problem before testing any hypothesis is, of course, how to capture naturally occurring experiential, behavioural and social events in such a way that they can be handled scientifically. Two ways suggest themselves. The first involves natural settings that already exist, in which one can use computing techniques and equipment to gather naturally occurring events or states either by self-protocols (Perrez and Reicherts, 1992) or with the help of observers. This approach can be called the 'touring model'.

The other way first constructs permanent physical, technical and natural social settings so that natural data gathering is easy. This approach can be realized through installations of special physical, technical and social facilities within institutions such as hospitals, schools or kindergartens. At the Department of Psychology in Berne there is a unique prototype of this sort – the BEO site – which was built for controlled field diagnostic and field research (Faßnacht, 1995: 298ff; Haehlen and Neuenschwander, 1998). Although, being permanent, it is restricted to a particular institution, this facility has the great advantage of being functional, controllable and instantaneously adaptable. By and large, it is similar to constructing radio-telescopes, satellites and meteorological stations which monitor relevant natural data continuously. I call it the 'stationary model'.

Both approaches are field diagnostic models, and both rely heavily on new technologies or are forced to develop new technologies themselves. Developing distinctive technologies is something quite usual for natural scientists: it seems to be their predominant and real work. In psychology, researchers are usually preoccupied with theories. Technological development is often cognitively more demanding, and – at least by psychology – it is belittled as being unscientific and so delegated to technicians. This negative evaluation hinders scientific research that would otherwise have been possible long ago (Faßnacht, 1974; 1995: 297f).

The following two paradigmatic studies represent the two ways of gathering naturally occurring events. Both aim at one of the 'big five' personality factors (Goldberg, 1981; 1990).

The touring model

The example of the touring model shows how a continuous description was made of the emotionality – factor IV of the big five – of a single person (Jöri, 1997). For three months Jöri self-monitored her feelings continuously, from when she got up in the morning until she went to bed in the evening, day after day. Before she started her three-month period of data collection, she developed a coding scheme with 35 qualitative units of feeling. These were mutually exclusive, representing a true category system. At any time, there was one and only one possible valid category. She coded whether she could detect the type of event that triggered the particular feeling: social, external, internal or no trigger found. This enormous achievement was accomplished alongside her daily activity as a student. As soon as she judged that her state of feeling was changing, she coded that new state and the type of trigger.

Data collection was realized with a Newton Message Pad (Macintosh), which Jöri took with her everywhere. Two menus allowed access to the category list of feelings and to the triggering events. This basic equipment had been extensively trialled for collection of geological field data, and adapted for data transfer of the feeling codes to a PC. Code interpretation into meaningful units and data management on the PC site was accomplished in accordance with the scheme of cascade predication by the programme package BEDAMAN (Faßnacht, 1997). Jöri amassed and computed 2360 feeling events over 93 consecutive days.

Substantial arguments against such an approach have been put forward since the early days of introspection: continuous conscious self-attention is impossible, so that self-attention must be seen as mostly being rather slight, and is only altered when one feeling becomes very dominant over other events of consciousness. Self-attention itself could have influenced the flow of feelings. All that is true and well known. Yet, one of Jöri's aims was to see whether such dynamical feedback could be detected by sequential analysis of time series, which was actually the case. But in addition she found a lot of 'noisy' feelings that could not be explained either by dynamical feedback or by any other triggering event. And by aggregating over periods of time by comparing the second with the third month of data collection, she found her distribution of feelings to be relatively stable: correlation of absolute frequencies was $r = 0.85$, and correlation of the absolute time each feeling took up was $r = 0.89$.

The stationary model

The example for the stationary model aimed at factor I of the big five, extraversion/surgency, and studied sociability. According to the EAS concept of Buss and Plomin (1984), sociability is seen as a main facet of temperament. As such, it is expected to develop early in childhood and be relatively stable over time. The question asked was: does sociability observed naturally by means of a qualitative coding system change intra-individually over time?

To give a tentative answer Baumgartner et al. (1997) observed the intra-individual variation of social behaviour of three-year-old toddlers engaged in free play at the BEO site in our department. Three sides of the pentagonal playroom are made of one-way screens, and the others are windows. The room has the usual toys – blocks, dolls, and movable objects such as carts and doll's prams. Each toy is stored in a particular place, and after the session the teacher puts the toys away so that the children will always encounter the same physical situation. There is a table in a standard position where breakfast is taken, and which is also used for play.

Usually, behaviour is coded live by up to 18 observers behind the one-way screens, on a huge event recorder which has 512 channels that can be divided up into keyboard units of different size (Zaugg, 1994). Configuration and designations of the keyboards, in terms of the coding system and the names of the observers and of the children, are managed by BEDAMAN (Faßnacht, 1997). For quick control, behaviour is videotaped from different perspectives on four recorders. The time code of the recordings is the same as that used by BEDAMAN. Normally, recordings are only used to collect prototypes of behaviour.

In the study three girls (F1, F2, F3) and one boy (M4) were observed over a period of six months in 1997. All came to the same playgroup of 12 children at the BEO site on Monday and Friday mornings from 9.00 a.m. to 12.00 noon. Breakfast was at 10.00–10.15 a.m. Part way through the study the composition of the playgroup changed distinctly: only five of the 12 children stayed – among them all four children of the study – and seven newcomers joined the group. For that reason the study was divided up into two social situations: the old group and the new group. The same single teacher was involved throughout the study, and was mostly passive, so the children were engaged in free play.

Eight observers made live observations between 11.00 a.m. and 12.00 a.m. In total 37 sessions were held, resulting in approximately 33 hours of observation per child. Each child was observed simultaneously by two observers throughout the whole study, and each observer always looked at the same child. During coding, two students videotaped and edited proto-typical behaviours as references. By means of a time and date code, videotapes and MCR data were synchronized. The category system was made up of the following 12 mutually exclusive codes:

Social participation: no

01   *Occupied alone*: The child is alone and occupied with an apparently significant specific activity. The child could not be distracted. Their activity is meaningful in so far as it performs something, even if the activity is not comprehensible for the observer, or if the activity's subject cannot be identified and designated. The child represents something while playing, or uses toys, but always acts or runs around on their own.

02   *Hanging around alone*: The child acts on their own, but unlike category 01, without representing anything. Examples: walking around apparently aimlessly, looking around undecided, and sitting around without company. The child looks bored.

03   *Alone, onlooker*: Solitary watching of other children or teacher. The attention is directed at others: the child's gaze is wandering. Onlooking

in pairs, and interrupting an activity to have a quick look around, are not part of this code. The child's observing can be clearly recognized as their main occupation.

04   *Alone, unclear*: This code is given if the child clearly shows no social participation and none of the previous codes (01, 02, 03) is applicable.

Social participation: yes

05   *Parallel behaviour 1*: Simultaneous, identical activity. Examples of adult behaviour: watching TV together; reading the paper together; sitting together in a café. Examples of child behaviour: sitting together at a table; sitting together in a row, alongside the wall or the window; shared onlooker behaviour, i.e. directed at the same object; writing, painting or kneading together but individually. Interactions are rare.

06   *Parallel behaviour 2*: Matched, identical behaviour that reveals mutual reference or reciprocal consideration. Examples: making noise together, running around together, doing the same but in succession. Unlike in category 05, interactions are more frequent.

07   *Loosely associated interactive behaviour*: Organized dissimilar behaviour, mutually related and coordinated behaviour, without being clearly interpretable for the observer. The behavioural theme can be identified and designated only partially or not at all.

08   *Role play, distinct designation*: Organized dissimilar behaviour, mutually related and coordinated, with a division of labour or of tasks. The behaviour is interpretable for the observer; the behavioural theme is identifiable and can be designated. The behaviour definitely represents something. Examples: hide-and-seek, circus, performing physical exercises, playing with a train set, doctors, etc.

09   *Social participation, unclear*: This code is given if the child clearly shows social participation and the four previous codes (05, 06, 07, 08) are not applicable. For example, the following case is unclear: two children are together in a house but we cannot see what they are doing.

Social participation: decision impossible

10   *Child out of sight*: The child is temporarily outside the playroom, or is hidden.

11   *Generally unclear*: Behaviour and situation are generally unclear. None of the above codes applies. This code should be reserved for when the observers are really uncertain.

12   *Child or observer absent*: Child or observer arrives late, goes home before the end of the observation period, or is absent during the whole period.

For a general overview, the percentage of time was computed that each child spent in the different categories during the whole period. Because for category 10 (out of sight) and for category 12 (observer or child absent) the computations make no sense, these categories were left out. As each child was observed twice, computation was made twice. The results are shown in Figure 7.1. As category 11 (generally unclear) was practically never used by any of the observers, it is not represented in the figure. The overlapping bars represent the two observers.

First, it can be seen that except for pair F and H, the observers give very similar profiles of the same child. Secondly, the profiles of the toddlers – their social behaviour – differ markedly. Thirdly, there is a general tendency of some categories to take more time than others. In particular, the ratio of category 9 (social participation of type unclear) is high for all toddlers. This is probably not an observer effect, because with one exception observers agree relatively well on that category. So, it is the behaviour itself that seems to be ambiguous and, as can be seen, toddlers differed in exhibiting this ambiguous social behaviour over the whole period. One may speculate that category 09 – ambiguous social behaviour (ASB) – is an unknown qualitative category for which there exists as yet no concise designation. And because the theory of social behaviour itself is insufficiently concise to deduce it, that behaviour could only be discovered by chance and a qualitative observational approach.

Besides such speculations, the bemetological approach is best suited to questions of stability and consistency on an extended intra-individual basis. If the profiles found are characteristic of a child, they should be stable over time and occasions. This was studied by dividing up the whole period into four intervals. Two social situations (old versus new group) are compared to compute cross-situational consistency. Within each situation a further division was made to assess temporal stability (see consistency debate: Mischel, 1968; 1973; Epstein, 1979; 1980). The resulting consecutive intervals were: old group period 1 (21 April to 28 May), old group period 2 (29 May to 4 June), holidays (5 June to 17 August), new group period 3 (18 August to 10 September) and new group period 4 (11 September to 24 October). Correlating intra-individually the profile of every interval with every other results in six comparisons per child. Two comparisons refer to temporal stability and four to cross-situational consistency. This is what Cattell (1957) calls the O-technique. Table 7.2 gives the results.

The table is open to several interpretations and speculations. Three of them should be pointed out immediately because they demonstrate the usefulness of the bemetological approach. First, stability of social behaviour seems to be an individual characteristic of the four children during the period observed. Two toddlers (F1, F3) seem to show a very stable social behaviour, and two (F2, M4) are less stable in this respect. Secondly, as to be expected the partial renewal of the playgroup resulted in a destabilization of the social behaviour profiles (comparisons of periods 1 and 3, 2 and 3). This happens probably because social structures within the group had to be negotiated with the newcomers. Thirdly, at the end of the observation period the original profile structures of the four 'senior' toddlers seemed to be re-established (comparisons of periods 1 and 2, 1 and 4).

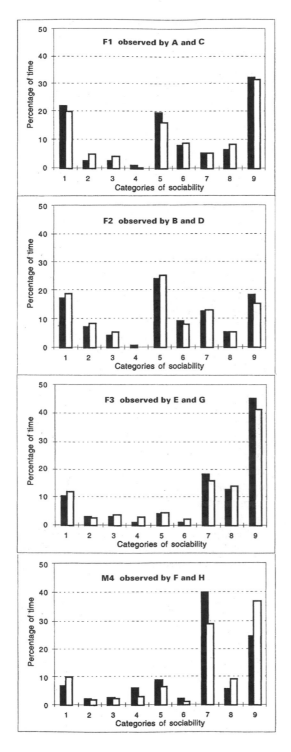

Figure 7.1 *Percentage of time spent in categories of sociability during the whole period*

Table 7.2   *Intra-individual correlations between four occasions over different categories: O-technique of correlation (measure: percentage of time spent in 10 categories)*

| | Temporal stability | | | | Cross-situational consistency | | | | | | | |
| | Old group Period 1–2 | | New group Period 3–4 | | Old–new Period 1–3 | | Old–new Period 2–4 | | Old–new Period 2–3 | | Old–new Period 1–4 | |
Child	r	p	r	p	r	p	r	p	r	p	r	p
F1	0.83	ss	0.92	sss	0.79	ss	0.90	sss	0.83	ss	0.86	ss
F2	0.75	s	0.59		0.85	ss	0.19		0.74	s	0.69	s
F3	0.99	sss	0.81	ss	0.71	s	0.98	sss	0.70	s	0.96	sss
M4	0.92	sss	0.65	s	0.74	s	0.50		0.61		0.78	ss

s: if r > .63, then p < .05, ss: if r > .76, then p < .01, sss: if r > .87, then < .001.

Conclusion: give discovery and change a chance

It has been argued that empirical laws can be interpreted as an aggregation of a huge mass of chance events. As far as we know, no such masses of single events are at work during actual psychic functioning, as is the case in classical physics. This may explain why we do not find strict natural laws in psychology.

Yet, the notion of latent personality factors as dimensions, that is, quantitative objects, presupposes that psychological laws are backstage features disguised by surface behaviours which are interpreted as being to some degree random events. Consequently, measuring instruments are devised to detect those stable states. If we abandon that conjecture, which actually derives from the old philosophical notion of identity of a person, there is no further need to seek general personality factors that are assumed to be valid, stable and the same for all individuals. Because the question of which cognitions, motives, feelings and behaviours should be seen as facets of personality cannot be answered empirically, we may instead decide it by convention. If, as in our culture and society, emotionality, sociability or any other psychological aspects are valued as important features, they are probably called personality factors. Such a quasi-arbitrary but culturally founded decision does not ignore the possibility of constancy. It only represents at first hand the concession that psychological events involve bargaining.

Nevertheless, constancy is still possible on three different levels of generality. The most general one is regularity, which should be valid for all human beings. There are doubts whether we will ever find a psychological law in this strict sense. The second level of generality can be called individuality: it is the differential point of view aiming at laws that are valid for a certain culture, a certain class of people, or perhaps only for some individuals. The third and lowest level of generality is peculiarity. As Schrödinger has indicated, laws are not carbon copies printed through all layers of resolution. Therefore the three levels of generality – regularity, individuality and peculiarity, or 'the RIP triplet' – must not form a functional unit in such a way that they are dependent on each other.

From this point of view, peculiarity must have nothing in common with what is usually called a law. Yet, peculiarities are well-established stabilities within psychopathology. There we find on an individual basis all varieties of strange but stable and hence predictable behaviours, like stereotypes of movements, paranoid reactions, linguistic reverberations, hallucinations, schizoid cognitions and so on.

The important point we have ignored thus far is that within the range of normality there are also peculiarities, which are probably more stable than we admit at first sight. That Mary has a swaying gait, which identifies her with high precision from others, that she typically holds her head in a slightly tilted position, sits on a chair in a stiff posture, glances with wide-eyed innocence, dresses strikingly, takes life seriously, admires Schopenhauer, eats with the knife in her left and the fork in her right hand even though she is right-handed, that she doesn't like lime pie but does like apple pie, that she is fascinated by the Inca culture and people, that her favourite colour is indigo, that she often scratches her head when she starts saying something: all these are peculiar and stable characteristics of her.

Thus, constancy in terms of peculiarity is a well-known fact of normal life. But which of our anonymous peculiar yet normal stable behaviours have the greatest impact on our individual lives cannot be answered on a general basis. Some behaviours are irrelevant, while others are decisive. It would be unwise to conclude that normal peculiarities are superficial facts whose importance ranges beyond those lawful ones that are taken to reside in the unknown depths of our minds. Idiosyncratic routines, strange behaviours or extravagant attitudes of a person are often much more influential in our lives than any of the big five. But whereas the big five are accessible by established standard procedures of research, peculiar laws are not.

To capture them we need research strategies and eventually theories that allow for change and chance events, and that can be described, perhaps deceptively, as qualitative. The reason why we often feel uncomfortable about accepting such an approach as a scientific one probably lies in our implicit notion of what laws are: a few quantitative forces agitating homogeneously from behind the scenes of our phenomenal world, and in opposition to its superficial disorder. Refraining from this notion and seeing laws as the mass aggregation of random events opens up an alternative perspective. The bemetological approach tries to do that by beginning at the bottom of the RIP triplet. Although ambiguous, RIP does not signify the peaceful end of scientific endeavours. Seriously taken, it gives discovery and change a chance.

STEPS TOWARDS A BEMETOLOGY

1 Select naturally occurring behaviour or experience for study; decide on following the touring or the stationary model of observation.
2 Decide on data collection by observer or by self-protocol.

3   Decide to record observations with paper and pencil or by using electronic recording devices (personal computer).
4   Observe a single unit: one person, one dyad, one interacting group, or one situation.
5   At the level of predicator, observe one naturally occurring behaviour/ experience of the unit.
6   At the level of predicator values, observe relatively few qualitative values of that behaviour.
7   Observe continuously during blocks of time, repeatedly over long periods of time.
8   Aggregate the observations across units, predicators, predicator values or across time, depending on the requirements of the analysis.

References

Argyle, M. and Dean, J. (1965) 'Eye-contact, distance and affiliation', *Sociometry*, 28: 289–304.

Baumgartner, L., Burren, F., Flammer, I., Geiser, C., Morgenthaler, C., Laupper, E., Sprenger, I., Studer, G., Zoller, P. and Zürcher, M. (1997) 'Temperamentsentwicklung im Vorschulalter. Vier Einzelfalluntersuchungen zur Entwicklung der Soziabilität'. Unveroffentliche Vordiplomarbeit aus dem Beobachtungskindergarten der Universität Bern, Berne, Institut für Psychologie.

Buss, A.H. and Plomin, R. (1984) *Temperament: Early Developing Personality Traits.* Hillsdale, NJ: Erlbaum.

Campbell, N.R. (1921) *What is Science?* Unabridged reprint, 1952. New York: Dover.

Carnap, R. (1956) *Meaning and Necessity: a Study in Semantics and Modal Logic*, 2nd edn. Midway Reprint. Chicago, IL: University of Chicago Press.

Cattell, R.B. (1957) *Personality and Motivation: Structure and Measurement.* New York: World Books.

Eagly, A.H. (1987) *Sex Differences in Social Behavior: a Social-Role Interpretation.* Hillsdale, NJ: Erlbaum.

Eaton, W.O. and Enns, L.R. (1986) 'Sex differences in human motor activity level', *Psychological Bulletin*, 100: 19–28.

Ekman, P. and Friesen, W.V. (1978) *Manual:Facial Action Coding System.* Palo Alto, CA: Consulting Psychology Press.

Epstein, S. (1979) 'Stability of behavior. I: On predicting most of the people much of the time', *Journal of Personality and Social Psychology*, 37 (7): 1097–126.

Epstein, S. (1980) 'The stability of behavior. II: Implications for psychological research', *American Psychologist*, 35 (9): 790–806.

Epstein, S. (1990) 'Comment on the effects of aggregation across and within occasions on consistency, specificity, and reliability', *Methodika*, 4: 95–100.

Exner, F. (1919) *Vorlesungen über die physikalischen Grundlagen der Naturwissenschaften.* Vienna: F. Deuticke.

Faßnacht, G. (1974) 'Entwicklung eines Beobachtungssystems zum Sozialverhalten gestörter und behinderter Kinder in Heimen'. Unveroffentliches Forschungsgesuch, Schweizerischer Nationalfond, Berne, Institut für Psychologie.

Faßnacht, G. (1982) *Theory and Practice of Observing Behaviour*, 2nd edn. London: Academic Press.

Faßnacht, G. (1995) *Systematische Verhaltensbeobachtung. Eine Einführung in die Methodologie und Praxis. Dritte, völlig neubearbeitete Auflage*. Munich: Reinhardt.

Faßnacht, G. (1997) *BEDAMAN. Behavioral Data Management. Basic Programs for Managing Data in Terms of Cascade Predications*, 3rd release (1st release, 1987), unpublished DOS version. Berne: Department of Psychology.

Goldberg, L.R. (1981) 'Language and individual differences: the search for universals in personality lexicons', *Review of Personality and Social Psychology*, 2: 141–65.

Goldberg, L.R. (1990) 'An alternative "description of personality": the Big-Five factor structure', *Journal of Personality and Social Psychology*, 59: 1216–29.

Grassberger, P. and Procaccia, I. (1983) 'On the characterization of strange attractors', *Physics Review Letters*, 50: 346–50.

Haehlen, A. and Neuenschwander, S. (1998) 'BEO Play Group. Behavioural Observation at the Department of Psychology, University of Berne'. Prediploma, Video Film. Department of Psychology, University of Berne.

Hartshorne, H. and May, M.A. (1928) *Studies in the Nature of Character*. New York: Macmillan.

Hartshorne, H. and May, M.A. (1929) *Studies in the Nature of Character*. New York: Macmillan.

Hartshorne, H. and May, M.A. and Shuttleworth, F.K. (1930) *Studies in the Nature of Character*. New York: Macmillan.

Hollis, M. (1994) *The Philosophy of Social Science: an Introduction*. Cambridge: Cambridge University Press.

Jöri, M. (1997) 'Individuelle Gefühlsmuster. Eine über drei Monate laufende Einzelfallanalyse unter Verwendung der Event-sampling-Methode'. Berne, Institut für Psychologie.

Kamlah, W. and Lorenzen, P. (1973) *Logische Propädeutik. Vorschule des vernünftigen Redens 2, verbesserte und erweiterte Auflage*. B.I.-Hochschultschenbücher, Vol. 227. Mannheim: Bibliographisches Institut.

LaFrenière, P., Strayer, F.F. and Gaulthier, R. (1984) 'The emergence of the same-sex affiliative preferences among preschool peers: a developmental/etiological perspective', *Child Development*, 55: 1958–65.

Lindley, D. (1993) *The End of Physics: the Myth of a Unified Theory*. New York: Basic Books.

Lorenz, E.N. (1963) 'Deterministic nonperiodic flow', *Journal of the Atmospheric Sciences*, 20: 130–41.

Magnusson, D. (ed.) (1981) *Toward a Psychology of Situations: an Interactional Perspective*. Hillsdale, NJ: Erlbaum.

Magnusson, D. and Endler, N.S. (eds) (1977) *Personality at the Crossroads: Current Issues in Interactional Psychology*. Hillsdale, NJ: Erlbaum.

McGrew, W.C. (1972) *An Ethological Study of Children's Behavior*. New York: Academic Press.

Mischel, W. (1968) *Personality and Assessment*. New York: Wiley.

Mischel, W. (1973) 'Toward a cognitive social learning reconceptualization of personality', *Psychological Review*, 80 (4): 252–83.

Mischel, W. (1984) 'On the predictability of behavior and the structure of personality', in R.A. Zucker, J. Aronoff and A.I. Rabin (eds), *Personality and the Prediction of Behavior*. Orlando, FL: Academic Press. pp. 269–305.

Nagel, E. (1961) *The Structure of Science: Problems in the Logic of Scientific Explanation*. New York: Harcourt, Brace and World.

Newcomb, T.M. (1929) *Consistency of Certain Extrovert–Introvert Behavior Patterns in 51 Problem Boys*. New York: Columbia University, Teachers College.

Perez, M. and Reicherts, M. (1992) *Stress, Coping, and Health: a Situation-Behavior Approach. Theory, Methods, Applications*. Seattle, WA: Hogrefe and Huber.

Popper, K.R. (1959) *The Logic of Scientific Discovery*. London: Hutchinson.

Schleidt, M. (1989) 'Temporal structures of behaviour', *Human Ethology Newsletters*, 5 (10): 2–4.

Schrödinger, E. (1962) *Was ist ein Naturgesetz, Beiträge zum naturwissenschaftlichen Weltbild*. Munich: Oldenburg.

Stewart, I. (1992) *Does God Play Dice? The Mathematics of Chaos*. Cambridge, MA: Blackwell.

Vallacher, R.R. and Nowak, A. (eds) (1994) *Dynamical Systems in Social Psychology*. San Diego, CA: Academic Press.

Windelband, W. (1894) 'Geschichte und Naturwissenschaft. Straßburger Rektoratsrede', in W. Windelband (1924), *Präludien. Aufsätze und Reden zur Philosophie und ihrer Geschichte*, vol. 2. Tubingen: J.C.B. Mohr. pp. 136–60.

Zaugg, W. (1994) *The Multi Channel Event-Recorder MCR-128/512*, second prototype (1st prototype 1988), unpublished manual. Berne: Department of Psychology, University of Berne.

Part II

Analytic Approaches for Text, Image and Sound

8

Classical Content Analysis: a Review

Martin W. Bauer

KEYWORDS

ambiguity	cultural indicators
artificial week	dictionary
CAQDAS	keyword in context (KWIC)
codebook	keyword out of context (KWOC)
code value	lemmatization
coding frame	metric: categorical, ordinal,
coding pathologies	interval, ratio
coding sheet	modularity
coding unit	parallel design
coherence	random sampling
computer-assisted analysis	reliability–validity dilemma
concordance	sampling unit
co-occurence	

Most social research is based on interviewing: researchers ask people about their age, what they do for a living, how they live, what they think and feel about X, Y and Z; or they ask them to tell their story of events. Interviewing, structured or unstructured, is a convenient and established method of social research. But as well as expressing their views in talk, people also write – to create records, to plan, play or entertain, to establish norms and rules, and to argue over controversial issues. So texts, as well as talk, are about people's thoughts, feelings, memories, plans and arguments, and are sometimes more telling than their authors realize.

Social researchers tend to undervalue textual materials as data. Research methods go through cycles of fashion and oblivion, but the World Wide Web and on-line archives for newspapers, radio and television programmes have created a window of opportunity for text as data. As the effort of data collection is tending to zero, we are seeing a renewed interest in content analysis (CA) and its techniques, and in particular in computer-assisted techniques.

How do quality and popular newspapers differ in their reporting of science and technology? Does commercial television address its audiences differently from public television? How was the myth of the storming of the Bastille cultivated by newsprint of the time? When and how does the 'achievement' theme appear in children's books? What information do internal memos in a business organization communicate? Can we reconstruct changes in social values from lonely hearts columns or obituaries? These are just some of the questions that researchers have addressed through content analysis.

Content analysis is the only method of text analysis that has been developed within the empirical social sciences. While most classical content analyses culminate in numerical descriptions of some features of the text corpus, considerable thought is given to the 'kinds', 'qualities' and 'distinctions' in the text before any quantification takes place. In this way, content analysis bridges statistical formalism and the qualitative analysis of the materials. In the quantity/quality divide in social research, content analysis is a hybrid technique that can mediate in this unproductive dispute over virtues and methods.

In the seventeenth century, a Swedish court classified, counted and compared the symbols used in the songs of a religious sect, but failed to find evidence of heresy (Krippendorff, 1980: 13). In the late nineteenth century CA demonstrated the 'moral decay' in the news coverage in the newly emerging yellow press (Speed, 1893). In Germany, Max Weber (1965 [1911]) envisaged a cultural sociology engaged in the analysis of newspapers. Later, several UK Royal Commissions on the Press contained comparative content analyses of news coverage (McQuail, 1977). The CA of enemy propaganda serves intelligence in wartime, and furthers business interests in its civil form of corporate media monitoring. During the 1960s, the advent of the computer intensified the level of methodological reflection (see Stone et al., 1966; Gerbner et al., 1969; Holsti, 1968; 1969; Krippendorff, 1980; Merten, 1995).

The interpretation of sacred or dignified texts, literary criticisms of aesthetic values, the philological scrutiny involved in reconstructing 'originals' and revealing 'fakes', or the semiotic analysis of advertisements, all increase the complexity of a text: one paragraph warrants extended commentaries exploring all ambiguities and nuances of language. Content analysis, by contrast, reduces the complexity of a collection of texts. Systematic classification and counting of text units distil a large amount of

Table 8.1   *Some definitions of content analysis (emphasis added)*

The *statistical semantics* of political discourse. (Kaplan, 1943: 230)

A research technique for the *objective, systematic, and quantitative* description of the manifest content of communication. (Berelson, 1952: 18)

Any technique for *making inferences* by *objectively and systematically* identifying specified characteristics of messages. (Holsti, 1969: 14)

Information processing in which communication *content is transformed*, through objective and systematic application of *categorisation* rules. (Paisley, 1969)

A research technique for making *replicable and valid inferences* from data to their context. (Krippendorff, 1980: 21)

A research methodology that utilizes a *set of procedures* to make valid inferences from text. These inferences are about senders, the message itself, or the audience of the message. (Weber, 1985: 9)

material into a short description of some of its features. A library can be contained in a single graphic: CA is a means of characterizing differences in an estimated 700,000 items written on science and technology in the post-war British press (Bauer et al., 1995). To read all those articles would be more than a life's work.

The definitions in Table 8.1 highlight several features of CA. It is a technique for making inferences from a focal text to its social context in an objectified manner. This context may be temporarily or in principle inaccessible to the researcher. CA often involves statistical treatment of text units. 'Objectified' refers to systematic, procedurally explicit and replicable procedures: it does not suggest a single valid reading of the texts. On the contrary, the irreversible coding of a text transforms it in order to create new information from this text. It is not possible to reconstruct the original text once it is coded; irreversibility is the cost of new information. The validity of a CA must be judged not against a 'true reading' of the text, but in terms of its grounding in the materials and its congruence with the theory of the researcher, and in the light of his or her research purpose. A text corpus offers different readings depending on the prejudice that is brought to bear. CA is no exception; however, it steers a middle course between the single truthful reading and 'anything goes', and is ultimately a class of explicit procedures for textual analysis for the purposes of social research. It can neither assess the beauty, nor explore the subtleties, of a particular text.

One may distinguish two basic purposes of content analysis by reflecting on the triple nature of symbolic mediation: a symbol represents the world; this representation expresses a source and appeals to an audience (Buehler, 1934). By reconstructing representations, content analysts infer the expression of, and the appeal in and across, contexts. With the focus on the source, the text is a *medium of expression*. Source and audience are the context and focus of inference. A text corpus is the representation and expression of a community that writes. In this light, the result of a CA is the dependent variable, the thing to be explained. Attributed texts contain records of events, values, rules and norms, entertainment, and traces of conflict and argument. CA allows us to construct indicators of worldviews, values, attitudes, opinions, prejudices and stereotypes, and compare these across communities. In other words, CA is public opinion research by other means.

With the focus on the audience, the text is a *medium of appeal*: an influence on people's prejudices, opinions, attitudes and stereotypes. Considering texts as a seductive force, the results of a CA are independent variables, the variables that explain things. The modality of this influence is still controversial; however, CA provides the independent variables in the design of media-effect studies on agenda-setting or cultivation studies (Neumann, 1989).

CA procedures reconstruct representations in two main dimensions: the syntactical and the semantic. Syntactical procedures focus on sign vehicles and their interrelation. Syntax describes the means of expression and influence – how something is said or written. The frequency of words and their ordering, the vocabulary, the types of words, and grammatical and stylistic features are indicative of a source and of the likelihood of influence over some audience. The unusually frequent use of a form of words may identify a likely author, and a certain vocabulary may indicate a likely type of audience.

Semantic procedures focus on the relation between signs and their common-sense meaning – denotational and connotational meanings in a text. Semantics concerns the 'what is said in a text?', the themes and valuations. Words, sentences and larger text units are classified as exemplars of predefined themes and valuations. The frequent co-occurrence of words within the same sentence or paragraph is taken to indicate associative meanings. For example, between 1973 and 1996, the theme 'biotechnology' became a more and more prominent part of science news in the national media; the coverage differentiates, and the valuation varies, with the particular application that is in focus (Durant et al., 1998).

Syntactical and semantic features of a text corpus allow the researcher to make informed guesses about uncertain sources, such as false claims to authorship, or uncertain audiences, either when information on these is inaccessible, or because good results can be achieved more cheaply through CA. Such guesses may infer the values, attitudes, stereotypes, symbols and worldviews of a context about which little is known. We profile a sender–audience context, or we attribute to a sender–audience context whose profile we already know. Profiling and the matching of profiles to identify a context are basic inferences of a CA. It is possible, for example, to measure the value structure, and its stability and changes, of the British establishment by analysing the London *Times* over the last 100 years; or to assess the basic motives of a person from personal letters and diary entries. However, the idea that one can infer any particular intention of a communicator or any particular reading of an audience is considered the fallacy of content analysis (Eco, 1994; Merten, 1995). Expression and impression are assessed only in aggregate, and probabilistically.

Krippendorff (1980) distinguishes different research strategies. First, one can construct a text corpus as an open system in order to pick up trends and changing patterns. This means that the text corpus is never complete; additional texts are continuously added. This is the practice of media monitoring. A sample of media outlets is regularly coded to detect shifting emphases and clusters in a set of themes.

Secondly, comparisons reveal 'differences' that may be observed between the coverage of different newspapers (by sources), in speeches of a politician to different constituencies (by audiences), and between scientific papers and popularized versions of them (input–output). Other comparisons consider 'standards' as part of an auditing process to identify and evaluate achievements against established norms, for example on obscenity, discrimination or 'objective reporting'. This may be relevant in a court action where a media proprietor is accused of biasing news coverage to function as hidden advertising.

Thirdly, CA is used to construct indices. An index is a sign that is causally related to some other phenomenon, just as smoke is an index or a symptom of fire. Changes in vocabulary in lonely hearts columns over 100 years are an index of societal values: the assumption is that the way people describe themselves and their ideal partners is an expression of what is desirable in a society. The amount of science coverage in newspapers may be a measure of the position of science and technology in society, or equally an indicator of the uncertainty of science over its position in society. Considering the content together with the intensity may define the index.

Finally, CA may reconstruct 'maps of knowledge' as they are embodied in texts. People use language to represent the world as knowledge and self-knowledge. To reconstruct this knowledge, CA may have to go beyond the classification of text units and work towards networking the units of analysis to represent knowledge not only by elements, but also in their relationships.

There are six CA research designs. The simplest and least interesting is the purely descriptive study that counts the frequency of all the coded features of the text. More interesting are normative analyses that make comparisons with standards, for example of 'objective' or 'unbiased' reporting. In cross-sectional analyses, empirical comparison may involve texts from different contexts, for example two newspapers covering a particular news story during one month. In longitudinal analyses, comparisons span the same context over a longer period. This allows us to detect fluctuations, regular and irregular, in content, and to infer concomitant changes in the context. More elaborate studies act as cultural indicators: they may consider several contexts over many years, such as the different public spheres in which biotechnology has become an issue (Durant et al., 1998). This kind of analysis may be a viable substitute for opinion polling (see Neisbitt, 1976 or Janowitz, 1976). The most ambitious designs are parallel designs, involving longitudinal analyses in combination with other longitudinal data such as from opinion polling or repeated waves of unstructured interviewing (see, for example, Neumann, 1989; Durant et al., 1998).

Conducting a content analysis

Theoretical considerations and texts

Methods are no substitute for good theory and a substantive research problem. The theory and the problem – which embody the prejudices of the researcher – will inform the selection and categorization of the text materials, either implicitly or explicitly. Being explicit is a methodical virtue. Say a researcher wants to attribute or dispute the authorship of a text. An implicit assumption suggests that text authorship is important; the researcher will then need explicitly to formulate a strong theory on how individuality manifests itself in the text.

CA traditionally deals with written textual materials, but similar procedures can be applied to images (see Rose, Chapter 14 in this volume) or sounds (see Bauer, Chapter 15 in this volume). There are two kinds of texts: texts that are made in the process of research, such as interview transcripts and observation protocols; and texts that have already been produced for some other purpose, such as newspapers or corporate memos. The classic materials of CA are written texts that have already been used for some other purpose. However, all these texts can be manipulated to provide answers to the researcher's questions.

Some years ago colleagues and I started to map the media cultivation of biotechnology between 1973 and 1996 in Europe and North America. In a cross-national and longitudinal study, we analysed media coverage of biotechnology in 12 European countries. Such media coverage constitutes a linguistic, and at times also pictorial, representation of a new technology in society (Bauer and Gaskell, 1999). Variations in media coverage across time and space are compared, in a parallel design, with public perceptions and the policy process, in order to explain the technological trajectory in different contexts. We analyse elite newspapers as proxies of media coverage of biotechnology. As aggregates over a longer period, they represent an important aspect of public opinion in modern societies.

Definition and sampling of text units

CA analysis often uses random sampling to select its materials (Krippendorff, 1980; Holsti, 1969; Bauer and Aarts, Chapter 2 in this volume). There are three problems of sampling: its representativeness, the sample size, and the unit of sampling and coding.

Statistical sampling provides a rationale for studying a small number of texts and still drawing conclusions about the whole collection of texts. The history of CA in studying newspapers has supported this rationale. Newsprint can be easily stratified into a hierarchical typology, for example daily papers and weekly magazines, left and right by political orientation, high or low circulation figures, national or regional distribution, popular and quality, or according to ownership.

A common sampling strategy for regular publications is the 'artificial week'. Calendar dates are a reliable sampling frame from which to select strictly randomly. However, random dates may include Sundays, when some newspapers are not printed, or papers may run coverage in a cycle, such as a science page on Wednesdays. So in this case, in order to avoid distortions in the sampling of science news, it would be necessary to ensure an equal distribution of weekdays in the sample. A week has seven days, so by choosing every third, fourth, sixth, eighth, ninth, etc. day over a longer period, a sample without periodicity is created. For every selected issue, all relevant articles are selected.

Sampling newspapers by dates, when articles or even sentences are the unit of analysis, makes a cluster sample. In cluster samples the randomly selected unit, in this case a newspaper, is larger than the units of analysis, the articles or sentences, all of which are collected.

Random sampling requires a complete list of units to select from. Sometimes such a list already exists, as with serial numbers or calendar dates, and sometimes one has to create it. Consider sampling press articles on genetics from a database such as FT-Profile. Typing in the word 'genetic*' may yield 5000 articles over several years. If you are able to analyse only 200 of these, save or print all 5000 articles as headlines and number them from 1 to 5000. Then decide on a random procedure: either generate 200 random numbers between 1 and 5000, or decide to take, say, every 25th article. Irrelevant articles can be rejected in favour of other articles as you go along.

Stempel (1952) has shown that 12 randomly selected issues of a daily newspaper provide a reliable estimate of its yearly news profile. A small sample, systematically selected, is far better than a large sample of materials collected conveniently. Ultimately all considerations of sample size are practical. How many articles can the researcher handle? How many codes and variables are used? What is a suitable distribution of a variable for multivariate analysis?

Sampling units are normally physically defined as a newspaper, a book, a television newscast and so on. The exclusion or inclusion of any one unit is irrelevant; the assumption is that sampling units are replaceable by each other. Recording units are for the most part the same as sampling units, except in the case of cluster sampling. Often it is easier to sample newspaper issues and to take all the relevant articles in any one issue. In these cases the recording unit, the article, is contained in the sampling unit, the newspaper issue.

Krippendorff (1980: 61ff) distinguishes the following types of sampling and recording units:

- *Physical units* are books, letters, television newscasts, films and so on.
- *Syntactical units* are apparent 'natural' building blocks: chapters in a book; headlines, articles or sentences in a newspaper; film scenes or shots in a film. The most obvious syntactical unit is the single word.
- *Propositional units* are logical kernels of sentences. Complex statements are deconstructed into kernels of the form subject/verb/object. Take the

sentence: 'Biotechnology, the most recent among post-war base technologies, enters the public arena in the 1990s.' It can be split into several propositions: 'biotechnology enters the public arena in the 1990s', 'biotechnology is a base technology', 'biotechnology is a base technology of the post-war period', 'biotechnology is the most recent base technology'. Most text analysis computer programs support automatic segmentation of syntactical units such as paragraphs, sentences or single keywords out of context; more specialized programs also support the deconstruction of complex sentences into propositional kernels.

● *Thematic or semantic units* are defined by features of texts that involve human judgement. For example, fairy-tales may be classified by basic motives; letters may be classified as love letters or business letters. The definition of sampling units often involves such judgements of stratification. Thematic units separate on theoretical grounds, and are often contrasted against irrelevant residual materials.

Representation, sample size and unitization ultimately depend on the research problem, which also determines the coding frame. What appears as a sequence from conceptualization to sampling to coding is actually an iterative process, and piloting is essential. But piloting and revising have to stop, at least temporarily, if the analysis is to deliver results.

In our study on biotechnology news we decided to sample opinion-leading newspapers between 1973 and 1996. The criterion 'opinion-leading newspaper' is a theoretical entry right at the beginning of the study. Each team identifies one or two key newspapers: the ones that journalists and politicians are most likely to read. The year-by-year sampling procedure varies from country to country, and the archives demand different techniques: manual scanning of hard copies of newspapers; using an in-house index of keywords such as *The Times* Index; accessing on-line databases; using existing collections of newspaper cuttings; and so on. In some years, teams select newspaper issues and sample relevant materials as clusters. For other years, they use on-line research, retrieve all relevant articles, and draw a strict random sample to a fixed number of articles for every year. Other teams create an artificial week and pick the papers as a cluster sample. The final international text corpus contains 5404 newspaper articles on biotechnology from 12 countries over 24 years (Bauer, 1998a). It is envisaged that the corpus will be updated to the year 2001. Sampling, in particular for international studies, can only progress pragmatically, making the best out of imperfect and varied circumstances.

Categories and coding

Coding and therefore classifying the sampled materials is a constructive task that brings together the theory and the research material. This match is not achieved immediately: the researcher needs to allow sufficient time for piloting, amendments and coder training. Constructing a coding frame is an iterative process, and, if several coders are involved, a collective process, that at some point must be closed.

A coding frame is a systematic way of comparing. It is a set of questions (codes) with which the coder addresses the materials, and to which the coder reaches answers within a predefined set of alternatives (code values). While a text corpus is open to a multitude of possible questions, the CA interprets the text only in the light of the coding frame, which constitutes a theoretical selection that embodies the research purpose. A CA re-presents what is already a representation, binding the researchers to a text and a research project (Bauer and Gaskell, 1999). CA is not the last word on any text, but an encounter objectified by systematicity and referring beyond itself to other texts and research activities (Lindkvist, 1981). Ultimately, however, even the positivist approach of counting text units is just another contribution to the open interpretation of a text corpus.

Categories and categorization

A number of considerations come into play for the construction of a coding frame or category system: the nature of categories, the types of codes variables, the organizing principles of the coding frame, the coding process and coder training. Each code in the frame has a finite number of code values. In our example in Table 8.2, the code 'size' may have the values of 'small', 'medium' and 'big'; or the code 'news format' may include 'latest news', 'reportage', 'interview', 'commentary', 'editorial', 'review' and 'other'. While the values of 'size' are common sense, the values of 'news format' are the outcome of extensive pilot work of reading through newspapers in different countries and trying to define a finite number of formats of reporting in elite newspapers. One may be able to rely on standard categories if a similar code has been used in previous research.

Every text unit must fit a code, and none can be left over. By adding a value 'other' or 'does not apply', one ensures that every unit fits. Codes

Table 8.2 *Example categories for press articles*

c1 size (ordinal scale)
1 = small
2 = medium
3 = big

c2 news format (categorical scale)
1 = latest news
2 = reportage
3 = interview
4 = commentary
5 = editorial
6 = review
7 = other

c3 word count (interval and ratio scale)
100, 165, 367 or 658 words

must be exclusive: every unit is assigned one value only on each code, e.g. an article is either small or big but never both. Codes are independent of each other: the coding of size has no direct influence on the coding of the news format (the observation that editorials are larger than latest news may show up as an empirical 'fact'). The mixing of categories is to be avoided: codes need to derive from a single dimension, e.g. to consider 'red' alongside 'small' violates the principle. Equally, the value 'television news' as a news format would violate the principle: it mixes the principle of news medium and the principle of news format. Confusions of this kind are normally resolved by splitting them into two codes: mass medium (television, radio and newsprint) and news formats (reportage, interview, etc.). Lastly, codes need to be derived theoretically and to reflect the purpose of the research. Both 'size' and 'news format' are codes derived from a theory that the size of a story expresses the editorial importance attributed to it, and serves as an indicator of the values in the newsroom. On the other hand, size may be format-specific. The code 'news format' is derived from an idea about the different functions of different formats in public debates.

For statistical analysis one assigns numbers to code values, as shown in Table 8.2 (here 1 = latest news). The meanings of these numbers vary. Categorical variables merely distinguish, and the numbers have no other significance: in code 2, '5 = editorial' could equally be '7 = editorial'. By contrast, ordinal or rating scales preserve an order among values: small, medium, big is mapped into a ranking 1, 2, 3 whereby 3 > 2 and 2 > 1. A word count for each article constitutes a scale that preserves the difference between the values; a 165-word article is 65 per cent larger than a 100-word article. The type of metric has bearings on the types of statistical analyses that can be applied.

CA is theory-laden coding (Franks, 1999). A text unit A may be coded 'commentary' in relation to a given theory embodied in the category 'news format'. The text unit A may be something else: it is not by nature 'commentary'. However, text unit A is either commentary' or 'latest news', but not both. Sharp distinctions between units are a construction rule, allowing us to ignore the fuzzy differences and ambiguities in the world of newspapers. Coder training and collective practice will make text unit A appear naturally as 'commentary', and any remaining ambiguity will reveal itself in problems of reliability. This constructive imposition of a code system is an act of semantic violence that must be justified by surprising results, rather than condemned out of hand.

The coding process: paper and pencil, or computer

The actual coding can be done either with paper and pencil, or directly into computer. In the paper-and-pencil format the coder will have instructions in the form of a codebook (see below), and the text material and coding sheets. A coding sheet is a single-page grid with a cell assigned for each code. The coder will write his judgement for each code in the assigned cell.

Once the coding is complete, all coding sheets are collated and entered into a computer for data analysis. Computer-assisted coding allows the coder to enter his judgements directly into the computer. CAPI, CATI (computer-assisted personal or telephone interviewing) or NUD*IST or ATLAS/ti (see Kelle, Chapter 16 in this volume) support the coding process directly. In the case of CAPI or CATI, a shell is created that presents a sequence of screens to the coder, one for each code, with all the necessary instructions and a field to record the coding judgement. NUD*IST and ATLAS/ti take on-line text and the coder tags the text units with a predefined code, thereby never losing the link between the code and the text unit, and linking text units with the code. An output file for statistical analysis will be created automatically. It is important always to create an additional code with the serial number of the text unit, and to identify the coder in cases where several coders are employed. The CA of large text corpora with several coders, such as the continuous monitoring of mass media, may develop into an undertaking on an industrial scale requiring organization, training, coordination and quality control.

Quality in content analysis

Content analysis is a social construction. Like any viable construction, it takes into account some reality, in this case the text corpus, and it needs to be judged by its outcome. However, this outcome is not the only grounds for assessment. In research, the outcome means whether the analysis delivers interesting results and withstands scrutiny; but elegance may also be part of the assessment. Content analysis methodology has an elaborate discourse of quality, with the key concerns being the traditional reliability and validity derived from psychometrics. However, the limitations of these criteria show themselves in the reliability–validity dilemma. I add coherence and transparency as two further criteria for evaluating good practice in CA.

Coherence: the beauty of a coding frame

Most CA analyses operate with many codes. The construction of a coding frame or category system is a conceptual issue that bears on the aesthetic value of research. The seasoned content analyst may well develop a sense of beauty: a beautiful coding frame is one that is internally coherent and simple in the sense that all codes flow from a single principle, rather than being grounded in the 'dust-bowl' empiricism of coding whatever comes to mind. Coherence in the construction of a coding frame derives from superordinate ideas that give order to a coding frame.

Table 8.3 compares several concepts and derived primary notions that provide coherence in the construction of a coding frame. Each primary notion is derived from a principle, and can be further specified by secondary codes. North et al. (1963) investigated diplomatic exchanges at the onset

Table 8.3   *Concepts that bring coherence in the construction of a coding frame*

Concept	Derived primary notions
Public message system (e.g. Gerbner et al., 1969)	Attention, emphasis, tendency, structure
Perception of action (e.g. North et al., 1963)	Perceiver, actors, effects on target, evaluation
Rhetoric (e.g. Bauer, 1998b)	Logos markers, ethos markers, pathos markers
Arguments (e.g. Toulmin, 1958)	Claim, data, warrant, backing, rebuttal, qualifier
Narrative (e.g. Bauer et al., 1995; Rose, Chapter 14 in this volume)	Narrator, actor, event, background, consequences, moral

of World War I. Their organizing principle was 'actions and their perception': who perceives which actions with what effects and with what qualifiers. Thematic units, paraphrased from the original texts, were coded for (a) perceivers, (b) actors, (c) effects on targets, (d) evaluative descriptors of these effects.

Rhetoric is another useful principle of analysis. Logos, pathos and ethos are the 'three musketeers' of persuasion (Gross, 1990). Logos refers to drawing conclusions from premises and observations; pathos stirs the emotions of the audience; and ethos refers to display of the speaker's own authority and claim to fame. This can be used to code text units in terms of argument (logos markers), their function of attracting the attention of a listener/reader (pathos markers), or as references to the authority and claim to fame of the speaker/writer (ethos markers) (Bauer, 1998b; Leach, Chapter 12 in this volume). The analysis of argumentation has inspired content analysis. Toulmin's (1958) analysis of a practical argument provides a principle on which to classify text units as claims, warrants, backings, data, qualifiers and rebuttals (see Leach, Chapter 12 in this volume). This can be used to analyse the arguments attributed to different actors in the media or in policy documents, both to compare across actors and to assess the complexity of argumentation in different public arenas (Liakopoulos, Chapter 9 in this volume). Finally, the narrative is a stimulating principle. To consider news as a story immediately suggests a number of primary notions: a story-teller, an actor, events, a background situation, consequences and a moral. Rose (Chapter 14 in this volume) has applied the narrative principle to analyse the portrayal of mental illness in soap operas.

Modularity is a trick in the construction of a coding frame to guarantee both efficiency and coherence. A module is a building block of a coding frame that is used repeatedly. Take, for example, a set of secondary codes specifying the primary notion 'actor' in a narrative: type of actor (individual, collective), gender (male, female, unknown) and sphere of activity (private, semi-private, public, etc.). These three codes constitute a module to specify actors. Actors appear in different functions in a narrative: as the author, the main actor, the background actor; as being on the receiving end of consequences of events; or as the target of the moral of the story. The actor module can now be used to specify each of the different actor functions in the narrative. Modular construction increases the complexity of the coding frame without increasing the coding effort, and while maintaining its coherence; it also makes both coding and training easier. Once the module is memorized, repeated application requires little additional effort, and reliability will be enhanced.

The coding frame for the analysis of news coverage of biotechnology finally comprised 26 codes arranged on the principle of a narrative: author, actor, themes, events, event location, and consequences in terms of risk and benefits. Modularity was used to code multiple actors and multiple themes. The coding process was developed over a year: the 12 teams met twice to negotiate and revise the structure of the coding frame. The whole process of sampling, developing a reliable coding process, piloting and coding the corpus in each country took two-and-a-half years (Bauer, 1998a).

Transparency through documentation

A coding frame is normally reported as a booklet that serves both as a guideline for coders and as a document of the research process. This codebook will normally include (a) a summary list of all codes; and (b) the frequency distribution for each code, each with the total number of codes (*N*). Each code will be reported with an intensional definition, its code name (such as 'c2'), its code label (such as 'news format'), and an illustrative text unit that applies to each code. A complete codebook will include (c) an account of the coder reliability, both for each code and for the coding process overall, and a note on the time required to achieve an acceptable level of reliability. This serves as an estimate of the training that is required for that particular coding frame. Documenting the coding process in detail ensures public accountability, and that other researchers can reconstruct the process should they want to emulate it. Documentation is an essential ingredient of the 'objectivity' of the data.

Reliability

Reliability is defined as agreement among interpreters. Establishing reliability involves some doubling of effort: the same person may make a second interpretation after a time interval (to determine intrapersonal reliability, consistency, stability), or two or more people may interpret the same material simultaneously (interpersonal reliability, agreement, reproducibility). Reliability indices – phi, kappa or alpha – measure the agreement among coders on a scale between 0 (no agreement) and 1 (perfect agreement) weighted against chance (Scott, 1955; Krippendorff, 1980: 129ff; Holsti, 1969: 135ff).

Most content analysis projects face two reliability problems: the demarcation of units within the sequence of materials, and the coding of contents. Semantic units of analysis are a matter of judgement. Suppose you have randomly selected some dates for old magazines, and you are flicking through those issues searching for articles on biotechnology. Although you have defined 'biotechnology' with circumspection as 'reportage on intervention at the level of the gene', room for judgement and disagreement remains. For the analysis of moving images, the unit of analysis is often a matter of judgement: some selectors may demarcate a scene to start several frames earlier, or to end several frames later, than others (see Krippendorff, 1994).

No content analyst expects perfect reliability where human judgement is involved, and so the question of an acceptable level of reliability arises. As different measures yield different values of reliability, kappa and alpha are more conservative than phi; different standards need to be defined for different measures. Furthermore, reliability may differ across codes, some being more ambiguous than others. How do we integrate reliability across many codes: as a simple average, a weighted average, by a range of values or by the lowest value? Low reliability adds to the error margin of statistical estimates derived from the data. Standards need to consider the possible consequences of an increased error margin: results that influence life-or-death decisions require very high reliability; but for studies that attempt only tentative and cautious conclusions, the standard can be relaxed. Reliability is generally considered to be very high at $r > 0.90$, high at $r > 0.80$, and acceptable in the range $0.66 < r < 0.79$.

Researchers should use reliability to improve the coding process. Reliability depends on the amount of training, the definition of categories, the complexity of the coding frame, and the material. Low reliability can mean several things. First, coders need training. Intensive coder training is likely to lead to higher reliabilities by building up a common 'mindset' among coders for some given material. Secondly, reliability can be used to order categories by their degree of ambiguity. Some codes may be poorly defined, and adding examples will improve the agreement among coders. Thirdly, coders inevitably memorize codes and speed up their coding. The more varied and numerous the codes, the less likely they are to be memorized, the more training will be required, and the more likely are ambiguities and errors due to fatigue. Thus reliability is limited by the complexity of a coding frame. Finally, reliability may be an indicator of the polysemy of the text. Low reliability may indicate that the boundaries of the code values are rather fuzzy. Furthermore, complex coding frames increase the likelihood of consistent but different readings of the same text units.

Validation

Validity traditionally refers to the degree to which a result correctly represents the text or its context. Krippendorff's (1980) distinction between the validity of data, results and procedure is useful. For the data, one wants to ensure that codes relate to the words used in the text (semantic validity), and that the sample represents the whole body of text (sampling validity). The results can be validated by correlation with external criteria. Previous results can validate a content analysis, for example by comparing a simple and a complex procedure. This is, however, tautological, and not always desirable. On the other hand, one could predict public opinion polls from press coverage and test this prediction under specified circumstances (predictive validity). Finally, a coding frame needs to embody the theory underlying an analysis (construct validity). However, the nature of interpretation suggests that challenging results methodically obtained may have value independently of external corroboration. Sometimes, internal coherence is sufficient to insinuate credibility. Indeed, unexpected but methodically derived results can yield meaningful information.

The main fallacy of content analysis is the inference of particular intentions or understandings from the text alone (Merten, 1995; Eco, 1994). Intentions and reception are features of the communicative situation and do not depend on the text alone: they are co-determined by situational variables. Particular readings are a matter for audience studies; particular intentions are a matter for production studies. Texts are open for different readings depending on prejudices. It may be possible to exclude certain readings or intentions, especially if the coders share an understanding of the world with the sender or the audience. However, no particular reading of an audience or particular intention of a communicator lies within the text alone. At best, content analysis maps the space of readings and intentions by exclusion or by trend, but never the actual state of affairs.

Dilemmas

CA researchers face a number of dilemmas. The first is between sampling and coding: a research project will have to balance the effort put into sampling and the time put into establishing the coding procedure. A perfect sample is of little value if it leaves insufficient time to develop a coding frame or to instruct coders for a reliable process.

The second dilemma is between trend analysis and complex coding, in other words between few observations over a long period and many observations over a short period. The more complex a coding frame, the more likely it is to suit only a small historical window. To adapt a complex coding frame to different historical contexts may not be worth the effort. Hence, a simple coding frame is indicated for a longitudinal study to avoid anachronisms in the coding as the coders go beyond their lifetime memory (see Boyce, Chapter 18 in this volume). Unlike survey research, where a panel design encounters enormous complications, content analysis is well suited to longitudinal analyses. The content analyst will therefore often favour long-term sampling over complex coding procedures.

The third dilemma is between reliability and validity. In psychometrics, validity can axiomatically never exceed reliability. In content analysis, however, we have a trade-off between the two. Content analysis cannot assume a 'true value' of the text that is confused by coding error: the coding is the value. Reliability only indicates an objectified interpretation, which is not a necessary condition of a valid interpretation. Inter-objectivity defends the researcher against the allegation of arbitrariness or lunacy. However, unlike in psychometrics, low reliability does not invalidate an interpretation

(Andren, 1981): the ambiguities of the material are part of the analysis. A simplistic coding may yield reliable but uninformative results. On the other hand, a high reliability is difficult to achieve for a complex coding, while the results are more likely to be relevant for theory and the practical context.

Computer-assisted content analysis

The advent of computing has stimulated enthusiasm for content analysis, and there are several types of computer-assisted analysis of textual materials. The latest wave of enthusiasm for computerization was simultaneous with the proliferation of text databases such as Reuters or FT-Profile. Because of the extended specialist literature on this (see Nissan and Schmidt, 1995; Fielding and Lee, 1998), I will only briefly characterize three basic strands.

The first strand in computer-assisted CA is KWOC – keyword out of context (word counts) – which classifies single words into concepts. It is in the tradition of the General Inquirer (Stone et al., 1966). A computer can easily list all the words in a text, and group them into a dictionary. This is a list of theoretically interesting concepts each defined by a list of tokens. For example, words like 'approach', 'attack' and 'communicate' may count as tokens of 'socio-emotional action'. A computer easily recognizes strings of letters as token words, assigns them to a concept according to a dictionary, and counts the frequencies of concepts in a text. The General Inquirer lives on in the PC package TEXTPACK. The most ambitious study to have used this approach is Namenwirth and Weber's (1987) cultural indicator project, which detected long waves of political values in political speeches in Britain and the USA over the last 400 years.

The main problem with KWOC is that in the dictionary, tokens can be assigned to only one concept. This is a fundamental shortcoming, since words are ambiguous. This problem has blunted much of the initial enthusiasm for the automatic approach.

The second strand of computerization is concordance and co-occurrence analysis, which consider keywords in their context (KWIC). A concordance presents a list of words together with co-text. Many text analysis packages offer concordances as a subroutine, and they are very useful for exploring the meaning of words in a corpus, or for checking the relevance of materials. For example, a concordance routine would quickly help to weed out articles on BSE (the Bombay Stock Exchange) from a study of press coverage of BSE (bovine spongiform encephalopathy or 'mad cow disease').

Co-occurrence analysis, on the other hand, is a statistical analysis of frequent word pairs in a text corpus. This procedure assumes that the frequent occurrence of two words together is semantically significant. Co-occurrence programs such as ALCESTE start with a lemmatization routine and establish the vocabulary of the text corpus. Then they exclude very frequent and very rare words, and count the co-occurrences of words within a defined text unit into a matrix. From this, an algorithm will extract a geometrical representation where points are words clustered into groups of association (see Kronberger and Wagner, Chapter 17 in this volume). Such programs can handle more or less amounts of text and only certain languages; they can vary the parameters of the analysis, the algorithms to extract a cluster solution, and the textual or graphical output on offer.

The third strand of computer-assisted CA is CAQDAS, computer-assisted qualitative data analysis software. This is the most recent development in supporting textual analysis (see Kelle, Chapter 16 in this volume; Fielding and Lee, 1998). CAQDAS supports tagging, coding and indexing of texts, thereby supporting segmentation, linking, ordering and reordering, structuring and the search and retrieval of texts for analytic purposes. An innovative function is 'memoing': the coder can comment on each act of tagging, thereby tracking a thinking protocol during coding. These memos can later be used to report the reflexivity of the research process: the researcher demonstrates how she herself changed in the act. Good programs offer Boolean search operators to retrieve text segments, graphics to map linkages in the text, and interfaces for statistical data analysis. CAQDAS and classical content analysis meet in the human coder.

Teachers often welcome CAQDAS as a corral for instilling discipline into inexperienced students, who might think that qualitative research equals 'anything goes'. However, its widespread use may foster undesirable practices such as the proliferation of tree structures in representing interview data, or various pathologies of open coding (Fielding and Lee, 1998: 119ff). The analyst, while ordering and reordering her codes and linkages, loses sight of the purpose of the research. When the analysis goes wild – for example, with 2000 codes for six interviews – the project is in crisis.

Computers, useful as they are, are unlikely to replace the human coder. Content analysis remains an act of interpretation, the rules of which cannot be realistically implemented into a computer within practical limitations. The human coder is good at making complicated judgements quickly and reliably if assisted.

Strengths and weaknesses of content analysis

CA was developed for the analysis of textual materials, namely newsprint, in social research. It is a very general approach, and the range of data has widened over the years to embrace nearly any cultural artifact (Gerbner et al., 1969). The main import of content analysis may well have been to continue challenging the curious primacy of interview data in social research.

The strengths of CA are that it is systematic and public; it mainly uses 'naturally' occurring raw data; it can deal with large amounts of data; it lends itself to historical data; and it offers a set of mature and well-documented procedures.

CA makes use of naturally occurring materials: it finds traces of human communication in materials stored in libraries. These relics have been created for other purposes, and in using them for research, CA is unobtrusive (Webb et al., 1966). 'Naturally occurring' does not imply that the researcher does not invest in the construction of an interpretation: the researcher comes in through the selection, unitization and categorization of the raw data, while avoiding the direct reactivity of the respondent during primary data collection.

CA can construct historical data: it uses relics of past activity (interviews, experiments, observation and surveys are bound to the present). Thus it can be a cheap way of establishing social trends, at a fraction of the cost of a panel survey. The downside is that CA mostly provides collective-level data, thus characterizing a collective by its relics of communication and expression.

The systematic approach and the use of computers allow researchers to deal with large amounts of material. Size is not in itself a virtue, but the amount of material on some topics may just be overwhelming. For example, I estimated for our study of science in the UK national press that we might need to consider up to 700,000 articles. This demanded a systematic approach. Far from being the last word on a corpus, a CA may be the first step in ordering and characterizing materials in an extended research effort.

Many weaknesses of CA have been highlighted in its short history. Kracauer (1952) pointed out that separating units of analysis introduces 'inaccuracies' of interpretation: citations out of context can easily be misleading. Although it is always preferable to consider a single unit within the context of the whole corpus, coders will make their judgements within the immediate co-text and through an overall familiarity with the material. Contextual coding is important for any unit of analysis, be it an article, a paragraph, a sentence or a word. Here, automatic and computerized coding has shown its limitations, and the human coder/interpreter is far from obsolete.

CA tends to focus on frequencies, and so neglects the rare and the absent: considerate analysts introduce theoretical codes that may well show significant absences in the text. This is a problem of focus: does one note presence or absence? In principle, CA can do both (see Rose, Chapter 14 in this volume), though it is biased towards presence.

The relationship between segmented text units coded into a frequency distribution and the original text is lost in CA: categorization loses the sequentiality of language and text (see Penn, Chapter 13 in this volume). The moment at which something was said may be more important than what was said. One could argue that CA constructs paradigms of potential meaning rather than understands actual meaning. Longitudinal analysis reintroduces some form of sequence, where the structure of one period can be compared with the structure of another while trends are established.

The pursuit of automatic content analysis – text in, interpretation out – has proved to be absurd: semantic coding privileges the efficient human coder (Markoff et al., 1974). Much CA with human coders suffers from overscrutiny that at times approaches a reliability fetish. In the analysis of most interviewing and opinion polling, researchers confidently attribute the observed variance to the respondents, while they black-box the various effects of interviewers, situations and question structures into 'quality control'. Content analysts must develop equal trust in their procedures, and attribute the observed variance to text differences for most practical purposes.

As social research methods, the sampling survey, the interview and content analysis are of about the same age, so how might we explain their different status in the social scientific toolbox? Neumann (1989) points to several institutional problems that have plagued CA for much of its short history. CA has failed to stimulate a continuous scholarly interest, moving in a 'methodological ghetto' with occasional bursts of external attention in the 1940s, 1970s and 1990s. It lacks a convergence of research activities. There are no data archives to store and make available raw data for secondary analysis. Individual researchers draw their own sample, and construct their own coding frame. CA has suffered from the fallout of much 'quick and dirty' research which has given the impression that CA can prove anything. Simplistic conceptions, limited time-scales, and small research issues have confined CA to small-scale student projects. A method is no substitute for ideas. The descriptive use of much CA reflects the difficulties of the inference problem: what does it tell us about whom? The gap between potential and reality must be confidently bridged with parallel multi-method research designs: coordinated longitudinal research including opinion surveys, unstructured interviews and text corpora is the way forward, thus integrating qualitative and quantitative research on a large scale. Conversation and writing are both manifestations of public opinion; and public opinion that is reduced to only one of its constituents is quite likely to be fake.

STEPS IN CONTENT ANALYSIS

1 Theory and circumstances suggest the selection of particular texts.
2 Sample texts if there are too many to analyse completely.
3 Construct a coding frame that fits both the theoretical considerations and the materials.
4 Pilot and revise the coding frame and explicitly define the coding rules.
5 Test the reliability of the codes, and sensitize coders to ambiguities.
6 Code all materials in the sample, and establish the overall reliability of the process.
7 Set up a data file for the purpose of statistical analysis.
8 Write a codebook including (a) the rationale of the coding frame; (b) the frequency distributions of all codes; and (c) the reliability of the coding process.

References

Andren, G. (1981) 'Reliability and content analysis', in K.E. Rosengren (ed.) *Advances in Content Analysis*. Beverly Hills, CA: Sage. pp. 43–67.

Bauer, M.W. (1998a) 'Guidelines for sampling and content analysis', in J. Durant, M.W. Bauer and G. Gaskell (eds), *Biotechnology in the Public Sphere*. London: Science Museum. pp. 276–98.

Bauer, M. (1998b) 'The medicalisation of science news – from the rocket-scalpel to the gene-meteorite complex', *Social Science Information*, 37: 731–51.

Bauer, M.W. and Gaskell, G. (1999) 'Towards a paradigm for research on social representations', *Journal for the Theory of Social Behavior*, 29 (2): 163–86.

Bauer, M., Ragnarsdottir, A., Rudolfsdottir, A. and Durant, J. (1995) *Science and Technology in the British Press, 1946–1990*. Technical Report to the Wellcome Trust for the History of Medicine, July.

Berelson, B. (1952) *Content Analysis in Communication Research*. Glencoe, IL: Free Press.

Buehler, K. (1934) *Sprachtheorie. Die Darstellungsfunktion der Sprache*. Stuttgart: Gustav Fischer.

Durant, J., Bauer, M.W. and Gaskell, G. (eds) (1998) *Biotechnology in the Public Sphere*. London: Science Museum.

Eco, U. (1994) *Apocalypse Postponed: Does the Audience have Bad Effects on Television?* Bloomington, IN: Indiana University Press. pp. 87–102.

Fielding, N.G. and Lee, R.M. (1998) *Computer Analysis and Qualitative Research*. London: Sage.

Franks, B. (1999) 'Types of categories in the analysis of content', in M. Bauer (ed.), *Papers in Social Research Methods – Qualitative Series*, Vol. 6. London: London School of Economics, Methodology Institute.

Gerbner, G., Holsti, O.R., Krippendorff, K., Paisley, W.J. and Stone, P.J. (eds) (1969) *The Analysis of Communication Contents: Developments in Scientific Theories and Computer Techniques*. New York: Wiley. pp. 123–32.

Gross, A. (1990) *The Rhetoric of Science*. Cambridge, MA: Harvard University Press.

Holsti, O.R. (1968) 'Content analysis', in G. Lindzey and E. Aronson (eds), *Handbook of Social Psychology*. Reading, MA: Addison-Wesley. pp. 596–692.

Holsti, O.R. (1969) *Content Analysis for the Social Sciences and Humanities*. Reading, MA: Addison-Wesley.

Janowitz, M. (1976) 'Content analysis and the study of socio-political change', *Journal of Communication*, 26: 10–21.

Kaplan, A. (1943) 'Content analysis and the theory of signs', *Philosophy of Science*, 10: 230–47.

Kracauer, S. (1952) 'The challenge of quantitative content analysis', *Public Opinion Quarterly*, 16: 631–42.

Krippendorff, K. (1980) *Content Analysis: an Introduction to its Methodology*. London: Sage.

Krippendorff, K. (1994) 'On reliability of unitizing continuous data', *Sociological Methodology*, 25: 47–76.

Lindkvist, K. (1981) 'Approaches to textual analysis', in K.E. Rosengren (ed.), *Advances in Content Analysis*. London: Sage. pp. 23–41.

McQuail, D. (1977) *Analysis of Newspaper Content*. Royal Commission on the Press, Research series 4. London: HMSO.

Merten, K. (1995) *Inhaltsanalyse*, 2nd edn. Opladen: Westdeutscher.

Markoff, J., Shapiro, G. and Weitman, S.R. (1974) 'Toward the integration of content analysis and general methodology', in D.R. Heise (ed.), *Sociological Methodology 1975*. San Francisco, CA: Jossey-Bass. pp. 1–58.

Namenwirth, J.Z. and Weber, R.P. (1987) *Cultural Dynamics*. Winchester, MA: Allen and Unwin.

Neisbitt, J. (1976) *The Trend Report: A Quarterly Forecast and Evaluation of Business and Social Developments*. Washington DC: Center for Policy Process.

Neumann, W.R. (1989) 'Parallel content analysis: old paradigms and new proposals', *Public Communication and Behavior*, 2: 205–89.

Nissan, E. and Schmidt, K. (eds) (1995) *From Information to Knowledge: Conceptual and Content Analysis by Computer*. Oxford: Intellect.

North, R.C., Holsti, O.R., Zaninovich, M.G. and Zinnes, D.A. (1963) *Content Analysis: a Handbook with Applications for the Study of International Crisis*. Evanston, IL: Northwestern University Press.

Paisley, W.J. (1969) 'Studying style as deviation from encoding norms,' in G. Gerbner, O.R. Holsti, K. Krippendorff, W.J. Paisley and P.J. Stone (eds), *The Analysis of Communication Contents: Developments in Scientific Theories and Computer Techniques*. New York: Wiley.

Scott, W.A. (1955) 'The reliability of content analysis: the case of nominal scale coding', *Public Opinion Quarterly*, 19: 321–2.

Speed, G. (1893) 'Do newspapers now give the news?', *Forum*, 15: 705–11.

Stempel, G.H. (1952) 'Sample size for classifying subject matter in dailies: research in brief', *Journalism Quarterly*, 29: 333–4.

Stone, P.J., Dunphy, D.C., Smith, M.S. and Ogilvie, D.M. (1966) *The General Inquirer: a Computer Approach to Content Analysis*. Cambridge, MA: MIT Press.

Toulmin, S. (1958) *The Uses of Arguments*. Cambridge: Cambridge University Press.

Webb, E.J., Campbell, D.T., Schwartz, R.D. and Sechrest, L. (1966) *Unobtrusive Measures: Nonreactive Research in Social Sciences*. Chicago: Rand-McNally

Weber, M. (1965 [1911]) 'Soziologie des Zeitungswesen', in A. Silbermann (ed.) *Reader Massen Kommunikation, Band I*. Bielefeld, pp. 34–41.

Weber, R.P. (1985) *Basic Content Analysis*. Beverly Hills, CA: Sage.

9

Argumentation Analysis

Miltos Liakopoulos

KEYWORDS

argumentation	rebuttal
backing	rhetoric
claim	warrant
data	

According to Aristotle we are 'political animals', by which he meant that humans are organized in societies around common principles and with commonly agreed practices of behaviour. Politics was the name given to the institution that allowed for the elaboration and organization of the common practices in society. The main form of communicating within that institution was speech, but not any kind of speech: there was a specific type of formalized speech used in politics called rhetoric.

The meanings of the words 'politics' and 'rhetoric' have changed since the time of Aristotle, but the manner in which people organize society, and debate it, is still the same. Debates emerge on issues of social interest and, as the information age is reaching maturity, more and more people are becoming active in these debates. The greater numbers of people taking part in social debates have an important consequence: the preferred form of speech becomes less formal. Despite its changing form, every debate speech evolves around a basic building-block: the argument. The argument forms the backbone of the speech. It represents the central idea or principle upon which the speech is based. Moreover, it is a tool for social change, as it aims at persuading the target audience.

This chapter is about argumentation analysis. It is about bringing argument into the foreground of social research on public debates. It aims to offer a comprehensive methodological view of the analysis of argument structures, for the purpose of understanding better the parameters that influence the development of public debates.

The term 'argumentation' refers to a verbal or written activity consisting of a series of statements aiming at justifying or refuting a certain opinion, and persuading an audience (van Eemeren et al., 1987). The aim of argumentation analysis is to document the manner in which statements are structured within a discursive text, and to assess their soundness. The analysis usually centres on the interaction between two or more people who argue as a part of a discussion or debate, or on a text in which a person makes an argument (van Eemeren et al., 1997).

The traditional approach views arguments as both a process and a product. The process refers to the inferential structure of the argument: it is a series of statements used as claims, with another series of statements used as justification for the previous statements. The argument as product refers to the way in which arguments become part of an activity within the general context of the discourse. The basic characteristics of an argument are (Burleson, 1992):

(a) the existence of an assertion construed as a claim
(b) an organization structure around the defence of the claim
(c) an inferential leap in the movement from support to assertion.

Argumentation theory and Toulmin

In the past, theories of argumentation focused on the logic of the argumentation structure, and aimed at devising rules that expose fallacies in thinking (Benoit, 1992). Aristotle's theory of reasoning, for example, was an influential approach in evaluating an argument from the perspective of formal logic. In this view, the argument is as good as the reasoning behind it, and there are certain universal rules that can be used in assessing the logic of the argument.

In the modern era of mass media influence, where argumentation reaches the many rather than the privileged few, new theories have developed. These theories have shifted to an interactional view of argumentation, their focus being on the informal use of arguments in everyday discourse and within a particular context. An outstanding example of the new type of theory is Stephen Toulmin's theory of argumentation, which is presented in his book *The Uses of Arguments* (1958). It is an example of a theory of informal logic that suits better the modern era of informal interaction, propaganda and advertising. Toulmin's emphasis on persuasiveness and convincingness over formal validity, and his more functional account of language, has made his theory a very influential framework for research in the area of argumentation (Antaki, 1994).

Toulmin (1958) proposes an analogy between an argument and an organism, and characterizes both as having an anatomical and a physiological structure. The anatomical structure of an argument, as with an organism, can be represented in a schematic form. The schematic representation of the argument structure is the basis for its critical evaluation and soundness (that is, its physiological function). In that sense, the merit of an argument is judged according to the function of its interrelating parts, and not on the basis of its form.

The simplest argument takes the form of a 'claim' or conclusion preceded by facts (data) that support it. But often, a qualifier of the data is required: in other words, a premise that we use to assert that the data are legitimately used to support the claim. This premise is termed a 'warrant'. Warrants are crucial in determining the validity of the argument because they explicitly justify the step from data to claim, and describe the process in terms of why this step can be made. A graphic representation of the argument structure is given in Figure 9.1 (adapted from Toulmin, 1958).

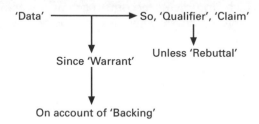

Figure 9.1   *Argument structure (adapted from Toulmin, 1958)*

Toulmin admits that in some arguments it is difficult to distinguish between data and warrants, although the distinction is crucial in the analysis of the argument. A way to distinguish them is to consider that overall, data are explicit, while warrants are implicit. While data are used to legitimate the conclusion by explicit reference to facts, warrants are used to legitimate the process from data to claim and to refer it back to other steps involved in that legitimization – steps whose legitimacy is presupposed.

Different types of 'warrant' give different force to the claim. Sometimes there is a need to make a specific reference to the force of the process from data to claim by virtue of a warrant. This reference is called a 'qualifier', and takes the form of words such as 'necessarily', 'presumably', 'probably', etc.

The process from 'warrant' to 'claim' can sometimes be conditional (for example, the claim is probably true unless . . .). That refers to conditions under which the warrant does not have authority. In such cases, 'rebuttals' are used as conditional statements close to 'qualifiers'.

In a more complex argument one needs to explain why the warrant used has authority. In this case the warrant needs a 'backing' (see Figure 9.1). Usually, backings are categorical statements or facts (such as laws), not unlike the data that lead initially to the claim. The appearance of warrant backings depends on whether the warrant is accepted as straightforward. Warrant backings are not used very often in a discussion because that would make practical discussion impossibly complex.

The categorical nature of the 'backings' creates certain similarities with the 'data' part of the argument. The difference between 'data' and 'backing' is usually that 'data' are particular and 'backing' is a universal premise. For example, where 'data' would refer to a frame directly related to the claim, a 'backing' would consist of a general statement that would apply to many other cases.

In Toulmin's view, argumentation is a social act that includes every activity around making claims, supporting them, backing the reasons, etc. (Toulmin et al., 1979). For that reason, he introduces the notion of the argument fields. He suggests that some aspects of the argument are basically the same regardless of the context in which they are developed; these are field-invariant. On the other hand, some other aspects differ from context to context, and as such are field-dependent. Examples of fields are politics, law and art. Each field has its own standards of developing and understanding arguments, with the result that disagreements between fields are difficult to resolve since they take place in different 'spheres'.

The notion of argument fields or 'contextualization' of the argumentation is directly linked with that of the 'formal validity' and the type of the argument. There are different types of arguments, according to Toulmin, and their classification is based on the different qualities of their components. The most important distinction is between 'substantial' and 'analytic' arguments. The difference is that the analytic argument contains backing for the warrant whose information authorizes, explicitly or implicitly, the conclusion itself. In other words, an understanding of the argument presupposes an understanding of its legitimacy. In this case the warrant is used in the traditional form of enforcing the process of the logic from data to claim, but being independent of them. This is a typical scientific argument of the kind found in logic or mathematics, where the conclusion 'necessarily' follows from the premises. The evaluation of these arguments follows the rules of formal validity.

Toulmin, though, asserted that formal validity is neither a necessary nor a sufficient condition for the soundness of an argument. For example, in a substantial argument the conclusion is not necessarily contained or implied in the premises, because the premises and the conclusion might be of different logical types. Understanding the evidence and the conclusion may not help to understand the process, and so warrants and backings of another logical type are used to cover the understanding gap. Consequently, the use of qualifiers such as 'possibly' or 'with probability' becomes unavoidable. An example of this argument could include a conclusion about the past with premises containing data about the present. In that case the logical chasm between premises and conclusion can be bridged only with reference to the specific field in which the argument is developing.

Toulmin's theory of argumentation has been influential in the field of argumentation research as it signifies a break with the rigid subject of formal logic and offers a basic and flexible quasi-geometrical form of argumentation analysis. His ideas have been explored in a number of studies. For example, in the area of formal textual argumentation, Weinstein (1990) used Toulmin's scheme to analyse the structure of the typical science argumentation. Ball (1994) used a computerized adaptation of Toulmin's model to analyse public policy arguments. In developmental psychology, de Bernardi and Antolini (1996) compared the argumentation type and structure in essays of different school grades. Putnam and Geist (1985) have studied the bargaining process between school teachers and administrators in a local school district to examine the way argumentation shapes outcomes. Similarly, Chambliss (1995) and Garner (1996) have employed Toulmin's structure to research the effect on readers of persuasive/ argumentative text about the Gulf War.

Toulmin's model is a generalization from a theory developed in the context of law, as he explains:

> In the studies which follow, then, the nature of the rational process will be discussed with the 'jurisprudential analogy' in mind: our subject will be the prudential, not simply of *jus*, but more generally of *ratio* . . . Our extra-legal claims have to be justified, not before Her Majesty's Judges, but before the Court of Reason. (1958: 8)

However, Toulmin's claims concerning the generality of his model have been questioned by other argumentation scholars. The model has been criticized as being too simple for the analysis of the complex structures that occur in the real world (Ball, 1994); and as being ill-defined in terms of its structural parts and its types (van Eemeren et al., 1987). Hample (1992) has even asserted that the model does not hold true for the examples Toulmin gives in his book *The Uses of Arguments*.

The flexibility of Toulmin's argument structure that allows for various interpretations of the argumentation components is another problem. For example, it has been argued that Toulmin's terms 'backings' and 'warrants' are not clearly distinguishable, and also that he offers no consistent way of telling 'data' from 'warrant' (Hample, 1992; van Eemeren et al., 1987).

Toulmin recognizes these limitations in the model. By using examples of arguments from a particular subject area (law), he avoided the problem of inconsistencies in his definition of the argument parts. Nevertheless, as described above, he introduced the important notion of context specificity in his model. The apparent inconsistencies can be resolved if one takes into consideration Toulmin's notion of the context in which the argument is used. In other words, the context will provide the structure in which the identification of the argument components becomes clear (Burleson, 1992).

Case study and definition of argument parts

In this section I illustrate argumentation analysis in a case study. The case concerns genetically modified (GM) soya beans, which entered the European market in October 1996 and led to the first public debate in Britain over applications of modern biotechnology.

As discussed above, the definitions of the argument parts (data, claims, warrants, backings and rebuttals) are not always clear. Researchers using

Toulmin's method have found it appropriate to devise their own definitions of the argument parts based on Toulmin's conceptualization (see de Bernardi and Antolini, 1996; Marouda, 1995; Simosi, 1997). Their definitions depend on the context in which the research is taking place (for example, the organizational or educational setting), and on the means of uncovering the argumentation structure (for example, essays or interviews).

In the study of the soya-bean debate, the argumentation structure is located in newspaper articles. The formality of the subject and the sources of argumentation allow for a less controversial approach to the issue of definition and identification of the argument parts, as the actors themselves have every reason to be formal and strict in their argumentation layout. This is because in a public debate that involves serious issues such as public health, big financial gains and even international relationships (as was the case in the soya-bean debate), every participant is very careful in articulating and using clear and proper backing for their claims. Therefore our definitions of the argument parts will be in the context of a formalized social debate that relies on explicit facts and with a view to supporting legal decision-making, not unlike the context in which Toulmin developed his original model.

Our unit of analysis is written texts (newspaper articles) that refer explicitly to views, beliefs and convictions of actors in the soya-bean debate. An actor is defined as any interested party in the debate who expresses a structured opinion. As the views of the actors are sometimes dispersed in the article, depending on the space available and the journalistic style, we considered it necessary to summarize the views in a paragraph that was used subsequently as the source for the deconstruction of the argumentation.

Furthermore, and in the light of the above, we have defined the argument parts as a point of reference for the coder who is required to deconstruct a given argument. We have found de Bernardi and Antolini's (1996) and Simosi's (1997) attempts to define the argument parts particularly helpful, and we have adapted them to our own purposes:

> *Claim* A statement that contains structure and is presented as the outcome of the argument supported by facts. There might be numerous claims in a unit of analysis, but our interest lies in the central claim that is part of the argumentation structure.

Examples of claims are:

Biotechnology is the solution to world hunger.

Genetically engineered foods have unpredictable long-term effects on health.

The risk assessment of the genetically engineered soya is not appropriate.

> *Data*   Facts or evidence that are at the disposal of the creator of
> the argument. Data might refer to past events or to the current
> situation, action or opinion, but in any case they refer to informa-
> tion that is related to the main claim of the argument.

Examples of data are:

> Population growth is rapid and there is lack of food.

> Regulators in the European Commission have already approved of
> genetically engineered crops.

> Ninety-three per cent of the public have answered 'yes' to the question:
> 'Do you believe that foods that contain genetically engineered foods
> should be labelled?'

Sometimes data can be claims which have been validated in previous
arguments. For example, in arguments that are generated from a scientific
source, the data might be the outcome (claim) of a past scientific experiment. For example:

> Foreign genes can pass into the intestinal cells [data], so genetically
> engineered foods can alter the DNA of those who eat them [claim].

In this argument the data derive obviously from a previous scientific
argument in which they were the main concluding comment (claim), the
structure of which was:

> The intestinal cells of subjects have been found to contain the foreign
> protein X [data], so foreign genes can pass into the intestinal cells
> [claim].

It is also in the same realm of the scientific argument that statements can
play the roles of both data and warrant at the same time. This is due to the
authoritative style of scientific arguments (Weinstein, 1990). For example:

> Scientists have discovered that foreign genes in genetically engineered
> crops can incorporate into weeds, so genetically engineered soya can pass
> the pest-resistant gene into weeds too [claim].

In this argument it is apparent that the first statement is both the evidence
on which the claim is based, and the support for the validity of the process
from data to claim.

> *Warrant*   A premise consisting of reasons, guarantees or rules
> used to assert that the data are legitimately utilized to support the
> claim. It is the logical step that leads to the conclusion not by
> means of a formal rule, but by the rule of the logic of the particular
> argument.

For example:

Risk assessment of genetically engineered foods does not include full environmental impact assessment.

Our society has the ability to work out the costs and benefits of new technology and decide about it.

These statements include a rule and a personal reasoning respectively, which are claims themselves if seen out of the argument context but are used as legitimization of the argument conclusion (the 'because' or 'since' that precedes the conclusion).

> *Backing* A premise that is used as a means of supporting the warrant in the argument. It is the source that guarantees the acceptability and truthfulness of the reason or rule that the warrant refers to. Similar in style to the data, it usually offers explicit information.

For example,

Chemists developed chlorine gas and physicists developed the atomic bomb

is used to legitimate the warrant:

Scientists are responsible for the consequences of their work and science is not ethically neutral.

It is also common that backings are not explicitly stated, but are rather alluded to or left to be assumed by the reader of the argument (Govier, 1987). For example, the warrant

Risk assessment of genetically engineered foods does not include full environmental impact assessment

alludes to the regulations of full environmental impact assessment 'that include articles X, Y, etc.'.

The incorporation in the argumentation of hidden premises such as these is left to the decision of the researcher, and depends on their need to include them in their analysis. In our case, we decided to include these hidden premises in our schematic representation of the arguments, whenever they are alluded to, as they are part of the implicit argument structure, and therefore aid our effort to understand the process of the argumentation.

> *Rebuttal* A premise that authorizes the refusal of the generality of the guarantee [warrant]. It shows the exception to the rule that is stated in the argument, or the conditions under which the argument does not have legitimation and therefore the claim does not hold true.

For example,

Consumer reaction might undermine the biotechnology trend

is used as a rebuttal for the claim that

The trend of biotechnology is unstoppable since it gives huge financial gains.

Rebuttals are not used often in formal argumentation as they were in our case, because they might undermine the very essence of the argument which is to persuade the public of the legitimacy of the conclusion. This is a difference from Toulmin's examples from law, where the rebuttals even contain separate backing premises since every law has also rules for exemptions.

From text to Toulmin: an example

I will now give an example of identifying and decomposing the arguments that are found in printed media material on the subject of genetically engineered soya beans. The example comes from a letter to the editor that appeared in the *Financial Times* on 27 June 1996, shortly before the introduction of genetically engineered soya beans into the market:

> Sir, Henry Miller's Viewpoint column 'Left standing by the agricultural revolution' (June 14) contained several statements worthy of challenge.
> (1)   The generation of genetically modified ('transgenic') plants and animals involves the random integration of the desired genetic material into the DNA of the host organism and can therefore hardly be called precise. This procedure results in disruption of the genetic blueprint of the organism with totally unpredictable long-term consequences.
> (2)   The transgenic approach to generating new varieties of plant and animal foods cannot be viewed as a natural extension of classical breeding methods as it allows the normal species barriers to be circumvented. Therefore, even animal proteins can now be made in plants.
> (3)   Foodstuffs from genetically engineered sources have already caused health problems (and in at least one case fatalities) from unpredicted production of toxic substances (tryptophan-like metabolites from engineered bacteria) and allergic reactions (Brazil nut protein in soybeans).
> (4)   Most transgenic plants (57 per cent) that are under development are being engineered to be resistant to herbicides to allow the more liberal use of agrochemicals rather than less as stated.
> (5)   Transgenic crops engineered to be resistant to herbicides (e.g. potatoes, oilseed rape) have already been found to cross-pollinate with related wild-type species, generating potential super weeds. These environmental problems threaten to undermine laudable initiatives such as the LEAF scheme of integrated crop management to which most of Britain's supermarket chains now subscribe.

Unfortunately, the EU seems to be following the US example and is poised to introduce dozens of different varieties of genetically modified crops in the near future without adequate safety checks and concern for the long-term impact of these plants on the environment. In addition, no mandatory labelling of genetically engineered foods is required. Surely, given the problems that have already arisen, even greater caution is needed, with tighter legislation on the assessment of the safety of what are essentially 'experimental' foods.

Also, clear labelling of these novel foods will ensure that the consumer not only has a choice, but also if unforeseen problems arise the source can more easily be traced. It should be obvious that an open and honest policy is necessary to build consumer confidence in these products and ensure a healthy economic future.

Lecturer in molecular biology

First, we identify the source of argumentation because it gives an indication of the actors in the debate. It is common in the journalistic tradition of broadsheet newspapers to give a full account of the perspectives on a particular issue before the journalist puts forward their own. As such, a single article might contain different sources for the different arguments. In this case the author of the text is identified as a doctor (PhD) and a lecturer in molecular biology. Therefore the source of the argumentation in this text is identified as 'science'.

As a practical aid to decomposing the argument, we next summarize the main points. This helps both to collect the dispersed parts of the argumentation in one continuous text, and to identify possible connections that might not be so obvious on the first reading of the article.

Genetically engineered food production uses random techniques that disrupt the genetic blueprint of an organism and therefore there are unpredictable long-term consequences.

Genetic engineering is not a natural process because it allows the circumvention of the species barriers by moving animal proteins into plants.

The approval by the EU of genetically modified crops is not based on the appropriate safety checks for the long-term effects on health and the environment since foodstuffs from genetically engineered sources have caused health problems, as with the case of the allergic reactions to genetically engineered soya with the Brazil nut protein, and genetically engineered crops have been found to cross-pollinate with related wild species.

In terms of Toulmin's schematic representation of the argument, we can represent the above arguments as in Table 9.1.

A note on the reliability of the argumentation coding scheme

I have discussed above the problems of definition and, consequently, of identification of the argument parts in argumentation analysis. We have

Table 9.1   *Letter on GM soya: representation of arguments*

Argument I

Data	Claim (so)
Genetic engineering food production uses random techniques	Genetically engineered foods have unpredictable long-term consequences
Warrant (since) The techniques disrupt the genetic blueprint of the organism	

Argument II

	Claim (so)
	Genetic engineering is not a natural process
Warrant (since) Genetic engineering allows the circumvention of the species barrier	
Backing (because) Genetic engineering can be used to move animal proteins into plants	

Argument III

Data	Claim (so)
The European Union has approved genetically modified crops	The European Union has not made the appropriate safety checks for long-term effects on health and the environment
Warrant (since) Genetically engineered foods have caused health problems and genetically engineered crops have cross-pollinated with wild species	
Backing (because) A genetically engineered soya with a protein from Brazil nut has caused allergic reactions	

seen that Toulmin's model has been criticized for lacking clear definitions, and how the concept of 'contextualization' can be of great help in over-coming identification difficulties. The definitions we have given to the argument parts were an attempt to solve identification problems and to create an objective coding frame that can be used by many coders.

A measure of objectivity is 'inter-coder reliability', whereby two coders use the same coding frame to code independently the same units. The amount of agreement between them is the estimation of the inter-coder reliability (see also Krippendorff, 1980). In an attempt to clarify the methodological process we have followed in this study, we performed an inter-coder reliability test. The overall reliability in the coding of the two independent coders used in this study was 0.77 (the reliability for the individual concepts fluctuates between 0.69 and 0.89). This is a satisfactory result as it denotes significant clarity in the definition of the parts and the text material we are using for our research.

Some results from the case study

Having explained the process of identifying and deconstructing the arguments from text material to Toulmin's schematic representation, we can now turn to an example from a case study of argumentation analysis. Our case study, as in the example above, refers to the public debate that sprung out of the first introduction of GM food – soya beans – into the European market.

The analysis of the soya-bean debate in newspaper articles was part of a PhD thesis by the chapter author (Liakopoulos, 2000). The first level of the analysis was the identification of the argumentation structure of each interested party in the controversy. For that purpose we identified media articles that referred to the soya-bean issue during the period of its introduction to the market (October 1996 to January 1997), and following the procedure discussed above, we deconstructed the argumentation for each main actor of the debate.

We identified a total of 37 articles containing argumentative material. The deconstruction of the argumentation resulted in 59 main arguments. The arguments were then summarized for each actor in the debate (source of argumentation). Here are some preliminary results for the three actors in the debate: industry, environmental groups and science.

Industry argumentation

The summary of the industry argumentation in Toulmin's schematic representation is shown in Table 9.2.

Table 9.2   *Industry argument on GM soya*

Data	*Claim (so probably)*
GM soya has been approved by the EC	Segregation of soya is not necessary
World population is increasing	GM soya is not new
World lacks food	GM soya is safe
	Labelling of GM soya is not necessary
	Biotech is the solution to world hunger
	Biotech is the key to sustainable development
	Consumers should learn more about biotech
	Biotech investment trend is unstoppable
Warrant (since)	*Rebuttal (unless)*
The same techniques have been used for hundreds of years	Consumer reaction undermines the biotech trend
GM soya has been approved as safe from regulators around the world	
Labelling would imply that GM soya is different	
Biotech gives cheaper and environment-friendly crops	
Biotech promises great revenues	
Backing (because)	*Backing (because)*
GM soya is identical to ordinary soya	Consumer reaction is based on ignorance and misunderstanding
GM crops yield 20% more and need less pesticide	

We see that the argumentation of industry for GM soya follows a variety of parallel lines. GM soya is primarily viewed as a safe and economical product, and a step toward the elimination of world hunger. The backing for these claims comes from the outcome of the regulatory process and data from trials. The problem of image is also acknowledged, and is attributed to ignorance and misinformation. Moreover, data are also used as warrants of claims: for example, the fact that the soya bean is approved by the regulatory authorities is used as a warrant for its safety credentials. Overall, the argument structure is clear, with backings and a simplicity that can appeal to common-sense reasoning.

The official regulatory stance over GM soya, as represented in the reasoning by the points on which the US Food and Drug Administration has approved the soya, is reflected in this argumentation. It is used as a warrant to the claims over its safety.

The only rebuttal in the industry argumentation is the consumer acceptance issue. Industry clearly sees consumer acceptance as the hindrance to the biotechnology promise, thus acknowledging the need for an information and image campaign (indeed, the European biotechnology industry has launched a major information and image campaign).

Regardless of the clarity of the argumentation, its understanding and acceptance depends on the acceptance of its implicit assumptions. These assumptions might be gaps in the deductive reasoning of the argument (that is, missing premises), or simply universal truths about the state of affairs in the particular context in which the argument takes place (Govier, 1987). In any case, these assumptions provide important clues to the validity of the argument. The industry argumentation leaves certain facts and warrants unexplained by presupposing that the reader is in agreement with their truth *ipso facto*. These assumptions can be summarized as follows:

1 The regulatory process for approval of new foods is rigorous and faultless (since regulatory approval is equated in the argument with product safety).
2 World hunger is the result of lack of food (since more and cheaper crops that biotechnology provides are seen as the solution to world hunger).
3 Biotechnology is a natural and benign process (since biotechnology is viewed as identical to traditional breeding methods).
4 Risks can be quantified (since the GM soya is claimed to be identical to ordinary soya because they are similar in more than 99 per cent of their genetic structure).

Science argumentation

The science argument can be represented as in Table 9.3.

The science argumentation is quite technical, as one might expect. It refers to specific technical aspects of the GM soya bean, the regulatory safety check procedures, and past genetic engineering research. It questions

Table 9.3 *Science argument on GM soya*

Data	Claim (so probably)
GM food production is using random techniques	GM foods have unpredictable long-term effects
Regulators have approved GM soya	GM is not a natural process
Foreign genes can pass into the intestinal cells	Regulatory process is not making appropriate safety checks
People worry about GM	GM soya can alter the DNA of those who eat it
	GM soya can pass the pest-resistant gene into weeds
	Scientists should react to people's worries

Warrant (since)
GM techniques are not precise
GM allows for the passing of animal proteins to plants
GM crops have already caused health problems
Living things are very complicated and unpredictable
The risk assessment of GM foods should include full environmental impact
Scientists are responsible for the consequences of their work

Backing (because)
In nature there is no overcoming of the cross-species barrier
A test trial of a GM soya with a Brazil nut protein caused health problems to people with Brazil nut allergy
Scientists were responsible for destructive discoveries such as chlorine gas and the atomic bomb

the naturalness of the technology of genetic modification, the integrity of the regulatory procedures for the acceptance of biotechnology products, and even the ethical credentials of scientific research.

Typically of official scientific argumentation, the data are also used as warrants to claims since they sometimes constitute a discovery in themselves (see also Weinstein, 1990). For example, the discovery that foreign genes can pass into the intestinal cells is used both as data and as warrant to the claim of the safety of genetic engineering.

The complete lack of rebuttals is indicative of the authoritative nature of the scientific argument. Based on hard facts, the only thing that can disqualify or cast doubt on a scientific claim is further research on the subject. One could, therefore, include a general rebuttal reading 'unless further research proves this to be wrong'.

Overall, the science argument is well constructed with solid backing that leaves very little space for assumptions. The only general assumption of this argumentation could be that the scientific research paradigm is objective and trustworthy. Moreover, the arguments directly attack the official line of the regulatory authorities, especially the claims that the GM soya is identical to ordinary soya and unlikely to produce any negative side-effects in human consumption.

The environmental argument

The summary representation of the environmental argument is given in Table 9.4.

Table 9.4   *Environmental argument on GM soya*

Data	Claim (so probably)
Consumers want labelling (survey results)	GM foods pose unknown risks
GM soya has passed regulatory tests	It is unlikely that the GM soya will be labelled
	There should be labelling of GM foods
	GM is not a natural procedure
	Regulatory process is unreliable
Warrant (since)	*Rebuttal (unless)*
GM has caused health problems in the past	Public is denied the right to choose
Monsanto has not segregated the GM soya beans	
Most people want labelling of GM foods	
GM allows for the passing of animal proteins to plants	
Regulatory processes test for short-term and not long-term effects	
Backing (because)	
A test trial of a GM soya with a Brazil nut protein caused health problems to people with Brazil nut allergy	
Monsanto is an irresponsible company	
Nature does not allow passing of the cross-species barrier	

We see that the environmental argumentation is developed at three levels. One is the level of science, where we see the repetition of some arguments that were originally developed by the scientific side. For example, the claim that GM foods pose unknown risks, based on the fact that past test trials with a GM food (soya beans) proved that its foreign gene produced allergies in some people, is a clear repetition of the scientific argument. The second level of argumentation refers to the credentials of the technology as a whole. Again the technology is portrayed as unnatural, and the backing for that claim comes from one of its technical procedures (the fact that a gene from an animal can be transferred to a plant). The third level has to do with the morality of political decision-making about GM soya beans, and especially with the labelling issue. The prominence of this argument is so clear that one could say that the environmental argument is centred around the labelling of approved GM foods in general and GM soya beans in particular. There are many possible reasons for this. First, the labelling issue is one associated with a clear and strong public attitude, since many surveys show an impressive majority of people wanting labelling of GM foods. Secondly, labelling is a moral argument that goes beyond the deadlocks of technical argumentation. Thirdly, labelling is an issue that brings to the surface many more political issues close to the environmental agenda (such as the industry–regulators relationship, and public knowledge and attitudes toward regulatory procedures).

Overall, the environmental argument is intelligently constructed with proper backing for each level and simple reasoning. The rebuttal is used not as a negation of the warrant, but rather as a reminder of the moral dimension of the issue. There are also two assumptions implied in the argument that can be summarized as follows:

1 The existing condition of the crops is natural (since the addition of a single gene makes them unnatural).
2 The usefulness of a technological development is outweighed by its moral and risk aspects (since the use of the GM soya does not even merit a mention in the argument).

Argumentation analysis as a form of content analysis

Content analysis is a data reducing exercise where text is coded into certain categories. The transformation of the original text into quantified categories is done through a coding frame that covers every important aspect of the research subject matter. The challenge is to reduce a large amount of material into meaningful units of analysis without losing the essence (content, intention) of the original writing (see Bauer, Chapter 8 in this volume). Reliability measures, such as inter- and intra-coder reliability, have been developed to assess objectivity during the transformation process.

Argumentation analysis can also be conceptualized as a form of content analysis. Both analyses try to reduce large amounts of material by capturing certain important aspects of the text and transforming them into units of analysis. One needs only to envisage the parts of the argument (data, claim, warrant, backing, rebuttal) as categories, and content analysis becomes a viable alternative process. For example, a typical content analysis exercise would result in a table with category variables v and cases c:

	$v1$	$v2$	$v3$	$v4$
$c1$	x	x	x	x
$c2$	x	x	x	x
$c3$	x	x	x	x
$c4$	x	x	x	x

In argumentation analysis the same table would consist of argument parts (data D, claims C, warrants W, backings B and rebuttals R) and cases c:

	D	C	W	B	R
c1	x	x	x	x	x
c2	x	x	x	x	x
c3	x	x	x	x	x
c4	x	x	x	x	x

Of course, not all cells in such tables would be filled with data, since each argument part could be related to more than one of the other argument parts. For example, the previous table could look like the following:

In this example the same data lead to different, but perhaps similar, claims. In turn, different warrants support a single claim, and so on. This is a realistic depiction of an argumentation structure deriving from a large amount of text. Such depiction allows for the description of category relations: for example, what type of data produces certain claims and warrants, what type of backing fits with certain warrants, and so on.

The challenge is to identify a process that would account for all relations between the categories as depicted above. An ordinary data sheet of the SPSS type could not, in our opinion, function properly as it would not be able to account for all possible combinations between categories. A software content analysis package such as ATLAS/ti would be better suited, as it allows for a schematic presentation of categories' relations.

Virgil is a database program for qualitative information, not unlike ATLAS/ti, that is a first step towards a complete implementation of argumentation analysis as content analysis. Ball (1994) has used Virgil under HyperCard 2.0 to analyse policy arguments with Toulmin's model. The software can analyse Toulmin's schematic in relatively simple arguments by allowing the display of many elements (such as argument parts) at the same time and in different versions. In the simple version the argument is represented in a concise form according to elements, with the possibility of adding extensive notes for each element. In the complex form, each element is referred back to parts of the original text, thereby contextualizing it according to Toulmin's theory.

From preliminary results to full-scale analysis

The preliminary results of the case-study argumentation analysis offered above constitute the first step towards a better understanding of the argument structure in the debate. The description of the argument content and analysis of the implicit premises in the argument are only one way to approach the issue. Other perspectives from which to approach the analysis of arguments are as follows.

Argument parts completeness

Toulmin's example of an argument contains all parts (data, claim, warrant, backing, rebuttal) in a meaningful whole. In ordinary text it is not usual to find a 'complete' argument, as many parts are left to the interpretation of the reader. One might argue that a successful argument is one that leaves no space for subjective interpretation, but rather includes all relevant parts. A measure of argumentation 'completeness' would therefore be an indication of argument strength. That measure could take the form of comparison between group argumentation in the debate as a function of their 'completeness index' (for example, the percentage of arguments that contain all necessary premises minus those that do not).

Warrant types

The significance of the warrant in the argumentation is indisputable. It is the single most important logical justification of the claim. Differences in the argumentation structure are also reflected in the types of the warrants. Brockriede and Ehninger (1960) offer three categories of arguments according to the way the warrants are used:

- In a substantive argument, the warrant is telling us something about the relationships of the things in the world about us.
- In a motivational argument, the warrants tell us something about the emotions, values or motives that make the claim acceptable by the person to whom the argument is addressed.
- In an authoritative argument, the warrants say something about the reliability of the source from which the data are drawn.

Comparison between the warrant types in the group argumentation would provide a better view of the intended use of the argument in the public sphere.

Logos, ethos, pathos

Related to the above is the Aristotelian idea that there are three main qualities in a speech: logos (reason, logic), ethos (morality, moral code), and pathos (emotion, affection). Each argument structure gives special weight to one of the three principles according to the target audience it tries to influence. For example, Aristotle believed that public speaking is bound to contain more pathos, as the emotional component has a strong influence on lay people.

Transposing this idea to modern-day analysis, we could pursue an argument structure comparison based on these three characteristics. Each argument can be assigned a numerical value on three scales (logos, ethos, pathos) which, provided they prove reliable, can be used for descriptive comparisons.

Semiotic reading and argumentation analysis

It is true, as Aristotle pointed out, that argument can also have an emotive component that functions at a different level from pure reason. In debates that introduce new concepts into the public realm, metaphors and images are important constituents of the argumentation structure that function on the emotive level. Semiotics is the science of understanding and analysing such symbolic concepts in everyday discourse. A fruitful combination between semiotics and argumentation analysis could provide a deeper understanding of the dynamics that affect the development of public discourse (Manzoli, 1997). For example, pictorial representations (documentary photographs, cartoons, graphics, etc.), which are commonly used in media texts, can be analysed as parts of the argument structure (for example, as warrants for the main claim).

STEPS IN ARGUMENTATION ANALYSIS

1 Collect a representative sample that incorporates the views of all interested parties in the debate.
2 Summarize the main points in a paragraph with minimum paraphrasing.
3 Identify the parts using the definitions provided and test them for reliability.
4 Collate all argument parts in a schematic presentation in order that they may be read relative to each other.
5 Offer interpretation in terms of the general context and the merit of the completeness of the argument.

References

Antaki, C. (1994) *Explaining and Arguing: the Social Organization of Accounts*. London: Sage.

Ball, W. J. (1994) 'Using Virgil to analyze public policy arguments: a system based on Toulmin's informal logic', *Social Science Computer Review*, 12 (1): 26–37.

Benoit, W.L. (1992) 'Traditional conceptions of argument,' in W.L. Benoit, D. Hample and P.J. Benoit (eds), *Readings in Argumentation*. Berlin: Foris.

Bernardi, B. de and Antolini, E. (1996) 'Structural differences in the production of written arguments', *Argumentation*, 10: 175–96.

Brockriede, W. and Ehninger, D. (1960) 'Toulmin on argument: an interpretation and application', *Quarterly Journal of Speech*, 46: 44–53.

Burleson, B.R. (1992) 'On the analysis and criticism of arguments: some theoretical and methodological considerations', in W.L. Benoit, D. Hample and P.J. Benoit (eds), *Readings in Argumentation*. Berlin: Foris.

Chambliss, M.J. (1995) 'Text cues and strategies successful readers use to construct the gist of lengthy written arguments', *Reading Research Quarterly*, 30 (4): 778–807.

Garner, R. (1996) 'Do adults change their minds after reading persuasive text?', *Written Communication*, 13 (3): 291–313.

Govier, T. (1987) *Problems in Argument Analysis and Evaluation*. Dordrecht: Foris.

Hample, D. (1992) 'The Toulmin model and the syllogism', in W.L. Benoit, D. Hample and P.J. Benoit (eds), *Readings in Argumentation*. Berlin: Foris.

Krippendorff, K. (1980) *Content Analysis: an Introduction to its Methodology*. London: Sage.

Liakopoulos, M. (2000) 'The debate on biotechnology in Britain: a social-psychological analysis of arguments, images and public perceptions'. PhD thesis, Social Psychology Department, London School of Economics.

Manzoli, F. (1997) 'Popularisation or pretension: representations of cloning in the daily press'. Dissertation, Department of Literature and Philosophy, University of Siena, Italy.

Marouda, A. (1995) 'The process of representation and development of knowledge in career decision making and counselling'. PhD thesis, Social Psychology Department, London School of Economics.

Putnam, L.L. and Geist, P. (1985) 'Argument in bargaining: an analysis of the reasoning process', *Southern Speech Communication Journal*, 50: 225–45.

Simosi, M. (1997) 'The processing of conflict in organizational groups'. PhD thesis, Social Psychology Department, London School of Economics.

Toulmin, S., Rieke, R. and Janik, A. (1979) *An Introduction to Reasoning*. New York: Macmillan.

Toulmin, S.E. (1958) *The Uses of Arguments*. Cambridge: Cambridge University Press.

van Eemeren, F.H., Grootendorst, R. and Kruiger, T. (1987) *Handbook of Argumentation Theory*. Dordrecht: Foris.

van Eemeren, F.H., Grootendorst, R., Jackson, S. and Jacobs, S. (1997) 'Argumentation', in T.A. van Dijk (ed.), *Discourse as Structure and Process*. London: Sage.

Weinstein, M. (1990) 'Towards an account of argumentation in science', *Argumentation*, 4: 269–98.

10

Discourse Analysis

Rosalind Gill

KEYWORDS

action orientation
construction
discourse
reflexivity

rhetorical organization
sceptical reading
talk/text as occasioned

Discourse analysis is the name given to a variety of different approaches to the study of texts, which have developed from different theoretical traditions and diverse disciplinary locations. Strictly speaking, there is no single 'discourse analysis', but many different styles of analysis that all lay claim to the name. What these perspectives share is a rejection of the realist notion that language is simply a neutral means of reflecting or describing the world, and a conviction in the central importance of discourse in constructing social life. This chapter will discuss one approach to discourse analysis that has been influential in fields as diverse as the sociology of science, media studies, technology studies, social psychology and policy analysis.

The chapter is divided into four broad sections. In the first, I consider the intellectual context of the development of discourse analysis, and set out its central tenets. Secondly, I discuss the practice of discourse analysis. The third section is a case study of the use of this approach to analyse a short passage of text from a newspaper article. It gives an indication of the kind of material generated by discourse analysis, and fleshes out readers' understanding of doing discourse analysis. Finally the chapter will offer an evaluation of discourse analysis, highlighting some of its advantages and disadvantages.

Introducing discourse analysis

Intellectual context

The extraordinarily rapid growth of interest in discourse analysis in recent years is both a consequence and a manifestation of the 'turn to language' that has occurred across the arts, humanities and social sciences. The 'linguistic turn' was precipitated by critiques of positivism, by the prodigious impact of structuralist and poststructuralist ideas, and by postmodernists' attacks on epistemology (Burman, 1990; Gill, 1995; Parker, 1992; Potter, 1996a). The origins of discourse analysis in critiques of traditional social science mean that it has a rather different epistemological basis from some other methodologies. This is sometimes called social constructionism, constructivism or simply constructionism. There is no single agreed definition of these terms, but the key features of these perspectives include:

1   a critical stance towards taken-for-granted knowledge, and a scepticism towards the view that our observations of the world unproblematically yield its true nature to us
2   a recognition that the ways in which we commonly understand the world are historically and culturally specific and relative
3   a conviction that knowledge is socially constructed – that is, that our current ways of understanding the world are determined not by the nature of the world itself, but by social processes
4   a commitment to exploring the ways that knowledges – the social construction of people, phenomena or problems – are linked to actions/ practices (Burr, 1995).

One outcome of this epistemological position is that discourse analysis cannot be used to address the same sorts of questions as traditional approaches. Instead it suggests new questions or ways of reformulating old ones (see below).

57 varieties of discourse analysis

The terms 'discourse' and 'discourse analysis' are highly contested. To claim that one's approach is a discourse analytical one does not necessarily tell anybody much; it is not a simple definitional issue, but involves taking up a position in an extremely charged – though important – set of arguments. Although there are probably at least 57 varieties of discourse analysis, one way of making sense of the differences between them is to think about broad theoretical traditions. I will discuss three.

First, there is the variety of positions known as critical linguistics, social semiotics or critical language studies (Fowler et al., 1979; Kress and Hodge, 1979; Hodge and Kress, 1988; Fairclough, 1989). Compared with many types of discourse analysis this tradition has a close association with the discipline of linguistics, but its clearest debt is to semiotics and structuralist analysis (see Penn, Chapter 13 in this volume). The central semiological idea that a term's sense derives not from any inherent feature of the relationship between signifier and signified, but from the system of oppositions in which it is embedded, posed a fundamental challenge to 'word-object' accounts of language which viewed it as a process of naming. This has been developed in recent critical linguistic work which has an explicit concern with the relationship between language and politics. The tradition is well represented in media studies, particularly in research on the press, and has highlighted – among other things – the ways in which particular linguistic forms (such as agent deletion, passivization or nominalization) can have dramatic effects upon how an event or phenomenon is understood.

A second broad tradition is that influenced by speech-act theory, ethno-methodology and conversation analysis (see Myers, Chapter 11 in this volume; Garfinkel, 1967; Sacks et al., 1974; Coulthard and Montgomery, 1981; Heritage, 1984; Atkinson and Heritage, 1984). These perspectives stress the functional or action orientation of discourse. Rather than looking at how accounts relate to the world, they have been interested in what accounts are designed to accomplish, and in looking in detail at the organization of social interaction.

The third body of work that sometimes identifies itself as discourse analysis is that associated with poststructuralism. Poststructuralists have broken with realist views of language, and have rejected the notion of the unified coherent subject that has long been at the heart of Western philosophy. Among poststructuralists, Michel Foucault (1977; 1981) is notable for characterizing his genealogies of discipline and sexuality as discourse analyses. In contrast to most discourse analysis, this work is interested not in the details of spoken or written texts, but in looking historically at discourses.

Themes of discourse analysis

The approach to be elaborated here draws on ideas from each of the three traditions outlined above, as well as from the growing field of rhetorical analysis (see Leach, Chapter 12 in this volume; Billig, 1987; 1988; 1991; see Potter and Wetherell, 1987 for a fuller discussion of the different influences upon discourse analysis). Developed initially in work in the sociology of scientific knowledge and social psychology, it has now produced analyses in a diverse range of fields, and constitutes a theoretically coherent approach to the analysis of talk and texts.

It is useful to think of discourse analysis as having four main themes: a concern with discourse itself; a view of language as constructive and constructed; an emphasis upon discourse as a form of action; and a conviction in the rhetorical organization of discourse. First, then, it takes discourse itself as its topic. The term 'discourse' is used to refer to all forms of talk and texts, whether it be naturally occurring conversations, interview material, or written texts of any kind. Discourse analysts are interested in texts in their own right, rather than seeing them as a means of 'getting at' some reality which is deemed to lie behind the discourse – whether social, psychological or material. This focus clearly marks discourse analysts out from some other social scientists, whose concern with language is generally limited to finding out 'what really happened' or what an individual's attitude to X, Y or Z really is. Instead of seeing discourse as a pathway to some other reality, discourse analysts are interested in the content and organization of texts.

The second theme of discourse analysis is that language is constructive. Potter and Wetherell (1987) argue that the metaphor of *construction* highlights three facets of the approach. First, it draws attention to the fact that discourse is built or manufactured out of pre-existing linguistic resources:

> language and linguistic practices offer a sediment of systems of terms, narrative forms, metaphors and commonplaces from which a particular account can be assembled. (Potter et al., 1990)

Secondly, the metaphor illuminates the fact that the 'assembly' of an account involves choice or selection from a number of different possibilities. It is possible to describe even the simplest of phenomena in a multiplicity of different ways. Any particular description will depend upon the orientation of the speaker or writer (Potter and Wetherell, 1987; Potter et al., 1990).

Finally, the notion of construction emphasizes the fact that we deal with the world in terms of constructions, not in a somehow 'direct' or unmediated way; in a very real sense, texts of various kinds construct our world. The constructive use of language is a taken-for-granted aspect of social life.

The notion of construction, then, clearly marks a break with traditional 'realist' models of language, in which it is taken to be a transparent medium – a relatively straightforward path to 'real' beliefs or events, or a reflection of the way things really are.

The third feature of discourse analysis that I want to stress here is its concern with the 'action orientation' or 'function orientation' of discourse. That is, discourse analysts see all discourse as *social practice*. Language, then, is not viewed as a mere epiphenomenon, but as a practice in its own right. People use discourse to *do* things – to offer blame, to make excuses, to present themselves in a positive light, etc. To highlight this is to underline the fact that discourse does not occur in a social vacuum. As social actors, we are continuously orienting to the *interpretive context* in which we find ourselves, and constructing our discourse to fit that context. This is very obvious in relatively formal contexts such as hospitals or courtrooms, but it is equally true of all other contexts too. To take a crude example, you might give a different account of what you did last night depending upon whether the person inquiring was your mother, your boss or your best friend. It is not that you would be being deliberately duplicitous in any one of these cases (or at least, not necessarily), but simply that you would be saying what seems 'right' or what 'comes naturally' for that particular interpretive context. Actions or functions should not be thought of in cognitive terms, for example, as related to an individual's intentions; often they can be global or ideological and are best located as cultural practices rather than confined to someone's head. Discourse analysts argue that all discourse is occasioned.

It is important to note that the notion of 'interpretive context' is not a narrow or mechanistic one. It is used not simply to refer to the gross parameters of an interaction, such as where and when it takes place, and to whom the person was speaking or writing, but also to pick up on more subtle features of the interaction, including the kinds of actions being performed, and the participants' orientations. As a discourse analyst, one is involved *simultaneously* in analysing discourse and analysing the interpretive context.

Even the most apparently straightforward, neutral sounding description can be involved in a whole range of different activities, depending upon the interpretive context. Take the following sentence: 'My car has broken down.' This sounds like a straightforwardly descriptive sentence about a mechanical object. However, its meaning can change dramatically in different interpretive contexts:

1   When said to a friend on leaving a meeting, it may be an implicit request for a lift home.
2   When said to the person who sold you the car only a few days earlier, it may be part of an accusation or blaming.
3   When said to a tutor for whose lecture you were half-an-hour late, it may be offered as an excuse or mitigation.

And so on. One way of checking your analysis of the discourse is to look at how the participants involved responded, as this can offer valuable analytical clues. For example, if the car salesperson responded by saying, 'Well, it was working fine when I sold it to you', this indicates that the sentence was heard as an accusation – even though no explicit accusation was made. But interpretive context does not simply vary by whom you are speaking to: you can talk with the same person – and even use the same words – and generate many different interpretations. Think about how the question 'Are you going out tonight?' can have multiple meanings when said by someone to their partner. The key point here is that there is nothing 'mere' or insubstantial about language: talk and texts are social practices, and even the most seemingly trivial statements are involved in various kinds of activities. One of the aims of discourse analysis is to identify the functions or activities of talk and texts, and to explore how they are performed.

This brings me to the fourth point: discourse analysis treats talk and texts as *organized rhetorically* (Billig, 1987; 1991). Unlike conversation analysis, discourse analysis sees social life as being characterized by conflicts of various kinds. As such, much discourse is involved in establishing one version of the world in the face of competing versions. This is obvious in some cases – politicians, for example, are clearly attempting to win people round to their view of the world, and advertisers are attempting to sell us products, lifestyles and dreams – but it is also true of other discourse. The emphasis on the rhetorical nature of texts directs our attention to the ways in which all discourse is organized to make itself persuasive.

The practice of discourse analysis

It is much easier to discuss the key themes of discourse analysis than it is to explain how actually to go about analysing texts. Pleasant as it would be to be able to offer a cookbook style recipe for readers to follow methodically, this is just not possible. Somewhere between 'transcription' and 'writing up', the essence of doing discourse analysis seems to slip away: ever elusive, it is never quite captured by descriptions of coding schemes, hypotheses and analytical schemata. However, just because the skills of discourse analysis do not lend themselves to procedural description, there is no need for them to be deliberately mystified and placed beyond the reach of all but the cognoscenti. Discourse analysis is similar to many other tasks: journalists, for example, are not given formal training in identifying what makes an event news, and yet after a short time in the profession their sense of 'news values' is hard to shake. There really is no substitute for learning by doing.

Asking different questions

Discourse analysis is not an approach that can be used 'off the shelf' as a substitute for a more traditional form of analysis – for example, content analysis or the statistical analysis of questionnaire data. The decision to use discourse analysis entails a radical epistemological shift. As I have indicated, discourse analysts do not regard texts as vehicles to find out about some reality assumed to lie beyond or behind language. Instead they are interested in the text in its own right, and therefore ask different questions. Faced with a transcript of a discussion among vegetarians, for example, the discourse analyst would not seek to discover from this why the people involved gave up eating meat and fish, but instead might be interested in analysing how the decision to become vegetarian is warranted by the speakers, or how they orient to potential criticisms, or how they establish a positive self-identity (Gill, 1996b). The potential list of questions is endless; but, as you can see, they are rather different from conventional social scientific questions.

Transcription

Unless you are analysing a text that already exists in the public domain – for example, a newspaper article, a company report or a record of a parliamentary debate – the first requirement is a transcript. A good transcript should be as detailed a record as possible of the discourse to be analysed. A transcript should not summarize speech, nor should it 'clean it up' or correct it; it should record verbatim speech with as many features of the talk as possible. The production of a transcript is hugely time-consuming. Even if only the grossest features of talk are noted – such as emphasis and hesitation – the development of the transcript can take as much as 10 hours for each hour of taped material. Conversation analysts and some discourse analysts argue that much more detailed transcripts are essential if key features of the speech are not to be missed. A transcription system that notes intonation, overlapping speech, intakes of breath, etc. – like the one designed by Gail Jefferson – may involve a time ratio of 20:1 (see Chapter 11 in this volume).

However, as Jonathan Potter has argued, the production of a transcript should not be thought of as 'dead' time before the analysis proper begins:

> Often, some of the most revealing analytical insights come during the transcription because a profound engagement with the material is needed to produce a good transcript. (1996b: 136)

For this reason, it is always useful to make analytical notes while you are doing the transcription.

One of the things that strike new discourse analysts most forcefully when they look at – or, better, have to produce – a transcript is the sheer *messiness* of speech. Aspects of speech that are so familiar that we often literally do not 'hear' them, become visible in transcripts. This includes multiple 'repairs' to speech, changes of gear or topic, pauses, overlaps, interruptions and liberal use of phrases such as 'you know'. Indeed, doing discourse analysis makes one realize the extent to which we all habitually 'edit' the speech we hear. The second thing that becomes striking is (seemingly contradictorily) how *orderly* the speech is. Repairs and changes of gear happen as speakers orient to the interpretive context; overlaps and interruptions are attended to conversationally; and so on (see Myers, Chapter 11 in this volume).

The spirit of sceptical reading

Once the transcript is produced (or other data are obtained), the analysis can begin. The most useful starting point is the suspension of belief in the taken for granted. This is analogous to the injunction by anthropologists to 'render the familiar strange'. It involves changing the way that language is seen in order to focus upon the construction, organization and functions of discourse rather than looking for something behind or underlying it. As Potter and Wetherell have pointed out, academic training teaches people to read texts for gist, but this is precisely the *wrong* spirit in which to approach analysis:

> If you read an article or book the usual goal is to produce a simple, unitary summary, and to ignore the nuance, contradictions and areas of vagueness. However, the discourse analyst is concerned with the detail of passages of discourse, however fragmented and contradictory, and with what is actually said or written, not some general idea that seems to be intended. (1987: 168)

Doing discourse analysis involves interrogating your own assumptions and the ways in which you habitually make sense of things. It involves a spirit of scepticism, and the development of an 'analytic mentality' (Schenkein,

1978) that does not readily fall away when you are not sitting in front of a transcript. You need to ask of any given passage: 'Why am I reading this in this way?', 'What features of the text produce this reading?', 'How is it organized to make it persuasive?' and so on. In my opinion, discourse analysis should carry a health warning, because doing it fundamentally changes the ways in which you experience language and social relations.

Coding

Like ethnographers, discourse analysts have to immerse themselves in the material being studied. A good way of starting is simply by reading and rereading your transcripts until you are really familiar with them. This process is a necessary preliminary to coding. The categories used for coding will obviously be determined by the questions of interest. Sometimes they will seem relatively straightforward: for example, one part of my analysis of interviews with broadcasters involved examining the accounts they gave for the lack of women working in radio (Gill, 1993). The initial coding for this involved going through the transcripts and highlighting or selecting out all occasions when the broadcasters referred to female broadcasters. On other occasions coding can be much more difficult, and the phenomenon of interest may not be clear until after some initial analysis. Potter and Wetherell (1987) describe how, in their study of white New Zealanders' accounts of racial inequality, their understanding of what should be coded changed repeatedly as their analysis became more sophisticated. And, indeed, in my own study of accounts for the lack of women DJs, it became clear that many other aspects of the interview material, besides direct references to female broadcasters, were relevant to the analysis: for example, references to the 'qualities' that 'all good DJs should possess' turned out to contain a number of hidden assumptions about gender.

This highlights an important point about coding: that in the initial stages it should be done as inclusively as possible, so that all borderline instances can be counted in rather than out. People use various strategies for coding, and you will develop your own, but essentially it is a way of organizing the categories of interest. For example, if we were interested in looking at how people accounted for their decision to become vegetarian, then one way of coding initially might be to sort out the transcripts into different kinds of account: some people may claim that they stopped eating meat for health reasons, others may discuss animal welfare, still others may have ethical concerns about the use of global food resources, and so on. It is important to note that individuals may draw on and combine different accounts, and that discourse analysts' interest is not in individuals' attitudes but in the cultural construction of vegetarianism.

Analysing discourse

With the initial coding complete – and your piles of photocopies or filecards in place – it is time to begin the analysis proper. It can be helpful to think of analysis as being made up of two related phases. First there is the search for pattern in the data. This will be in the form of both variability (differences within and between accounts) and consistency. Secondly, there is the concern with function, with forming tentative hypotheses about the functions of particular features of the discourse, and checking these against the data (Potter and Wetherell, 1987). Of course, presenting it like this makes it sound easy, and it glosses over hours of frustration and apparent dead-ends. In practice, identifying the patterning and functions of discourse is often difficult and time-consuming.

One useful analytical strategy, suggested by Widdicombe (1993), is that of regarding the ways in which things are said as being potential solutions to problems. The analyst's task is to identify each problem and how what is said constitutes a solution. In my study of how broadcasters accounted for the small number of women in radio, one of the discursive problems to which the broadcasters had to orient was that of being heard as sexist while still wanting to offer 'legitimate' reasons for the lack of women. The transcripts are full of disclaimers (Hewitt and Stokes, 1975) such as 'I'm not being sexist but . . .', which preceded the expression of remarks that could easily be heard as sexist. Staying with our example about vegetarianism, we might expect to find our vegetarian speakers orienting to a variety of potential criticisms – for example, sentimentality, 'political correctness' and inconsistency.

Although suggestions like Widdicombe's are helpful in thinking about analysis, in the end there is no escape from the fact that discourse analysis is a craft skill that can be difficult and is always labour-intensive. As Wetherell and Potter (1988) have noted, it not unusual to work with one analytical schema for several days, only to have to revise it or discard it because the linguistic evidence does not fit precisely. Unlike some styles of analysis which suppress variability or simply gloss over instances which do not fit the story being told, discursive analyses require rigour in order to make analytical sense of texts in all their fragmented, contradictory messiness.

As well as examining the way that language is used, discourse analysts must also be sensitive to what is not said – to silences. This in turn requires a significant awareness of the social, political and cultural trends and contexts to which our texts refer. Without this broader contextual understanding:

> we would be unable to see the alternative version of events or phenomena that the discourse we were analysing had been designed to counter; we would fail to notice the (sometimes systematic) absence of particular kinds of account in the texts that we were studying; and we would not be able to recognise the significance of silences. (Gill, 1996b: 147)

However, to argue that a familiarity with the context is vital is not to suggest that this context can be neutrally and unproblematically described. When a discourse analyst discusses context, he or she is also producing a version, constructing the context as an object. In other words, discourse analysts' talk is no less constructed, occasioned and action oriented than any other. What discourse analysts do is to produce readings of texts and contexts that are warranted by careful attention to detail and that lend coherence to the discourse being studied.

Case study: 'Death of the Dad'

In order to demonstrate the kinds of insights produced by discourse analysis, I am going to present a preliminary analysis of a short passage extracted from a current newspaper article ('Death of the Dad' by Melanie Phillips, *The Observer*, 2 November 1997). The article, which I came across while writing this chapter, is in many ways typical of the kind of 'think pieces' that are to be found in British Sunday broadsheet newspapers. Situated in debates about the Blair government's attitude towards single mothers, the article excoriates the architects of a crisis that apparently threatens the survival of fatherhood, men in general and the very future of the 'traditional family'.

The short passage I have extracted could be analysed in many different ways. My interest in the extract is in examining how the nature of the threat is discursively constructed and made persuasive. In analysing this, as you will see, I will touch upon other questions, beginning with how Phillips constructs her own identity, and moving to explore her characterization of the target of her attack. The text is as follows:

01	Many women want to work, and do. This is not an argument
02	for forcing women to stay at home. Nor is it an argument
03	for 'male domination'. This is an argument for
04	acknowledging the need for a balance of responsibilities.
05	This desire to eradicate sexual and gender differences
06	in order to re-engineer men arises from a kind of feminism
07	that has flowed into Britain from America to become the
08	orthodoxy among social science researchers, public
09	sector professionals and much of the chattering classes.
10	This feminism sees women only as victims of male
11	domination. It advocates the use of state power to
12	promote the independence of women from partnerships
13	with men, at least until men have redefined their role
14	and identity so that they become more like women.
15	This female supremacism, rather than feminism,
16	fundamentally despises, distrusts and dislikes men.
17	Female supremacism has placed the idea of
18	fatherhood itself under siege. Men in general and
19	fathers in particular are increasingly viewed as
20	superfluous to family life. There are no longer key
21	roles that only fathers can fill. Indeed, it holds that
22	masculinity is unnecessary or undesirable. It tells us
23	men are important as new fathers. But it undercuts
24	this by claiming that lone parenthood is perfectly

25   acceptable – and in some cases preferable.
26   Fatherhood must become surrogate motherhood, and
27   fathers and mothers must be turned into unisex parents.
28   But most men and women don't want to be unisex parents.
29   That's because there are profound sexually based
30   differences between mothers and fathers. Motherhood is a
31   biological bond fuelled by hormones and genetic impulses.
32   Fatherhood, on the other hand, is to a large extent a social
33   construct, but founded – crucially – on a biological fact.

Constructing the writer's identity

In the first few lines of the passage, Phillips lays the groundwork for her argument by telling her readers what it is *not*: it is 'not an argument for forcing women to stay at home. Nor is it an argument for "male domination".' This is a common rhetorical move, designed to protect or 'inoculate' an argument from criticism and to offer a 'preferred reading', indicating the way the argument should be interpreted. Implicit in these assertions is the idea that she is not against women's rights, nor is she against feminism *per se*. She rejects the extremism of those who would force women back into the home, and instead presents herself as moderate and reasonable – someone merely making a plea for 'acknowledging the need for a balance of responsibilities'.

The notion of 'balance' accomplishes considerable rhetorical work here. Positioned at the centre of a discursive organization which has few (if any) negative meanings, and used to sell everything from bottled water and breakfast cereal to religion and politics, 'balance' has connotations of health, harmony and, above all, naturalness. Like 'community', it has overwhelmingly positive meanings which can be managed and reworked in particular instances of use. Here the notion is tied to 'responsibilities', a word with particular resonances in discussions about lone parenthood, where much is made by politicians and journalists of people's *irresponsibility*. The idea of a balance of responsibilities, then, conveys a sense of moral rightness, and, because it is virtually platitudinous, is very difficult to rebut: who could mount a case against 'a balance of responsibilities'? Phillips's case is further strengthened by the suggestion that what she is calling for is merely an *acknowledgement* of the need for balance, implying, as it does, the existence of a pre-existing true or natural need (which we must simply not deny any more).

The targets of the attack: feminism and . . . female supremacism

As we have seen, Phillips is careful to construct her argument as one that is not straightforwardly anti-feminist. The opening passage of the extract can be read as a way of disclaiming an identity hostile to women's independence. In Widdicombe's (1993) terms, one of the problems to which she is orienting is that of being heard as attacking women. When she first elaborates the target of her critique it becomes clear why this disclaimer was necessary, because her target is precisely 'a kind of feminism'. It is not, however, all feminism that she berates, but a specific type that has 'flowed into Britain from America'. Here, 'America' is invoked to index a long-standing British fear of insidious Americanization, but it also references more recent concerns about the spread of 'political correctness' and a particular type of 'victim feminism' (lines 10–11) that is frequently perceived to accompany it.

One of the basic points made by discourse analysis is that description and evaluation are not separate activities. In most discourse, descriptions are produced that *contain* evaluations. A clear example of this is to be found in line 15. Here feminism is recast as 'female supremacism', a phrase which comes 'ready evaluated', replete with resonances of racism and fascism and of shadowy organizations whose goal is to elevate one group of people above all others. No exponent of female supremacism is identified in the article, nor yet is any source or reference for female supremacist ideas indicated. Indeed, part of the rhetorical force of 'female supremacism' is that it evokes ideas of chilling, all-encompassing threat, while protecting Phillips from critique by denying any leverage for criticism.

Orthodoxy and state power

A common way of attacking opponents' ideas is to call them dogmas, ideologies or orthodoxies. In this context, though, the notion of orthodoxy has particularly significant connotations, suggesting a set of ideas which cannot be challenged but must be unthinkingly accepted and adhered to. Again, fears about the spread of 'political correctness', with its perceived policing of thought and behaviour, are conjured, with the notion that these ideas, far from being a minority view, have 'become the orthodoxy among social science researchers, public sector professionals and much of the chattering classes' (lines 07–09).

Two of the three groups singled out by Phillips are significant for being regarded as key loci of campaigns for 'political correctness' in the USA, while also being familiar targets of the right-wing press – identified as socialists or soft liberals positioned outside the 'real' world of business and enterprise. The climax of the three-part list, 'the chattering classes', is particularly rhetorically effective. Coined in the 1980s, part of the force of this categorization is its very inexplicitness. With no clear referent, it is an entirely flexible discursive category that generates impressions of an affluent elite, largely employed in education, the media and the 'helping professions', whose dinner-party chatter is simultaneously inconsequential while also constituting the voice of the liberal establishment.

The evocation of female supremacist ideas which have already become the orthodoxy among a significant – though derided – segment of the population conveys a powerful sense of threat. It constructs female supremacism as a political project only moments away from seizing 'state power', with dire consequences for fathers and men in general.

The nature of the threat: men and fatherhood under siege

So far, I have looked at how Phillips assembled a powerful rhetorical image of the people she deems responsible for threatening the 'death of the Dad'. Now I will turn to how she characterizes the nature of the threat itself. It is first alluded to in lines 5–7: a 'desire to eradicate sexual and gender differences in order to re-engineer men'. This is a fascinating construction because it *inverts* the logical order of most feminist accounts. The argument that men may have to change in order to bring about gender equality is one that would be familiar to most readers as recognizably feminist. However, Phillips attributes to female supremacists another project entirely – one whose *primary goal* is to 're-engineer men'. Rather than the challenge to some masculine behaviour being a means to a socially desirable end (gender equality), the re-engineering of men is cast as the end itself. The implication is that this project is born of nothing more noble than hatred of men. This is made explicit in lines 15–16: 'This female supremacism, rather than feminism, fundamentally despises, distrusts and dislikes men.' The use of another three-part list (shown by studies of political speeches to be a highly persuasive rhetorical format that generates particular audience appreciation), combined with the use of alliteration ('despises, distrusts and dislikes'), enhances the impact of the claim.

The nature of the threat to men is further elaborated in lines 17–25. One of the most striking features of this passage is its vagueness. I noted earlier that the identity of the 'female supremacists' is never made explicit; the same inexplicitness affects Phillips's discussion of the nature of the threat posed by this clandestine group. She writes of 'fatherhood under siege', of 'men and fathers increasingly viewed as superfluous to family life', and of masculinity being portrayed as 'unnecessary or undesirable', but she provides neither example of nor evidence for these claims. The force of her argument rests on rhetoric alone. The powerful sense of threat to men is conveyed by the use of metaphors of war ('under siege'), references to supremacist movements, and a language that is redolent of fascist discourse, with its views of some groups as 'unnecessary', 'undesirable' and 'superfluous'.

It is not that Phillips is deliberately or consciously plundering fascist discourse – and as a discourse analyst I am less interested in her internal motivation than in the effect of her constructions – but that it is perhaps the most powerful cultural resource available in Western democracies for conveying threat. The use of language like this to characterize feminist beliefs is not new: the notion of 'feminazis' has been circulating in the USA for at least a decade, popularized by right-wing commentators and 'shock jocks' like Howard Stern. So potent is this imagery, that it does not appear to need any explanation or justification. Indeed, part of its force is its very vagueness. As other discourse analysts have pointed out (Drew and Holt, 1989; Edwards and Potter, 1992), when it is systematically deployed, vagueness can constitute an important rhetorical defence precisely because it provides a barrier to easy challenges and to the initiation of rebuttals.

Moreover, if this fails and challenges are made, speakers can deny the particular meaning being attributed to them.

The effectiveness of the passage is also enhanced through the use of particular rhetorical formats such as contrast structures. In political discourse like this, a typical form is the rhetoric–reality contrast – when an opponent's action is compared unfavourably with their rhetoric, as in the following example: 'They *say* the health service is safe in their hands, but they have cut spending on it by 10 million pounds this year.' In our extract the contrast is rather different: in lines 22–25 a contrast is made between what 'female supremacism' says on some occasions and how this is 'undercut' by what it says on others: 'It tells us men are important as new fathers. But it undercuts this by claiming that lone parenthood is perfectly acceptable – and in some cases preferable.' This is a highly effective form of attack because it suggests simultaneously that female supremacists are inconsistent and contradictory, and that even apparently reasonable assertions should be treated with suspicion. A hidden agenda of hatred of men lies behind innocuous claims to welcome 'new fathers'.

Going against nature

In the final part of this case study I will look back to lines 5–7 and to Phillips's claim that this 'kind of feminism' aims to 're-engineer men'. The notion of 're-engineering' accomplishes considerable discursive work here. The word suggests not simply a desire to change men, but the view that men are to be treated like objects or machines to be re-engineered or reprogrammed. It suggests a desire for intervention that is aggressive and invasive, and that fundamentally dehumanizes men. A psychoanalytic reading might even suggest that castration is symbolically implied. In asserting that feminists seek to 're-engineer' men, Phillips presents feminists as harsh, cold and inhuman. The notion also reinforces the implication of fascist tendencies. In the context of discussion of supremacism it powerfully evokes images of Nazi eugenics or human re-engineering programmes.

A newer discourse of genetic experimentation and of reproductive technologies is also indexed: the phrase implicitly draws on popular fears about a variety of biomedical technologies from cloning to 'test-tube babies'. Although this is not spelled out explicitly in the article, debates about genetic engineering – and especially about the introduction of eugenics 'by the back door' – constitute a key discursive resource upon which Phillips draws. Later in the extract (lines 26–27) the idea of surrogacy is invoked, with the suggestion that the re-engineering has the ultimate goal of turning men into women (reinforcing once more the depiction of female supremacism).

Underlying this discourse is the implication that men are threatened not simply by an ordinary political organization, but by a movement that seeks nothing less than to overturn nature. Men will have to be re-engineered, fathers will have to become mothers: nature itself, as we know it, is under threat from these people. The idea that they are going against nature is made explicit only towards the end of the extract (lines 28–33). Having constructed the nature of the threat facing men, Phillips argues: 'But most men and women don't want to be unisex parents.' This is a fairly standard rhetorical move, in which a speaker or writer claims to know and articulate the desires of another person or group. It is particularly effective, of course, in constructions of crisis or threat, since it also implies that the group (in this case men) are in danger of not being able to speak for themselves. Here, though, Phillips goes on to articulate *why* men and women do not want to become 'unisex' parents: 'That's because there are profound sexually based differences between mothers and fathers' of a biological, genetic and hormonal nature. What the 'female supremacists' want goes against this natural reality. In this way, then, feminists' putative attack on fatherhood becomes constructed as an attack on nature itself.

I hope that this brief case study has given some indication of the potential of discourse analysis for analysing language and social relations. In sum, the study has attempted to show that even a short passage extracted from a newspaper article is a complex rhetorical accomplishment. In this case, an apparently liberal article, which claimed explicitly that it was not anti-feminist, was shown to be highly ideological, constructing a society in which fathers, men in general and indeed nature itself are under siege from feminism. The powerful sense of threat generated by this passage was shown to be the outcome of a wide variety of different rhetorical strategies and formats.

Evaluating discourse analysis: questions and comments

In this final section, I turn to the evaluation of discourse analysis, which will be structured in terms of frequently asked questions, and their answers.

Does it produce broad empirical generalizations?

The short answer is no: for example, it does not seek to address questions such as why some people choose to become lone parents. Discourse analysis does not set out to identify universal processes, and, indeed, discourse analysts are critical of the notion that such generalizations are possible, arguing that discourse is always occasioned – constructed from particular interpretive resources and designed for particular contexts.

Is it representative?

There are occasions on which discourse analysts may want to make claims of representativeness for their analyses. For example, if I had done the necessary empirical research, I might have wanted to claim that Phillips's argument is representative of the kinds of discourses that are to be found in the literature of the contemporary UK men's movement (which, judging from material available on its websites, seems to argue that women have achieved dominance in society and are victimizing men in various different ways).

Generally speaking, however, discourse analysts are less interested in the issue of representativeness than in the content, organization and functions of texts. While discourse analysts do not reject quantification altogether (and indeed question the idea of a straightforward quality–quantity distinction), a prerequisite for counting the instances of a particular category is a detailed explication of how to decide whether something is or is not an instance of the relevant phenomenon. This usually proves to be far more interesting and complex than apparently straightforward attempts at quantification.

Does it produce data that are reliable and valid?

Discourse analysts have been extremely critical of many existing methods for ensuring reliability and validity. In psychology, for example, much experimental and qualitative research depends upon the suppression of variability, or the marginalization of instances that do not fit the story being told by the researcher (see Potter and Wetherell, 1987). Discourse analysts themselves are committed to producing new and appropriate checks for ensuring validity and reliability. Jonathan Potter (1996b) argues that discourse analysts can make use of four considerations to assess the reliability and validity of analyses:

1 *Deviant case analysis* That is, detailed examination of cases that seem to go against the pattern identified. This may serve to disconfirm the pattern identified, or it may help to add greater sophistication to the analysis.
2 *Participants' understandings* As I noted earlier, one way of checking whether your analysis holds water is to examine how participants responded. This is most relevant, of course, in records of interaction, but, even in the case of newspaper articles, letters and responses can provide useful checks.
3 *Coherence* Discourse analytic work, like conversation analysis, is building increasingly upon the insights of earlier work. For example, knowledge about the effectiveness of three-part lists, contrast structures, extreme case formulations, and so on is developed from insights from earlier studies. As Potter (1996b) argues, there is a sense in which each new study provides a check upon the adequacy of earlier studies. Those that lend coherence by capturing something about the discourse can be developed, while others are likely to be ignored.
4 *Readers' evaluations* Perhaps the most important way for the validity of the analysis to be checked is by presentation of the materials being analysed, in order to allow readers to make their own evaluation and, if they choose, to put forward alternative interpretations. Where academic

publishers permit it, discourse analysts present full transcripts to readers. When this is not possible, extended passages will always be presented. In this sense discourse analysis is more open than almost all other research practices, which invariably present data 'pre-theorized' or, as in ethnographic research, ask us to take observation and interpretations on trust.

Discourse analysts, like other qualitative researchers, argue that 'validity is not a commodity that can be purchased with techniques . . . Rather validity is like integrity, character and quality, to be assessed relative to purposes and circumstances' (Brinberg and McGrath, 1985: 13). Researchers are beginning the difficult task of fashioning an approach to validity that does not rely upon the rhetoric or norm of objectivity for its justification (see Henwood, 1999 for discussion).

What then is the status of an analysis?

A discourse analysis is a careful, close reading that moves between text and context to examine the content, organization and functions of discourse. Discourse analysts tend to be quite humble people who dislike overblown claims and would never argue that their way is the only way of reading a text. In the final analysis, a discourse analysis is an *interpretation*, warranted by detailed argument and attention to the material being studied.

What about reflexivity?

Critics of discourse analysis enjoy a sport that is a variant of traditional academic competitiveness: this involves pouncing on analysts with a triumphant 'Ha! Got you!', and asserting that if all language is constructive, then discourse analysts' language is too, and therefore their analyses are mere constructions. Discourse analysts are well aware of this: in fact, we told our critics! But this does not undermine the discourse analytic case in any way. Indeed, it merely serves to highlight the inescapable fact of language as constructed and constructive. There is nothing *mere* about language! Some discourse analysts have become particularly interested in this reflexive point and have begun experimenting with different ways of writing which eschew the traditional disembodied, monologic authority of conventional academic texts, and are more playful and exploratory (see Ashmore, 1989; Woolgar, 1988; Gill, 1995; 1998; Potter, 1996b; Myers et al., 1995).

STEPS IN DISCOURSE ANALYSIS

1 Formulate your initial research questions.
2 Choose the texts to be analysed.
3 Transcribe the texts in detail. Some texts, such as archive material, newspaper articles, or parliamentary records, will not require transcription.

4 Sceptically read and interrogate the text.
5 Code – as inclusively as possible. You may want to revise your research questions, as patterns in the text emerge.
6 Analyse, (a) examining regularity and variability in the data, and (b) forming tentative hypotheses.
7 Check reliability and validity through: (a) deviant case analysis; (b) participants' understanding (when appropriate); and (c) analysis of coherence.
8 Write up.

Note

I am extremely grateful to Bruna Seu for her helpful comments on this chapter.

References

Ashmore, M. (1989) *The Reflexive Thesis: Writing the Sociology of Scientific Knowledge.* Chicago, IL: University of Chicago Press.

Atkinson, J.M. and Heritage, J. (1984) *Structures of Social Action: Studies in Conversation Analysis*. Cambridge: Cambridge University Press.

Billig, M. (1987) *Arguing and Thinking: a Rhetorical Approach to Social Psychology.* Cambridge: Cambridge University Press.

Billig, M. (1988) 'Methodology and scholarship in understanding ideological explanation', in C. Antaki (ed.), *Analysing Everyday Explanation: a Casebook of Methods.* London: Sage.

Billig, M. (1991) *Ideology and Opinions: Studies in Rhetorical Psychology.* Cambridge: Cambridge University Press.

Brinberg, D. and McGrath, J. (1985) *Validity and the Research Process.* Newbury Park, CA: Sage.

Burman, E. (1990) 'Differing with deconstruction: a feminist critique', in I. Parker and J. Shotter (eds) *Deconstructing Social Psychology.* London: Routledge.

Burr, V. (1995) *An Introduction to Social Constructionism.* London: Routledge.

Coulthard, M. and Montgomery, M. (eds) (1981) *Studies in Discourse Analysis.* London: Longman.

Drew, P. and Holt, E. (1989) 'Complainable matters: the use of idiomatic expressions in making complaints', *Social Problems*, 35: 501–20.

Edwards, D. and Potter, J. (1992) *Discursive Psychology.* London: Sage.

Fairclough, N. (1989) *Language and Power.* Harlow: Longman.

Foucault, M. (1977) *Discipline and Punish: the Birth of the Prison.* Harmondsworth: Penguin.

Foucault, M. (1981) *The History of Sexuality.* London: Pelican.

Fowler, R., Kress, G., Hodge, R. and Trew, T. (1979) *Language and Control.* London: Routledge.

Garfinkel, H. (1967) *Studies in Ethnomethodology.* Englewood Cliffs, NJ: Prentice-Hall.

Gill, R. (1993) 'Justifying injustice: broadcasters' accounts of inequality in radio', in E. Burman and I. Parker (eds), *Discourse Analytic Research: Readings and Repertoires of Texts in Action*. London: Routledge.

Gill, R. (1995) 'Relativism, reflexivity and politics: interrogating discourse analysis from a feminist perspective', in S. Wilkinson and C. Kitzinger (eds), *Feminism and Discourse*. London: Sage.

Gill, R. (1996) 'Discourse analysis: practical implementation', in J. Richardson (ed.), *Handbook of Qualitative Research Methods for Psychology and the Social Sciences*. Leicester: British Psychological Society.

Gill, R. (1998) 'Dialogues and differences', in C. Griffin, K. Henwood and A. Phoenix (eds), *Standpoints and Differences: Essays in the Practice of Feminist Psychology*. London: Sage.

Henwood, K. (1999) 'Reinventing validity: reflections on principles and practices from beyond the quality-quantity divide', in Z. Todd, B. Nerlich, S. McKeown and D. Clarke (eds). *Mixing Methods in Psychology*. London: Routledge.

Heritage, J. (1984) *Garfinkel and Ethnomethodology*. Cambridge: Polity.

Hewitt, J.P. and Stokes, R. (1975) 'Disclaimers', *American Sociological Review*, 40: 1–11.

Hodge, R. and Kress, G. (1988) *Social Semiotics*. Cambridge: Polity.

Kress, G. and Hodge, R. (1979) *Language as Ideology*. London: Routledge.

Myers, G., Ashmore, M. and Potter, J. (1995) 'Discourse, rhetoric, reflexivity: seven days in the library', in S. Jasanoff, G. Markle, J. Petersen and T. Pinch (eds), *Handbook of Science and Technology Studies*. London: Sage.

Parker, I. (1992) *Discourse Dynamics: Critical Analysis for Social and Individual Psychology*. London: Routledge.

Potter, J. (1996a) *Representing Reality: Discourse, Rhetoric and Social Construction*. London: Sage.

Potter, J. (1996b) 'Discourse analysis and constructionist approaches: theoretical background', in J. Richardson (ed.). *Handbook of Qualitative Research Methods for Psychology and the Social Sciences*. Leicester: British Psychological Society.

Potter, J., Edwards, D., Gill, R. and Wetherell, M. (1990) 'Discourse: noun, verb or social practice', *Philosophical Psychology*, 3 (2): 205.

Potter, J. and Wetherell, M. (1987) *Discourse and Social Psychology: beyond Attitudes and Behaviour*. London: Sage.

Sacks, H., Schegloff, E.A. and Jefferson, G.A. (1974) 'A simplest systematics for the organisation of turn-taking in conversation', *Language*, 50: 697–735.

Schenkein, J. (1978) 'Sketch of the analytic mentality for the study of conversational interaction', in J. Schenkein (ed.), *Studies in the Organisation of Conversational Interaction*. New York: Academic Press.

Wetherell, M. and Potter, J. (1988) 'Discourse analysis and the identification of interpretative repertoires', in C. Antaki (ed.), *Analysing Everyday Explanation: a Casebook of Methods*. London: Sage.

Widdicombe, S. (1993) 'Autobiography and change: rhetoric and authenticity of "Gothic" style' in E. Burman and I. Parker (eds), *Discourse Analytical Research: Readings and Repertoires of Texts in Action*. London: Routledge.

Woolgar, S. (1988) *Knowledge and Reflexivity: New Frontiers in the Sociology of Knowledge*. London: Sage.

11

Analysis of Conversation and Talk

Greg Myers

KEYWORDS

adjacency pair
assessment
formulation
indexical expression

preferred turn
topic
turn

At some point in almost any social science research project, the researcher faces a mountain of data, piling up on desks and bookshelves and chairs and spilling out of file cabinets. Often these data are in the form of talk or writing: audiotapes, transcripts, survey forms, case notes and field notes. For most methodologies, the problem is reducing these raw data to the categories and forms the researcher can use in an argument; the actual moments of talk or the marks on the page get cut out. When social science research handbooks do talk about the wording of questions, or conducting interviews, or recording interactions (see, for example, Robson, 1993), they are usually concerned with locating and eliminating possible sources of bias or influence, or with making the research situation as much as possible like the real world. I will argue that it is sometimes appropriate to go back to the mountain of talk in the research materials and treat it as talk, looking at particular interactions in their particular situations. I will discuss some practical issues, and then present a short example to show the kinds of features that might be treated in such an analysis, after which I will raise some of the methodological issues that arise with such an approach.

Most research interactions are designed to be standardized and reduced, by following the same interview script, questionnaire or experimental protocol in every case, so that the researcher and the circumstances of the interaction can be disregarded. But a number of researchers have reminded us that even these carefully designed encounters are complex forms of social interaction. Interviews, surveys and group discussions can all be analysed in terms of what frames participants seem to be applying, how questions are asked and answered, how encounters open and close (on interviews see Gilbert and Mulkay, 1984; Briggs, 1986; Potter and Wetherell, 1987; Wooffitt, 1992; Schiffrin, 1996; on surveys see Antaki and Rapley, 1996; Maynard, 1998; and on group discussions see Kitzinger, 1994; Agar and MacDonald, 1995; Burgess et al., 1988). In conversation analysis, research data are not seen as having a special status that sets them apart from other talk. The analyst asks the same sorts of questions one might ask of a dinner table conversation between friends (Tannen, 1984; Schiffrin, 1984), interviews between doctors and patients (Heath, 1986), sessions of a marriage guidance counsellor (Edwards, 1997), broadcast talk (Scannell, 1991) or casual talk among graduate students (Malone, 1997). There is a large literature on conversational analysis: recent introductions include Hutchby and Wooffitt (1998), Malone (1997) and Psathas (1995). But researchers may get a better idea of the range and applications of conversation analysis by looking at some of the collections of specific studies: Atkinson and Heritage (1984), Button and Lee (1987), Boden and Zimmerman (1991) and Drew and Heritage (1992). Sacks's original lectures from the 1960s and 1970s on conversation (published in 1992) are not a systematic textbook, but remain the most profound and readable explorations of the methodological issues involved. For perceptive linguistic analysis of conversation, not within the conversation analysis model, see Schiffrin (1994) and Eggins and Slade (1997). Many researchers in other areas of social science ignore the literature on conversation analysis because it is concerned with how participants organize interaction from moment to moment; it does not seem to be concerned with the social structures, changes, attitudes, identities or groups studied in other social science approaches.

Conversation analysis is often promoted (and attacked) polemically as an alternative to these other science approaches, not as complementary to them. But I will argue here that the analysis of research data as talk can lead from very detailed analysis on to the social issues that typically concern social science researchers (and their sponsors). It can be used to explore the kinds of categories assumed by participants (rather than those of the researcher). It can show how participants link and contrast activities and actors (links that may be missed in content analysis) and how they present views to each other. It can lead to practical changes in the style and structure of interviewing or moderation. And it can be a step towards more reflexive research, enabling researchers to consider the kind of situation they have set up, the participants' orientation to it, and their own roles in it as researchers.

Practicalities

I take my example from the transcript of a discussion held as part of a study of media imagery of global citizenship. The study, 'Global Citizenship and the Environment', was conducted at Lancaster University with my colleagues John Urry (Sociology) and Bronislaw Szerszynski and Mark Toogood (Centre for the Study of Environmental Change). The project involved a survey of broadcast output over a 24-hour period and a series of interviews with media professionals, besides the focus groups discussed here (for an overview of the issues see Szerszynski and Toogood, 2000). Such a study provides opportunities for a number of different approaches, such as detailed analysis of a few selected media texts, more extensive and focused analysis of a representative corpus of media texts, depth interviews with producers or interpreters of these texts, questionnaires eliciting attitudes on scales, or exercises aimed at simulating some aspects of media reception and response. We decided to gather responses to some of the images we had collected by using focus groups, that is, group discussions, led by a moderator following a topic guide, with participants selected according to specified criteria.

There have been a number of introductory guides to conducting focus groups, such as Morgan (1988), Krueger (1994) and Stewart and Shamdasani (1990). But there are still relatively few studies that deal with the details of interaction, among them Kitzinger (1995), Agar and MacDonald (1996), Myers (1998), Wilkinson (1998), Puchta and Potter (1999) and the collection edited by Barbour and Kitzinger (1999). Focus groups produce a vast amount of data; the transcripts of our eight groups, each of which met twice, together run to 320,000 words, or longer than three academic monographs. One approach to such a mass of data is to use the transcripts as quarries, coding the transcripts according to categories derived from one's theoretical framework, for instance identifying different sorts of actors, actions and identification (for examples of this kind of content analysis on similar data see Myers and Macnaghten, 1998; Macnaghten and Urry, 1998; Hinchcliffe, 1996). Such analyses may be assisted by qualitative software (Catterall and Maclaran, 1997); in our project we are using ATLAS. But here I will outline an approach that tries to start with the evidence of the participants' own orderly management of the interaction. The basis of this approach is that the analyst looks for the interpretation of a turn (one person's utterance from start to finish) by seeing how another participant responds in the next turn; the key to the local organization is in the relations of adjacent turns, rather than assumptions about larger underlying structures (as in discourse analysis). This approach requires careful attention to exactly how each utterance was said, especially matters of timing such as pauses, overlaps and interruptions.

Because conversation analysis can only be done with rather detailed transcriptions (and ideally with access to the original tapes), one needs to take some practical matters into account from the beginning.

PLANNING The topic guide or interview schedule has to allow for clear taping. For instance, in the example I will present, the breaking of one group into two for part of the session meant that discussions within both groups were lost in a jumble; in later sessions we had the whole group work together so there would be one main line of talk. For interviews, the schedule would need to allow for some uncontrolled back and forth, not just a survey-like series of questions and answers, to be at all useful for conversation analysis.

RECORDING   The recording has to be clear enough to allow for good transcription, ideally with stereo microphones (we have also found that flat mikes on two separate tape recorders could give a useful check). Noisy settings such as pubs, or even open windows onto the street, can obscure crucial passages. This does not matter when the analyst is just looking for the gist of the session or for a few illustrations, but it can be frustrating when any particular utterance is potentially relevant, and when quiet asides and overlapping talk may be particularly interesting. Video can be useful (see Heath, 1986), but it is also much more intrusive.

TRANSCRIBING   Transcription is much debated among linguists and other social science researchers; in Elinor Ochs's (1979) phrase, it is important to treat 'transcription as theory'. One good overview, with references, is Cook (1995). A defence of the detailed transcriptions used in conversation analysis is in Sharrock and Anderson (1987); see Atkinson and Heritage (1984) for a fairly extensive list of the standard conversation analysis symbols. A full conversation analysis transcription could include pitch, loudness, pace, audible breaths and timings as well as what I have given here. Most transcribers who have worked as secretaries will be used to providing a cleaned-up version of what is said, automatically editing out repetitions, overlaps and disfluencies, and editing what is said into coherently punctuated sentences. They have to be told and trained if one wants something else. Each of the symbols in my appendix is needed in my particular example to suggest features that may be essential to interpretation of this passage. A conversation analysis project needs to plan from the beginning on a great increase in time for transcription: Potter and Wetherell (1987) figure on about 20 hours per hour of tape, as opposed to about four hours per hour of tape for a simpler transcription. In our case, we told the transcribers we wanted every word transcribed, even if it was not part of a complete sentence. Even simple checking of this already prepared transcription to make it accurate enough for our purposes took about five hours per hour of tape. The analyst can then go back to the tapes and enrich this transcription as needed. But this enrichment is not just a matter of linguistic detail; I have always found my interpretation changed somewhat when I transcribed more closely.

ATTRIBUTING   Transcribers may not attribute turns to specific participants in group discussions; attribution can be very difficult and add extra time to transcription. But for the purposes described here, it is crucial to be able to tell who says what. On the one hand, as my colleague Bronislaw Szerszynski points out, an analyst could take three examples of similar statements to show broad consensus, when in fact they may be the same person talking three times. On the other hand, one may fail to recognize the continuity when one participant makes a clear statement and goes on to state what seem quite different sentiments on the next page.

ANALYSING   As with transcription, analysis is likely to be much more time-consuming, and thus less extensive. Some relevant features can be found by an automatic search, but as I will show in the next section, there is no substitute for a close reading, preferably with the tape, as the first step of analysis.

REPORTING   The ideal form of report would be to play sections of the tape to illustrate our argument. But since most reports will be printed, as this one is, the interaction must usually be represented in print symbols, as I will do in my example. Detailed transcripts can be off-putting to readers used to seeing speech represented in the cleaned-up form of newspapers and play scripts (and can be especially off-putting if the speakers themselves read them). They also take up a lot of space (as my transcript does here) and there is always the temptation to want to include more and more. Arguments in conversation analysis are typically made by the comparison of a large number of short, very detailed extracts; these also take up space and demand a great deal of attention.

It might seem that these difficulties were simply all the result of print technology, to be overcome someday with videotaping, voice recognition, multimedia storage and sophisticated hypertext databases. Certainly there is always more that could be included in the transcript; many researchers have experimented with coding non-verbal elements of communication (see, for example, Heath, 1986; Avery and Antaki, 1997). But technology will not remove the need for the researcher to make choices of what is relevant, and as other chapters in this collection indicate, practical choices in research methodology are closely linked to theoretical assumptions about the kinds of entities and phenomena social science can address.

An example

My example comes from the second of two two-hour sessions with people in a small town in Lancashire; they are all over 60 and had travelled abroad in the last year. Earlier in this session, they discussed examples they had brought in, from newspaper reading and television watching, of actions done out of responsibility to humanity or the earth in general. Then they did an exercise in which they sorted out on the floor various pictures of people and activities in the news that we had collected from magazines. One group has made a category that includes pictures of Nelson Mandela, Mother Teresa, Prince Charles, a UN soldier, and a protester holding a placard against live animal exports. The other group has a category consisting of a picture of a demonstration against roads, and a picture of Swampy, a roads protester whom the newspapers picked up briefly as

emblematic of the movement. The moderator is following up and challenging their categories, asking people in the first group where they would have
put the various pictures from the other group; he has already established
that they would put a picture of the Greenpeace boat in with the category
they referred to as 'carers', and is now asking what they would do with the
roads protesters.

MOD   could I go back to what Dennis was saying about= =I was interested in
your= =I haven't . um probed much what you thought about these
demonstrations but you put you had no trouble putting the people who
protested live animal exports <u>in</u> with Mother Teresa and um the UN as as
trying to do something to repair=

F1   =in their way / their way

MOD   /um and is that the way you felt about about this . protest
it looks like a protest about roads/

F1   /[I don't really know]

F12   No I don't

MOD   and Swampy and Greenpeace.

F1   oh Swampy

MOD   you're saying that . because they are not being apathetic (2.0) you
um . you think they're doing something good

M1   Yeh

M2   I see them as completely different is that what you're saying

MOD   you see those

M2   I see them as being a nuisance in the world

MOD   OK so/

M2   /these people . they should be locked up.

MOD   one view is/that at least they're not apathetic

F3   /do you not think that they're

M2   I think they should be locked up/

F3   /who are they

M2   they cause more damage they cause more harm/

F3   /who are they

M3   at the end of the airport . the airport runway

F3   oh are they

M2   they cause more money and they never alter anything anyway it gets
done and it costs millions and millions of pounds for it to happen so, these
people are trespassers and criminals /and these people have done

M3   /you know . in the paper . you're
right [uses M2's name] . it was in the paper where they damaged more
trees . than the bulldozers /did . building them houses and things

M1   /yeah but this gentleman has just this gentleman has just said . haven't you . it will <u>happen</u> <u>anyway</u>=

M2   =it will happen
anyway

F1   yes

M1   that is apathy

M3   course it will

M2   possibly it is . but do you know any /place

F1   /well they they put lives at risk
don't they, where they've built tunnels and that sort of thing

M2   where they've stopped it happening

MOD   what about . did you put live animal exports in a different category from
         that

An appendix discusses some of the transcription symbols used here.

Some features for analysis

There is no simple checklist of which features might be relevant in
conversation analysis, as there would be in some approaches to discourse
analysis; previous studies have dealt with everything from 'oh' to laughter
to assessments to telephone closings. But a few comments on the example
can suggest possible starting points: sequence, topic, formulation and
indexicality.

Sequence and preference

Conversation analysis begins with the turn-by-turn sequencing of talk, as
the participants work out who speaks next and how each turn relates to the
previous one. Studies have identified a number of different kinds of
adjacency pairs – regular patterns of sequence in ordinary talk such as
question and answer or invitation and response. One such regular sequence
is the way one evaluative statement, or *assessment*, is followed by another;
what is predictable is that the second assessment will be put in a form that
sounds like agreement, or even strengthening of the assessment; or if the
turn is disagreeing, it will show signs of modification, preface or delay. In
conversation analytic terms, there is a *preference* for agreement in second
assessments (Pomerantz, 1984).

An analysis that looks at these assessments, comparing them with what
one expected from ordinary talk, can be useful in showing whether the
participants present themselves as disagreeing (not just whether the analyst
thinks they disagree). Unlike participants in ordinary talk, participants in a
focus group can address statements with which others might disagree to
the moderator, so they do not call for a response from other participants.
For instance, M2's first comment here is addressed to the moderator:

M2   I see them as completely different is that what you're saying

M1 then disagrees with him by addressing the moderator again:

M1   yeah but this gentleman has just

Only then does he address the other participant, M2, in a tag question
('haven't you'):

M1   this gentleman has just said . haven't you . it will <u>happen</u>

M2 begins his response with a concession:

> M2   possibly it is . but do you know anyplace where they've stopped it happening

F1 seems to be agreeing, but she begins her turn

> F1   well they they put lives at risk

with 'well', which typically signals a dispreferred turn, here a possible lack of agreement or difference (and indeed she goes on, later in the transcript, to defend the protesters).

The opinions here do not come out in the two-sided debate format in which broadcast discussions of public issues are framed; the participants make various contributions that lead in several different directions. The acknowledgement of risks can lead to praise for the protesters' spirit, or criticism of their irresponsibility; the attack on apathy can be used to support participatory mechanisms or to support the direct action of the protesters. By looking at the way disagreement emerges and how it is dealt with, the analyst can explore some of the complexity of these beliefs (Myers, 1998).

Topic

In coding a passage of transcript like this, an analyst decides what the topic is. But participants are also trying to decide what the topic is, and the current topic is not given, but negotiated and fought over by participants. Here the moderator names a topic, linking it back to earlier comments and then focusing on one aspect of it:

> MOD   Is that the way you felt about about this . protest it looks like a protest about roads and Swampy and Greenpeace

From that point, each participant refers to 'they' or 'them' as the current subject. But as we have seen, the participants also check who 'they' is. When M1 makes his comment, which might be taken to be a new topic ('apathy') he links it to what has been said two turns before:

> M1   This gentleman has just said

This could be seen by an analyst as a comment on the discussion itself, and the participants apathy. But the way it is picked up by others is as another comment on the protesters, and the ineffectiveness of their protest.

It is notoriously difficult to tell from utterances what will be taken as the current topic; the last utterance by F1 ('well they they put lives at risk don't they') could lead to a criticism of the protesters or a defence of them. But one can start with moves like 'this gentleman has just said' where participants try to link an apparently new topic onto some previous (usually not the immediately previous) turn. And one can note which shifts occur because, as happens at the end here, the moderator steps in after opposing opinions have been expressed and repeated (Myers, 1998). These boundaries, marked by interventions of the moderator, form a logical unit for presenting examples to readers, because they show how it was divided for participants.

Formulating

Much of the talk in focus groups is about talk itself. The moderator may formulate what the participants have just said, that is, repeat it in different words, to get further comments:

MOD   You're saying that . because they are not being apathetic . . .

Or the moderator may formulate an utterance to close off one part of a discussion:

MOD   OK so one view is that . . .

Formulations are a key device by which the moderator controls topic and demonstrates empathy. There is a great deal of worry in guides to focus group research about the way a moderator may guide the discussion; formulations and the responses to them are one place we see this guiding at work.

Participants can repeat what other people say or write, to criticize it or to use it as evidence (Holt, 1996; Myer, 1999):

M3   it was in the paper where they damaged more trees

They can also formulate contributions from other participants, as we have seen M1 do to M2. M1 does not give the exact words of the other participant; M2 said:

M2   they never alter anything anyway it gets done

M1 formulates this as:

M1   this gentleman has just said . haven't you . that it will <u>hap</u>pen anyway

At this point, M2 could reject this as not what he said, or meant, at all. Instead he repeats it back immediately, stressing his responsibility for the assessment.

M1   it will <u>hap</u>pen anyway=
M2   =it will happen anyway

Such quotation, formulation and response make up much of the transcript. They are important both in constraining analysis and in opening it up.

When we see how common echoes and formulations are in the back and forth of discussion, we see it can be dangerous to excerpt a participant's comments without looking back to the chain of talk that led to it; that is the constraint. The opening is in seeing these echoes and formulations in terms of the participants' sense of just what is relevant at the moment (Buttny, 1997).

Indexicality

Linguists and philosophers identify certain expressions, such as 'here' or 'now' or 'come', as indexical, that is, varying in meaning depending on the situation. 'Here' means something different depending on where the speaker is standing (Lancaster or Seattle); and how wide an area the term is taken to indicate (the living room or the nation). Conversation analysts hold that *all* expressions are in principle indexical; that is, they have their meaning by pointing to the immediate situation, not by reference to fixed symbolic codes (Schegloff, 1984). A word means what it means here and now, for these purposes. This challenge is relevant to our analysis because focus group techniques, and most other social science research techniques, assume that meanings are relatively stable between settings, so that one can ask each group the same questions, more or less, in the topic guide, and show them the same pictures, and compare responses across groups. But even if researchers do not accept the philosophical position underlying conversation analysis, they will find that indexicality is a practical issue in analysing their data. For instance, one reader of the transcript noted that the question by the moderator that opens my example seems particularly incoherent. This is not just because of the way transcription highlights hesitations and repetitions (though it is partly that). It is also because the moderator's opening question is not primarily about political groups, it is about the way pictures are arranged on the floor:

> MOD   I haven't . um probed much what you thought about *these demonstrations* but you put you had no trouble putting *the people* who protested live animal exports *in* with Mother Teresa and um the UN as as trying to do something to repair /um and is that the way you felt about about *this . protest* [emphasis added]

There is indexical reference not only in 'these demonstrations' and 'this protest' but also in 'the people who protested live animal exports', 'the UN', and (later) 'Greenpeace' as referring to particular pictures. The moderator's question gets the response it does because the participants have arranged these pictures in this way, and they assume they can be called to account for what they have done. Similar expressions are found throughout this and other focus groups, referring to what is present to all the members of the group but not, perhaps, to the listener to the tape recording or reader of the transcript.

There is another issue of indexicality in the quiet side discussion of 'who are they' in the middle of this example; it is not just a matter of information, but of what the picture represents for present purposes. All the pictures are polysemic in this way, but the participants settle on a meaning for present purposes. Close attention to the openness of the references helps us see the flexibility of the key categories of media images and environmental actions. Indexical references are not just a practical problem for the analyst, they are also indications of how the group takes on its setting, refers to what its members share, and becomes a group.

There is another kind of indexicality in this passage that any research must take into account: the silent features of the setting to which no one refers but of which they may be aware. Throughout this session, a second researcher sat in the corner, assisting with the taping, videos and note-taking, occasionally making a remark but generally remaining silent. He commented afterwards, recalling the abuse some participants heaped on the runway protesters, that he hoped they hadn't realized that he himself was one of them. One can only speculate about what sort of influence this may have, just as one can only speculate about the relevance of the moderator's American accent, one participant's mobility impairment, or the pattern of the carpet in shaping the arrangement on the floor, because none of these features was invoked in the discussion. The analytical relevance of these uninvoked features of participants or setting is one of the ongoing controversies in discourse analysis.

All these features – agreement sequences, topic, formulation and indexical expressions – link to the larger issues of the research. People do not just come with favourable or unfavourable attitudes towards given actors or actions. They work out stances in relation to the moderator's prompts, the other participants' offerings, the objects around them, and the actions and talk so far. They propose and explore possible positions in relation to the previous turn, so it is not surprising that their views are frequently complex, unstable and apparently contradictory. For the researchers, the interaction is a way of gathering opinions; for the participants, expressions of opinion are a way of interacting with a room full of strangers.

Methodological issues

Detailed analysis of talk raises questions about whether the source of the data is an interview, a group discussion, broadcast talk or informal inter-action. Some of the questions concern the persuasiveness of any inter-pretation (inference); the relation of the sample as a whole to larger society (generalizability); their relation to various social groups (identity); and the relation of what they do and say in focus groups to what they would do and say in other contexts (activity type).

INFERENCE   I have only presented a few examples to illustrate the kinds of features with which an analysis might begin. A more persuasive analysis would show how they are like or unlike patterns found in other transcripts of talk, for instance comparing one instance of disagreement with others. But that in itself would not make the point, because conversation analysis seeks to show what sorts of patterns participants take for granted. So an analyst would look for examples in which participants disagreed more directly and sharply, and show how other participants responded to these instances as a breach of their expectations (an example is Greatbatch, 1988).

GENERALIZABILITY   One might be tempted to generalize from this example to social groups if, for instance, many of the transcripts included some defence of roads protesters. But the members of focus groups were not chosen to represent society as a whole; they were chosen to constitute groups that might have something to say in relation to our theoretical issues. One cannot say that people in general defend roads protesters, but one can say that this man, in this situation, did defend the protesters in these terms. Often these findings are surprising, and go against expectations based on broad social overviews; for instance, M1 combines a social conservatism and an emphasis on discipline (in other passages) with the assertion here that even law-breaking is preferable to apathy.

IDENTITY   Researchers must also be careful in attributing statements to particular social groups. It is tempting, in the passage I have given, to note that the men in general come out against road protesters, and the women for them, and to try to generalize about gender. But these participants have a number of possible social identities, and the text analytical approach resists taking any of these identities as necessarily primary. In focus groups, participants tend to refer to an identity that they see as shared in the group, so these people often referred to their age, while in other contexts they might have referred to gender, parental status, health and disability, 'race', class and regional background (in this area, 'sand grown uns' versus 'off-comers'). Though the issue is highly controversial among researchers who assume that gender or cultural differences or power relations must always be relevant, researchers in conversation analysis pay attention to just those elements of identity foregrounded by the participants in the talk.

ACTIVITY TYPE   What do the participants think they are doing when they talk? In a world with so many institutions gathering opinions, it may seem completely natural for a group of strangers to meet and say what they think about various issues. But we can see in the transcripts various shifting frames for what they are doing here. I have argued elsewhere that many of the features of focus groups make sense if we see participants as displaying opinions for an overhearing tape recorder (Myers, 1998). But there are also places where they shift into interactions more like chat, therapy, play, jury or classroom; sometimes they respond directly to the moderator so much that there is practically a series of one-to-one interviews, and sometimes they seem to ignore the moderator entirely. Such shifts can be traced by close analysis of talk; they tend to get lost in summary or selective overviews.

Conclusion

I have argued here that close analysis of transcribed spoken data, following models drawn from conversation analysis, can lead to insights into the data produced by social science research projects. The disadvantages of such analysis are that it requires careful recording and transcription, and time-consuming analysis. To some researchers, it seems like adding a molehill to the mountain of their data. But such analysis can also provide a way of exploring participants' categories, finding what participants take to be relevant to these categories, providing an explicit account for what might otherwise be left as the analyst's vague intuitions, improving research techniques, and reflecting on the research situation and the researcher's place in it. In a project like ours, where we are investigating the possibility of new kinds of identities and new kinds of actions, it can complement other approaches to the data, linking to our theoretical concerns while keeping us open to what should surprise us.

STEPS IN ANALYSING TALK

1 Plan the research gathering to allow for clear audio (and possibly video) tape recording.
2 Include in the transcription all false starts, repetitions, filled pauses ('erm') and temporal features such as silences and overlapping speech.
3 Start with turn-to-turn transitions, looking for how each turn is presented as relevant to the previous turn or to earlier turns.
4 Consider especially *dispreferred* turns – those marked by prefaces, delay or modifications.
5 For any patterns you find, what happens in those cases when the pattern is not followed?
6 Check any patterns you find against those of ordinary speech.

Appendix: transcription conventions

underlined	stress
CAPITALS	loudness
/	
/	the beginning of overlapping talk
.	short pause
(2.0)	timed pause
==	continues without hearable pause
[ ]	uncertain transcription

For a more detailed transcription system and commentary on transcription, see Hutchby and Wooffitt (1998).

References

Agar, M. and MacDonald, J. (1995) 'Focus groups and ethnography', *Human Organization*, 54: 78–86.

Antaki, C. and Rapley, M. (1996) '"Quality of life" talk: the liberal paradox of psychology testing', *Discourse & Society*, 7: 293–316.

Atkinson, X. and Heritage, J. (1984) *Structures of social action: studies in conversation analysis*. Cambridge: Cambridge University Press.

Avery, C. and Antaki, C. (1997) 'Conversational devices in stories turning on appearance versus reality', *Text*, 17 (1): 1–24.

Barbour, R. and Kitzinger, J. (1999) *Developing Focus Group Research*. London: Sage.

Boden, D. and Zimmerman, D. (eds) (1991) *Talk and Social Structure*. Cambridge: Polity.

Briggs, C.L. (1986) *Learning How to Ask: a Sociolinguistic Appraisal of the Role of the Interview in Social Science Research*. Cambridge: Cambridge University Press.

Burgess, J., Limb, M. and Harrison, C. (1988) 'Exploring environmental values through the medium of small groups. 1: Theory and practice', *Environment and Planning A*, 20: 309–26.

Buttny, R. (1997) 'Reported speech in talking race on campus', *Human Communication Research*, 23 (4): 477–506.

Button, G. and Lee, J.R.E. (eds) (1987) *Talk and Social Organisation*. Clevedon: Multilingual Matters.

Catterall, C. and Maclaran, P. (1997) 'Focus group data and qualitative analysis programs: coding the moving picture as well as the snapshots', *Sociological Research Online*, 2 (1): <http://www.socresonline.org.uk/socresonline/2/1/6.html>.

Cook, G. (1995) 'Theoretical issues: transcribing the untranscribable', in *Spoken English on Computer: Transcription, Mark-Up, and Application*. Harlow: Longman. pp. 35–53.

Drew, P. and Heritage, J. (eds) (1992) *Talk at Work*. Cambridge: Cambridge University Press.

Edwards, D. (1997) *Discourse and Cognition*. London: Sage.

Eggins, S. and Slade, D. (1997) *Analysing Casual Conversation*. London: Cassell.

Gilbert, N. and Mulkay, M. (1984) *Opening Pandora's Box: an Analysis of Scientists' Discourse*. Cambridge: Cambridge University Press.

Greatbatch, D. (1988) 'A turn-taking system for British news interviews', *Language in Society*, 17: 401–430.

Heath, C. (1986) *Body Movement and Speech in Medical Interaction*. Cambridge: Cambridge University Press.

Hinchcliffe, S. (1996) 'Helping the earth begins at home: the social construction of socio-environmental responsibilities', *Global Environmental Change*, 6 (1): 53–62.

Holt, E. (1996) 'Reporting on talk: the use of direct reported speech in conversation', *Research on Language and Social Interaction*, 29 (3): 219–245.

Hutchby, I. and Wooffitt, R. (1998) *Conversation Analysis: the Study of Talk in Interaction*. Cambridge: Polity.

Kitzinger, J. (1994) 'The methodology of focus groups: the importance of interaction between research participants', *Sociology of Health and Illness*, 16: 103–21.

Kitzinger, J. (1995) 'Introducing Focus Groups', *British Medical Journal*, 311: 299–302.

Krueger, R.A. (1994) *Focus Groups: a Practical Guide for Applied Research*. Newbury Park, CA: Sage.

Macnaghten, P. and Urry, J. (1998) *Contested Natures*. London: Sage.

Malone, M.J. (1997) *Worlds of Talk*. Cambridge: Polity.

Maynard, D. (1998) *Refusal Conversation in the Survey Interview as a Local, Situated, and Embodied Achievement*. Seattle, WA: American Association for Applied Linguistics.

Morgan, D.L. (1988) *Focus Groups as Qualitative Research*. Newbury Park, CA: Sage.

Myers, G. (1998) 'Displaying opinions: topics and disagreement in focus groups', *Language in Society*, 27: 85–111.

Myers, G. and Macnaghten, P. (1998) 'Rhetorics of environmental sustainability: commonplaces and places', *Environment and Planning A*, 30: 333–53.

Myers, G. (1999) 'Functions of reported speech in group discussions', *Applied Linguistics*, 20: 376–401.

Ochs, E. (1979) *Transcription as Theory: Developmental Pragmatics*. New York: Academic Press. pp. 43–72.

Pomerantz, A. (1984) 'Agreeing and disagreeing with assessments: some features of preferred/dispreferred turn shapes', in J.M. Atkinson and J. Heritage (eds), *Structures of Social Action: Studies in Conversation Analysis*. Cambridge: Cambridge University Press. pp. 57–101.

Potter, J. and Wetherell, M. (1987) *Discourse and Social Psychology*. Beverly Hills, CA: Sage.

Psathas, G. (1995) *Conversation Analysis: the Study of Talk-in-Interaction*. Thousand Oaks, CA: Sage.

Puchta, C. and Potter, J. (1999) 'Asking elaborate questions: focus groups and the management of spontaneity', *Journal of Sociolinguistics*, 3: 314–35.

Robson, C. (1993) *Real World Research: a Resource for Social Scientists and Practitioner-Researchers*. Oxford: Blackwell.

Sacks, H. (1992) *Lectures on Conversation*. Oxford: Blackwell.

Scannell, P. (ed.) (1991) *Broadcast Talk*. London: Sage.

Schegloff, E.A. (1984) 'On some questions and ambiguities in conversation', in J.M. Atkinson and J. Heritage (eds), *Structures of Social Action: Studies in Conversation Analysis*. Cambridge: Cambridge University Press. pp. 28–52.

Schiffrin, D. (1984) 'Jewish argument as sociability', *Language in Society*, 13: 311–35.

Schiffrin, D. (1994) *Approaches to Discourse*. Oxford: Blackwell.

Schiffrin, D. (1996) 'Narrative as self-portrait, sociolinguistic constructions of identity', *Language in Society*, 25: 167–203.

Sharrock, W. and Anderson, B. (1987) 'Epilogue: the definition of alternatives: some sources of confusion in interdisciplinary discussion', in G. Button and J.R.E. Lee, (eds), *Talk and Social Organisation*. Clevedon: Multilingual Matters. pp. 290–321.

Stewart, D.W. and Shamdasani, P.N. (1990) *Focus Groups: Theory and Practice*. London: Sage.

Szerszynski, B. and Toogood, M. (2000) 'Mediating environmental citizenship', in S. Allen (ed.), *The Media Politics of Environmental Risk*. London: Routledge.

Tannen, D. (1984) *Conversational Style: Analyzing Talk among Friends*. Norwood, NJ: Ablex.

Wilkinson, S. (1998) 'Focus groups in feminist research: power, interaction, and the co-construction of meaning', *Women's Studies International Forum*, 21(1): 111–25.

Wooffitt, R. (1992) *Telling Tales of the Unexpected: the Organization of Factual Discourse*. Hemel Hempstead: Harvester Wheatsheaf.

Further reading

Bilmes, J. (1988) 'The concept of preference in conversation analysis', *Language in Society*, 17: 161–81.

Houtkoop-Steenstra, H. and Antaki, C. (1997) 'Creating happy people by asking yes/no questions', *Research on Language and Social Interaction*, 30(4): 285–313.

MacGregor, B. and Morrison, D.E. (1995) 'From focus groups to editing groups: a new method of reception analysis', *Media, Culture & Society*, 17: 141–50.

Psathas, G. (1979) *Everyday Language: Studies in Ethnomethodology.* New York: Irvington.

Silverman, D. (1993) *Interpreting Qualitative Data: Methods for Analysing Talk, Text, and Interaction.* London: Sage.

12

Rhetorical Analysis

Joan Leach

<table>
<tr><td colspan="2">KEYWORDS</td></tr>
<tr><td>accommodation</td><td>metaphor</td></tr>
<tr><td>analogy</td><td>metonymy</td></tr>
<tr><td>argument</td><td>pathos</td></tr>
<tr><td>discourse</td><td>rhetoric</td></tr>
<tr><td>ethos</td><td>rhetorical canons (parts of rhetoric)</td></tr>
<tr><td>genre</td><td>synecdoche</td></tr>
<tr><td>logos</td><td></td></tr>
</table>

> If only the Prime Minister's policies were as good as the policy rhetoric we hear, we would all be better off.

This common use of the word 'rhetoric' belies the long and celebrated history of an academic discipline and mode of critical analysis. In everyday talk, we contrast 'rhetoric' with 'action', and suggest that something 'rhetorical' is tantamount to a collection of lies and half-truths. This is unfortunate public relations for contemporary scholars who look at texts and oral discourses, developing theories of how and why they are compelling and persuasive, why they were developed when they were, what argument structures, metaphors and structuring principles are at work and, in some cases, what can be done to make different forms of communication work better in context.

One way to begin to clarify the term 'rhetoric' is to give working definitions that begin to shed some light on the multiplicity of uses of the word itself:

Rhetoric I   The act of persuasion.
Rhetoric II   The analysis of acts of persuasion.
Rhetoric III A worldview about the persuasive power of discourse.

The quote at the start of the chapter seems to be a comment on the first definition given here. Politicians perform 'acts of rhetoric'. That is, they organize discourse to be persuasive. Rhetorical scholars, however, seek to unpack such discourses and ask why they are persuasive, thus adopting the second definition of rhetoric. This seems simple, but an analogy from a different context is useful here to more clearly articulate some blurred boundaries. We refer to those people who commit crimes as criminals. Those who study criminals and their behaviour are called criminologists. The discourse of criminologists in sociology journals is never referred to as a discourse of criminality. Rhetoric, by comparison, is different. The big issue is that 'rhetorical' discourses can be analysed by rhetoricians, and rhetoricians are also responsible for producing rhetorical discourse. This might seem to be a problem of semantics, but it is also a rather interesting methodological issue. At what point does the 'analysis' of persuasion not become persuasive itself? A close example is the text that you are currently reading. At what point am I laying out some ground-rules for rhetorical analysis, and at what point am I trying to persuade you that rhetorical analysis is a valuable tool for social analysis? This issue of reflexivity comes up in many social science research methods, but it is arguable that it is most transparent here in the realm of rhetoric. Finally, there is a sense in which rhetoric is also a worldview, a belief in the power of language and discourse to fundamentally structure our thinking, our systems of representation, and even our perception of the natural world. This last issue brings rhetorical analysis very close to ideological analysis, ethical analysis and other issues in social theory.

If we foreground the analysis of persuasion or rhetoric II, some background to this area is useful. It was the classical Greeks who first had an interest in analysing discourses to know why they were persuasive, and they did so both in speaking and in writing (Cole, 1991; Poulakos, 1995). Aristotle and Plato both concerned themselves with this art, and were anxious to distinguish 'good' rhetoric from 'bad' rhetoric as well as to create categories of persuasive discourse and rules for creating 'good' rhetoric. Indeed, this classical argument about good versus bad rhetoric underlies many of Plato's dialogues. It is also Plato who begins to talk about rhetoric as if it were a tainted subject. Some of Plato's key concerns plague rhetorical analysis to this day. First, Plato suggested that rhetoric was somehow different from the 'truth'. That is, what people say in their lived world may not be how things really are in his world of ideals. This notion stays with us, and makes us sceptics in the face of individuals trying to persuade us to one view or another. Secondly, Plato asserted that rhetoric was unteachable. This assertion was in response to a group of teachers, called *sophistai* (sophists), who professed to be able to teach young students the ability to speak persuasively, as well as to analyse others' speech for successful and unsuccessful techniques. Plato held the position that rhetoric could not be taught, because 'good rhetoric' was related to individual virtue. If the person was not virtuous, then they could never be taught rhetoric as an art, nor would their analysis ever come to anything.

The Romans continued an interest in persuasive discourse and teaching rhetoric, and created elaborate schemes and names for rhetorical strategies. It is their legacy that gives us 'handbooks of rhetoric' that describe and interpret the figures of speech, grammatical patterns and aesthetic matters that made speeches and texts compelling. From classical times through the medieval period, rhetoric was a core discipline taught along with grammar, dialectic and later arithmetic and geometry. But this was to change: during the Enlightenment, rhetoric came under fire as both a practice and a discipline. The founding of the Royal Society in England was marked by Francis Bacon's motto *nullius in verba* (nothing in words) and the new 'sciences' were to avoid any taint of rhetorical flourish including metaphors, analogies and graceful prosaic elements (Montgomery, 1996). Bacon's chief concern in his disavowal of rhetoric was to get away from the scholasticism of the previous generation which relied on the texts of ancient and renaissance figures such as Ptolemy and Paracelsus. According to Bacon, scholasticism had relied on the rhetoric of the ancients without any new observations and induction from observation. In this way, science was to be 'unrhetorical'. Rhetorical analysis, however, continued to be popular in humanities disciplines and theology far into the twentieth century. Awareness of this tradition is important in the case of rhetoric since, as a discipline, it has had close to 2500 years to develop methodological refinement and diversity.

Object of analysis

One is immediately thrown into a quagmire when faced with trying to find the 'object' for rhetorical analysis. Traditionally, rhetorical analysis critiqued oral discourses such as those in the law courts, parliament and the political arena, or even oral discourses such as acceptance speeches and diatribes. As these oral discourses are usually now reported as written ones or are even underpinned by written documents, rhetorical analysts have chosen documentary sources as well as oral ones on which to use their methods. The recent elucidation of semiotics has also opened the door to the analysis of images, non-verbal communication, gestures and even the placement of objects within buildings, and semiotics claims a kinship to rhetorical analysis (Eco, 1979). The traditional object for rhetorical analysis is also persuasive. Historically speaking, the object of analysis was overtly persuasive, but since the theoretical elucidation of ideology and other more subtle forms of social cohesion, rhetorical analysis can easily handle discourses that claim to be objective (that is, claiming to be objective is itself a persuasive move). Whether one is choosing an oral discourse, an image or a written document, an overtly persuasive discourse such as political speeches and advertising or more covert persuasion such as a scientific article or a newspaper feature, the context of discourse should be the first port of call when embarking on rhetorical analysis.

It has been frequently asserted that rhetorical analysis assumes that rhetoric is produced by a cognizant, self-aware rhetor who orders her discourse in accordance with sets of formalized rules. This rhetoric is directed at a discrete audience which is persuaded by the arguments given and gives some sign to that effect (classically, a change in behaviour or opinion). Rhetoric, in this somewhat impoverished view, then, recovers the intentions of the speaker or author, discovers the systems of rules that organize the discourse, and evaluates the effectiveness of the intended persuasion by the effect on the audience. While an analysis can be rendered in this way, there are many dangers. Most importantly, this treats the analysis of discourse as merely the reverse of the construction of discourse, and assumes that the processes of construction are recoverable and the contexts of reception are transparent. Furthermore, this attitude toward analysis commits the intentionalist fallacy. That is, if we pursue rhetorical analysis as the reconstruction of the intention of authors and speakers and the intention 'behind' the behavioural or attitude changes of audiences, we proceed as if 'intentions' of authors can be divined by their texts or oral performances. This is a danger of many types of analysis, but one that has especially plagued rhetorical analysis.

The easiest way to avoid this pitfall is to analyse 'found' or 'natural' discourses and not those that are produced by social science methodologies. For example, consider the dangers of analysing a set of texts produced from an interview that you performed. While this text can be persuasive and benefit from rhetorical analysis, one might find oneself 'second-guessing' the persuasive impact of any one statement. It becomes very difficult to sort out the intentions of the interviewer, the intentions of the interviewee and the persuasive import of any one remark. Further, arguments should not be judged on their potential persuasive value to the analyst. They must always be judged in relation to the context and the entirety of the discourse.

Since rhetoric has analysed both written texts and oral performances, there exists quite a bit of confusion about where rhetorical analysis ends and some other type of analysis begins. This has become an interesting problem in light of interdisciplinarity and the so-called 'linguistic turn' in philosophy and the social sciences (Rorty, 1979). Considering the object of study for many social sciences and even philosophy, this object has become increasingly a linguistic one. Therefore, it becomes very difficult to say, for example, whether rhetoric is an overarching term for something like 'ideological analysis', or whether it is something different altogether – and many theorists and practitioners disagree (Gross and Keith, 1997). A brief example shows the difficulty. In reading a political text, a scholar doing rhetorical analysis will be looking for the available means of persuasion located within the text. One of those means of persuasion is making arguments with which the audience may already agree, in order to create a sense of identity between the implied author and the implied audience. Such shared political commitments may operate at the level of ideology. Should the rhetorical analysis, then, avoid commenting about those arguments? Most scholars think not. This is a simple and fairly straightforward example. Most texts do not present such easy ways to imagine the relationship between ideology and persuasion. But, increasingly, scholars are feeling more comfortable with these blurred boundaries, even in terms of methodology (Nelson et al., 1987). As the trend to interdisciplinarity looks to continue apace in the social sciences and humanities, scholars feel comfortable indicating that they use rhetorical methods to do 'argument analysis' or look to the rhetoric of a particular text to talk about ideology, or even that they use semiotic methods as part of a rhetorical approach to analysing film and other media (Martin and Veel, 1998).

But before this catholic approach to methodology and disciplinarity leads one to believe that, in the words of Paul Feyerabend, 'anything goes', there is a tradition to rhetoric that sits uneasily in the social sciences. As rhetoric is a classical 'art' or *techne*, its historical attitude toward knowledge production is much more at home with literary criticism than with sociology. Some scholars would even argue that rhetoric produces knowledge in the same way as a poem or a painting produces knowledge, and that analysing those forms of knowledge production is best done not by the social sciences, but by the art historian or the literary critic. While these are large issues about the attitude toward an object of research, they are important to consider when thinking about methods. The goal of rhetoric is never to be 'scientific', or to be able to categorize persuasion for all times and all places. The power of rhetorical analysis is its immediacy, its ability to talk about the particular and the possible, not the universal and the probable. And this brings us back to Plato's and Bacon's particular concerns about rhetoric. If one can analyse one text for its persuasive merits, what claims can one make about the knowledge produced? Bacon would say that it gets us nowhere as we cannot induce more knowledge from only one text. Plato might worry that just analysing the available means of persuasion gets us no closer to any universal truths. So, while a rhetorical approach can be used in conjunction with many types of humanities and social science methodologies, the fundamental attitude that rhetoric suggests comes from its tradition of being an art, not a science.

The rhetorical situation

Keeping these larger issues in mind, we return to the key question of how to avoid pitfalls while doing rhetorical analysis, and find that the problem becomes how to say something meaningful in analysis without assuming the processes that constructed the discourse in the first place. This is where contexts of discourse become so important. The following are some guiding questions and categories to consider when looking at an image, hearing an oral discourse or reading a text and thinking about it rhetorically. These categories will begin to flesh out the who/what/where/when/why aspects of rhetorical analysis in a concrete way (Bitzer, 1968). What is remarkable about these categories is that they have existed for over 2000 years, first as methods by which to practise oration, and then, via Aristotle, as a way to analyse and examine the structure of particular discourses.

Exigence

In the words of Bitzer (1968), 'Any exigence is an imperfection marked by urgency; it is a defect, an obstacle, something waiting to be done, a thing which is other than it should be.' Rhetoric responds to this exigence. In doing rhetorical analysis, then, it is crucial to identify the exigence for the rhetoric at hand. This situates analysis, and ensures that the analysis is contextualized. To further contextualize rhetoric, good rhetorical analysis attends to what the classical Greeks called *kairos* and *phronesis*. Loosely translated, *kairos* is the 'timeliness' of a persuasive text; *phronesis* is the appropriateness of a particular persuasive text. A recent example in a very public context points to the need for attention to these aspects. An analyst might like to look at the Queen's address to the nation after Princess Diana's untimely death, an exigence marked by public mourning. Surely this analysis would be severely lacking if it did not acknowledge the public outcry for the Queen to make a statement, which she ignored and which ultimately constrained the response she received from the audience. That is, the Queen's discourse did not have a sense of *kairos*. It was as untimely as the unexpected death: one occurred too early, the other too late. Likewise, the Queen was immediately condemned after this speech as being 'unfeeling and cold'. That is, the audience deemed something inappropriate about the Queen speaking about the Princess after her death: a sense of *phronesis* was lacking. In addition to giving the context and paying attention to the audience, considering these two concepts helps to link text, context and audience together.

Audience

Oral performances have a sense in which their audience is immediate and, in some ways, more identifiable. Texts and mass mediated forms of communication, however, do not exist in the same relationship to an immediate and identifiable audience. When approaching a text, for example, the audience does not reside in any clear way within the text itself. However, we can see in texts ways of positioning readers, or 'creating' audiences. Take, for example, the scientific paper that might appear in the journal *Nature*. The text and its context position readers in very particular ways as an 'audience'. The specialized language, the conventions of citation, the structure of the text with ordered sections, and the relationship between diagrams and the text, all select a certain audience of readers, as well as position them in certain ways. For example, the audience might be positioned as sceptics, as scientists possibly interested in reproducing the results of the experiment, or even, as in review articles, as novices in a particular area. So, while the audience does not always reside in the text in any obvious fashion, the text rhetorically positions its audience in ways that can be discerned through analysis.

Types of persuasive discourse: stasis theory

Looking at persuasive discourse, rhetorical theorists have identified three persuasive genres or stases: forensic, deliberative and epideictic (Gross, 1990; Fahnestock, 1986). These are categorized by purpose, audience, situation and time. Forensic rhetoric is the rhetoric of the law courts, where discussion centres around the nature and cause of past events. Interlocutors must persuade a third party that their account of past events is the 'true' account. Deliberative rhetoric is found in the arena of policy, where debate centres on the best possible course of future action. This persuasion is future oriented, and frequently speculative. Epideictic rhetoric is centred on contemporary issues, and on whether a certain individual or event deserves praise, blame or censure. The classical forms of epideictic rhetoric are funeral orations and award ceremonies. The usefulness of stasis theory is that it can classify a discourse by its persuasive genre and help to set your analysis in a particular direction. This said, many persuasive discourses participate in more than one stasis or genre, so identifying each argument by type is a useful exercise.

Parts of rhetoric

Traditionally, when an analyst began to consider rhetoric, she had to take into account the five 'canons' of rhetoric. The province of persuasion, or rhetoric, was conveniently divided by Cicero for pedagogical reasons, especially for the teaching of the 'art of persuasion' or rhetoric I. But these categories can still be useful. First, categorize a persuasive discourse by stasis, then consider the five canons. Each canon can be subdivided into yet further categories.

Invention

Medieval rhetoric scholars made a clear distinction between form and content (*res* and *verba*). Early rhetorical theorists thought that one must first clearly delineate the content of a discourse, and then look carefully at its style, organization and aesthetic elements. But contemporary scholars believe that the classical categories, while still useful, assumed that the form in which communication takes place was much less important than we now see it. Indeed, some have argued that the form of communication determines the arguments that can be made. These kinds of discussions are encountered when one looks into that province of rhetoric called 'invention'. The key questions that are invoked by rhetorical analysis in this canon are those that address where arguments come from or, more classically, how orators 'invent' arguments in relation to particular purposes.

ETHOS   One form of persuasive argument relies on the establishment of the credibility of the author or speaker. While who the author is does not make an argument more or less valid, subtle forms of persuasion play out in power relationships set up in texts. Take, for a brief example, scientific authorship and citation. The late twentieth century saw increasing prominence given to 'first' authors of scientific papers; those who are listed first, and whose names therefore appear first in the citation indexes. While formal peer review may ignore the name of the first author, readers in scientific communities cannot. Therefore, certain authors have 'ethos' to make stronger claims than other authors.

PATHOS   Another form of persuasive argument is the appeal to emotion. Advertising is full of examples of this form of argument. However, less noticed forms include the appeal to application in medical research. The persuasive call of 'more research is needed' is all the more persuasive when applications such as cures or remedies for painful diseases, or applications to the health of children, are mentioned.

LOGOS   The Greek word *logos* provides the basic root for our word 'logic'. Part of the province of rhetoric is to examine how logical arguments work to convince us of their validity. This is closely related to the discussion of disposition below. While people today find certain forms of logic persuasive, historical texts indicate that earlier audiences would not have found those forms of logic persuasive. This also relates to exploring rhetoric III, or the rhetorical worldview under which discourses operate. Thinking about logos in this way also suggests the power of discourse to shape or construct certain worldviews. While Aristotle found himself at the centre of the universe and argued accordingly, that structuring principle to Aristotle's logic has been lost to us in the West, while others have taken its place.

These elements – ethos, pathos and logos – are essential ingredients for exploring context as a beginning to rhetorical analysis. They provide forms of arguments that figure in different types of persuasive discourse. They are introductory forms from which persuasive arguments can be invented or developed. But there are many methods to go forward and analyse the discourse further within the structure of the classical five canons or parts of rhetoric.

Disposition

This rhetorical canon explores how discourse is organized. By what logic does it support its ultimate claims? How is the organization of the work related to the argument that it advances? Journalistic articles are usually written in what is sometimes referred to as 'the inverted pyramid', starting with a sentence telling us 'who, what, where, when and why' and finishing with detail. What effect might this type of organization have on audiences? Might this organizational feature actually persuade us that some things are more important than others?

Style

We talk in common parlance as if style were something extrinsic to discourse, something that can be removed at will. It is important to consider style as an intrinsic part of discourse, as a complex part of the relationship between form and content. Discourses are frequently persuasive on the basis of their style, which, of course, is related to context. Poetry, for example, is written in a style that persuades, in a certain context, one lover of the other's love. Merely waving a highly stylized scientific paper in front of an advisory committee has persuasive effect, as the style of the discourse suggests objectivity. Consider further the scientific document, one of the most highly stylized discourses of contemporary culture. Note the absence of the first person. This is an adopted conventionalized style. It works to persuade us that anyone can, in fact, perform any of the actions that the text describes; the 'I' need not be present. Legal documents are only persuasive when they are signed. They have adopted a style of presentation where the reader can find an empty space in which to sign their name after reading. The author of agony columns, however, is only persuasive when adopting a style of personal intimacy. Imagine if the agony columnist adopted the scientific style of omitting the first-person pronoun; persuasiveness suffers!

Aside from this notion of style, however, conventions form an elaborate ritual within discourse. Additionally, there are conventions of interpretation, reception, reading and listening as well as conventions of writing, speaking and representing. Let us take the example of the television news. News is a highly ritualized form of discourse. Families and communities have their favourite news programme which they watch without fail, a temporal ritual to mark the beginning or the ending of the day. They have conventions about the style in which they watch the news: they may ritually watch it with an air of distractedness, while they press a shirt, eat breakfast or open the mail. The news programme itself is highly ritualized, with relatively constant presenters, orders of segments and types of arguments. In this sense, watching the news becomes more like complex theatre than information dissemination. This has an important impact on rhetorical analysis. These rituals and conventions define boundaries and limits of both the creation of discourse and the reception of discourse. There was a famous episode on American television when a presenter walked off the air in order to make his position on an issue known. This notoriously failed, as confusion reigned both at the studio and among the audience. This was outside the ritual that is television news. The persuasiveness of the act was not appreciated because it could not be understood within the boundaries of the discourse.

'What, then, can rhetorical imagery effect?,' asked Longinus. His answer is quite striking: 'Well, it is able in many ways to infuse vehemence and passion into spoken words, while more particularly when it is combined with the argumentative passages it not only persuades the hearer but actually makes him its slave' (*On the Sublime*, XV, 9). This quality that rhetorical imagery has to make slaves is an important part of the analysis of texts. By 'rhetorical imagery', what is meant is the use of figurative language. Some rhetorical handbooks of the medieval period list hundreds of uses and categories of figurative language. Here, we will consider two: metaphor and, by association, analogy; and metonymy and, by association, synecdoche. These are two of the most common tropes that appear in discourse and have quite persuasive functions.

METAPHOR AND ANALOGY   Analysing metaphors has been second nature for rhetorical analysis since Plato. The notion that metaphors can 'transfer over' (*meta pherein*) meaning from one concept to another as an aid to our understanding and description, as well as being a persuasive tool, comes from the ancient Greeks. In this sense, metaphor works by creating an analogy between two concepts. When Burns says 'my love is like a red red rose that's newly sprung in June', he transfers the meaning associated with a rose to the notion of love, indicating passion, a sense of newness and of trueness. This use of metaphor is common in poetry and creative writing, but is also present in many persuasive discourses and in science. The following example is of a rhetorical analysis rendered by Evelyn Fox Keller (1995), who has written extensively on metaphor in the biological sciences and how they persuade us as well as provide heuristic models for our thinking.

Keller tells a history of the term 'information' and how it has been used metaphorically. Claude Shannon, a mathematician, appropriated the term and defined it as the precise measure of complexity of linear codes. Soon after, many other mathematicians, computer scientists and systems analysts became interested in what they called 'information theory', which was billed as the cutting edge in science and technology. Systems came to be graded for how much information they 'contained' – a move away from describing information as a quality, but toward describing information as a thing. Then, biologists came on the scene. Famously, Watson and Crick wrote in 1953 that they had discovered the 'basis of life' 'in a long molecule . . . it seems likely that the precise sequence of bases [DNA] is the code which carries the genetical information' (Watson, 1968). In this seemingly technical sentence, Watson and Crick had transferred the meaning of information as an exciting measure of complexity into a biological context, and had applied the meaning to DNA. Many geneticists objected that this use of 'information' as a technical term was incorrect and inappropriate to a mathematical understanding of the complexity of the DNA; but the term stuck and we now talk often of the information encoded on the DNA molecule. In this case, 'information' is a metaphor that was used persuasively by Watson and Crick to lend a sense of complexity, newness and mathematical rigour to their work.

Such uses of metaphor are quite common, quite subtle and quite complex. So, in addition to looking for more obvious metaphors such as 'on the final examination, students went down in flames', we must ferret out more complex metaphors. While the technical example given above would be quite difficult to recognize for non-specialists, metaphors exist on many levels and in all discourses. Many philosophers and semioticians even suggest that our fundamental relation to language is metaphoric (for more on this very radical claim see Gross, 1990).

METONYMY AND SYNECDOCHE Metonymy and synecdoche are figures of speech where the part stands for the whole. There are many examples of this in common speech. When we ask people at formal meetings to 'address remarks to the chair', we typically do not mean them to talk to the furniture on which the discussion leader is sitting, but to the person sitting in the chair. This use of language functions at very complex levels. It allows us to shift attributes and characteristics from one thing to another. In this sense, it is a close relation to metaphor. It also works alongside appeals to pathos. For example, a recent newspaper article referred to great chaos that would happen in Britain 'if the crown was lost'. The worry seems to revolve around the loss not of the gems and gold of the monarchy, but of the monarchy itself. This appeal to the 'crown' relates to a broader field of cultural imagery and items of heritage which the article invokes to encourage emotion in the audience.

Here, we have looked at some tropes or 'figures of speech'. That they operate to adorn our prose is without question, and that they are unavoidable to a certain extent is probable; but some scholars suppose that they tell us something profound about the way in which we think and the way that language itself works (see Fahnestock, 1999 for more on the power of the figures of speech).

Memory

This canon analyses the access that a speaker has to the content of his or her speech. In classical times, orators were judged by the length of their speeches, and by whether they could deliver them exactly twice running. In current theoretical circles there is a revived interest in the cultural aspect of memory, and how particular discourses call upon cultural memories shared by authors and their audiences (Lipsitz, 1990).

Delivery

While more obviously applicable to oral discourses, this canon explores the relationship between the dissemination of a work and its content. We can imagine the speaker who has 'ethos' to speak on a certain subject. While part of this ethos is a certain way of inventing an argument, part of it may be in the delivery of the talk itself. This can also be explored textually by looking at different dissemination patterns. The style of address or delivery in e-mail, for example, differs radically in some cases from delivery in written prose. A rhetorical analysis might use this category to explore what those differences are.

Strengths and weaknesses of rhetorical analysis

By its very nature, rhetorical analysis is a discursive act: it is creating arguments about arguments. Rhetorical analysis, then, is conducted to greatest effect on complete, conventionalized and socially purposive discourses. Politicians' speeches, newspaper editorials and lawyers' orations are traditional sources for rhetorical analysis. But equally carefully crafted documents and oral discourses can be analysed rhetorically to very good effect. These include the rhetoric of science, the rhetoric of the social sciences and the rhetoric of economics. These academic discourses are themselves highly crafted, and make use of traditional structures of argumentation, appeals to emotion and appeals to credibility. These last suggestions to look at texts within the social sciences lead us once again to the issue of reflexivity: why not analyse our own texts in this way, and evaluate them for meeting the goals we set for them?

The main weakness of rhetorical analysis is the extent of its formalisms. As one can see from looking above, the notion that there are 'five' canons with yet more categories for analysis related to them gives the impression of an elaborate edifice that must be applied at every turn. Such application of rhetorical analysis in this way would be unwieldy, and probably uninteresting. Thus, the rhetorical tools that one uses to analyse any one text can differ from those used in analysing another text. In short, rhetorical analysis is an interpretive art. The weakness here is that it fails by most social scientific standards, which applaud uniformity in analysis and consistency in application. This feature is both the greatest strength and the greatest weakness of rhetorical analysis: on the one hand, it is flexible and interpretive; and on the other hand, it is inconsistent and subject to the strengths and weaknesses of the analyst.

Toward quality in qualitative research

What marks quality in a rhetorical analysis? While answering that question is difficult for any social science methodology, given the history of argument over this topic by the sophists, Plato, Aristotle, Cicero, Vico and Scottish Enlightenment thinkers, contemporary commentators pale at the thought of adding their own opinions to those of past greats. However, some features do stand out in what the field of rhetoric recognizes as good analysis. Most crucially, serious attention to audience marks rhetorical analyses in the literature. Because the notion of truth in many other disciplines is looked upon as being universal in all times and places, they need not pay attention to specific audiences at specific times and in specific places. Rhetoric cannot afford this move. Instead, what is considered persuasive or even 'true', in a pragmatic sense, is due to the reception of the text or discursive act by the audience at hand. Rhetoric makes no such claims to universal truths, and therefore measures its successes and failures on whether it has addressed and even persuaded the identified audience in its real time and place. Thus, knowledge of the audience is central for any rhetorical discourse.

The second aspect of quality in rhetorical analysis relates to the first. In contemporary Western culture, where science and scientized philosophy influence heavily the agenda for knowledge production and the reception of that knowledge in the culture, this notion of specific truths from rhetoric sounds strange, foreign and, some may even say, irrelevant. But if one accepts the possibility of truth being place- and time-dependent, one pays special attention to the particular and not the general. Such rhetorical analysis will examine the movement and influence of a single text, perhaps. And from rhetorical analysis, it is not possible to generalize to other texts. That a single analysis reveals a pattern in argument does not mean that one should expect to see that pattern again. But while it is not possible to generalize to other texts for the sake of analysis, it is possible to make normative statements based on the analysis at hand. Good rhetorical analyses frequently do not hesitate to make normative proclamations. These may be in the form of suggestions about how the discourse being analysed failed to persuade an audience, and what might have won the day. They may be in the form of prescriptions about how other forms of persuasion could avoid particular pitfalls. They may be in the form of critiquing the persuasive devices used; a particular audience may be persuaded by arguments that are unsupported. They may be in the form of critiquing the evidence or the status of the evidentiary claims made in a text. This is a different position from most other methods, ideological analysis excepted. Description and analysis are usually considered to be 'good' when they avoid normative suggestions. The lack of normative suggestions usually suggests an 'objective' or unbiased account. But rhetorical theorists would suggest that description is really prescription under a rhetorical guise. Claiming to be only 'descriptive' and, thus, objective is a persuasive move made by social scientists to secure the rights of calling what they do a science, the most radical theorists would hold (see Nelson et al., 1987 and the 'Introduction to the project for the rhetoric of enquiry' in that volume for examples of these arguments). These two aspects of good rhetorical analysis – the attention to the particular and local, and the affinity for normative conclusions – set it apart from many other forms of analysis, and even make it 'unscientific' within many social science frameworks.

This brings us full circle to the definition of rhetoric. We have considered strategies under the heading of rhetoric II: the analysis of discourse. It can be equally helpful, however, to consider our own discourse production as we are doing analysis. Bazerman (1988), in a now canonical study, makes the following concrete suggestions for a rhetorical approach to policing one's own analytic discourse in the humanities and social sciences.

Consider your fundamental assumptions, goals and projects

The underlying epistemology, history, and theory of a field cannot be separated from its rhetoric. (Bazerman, 1988: 323)

Whatever specific field of study in which you find yourself doing research, it is important to remember that this field has set boundaries around what can be said about certain topics and what is meaningful to be said. Your research projects must come within these boundaries or challenge these boundaries in order for them to be 'meaningful', that is, understood by practitioners and researchers within that field. Do your assumptions about what research is and what constitutes successful research match up to those represented within the field? These assumptions can themselves be rhetorically analysed (as we have seen with introductory textbooks), but you must be clear about how your own rhetoric and argument strategies match up to those of the field in which you are working.

Consider the structure of the literature, the structure of the community, and your place in both

When you seek to write or present your research findings or positions, the literature of your field is already positioned around you. There is a prior literature that must be addressed; there is a rhetorical style in which it must be addressed (for more specifics on this see Swales, 1983). As you begin contributing to the literature, your work must address the rhetorical exigency established in that literature. In order to contribute, therefore, you must know the literature through reading. As Bazerman argues, reading the literature, through a developing schematic of what problems the discipline had addressed, what the discipline has learned, where it is going, who the major actors are and how these things relate to your own project, can help you integrate your work with the work in the field. One strategy to help you do so in the introduction of your work is to create an intertextual web where you link the issues which are central to your project with the issues central to other projects in the field.

Consider your investigative and symbolic tools

Even if your research has developed some significant findings through the use of good methodology and investigative tools, your symbolic tools must be equally up to the task. This tends to mean that the claims you make about your investigations need to be supported by good arguments. Argument tends to hang on the quality and character of evidence. Toulmin's (1958) minimal model is a good start to test your own ability to construct arguments with which interlocutors can engage without discarding immediately. However, you have many other symbolic and rhetorical tools at your disposal. In addition to discerning the common arguments made within your own field, reflecting on the use of argument in other fields is also useful.

Consider the processes of knowledge production

When we begin doing research, we tend to think of the ends of the research – what gains we seek to make, what goals we have. But some concern about the processes we will use to reach these is equally important. Considering the way you will write up, report or discuss your results as you perform your research can be extremely helpful, and can allow you to imagine the range of possible forms it might take. Likewise, anticipating how your research might be received by others may help you to construct the boundaries in which your work will be received.

Example of analysis

A canonical example of rhetorical analysis has been given by Jeanne Fahnestock (1986). Fahnestock begins by asserting that every discourse has a persuasive element, even scientific discourse. This assertion is not universally admired, but it forms the basis or the fundamental assumption of Fahnestock's work. Indeed, from her position of teaching technical writing, she sees first-hand the problems that scientists and engineers face when attempting to persuade their audiences. Moving from this concrete situation, she also notices that persuasion in scientific discourse does not stop within the scientific community. In fact, in terms of knowledge production about science, scientific discourse also seeks to persuade lay audiences. So, from these basic reflexive and reflective positions, Fahnestock lays the groundwork for a rhetorical analysis of scientific discourse as it moves from the scientific community into the popular press.

The symbolic tools of rhetorical analysis are deployed in relation to two very particular types of text which are arranged in pairings for ease of analysis. The first text in each pair is from the scientific journal in which the original research was reported. The second text in each pair is what Fahnestock terms 'accommodated' science writing: these texts come from a popular science magazine. For example:

1(a)   No other protein sources are used by *T. hypogea*, and pollen transporting structures have been lost, making this species an obligate necrophage. (Roubik, *Science*, 1982, p. 1059)

1(b)   Though other bees have teeth, this is the only species that cannot carry pollen. ('Vulture bees', *Science '82*, p. 6)

The first text comes from the American scientific journal *Science*, and the second from its popular counterpart. To contextualize her analysis, Fahnestock first considers the rhetorical situation of these two texts, noting the massive growth in readership of popular science, the proliferation of popular science writers, and even the growth of the number of scientific journals aimed at scientists themselves. Further, analysis by sociologists and literary scholars provides some contextual information for her rhetorical analysis. From this 'rhetorical situation', Fahnestock proposes that her rhetorical analysis will reveal three related themes:

[first, on] the genre shift that occurs between the original presentation of a scientist's work and its popularization, second, on the change in 'statement types' that occurs when a larger audience is addressed, and third, on the usefulness of classical stasis theory in explaining what goes on in the 'rhetorical life' of a scientific observation. (1986: 228)

Following the methods previously explored, Fahnestock goes forward from the rhetorical situation to analyse using stasis theory the types of persuasive discourse in which science participates. According to Fahnestock, the original scientific texts are predominantly forensic in nature:

> scientific papers are largely concerned with establishing the validity of the observations they report; thus the swollen prominence of the 'Materials and Methods' and 'Results' sections in the standard format of the scientific paper and the prominence given to tables, figures, and photographs that stand in as the best possible representation of the physical evidence that the research has generated. (1986)

Scientific accommodations, however, are

> overwhelmingly epideictic; their main purpose is to celebrate rather than validate. (1986: 279)

Accommodations celebrate by appealing to their audience's sense of wonder and application. In the above example, this plays out in the following ways. First, note the forensic features of the original report. Here we have an author establishing facts that are necessary to his scientific argument. The accommodated version, in contrast, changes this in specific ways by giving the claim

> a greater degree of certainty than the first. The scientist who wrote the original report and who had just discovered a species of tropical bee unknown before was not about to claim that no other similar species existed and that he had found the 'only' one. (1986: 280)

In contrast, the accommodated version has shifted the claim up a notch in certainty by claiming its uniqueness, its one-of-a-kind status. Further:

> The accommodated version also claims that the bees 'eat any animal,' an inferential extension from the data observed and recorded in the *Science* piece. This change is perhaps no more than an innocent hyperbole. But again it is an exaggeration in an interesting direction because it helps to glamorize the danger of the bees . . . The claim of uniqueness serves the epideictic 'wonder' appeal. 1986: 281)

This part of Fahnestock's analysis establishes the rhetorical situation for her analysis, and outlines the types of persuasion she finds in her textual objects. But, in addition, the parts of rhetoric, or the five canons, also come into play in her analysis. While the categories of memory and delivery are absent, invention, disposition and style are all analysed to continue her themes of the genre shift and the construction of certainty in accommodated scientific texts. Invention, as explored above, is always in relation to a purpose. Fahnestock explores this in relation to the following textual pair:

2(a)   The cheetah is unusual but not the only mammalian species with low levels of variation in blood profiles. The northern elephant seal, the moose, the polar bear, and the Yellowstone elk have been reported to have diminished levels of variation. (O'Brien et al., *Science*, 1983, p. 461)

2(b)   Such remarkably high levels of genetic uniformity are usually found only in specially bred laboratory mice. ('Copycat cheetahs', *Science '83*, p. 6)

Says Fahnestock:

> The scientist-authors of [2(a)] want to diminish the singularity of the phenomenon they have observed; because their purpose is to convince readers of the validity of their observation, the rarer the phenomenon is, the harder their job. Their observations are more plausible if other similar ones have been made, so they naturally cite analogous reports. But the science accommodator wants to make readers marvel at something, so he leaves out any mention of species that have shown similar genetic invariance and makes his subject seem more wonderful by claiming in effect: 'here we have animals in nature exhibiting the genetic conformity of those bred for that very quality in the laboratory'. The science accommodator is not telling an untruth; he simply selects only the information that serves his epideictic purpose. (1986: 281)

Style, too, plays an important role in this rhetorical analysis. The following textual pair show the persuasive purpose to which style can be put:

3(a)   The estimate is derived from two conventionally studied groups of genes; 47 allozyme (allelic isozyme) loci and 155 soluble proteins resolved by two dimensional gel electrophoresis . . . The entire cheetah sample was invariant at each of the 47 loci. (O'Brien et al., *Science*, 1983, p. 460)

3(b)   But all the cheetahs carried exactly the same form of every one of the 47 enzymes . . . In another test of more than 150 proteins, 97% of them matched in the cheetahs. ('Copycat cheetahs', *Science '83*, p. 6)

Fahnestock analyses the style of these two passages. While the original does not add editorial comments, the accommodated version uses 'intensifying phrases' such as 'more than 150' when the total is precisely 155, and 'exactly the same form of every one' instead of the neutral 'invariant'. Style, even at the level of word choice, in this particular case serves to highlight epideictic purposes in the text.

Finally, disposition, or the arrangement of arguments within texts, is important to this rhetorical analysis. Fahnestock chooses a report from *Science* which made its way into *Newsweek*, *Time*, *The New York Times*, *Reader's Digest* and a number of other popular forums for accommodated science. The report was entitled 'Sex differences in mathematical ability: fact or artifact?' *Time* had a quite different title indicating a degree of certainty about the answer to that question: 'The gender factor in math'. In the original report, the scientists assert that their data

4(a)   are consistent with numerous alternative hypotheses. Nonetheless, the hypothesis of differential course-taking was not supported. It also seems likely that putting one's faith in boy-versus-girl socialization processes as the only permissible explanation of the sex difference in mathematics is premature. (Benbow and Stanley, *Science*, 1980, p. 1264)

Time accommodates this in the following way:

4(b)   According to its authors, Doctoral Candidate Camilla Persson Benbow and Psychologist Julian C. Stanley of Johns Hopkins University, males inherently have more mathematical ability than females. ('The gender factor in math', *Time*, December 15th 1980, p. 57)

The structure of the arguments, their disposition, also reveals a persuasive purpose. Says Fahnestock:

The popularizations give some coverage to pre-existing viewpoints that differ from Benbow and Stanley's, but this attention differs in the effect it can have depending on whether or not the article ends with a disagreement or with a reiteration of Benbow and Stanley's position. If Benbow and Stanley have the 'last word' about anything, then it seems as if they have made a successful rebuttal of their opponents. In other words, although the newsweekly pieces may be following some journalistic principle of organization, inverted pyramid or 'I' structure, they inevitably have argumentative structure and by their arrangement influence, even create, the reader's opinion. (1986: 286)

This final example shows the ideological import of this type of analysis. Stylistic and formalistic features do have rhetorical and ideological impact. In short, the structure and style of discourse can have a persuasive, or rhetorical, aspect.

The rhetorical worldview

We have considered rhetoric as both the production of persuasive communication and the analysis of persuasive communication, but perhaps it is as important to understand that there is a worldview at work among rhetorical theorists and analysts about the nature of communication. Rhetoric is, at root, a dialectical process between representation and audience. Frequently, the authors or initiators of communication are not part of the rhetorical analysis. Once discourse enters a communication arena, it is no longer under full control of those who produced it. This is central to remember in analysis. But perhaps, it is equally important to those producing rhetorical discourse. Further, if we do accept that rhetoric has the ability to contour issues and even to construct issues of importance, we must acknowledge that rhetoric is part of the fabric of knowledge itself. What we know, we rhetorically package; what we rhetorically package, we say that we know.

This can be a dangerous or a liberatory stance, but it does push us to acknowledge that rhetoric is more than 'mere rhetoric'.

STEPS TO RHETORICAL ANALYSIS

While rhetorical analysis tends to resist codification and every analysis differs just as every text differs, the following guidelines are a useful starting point:

1 Establish the rhetorical situation for the discourse to be analysed.
2 Identify the types of persuasive discourse using stasis theory.
3 Apply the five rhetorical canons.
4 Review and refine analysis using the reflexive guidelines.

References

Bazerman, C. (1988) *Shaping Written Knowledge*. Madison, WI: University of Wisconsin Press.

Bitzer, L. (1968) 'The rhetorical situation', *Philosophy and Rhetoric*, 1 (1): 1–14.

Cole, T. (1991) *The Origins of Rhetoric in Ancient Greece*. Baltimore, MD : Johns Hopkins University Press.

Eco, U. (1979) *The Role of the Reader: exploration in the semiotics of texts*. Bloomington and London: Indiana University Press.

Fahnestock, J. (1986) 'Accommodating science: the rhetorical life of scientific facts', *Written Communication*, 3 (3): 275–96.

Fahnestock, J. (1999) *Figures of Argument*. London: Oxford University Press.

Gross, A. (1990) *The Rhetoric of Science*. London: Harvard University Press.

Gross, A. and Keith, B. (eds) (1997) *Rhetorical Hermeneutics: Invention and Interpretation in the Age of Science*. Albany, NY: SUNY Press.

Keller, E.F. (1995) *Refiguring Life: Metaphors of Twentieth-Century Biology*. New York: Columbia University Press.

Lipsitz, G. (1990) *Time Passages: Collective Memory and American Popular Culture*. Minneapolis, MN: University of Minnesota Press.

Martin, J.R. and Veel, R. (1998) *Reading Science: Functional Perspectives on Discourses of Science*. London: Routledge.

Montgomery, S. (1996) *The Scientific Voice*. London: Guilford.

Nelson, J., Megill, A. and McCloskey, D. (1987) *The Rhetoric of the Human Sciences*. Madison, WI: University of Wisconsin Press.

Poulakos, J. (1995) *Sophistical Rhetoric in Classical Greece*. Columbia, SC: University of South Carolina Press.

Rorty, R. (1979) *Philosophy and the Mirror of Nature*. Princeton, NJ: Princeton University Press.

Swales, J. (1983) 'Aspects of article introductions'. Aston University ESP Research Report, Birmingham.

Toulmin, S. (1958) *The Uses of Argument*. Cambridge: Cambridge University Press.

Watson, J.D. (1968) *The Double Helix*. New York: Athenaeum.

Further reading

Bazerman, C. and Paradis, J. (eds) (1991) *Textual Dynamics of the Professions.* Madison, WI: University of Wisconsin Press.

Corbett, E. (1965) *Classical Rhetoric for the Modern Student.* Oxford: Oxford University Press.

Meyer, M. (1994) *Rhetoric, Language, and Reason.* University Park, PA: Pennsylvania State University Press.

13

Semiotic Analysis of Still Images

Gemma Penn

KEYWORDS

anchorage	recuperation
connotation	referent system
denotation	relay
icon	sign
index	signified
lexicon	signifier
myth	symbol
paradigm or associative set	syntagm

Semiology has been applied to a range of sign systems, including menus, fashion, architecture, fairy-tales, consumer products and publicity of all kinds. This chapter looks at its application to images, and in particular to the advertising image.

Conceptual tools

Semiology provides the analyst with a conceptual toolkit for approaching sign systems systematically in order to discover how they produce meaning. Much of its precision derives from a series of theoretical distinctions, which are captured in a distinctive vocabulary. This section introduces these conceptual tools.

The linguistic sign system: signifier and signified

Semiology grew out of the discipline of structural linguistics that originated in the work of the Swiss linguist Ferdinand de Saussure (1857–1913). The structural approach sees language as a system and attempts to discover 'all the rules that hold it together' (Hawkes, 1977: 19). The linguistic system comprises units, which Saussure called *signs*, and the rules that govern their relationships. Saussure proposed a simple and elegant model of the linguistic sign as the arbitrary conjunction of a *signifier*, or sound-image, and a *signified*, or concept or idea. These two parts can be analysed as if they were separate entities, but they exist only as components of the sign, that is, by virtue of their relation to each other. Saussure begins his account of the nature of the sign by asserting that language is not nomenclature (1915: 66). The signified does not exist prior to and independently of language: it is not simply a matter of attaching a label to it.

Further, the relationship between the two elements is arbitrary or non-motivated. There is no natural or inevitable link between the two. My furry, bewhiskered pet, my 'cat', might just as happily be a 'frizz' if it was accepted as such by members of my speech community. Language is thus conventional, a social institution that the individual speaker is relatively powerless to change. Similarly, although more controversially, the concept referred to by a particular signifier may change.

Saussure's key insight was the relativity of meaning. He summarizes the argument as follows:

> Instead of pre-existing ideas then, we find . . . *values* emanating from the system. When they are said to correspond to concepts, it is understood that the concepts are purely differential and defined not by their positive content but negatively by their relations with the other terms of the system. Their most precise character is in being what the others are not. (1915: 117)

Thus, a language comprising a single term is not possible: it would encompass everything and exclude nothing; that is, it would not differentiate anything from anything else; and without difference there is no meaning. To take an example: imagine a person who does not 'know about' hats. Now imagine teaching him what a beret is. It will not be sufficient to show him a beret, or a whole collection of berets. He will only be able to grasp the meaning of 'beret' when taught to distinguish a beret from other kinds of hat: deerstalkers, tam-o'-shanters, flat caps and so on.

Saussure distinguishes two types of relationship within the linguistic system. The value of a term within a text depends on the contrasts with alternative terms which have not been chosen (*paradigmatic* or *associative* relations) and on the relations with the other terms which precede and follow it (*syntagmatic* relations). A paradigm, or associative set, is a group of terms which are both related or similar in some respect, and different. The meaning of a term is delimited by the set of unchosen terms and by the way in which the chosen terms are combined with each other to create a meaningful whole. This may be clarified with an example. The sentence 'Alice's hat is green' constitutes a meaningful whole by virtue of the conjunction of a series of linguistic terms (informally, words). The value of each term is determined by its place in the syntagm, that is, by the other terms in the sentence which precede and follow it, and by the set of alternative terms which might replace it. This can be illustrated as follows:

	People	Clothing	'to be'	Colour
		←Syntagm→		
↑	Alice's	hat	is	green
Paradigm	My	coat	isn't	yellow
↓	The vicar's	pyjamas	were	pink

Saussure proposed that the study of the linguistic sign system would be one part of a wider discipline, which he designated semiology: 'a science that studies the life of signs within society' (1915: 16). The linguistic sign system would be the model for the analysis of other sign systems.

Language and non-linguistic sign systems

Barthes, to my mind, provides the clearest and most useful exposition of this new discipline in relation to the analysis of images. Whereas Saussure posited a special place for linguistics within semiology, Barthes begins his *Elements of Semiology* by inverting the relationship. Semiology is more usefully considered a part of linguistics, 'that part covering the *great signifying unities* of discourse' (1964a: 11). While images, objects and behaviours can and do signify, they never do so autonomously: 'every semiological system has its linguistic admixture'. For example, the meaning of a visual image is anchored by accompanying text, and by the status of objects, such as food or clothing, as sign systems require 'the relay of language, which extracts their signifiers (in the form of nomenclature) and names their signifieds (in the form of usages or reasons)'.

Rather than treat this as a philosophical argument about the relationship between thought and language, it is better taken as a pragmatic prescription. Whatever the medium of study, the analysis will usually require language for precise expression. For example, the stages in the progression of modern art can be seen as an evolving commentary, purely visual, on the nature and function of art and on its predecessors. The 'thought equals language' position would say that meaning only enters the system when it is articulated verbally, through interpretation or criticism. The pragmatic position would not deny the signifying potential of the visual medium, but would argue that it is only anchored or clarified in the linguistic medium. Another way of looking at this is through the signifier/signified distinction. The signifier, in whatever medium, points to a signified. But the signifieds of different media are of the same nature, clearly not reducible to their media of expression.

This highlights one important difference between language and images: the image is always polysemic, or ambiguous. This is why most images are accompanied by some form of text: text disambiguates the image – a relationship Barthes referred to as *anchorage*, in contrast to the more reciprocal relationship of *relay*, where both image and text contribute to the overall meaning. Images differ from language in another important way for the semiologist: in both written and spoken language, signs appear sequentially. In images, however, the signs are present simultaneously. Their syntagmatic relations are spatial rather than temporal.

A second important difference between language and images relates to the distinction between arbitrary and motivated. C.S. Peirce (1934), who developed an alternative, tripartite model of the sign (comprising object, sign or 'representamen', and interpretant, and usually referred to as semiotics), makes a relevant distinction (again triadic) between *icon*, *index* and *symbol*.

A further way of addressing the question of motivation is provided by Barthes's distinction between different levels of signification: the denotational or first level is literal, or motivated, while higher levels are more arbitrary, relying on cultural conventions. The relationship between the signifier and signified in the icon is one of resemblance. The photograph, for example, re-presents its subject more or less faithfully and is thus the least arbitrary or conventional type of sign. In the indexical sign, the relationship between signifier and signified is one of contiguity or causality. Thus, smoke is an index of fire and a stethoscope stands indexically for the doctor or medical profession. The role of convention is more important here. Finally, in the symbol, the relationship between signifier and signified is purely arbitrary. A red rose signifies love, and a red triangle on a UK traffic sign signifies warning, purely by convention.

Levels of signification: denotation, connotation and myth

In his outline of semiology (1964a) and mythologies (1957), Barthes describes what he calls 'second-order semiological systems'. These build on Saussure's structural analysis of the sign as the association of signifier and signified. The sign of this first-order system becomes the signifier of the second. In the first system, for example, the sign 'fox' comprises the association of a certain sound-image and a certain concept (reddish-coloured canine with a bushy tail, etc.). In the second order, this association becomes the signifier to the signified: sly or cunning. The first-order sign need not be linguistic. For example, a cartoon of a fox would serve equally well. Barthes illustrates the relationship between the two systems using the spatial metaphor shown in Figure 13.1.

Although the sign of the first order is 'full', when it takes part in the second-order system it is empty. It becomes a vehicle for signification. It expresses a further concept, not derived from the sign itself, but from conventional, cultural knowledge. This is the point at which the psychological user of the system makes his or her entry. In *The Rhetoric of the Image* (1964b), Barthes distinguishes the types of knowledge required to 'grasp' the signification at each level.

At the first level, which Barthes refers to as *denotation*, the reader requires only linguistic and anthropological knowledges. At the second level, which he calls *connotation*, the reader requires further cultural knowledges.

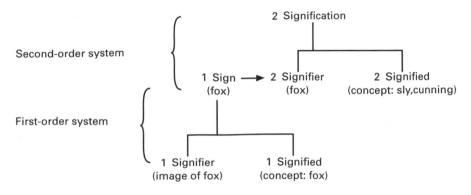

Figure 13.1 *Spatial metaphor of the relationship between first- and second-order sign systems (adapted from Barthes, 1957: 124)*

Barthes calls these knowledges *lexicons*. He defines a lexicon as a 'portion of the symbolic plane (of language) which corresponds to a body of practices and techniques' (1964b: 46). It may be practical, national, cultural or aesthetic, and can be classified. Other researchers use different terminology to refer to broadly the same thing, a socially shared interpretive resource: for example, Williamson (1978) uses the term *referent system*. The reader's interpretational freedom is dependent upon the number and identity of his or her lexicons. The act of reading a text or an image is thus a constructive process. Meaning is generated in the interaction of the reader with the material. The reader's meaning will vary with the knowledges available to him or her through experience and contextual salience. Some readings may be pretty much universal within a culture; others will be more idiosyncratic.

One form of second-order signification to which Barthes devoted much attention was that of myth. For Barthes, myth represents an unpardonable confusion of history and nature. Myth is the means by which a culture naturalizes, or renders invisible, its own norms and ideology.

> The mythological or ideological significance of a message pertains to systems of representation that often appear neutral and objectivated but which legitimate and sustain the power structure or a particular set of cultural values. (Curran, 1976: 9)

For example, in relation to the photographic advertising image, the denoted or literal message serves to naturalize the connoted message. That is, the work of interpretation, or grasping the connotation of the image, is under-lain and held together by the brute fact of the syntagm of denotation: the conjunction of the objects in the scene is natural or given, because it requires no translation, no decoding (Barthes, 1964a: 51). The semiologist's task is to demystify or 'unmask' this process of naturalization by drawing attention to the constructed nature of the image, for example, by identifying the cultural knowledges that are implicitly referred to by the image, or by contrasting the chosen signs with other members of their paradigmatic sets.

Undertaking a semiological analysis

In overview, the process of analysis can be described as dissection followed by articulation, or the reconstruction of the semanticized image, or 'intellect added to object' (George and George, 1972: 150). The aim is to make explicit the cultural knowledges which are required in order for the reader to understand the image.

Choosing material

The first stage is to choose the images to be analysed. The choice will depend upon the purpose of the study and the availability of material. For example, it is often time-consuming to track down specific advertisements or campaign materials that are no longer current. Semiotic analyses can be quite verbose – anything from a fair-sized paragraph to several pages – which will limit the quantity of material chosen. A further constraining factor is the nature of the material. Put simply, some materials are more amenable to semiotic analysis than others. If the purpose of the analysis is to provide an account of a representative sample of material, then appropriate (random) sampling should be employed, and any difficulties in applying semiological techniques should be acknowledged.

The material chosen here for the purposes of critical discussion is a contemporary perfume advertisement (Figure 13.2) from a national newspaper magazine. Barthes (1964b: 33) justifies the use of advertising for didactic purposes on the grounds that the signs in advertising are intentional and will thus be clearly defined, or 'graspable'. We also know that the intention will be to promote the reputation and sales of the product. This frees the analyst to concentrate on *how* rather than *what*.

A denotational inventory

The second stage is to identify the elements in the material. This may be done by listing the constituents systematically, or by annotating a tracing of the material (see Figure 13.3). Most commercial material contains both text and images, and neither should be ignored. It is important that the inventory is complete as the systematic approach helps to ensure that the analysis is not selectively self-confirming. This is the denotational stage of analysis: the cataloguing of the literal meaning of the material. All that is required is a knowledge of the appropriate language and what Barthes refers to as basic 'anthropological' knowledge. For the present material, our basic inventory would look something like this:

Text: 'Givenchy', 'Organza'
Image: bottle (of perfume), woman, background

Figure 13.2   *The Givenchy advertisement*

Each element may be dissected into smaller units. For example, the textual elements comprise two types of component at the level of denotation. The first is linguistic: the words 'Givenchy' and 'Organza', which both appear twice. Both are names: one a company name and the other a brand name. In addition the brand name, 'Organza', denotes a type of fabric – a thin, stiff silk or synthetic dress fabric. The second component of the textual elements is visual: typographical and spatial. For example, 'Givenchy' appears centre top and is upper case, dark red, widely spaced, sanserif and roman.

The same may be done for the images. For example, the woman is standing, facing forward with one knee slightly raised, just overlapping the bottle. She is slim with an 'hourglass' figure, light brown (tanned?) skin, and dark hair and so on.

Higher levels of signification

The third stage is the analysis of higher-order levels of signification. This will build on the denotational inventory and will ask of each element a

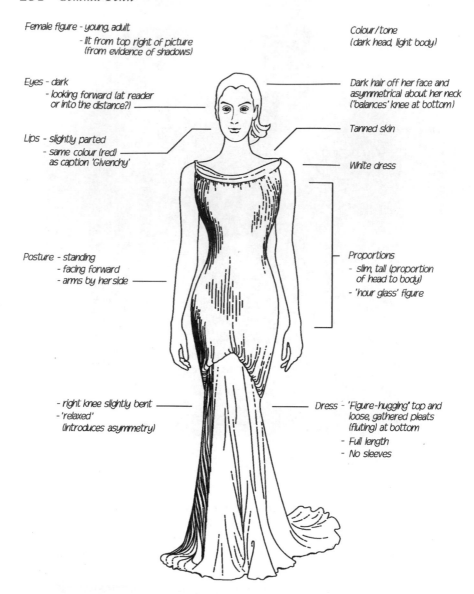

Female figure - young, adult
- lit from top right of picture
(from evidence of shadows)

Colour/tone
(dark head, light body)

Eyes - dark
- looking forward (at reader
or into the distance?)

Dark hair off her face and
asymmetrical about her neck
('balances' knee at bottom)

Tanned skin

Lips - slightly parted
- same colour (red)
as caption 'Givenchy'

White dress

Posture - standing
- facing forward
- arms by her side

Proportions
- slim, tall (proportion
of head to body)
- 'hour glass' figure

- right knee slightly bent
- 'relaxed'
(introduces asymmetry)

Dress - 'Figure-hugging' top and
loose, gathered pleats
(fluting) at bottom
- Full length
- No sleeves

Figure 13.3   *An annotated tracing of the female figure*

series of related questions. What does it connote (what associations are brought to mind)? How do the elements relate to each other (internal correspondences, contrasts, etc.)? What cultural knowledges are required in order to read the material?

At the level of denotation, all the reader requires to read the advertisement is a knowledge of written and spoken language and a knowledge of what a woman and a perfume bottle are. At the level of connotation, we require several further cultural knowledges. In relation to the linguistic code, the reader is required to 'know' that the company name 'Givenchy' signifies 'Frenchness' – at least to English ears. This, in turn, may connote high fashion and 'chic'. 'Fashion' may also be connoted by the fabric name 'Organza', and the sound of the word may call to mind a number of potential connotations: 'organic', perhaps, or 'extravaganza', or even 'orgasm'.

In relation to the typography of 'Givenchy', that of 'Organza' appears personalized (brushscript = handwritten) and thus individualized. 'Givenchy' is generic (the company name) while 'Organza' is specific (the brand name). This relationship is also signified by the layout of the advertisement. 'Givenchy' is the overarching heading, whereas 'Organza' appears in a subordinate position. The handwritten typography also suggests an afterthought: a caption supplied to the already complete image. The Z is drawn with a flourish and the letters are clearly formed italicized capitals, suggesting perhaps flair, optimism and extroversion.

Note that here the idea of paradigmatic choices is used implicitly. It is through the comparison of the choices that are present with each other, and with the potential choices that are absent (the unchosen), as well as with the combination of choices, that the value of each element is created. This may be expressed explicitly:

		Case	Orientation	Letter proportion	Typeface style
			←Syntagm→		
↑	GIVENCHY	upper case	roman	expanded	sanserif
Paradigm	ORGANZA	upper/lower case	italicized	condensed	brushscript
↓	UNCHOSEN	lower case	backslant	regular	serif etc.

In moving to the connotational or second order of signification, something of the specificity of the denoted, literal message is lost. The specific woman loses her individuality and becomes an instance of a glamorous model. She is recognized not by anything idiosyncratic or personal, but by her tall slim body, her posture, etc. We can note straight away the intended equivalence between the woman and the bottle: they are both about the same height; both have a 'head' and a 'body' in similar proportions, with the 'heads' darker than the 'bodies'. The 'anatomy' of the woman is reproduced in the shape of the bottle, together with the fluted texture of her dress. Both are slightly asymmetrical. These correspondences suggest their equivalence: the connotations of fashion and glamour are transferred from the model to the brand (the perfume is the woman).

Besides implying that the woman and the bottle are equivalent, it is also possible to draw on particular cultural knowledge to further interpret the image. For example, it occurs to me that the woman is intended to resemble a caryatid (see Figure 13.4) and thus brings with her classical connotations of ancient Greece. The correspondence between the model and the caryatid may be spelled out: both are female figures, standing upright and facing

Figure 13.4   *The caryatid and female figure*

forward with one knee slightly raised. The style of the dresses is similar: both are full-length, without sleeves. The fabric appears to be tucked in around the middle and hangs in pleats to the floor. The pleated effect in the dress and bottle may also recall the fluting that appears on many Greek columns, which are functionally equivalent to caryatids.

If this hypothesis is correct, then it is possible to treat the differences between the two as intended, as significant paradigmatic choices. Perhaps the most noticeable difference between the two is in their respective proportions or build. The paradigmatic set here is possible body shape: slim, athletic, curvaceous, etc. The model is considerably slimmer than the caryatid. This is accentuated by the closer fitting top of the model's dress. Two hypotheses present themselves to explain the difference. The first is simply that, besides being a representation of a woman, the caryatid is also a load-bearing architectural feature. The second, and probably more obvious, hypothesis is that the model's proportions signify the modern ideal of elegance and beauty: the etiolated and sometimes controversial catwalk model (displaying 'fashioned' fabrics – perhaps organza). The image modernizes the Greek ideal. However, the strong correspondence between the two figures connotes a perennial or 'classical' (and thus natural) image of beauty.

The reason for raising the first hypothesis is that some elements of an image may be simply a function of technical or financial constraints. For example, when photosetting superseded typesetting, graphics artists were keen to exploit the potential of this new technology and there was a vogue for unusual and especially 'squashed' letter spacing. A more recent example of technologically driven innovation is the computer-generated 'morphed' image.

The reference system of the caryatid places the advertisement within the world of classical Greece. A second set of signifiers shifts the location eastwards. The background with its golden colours and gently rippled texture suggests the sand of the desert. The other key signifier of the desert, the sun, is suggested by its effect: the bronzed skin tones of the model. More fancifully, the decorative bottle top may recall the hieroglyph for the Egyptian sun-god Ra: a snake entwined around the sun. A further Eastern myth aids this more exotic relocation. The equivalence between the bottle and the model suggests that the model may be read as the spirit of the bottle – the genie of the lamp – thus promising wish-fulfilment to the purchaser (the model is the perfume).

When to stop?

Theoretically, the process of analysis is never exhaustive and thus never complete. That is, it is always possible to find a new way of reading an image, or a new lexicon or referent system to apply to the image. However, for practical purposes, the analyst will usually want to declare the analysis finished at some point. If the analysis has been undertaken to demonstrate a specific point – for example, to investigate the workings of a particular myth structure – then the analyst will be justified in confining himself or herself to relevant aspects of the material. In more inclusive analyses, one

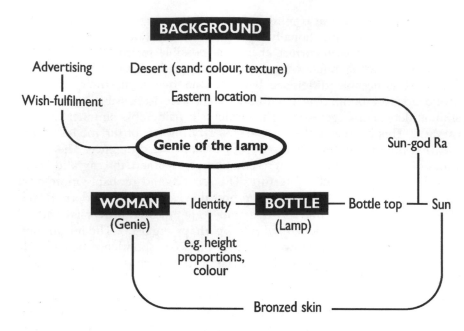

Figure 13.5   *An example of a mindmap*

way of ensuring that an analysis is relatively complete is to construct a matrix of all the identified elements and to check that the two-way relationships between each pair of elements have at least been considered ('What does element A signify in the context of element B, and vice versa?'). A more flexible way of examining the relationships among the elements, illustrated in Figure 13.5, is to construct a 'mindmap' around the denotational inventory. This allows for the identification of relationships among more than two elements at a time.

Doubtless the attentive analyst of the present advertisement will identify further signs in addition to those discussed here. I shall mention only one more. This final signifier comprises the whole advertisement and its signified is simply: 'this is an advertisement'. The juxtaposition of product and brand name recalls a hundred thousand such commercial communications (this is also signified by its placing within such a magazine, and by features such as the omission of a page number). More than this, through its Spartan simplicity and minimal text, the present advertisement signifies: 'This is a modern advertisement.' As Leiss et al. (1997: 199) observe, advertisements of an earlier era would have included an explanatory text, to orient the reader to the image, and to educate him or her in the ways of reading such an image. The present advertisement assumes that the image requires no such textual mediation or anchorage. Curiously, this final sign undermines the enterprise of semiology itself, suggesting that present-day advertising assumes a semiologically astute readership.

Table 13.1 *An example of tabular presentation of findings*

Denotation	Syntagm	Connotation/myth	Cultural knowledge
Female figure: posture, clothing, etc. Perfume bottle: proportions, 'fluting', etc.	Equivalence suggested by: asymmetrical 'hourglass' proportions; tone, e.g. dark 'head' and light 'body'; size, adjacent location, etc.	Classical elegance Perennial (and natural) beauty	Greek architecture: caryatid fluted columns

Reporting

There is no one way of presenting the results of semiological analyses. Some researchers like tables (see Table 13.1); others prefer a more discursive approach. Ideally, the presented analyses should make reference to each level of signification identified in both the image and the text (denotation and connotation/myth), and identify the cultural knowledge required in order to produce the reading. They should also comment on the ways in which the elements of the material relate to each other. For example, analyses may be structured by the higher-order signs identified in the material, stating the constituent signifiers and their syntagmatic relations for each.

Criticisms of semiology

Subjectivity: idiosyncratic and culturally shared readings

Critics argue that semiology is only capable of offering impressionistic insights into the construction of meaning, and that there is no guarantee that different analysts will produce similar accounts. This objection taps into one of the perennial debates of media studies: to what extent is meaning in the mind of the beholder? The consensus has shifted several times in the past few decades, between the extreme poles of the hypodermic needle approach which casts readers in a more or less passive role, dependent upon the image, and a vision of an endlessly creative reader, largely unconstrained by the image. The truth, no doubt, lies somewhere between these two extremes. Some readings, both denotational and connotational, will be pretty much universal while others will be more idiosyncratic. On the one hand, it would be expected that readers would agree that Figure 13.2 includes a bottle of perfume and a woman. If someone were to claim that the images were of a jar of peanut butter and a fish, we might reasonably question their sanity, eyesight or sincerity. That is, the image constrains potential readings. On the other hand, a reader might claim that the woman resembles a friend and that this similarity 'colours' the associations that spring to mind. In this case, the reading is merely idiosyncratic. Barthes's concept of the lexicon is useful here. What will be most important to the analyst is not the idiosyncratic, but the culturally shared associations and myths that readers employ.

Leiss and colleagues (1997: 214) raise a further issue of subjectivity. They note that the quality of the analysis is heavily dependent upon the skill of the analyst. They say that in the hands of a skilled analyst such as Roland Barthes or Judith Williamson:

> It is a creative tool that allows one to reach the deeper levels of meaning-construction in ads. A less skilful practitioner, however, can do little more than state the obvious in a complex and often pretentious manner. (1997: 214)

Their argument is that the importance of the analyst's skill militates against the possibility of establishing consistency and reliability, in the form of agreement among analysts. Other critics go further. Cook (1992: 71), for example, objects to the general tone of semiological accounts as claiming superior insight or truth. In some respects this is a stylistic point, and perhaps the social scientist should be cautious about displaying too much literary flair and should present analyses with more humility. However, Cook is also uneasy about the use of the metaphors 'deep' and 'surface', and the tendency to abstraction that results from prioritizing 'deep' levels of meaning.

Abstraction and mystification

Semiological accounts recognize the relationship between 'surface content' and 'interpretive content' in the distinctions between denotation and con-notation and between signifier and signified. However, much semiological research places greater emphasis on connotation and the signified. Cook (1992: 70–1) argues that the quest for hidden myths blinds the researcher to surface detail and structure. For example, advertisements are not remem-bered as abstract entities. Their minutiae are essential: detail and style are just as important as underlying myth. As Barthes (1964a: 45) puts it, there is always something left when one strips an advertisement of its messages: 'the message without a code'. A lizard crawls across a ringing telephone in a television advertisement for the chocolate bar Flake: here, the lizard may be a metaphor, but it is also a very concrete animal. Sift out the myth and you are still left with a lizard, representing itself, and this lizard is part of what is remembered by the reader, and what is lost in the process of abstraction.

The essence of this criticism is that the analysis aims at a unified statement of underlying meaning, and that this ignores surface variation and contradiction. It reduces myriad complexity to a handful of abstract dimensions. Leach comments upon the mythological analyses of Lévi-Strauss: 'at this point, some English readers may begin to suspect that the whole argument was an elaborate academic joke' (1970: 31). Yes, Lévi-Strauss has shown that it is possible to deconstruct complex social dis-courses into neat matrices of fundamental dimensions, but this is only possible by leaving out what is characterized as 'non-essential'. Similarly, Leiss et al. (1997) applaud Barthes and Williamson for their close analyses of detail, but they criticize the abstractions that Williamson presents in the second half of her book: they are banal and lacking in specifics. In a practical sense, they are not very practical.

In this way, Cook's and Leiss et al.'s criticism wrests the semiological account from its tendency to focus on the signified at the expense of the signifier, and on higher orders of signification at the expense of denotation. The detail should not be seen as purely secondary, dependent upon the myth structure: it is important in its own right, and especially useful as a potential social index. For example, the model's suntan in the Givenchy advertisement is an index of current ideals of beauty. A suntan connotes leisure in the contemporary Western world; whereas during the Regency period, say, it connoted outdoor labour, and the genteel, leisured classes adopted elaborate means of avoiding tanning. To conclude, an analysis should be reciprocal. Abstraction should feed into concretization, and vice versa. The irony of this otherwise well-made point is that detailed accounts of denotation tend to state the obvious and, of course, eat into the 'word count' budget.

Ecological validity and the problem of recuperation

Ordinarily we do not scrutinize images for their implicit cultural meanings. If the everyday reader does not engage with images in the painstaking and systematic manner of the semiologist, then what is the relevance of the semiologist's account? One answer may be precision: the semiological account sharpens and makes explicit that which is implicit in the image. For example, the casual reader may grasp the classical connotations of Figure 13.2 without recourse to the notion of a caryatid. Quite often we have only a vague sense of familiarity. Indeed, this vague familiarity is often intended. References that are too precise may distract the reader from the myth-work that an image is intended to accomplish: in the case of advertising, the transfer of meaning from the image to the product. The semiologist therefore performs the valuable task of drawing attention to the constructed nature of the image.

Barthes championed demystification as a means to political action, with sarcasm and irony as the principal tools. However, myth-makers, such as advertisers, always have a ready-made alibi: the simple denial of second-order meaning, or its intention. More interestingly, criticism entails a contribution to myth, a certain complicity with the object of scrutiny. In critiquing, say, the Marlboro Man, the mythologist merely adds another twist to his fame and endurance: he becomes an academic icon. That is, more often than not, criticism is recuperated by the myth itself and made to work for the myth.

This recuperative ability derives from the often-noted 'protean' quality of myths. This quality is the result of the draining of the content and history of the first-order sign so that it becomes an empty vehicle for second-order signification. In this way, anything may be used as a signifier of myth, and the myth is able to assimilate or deflect criticism. An example of recuperation at work can be found in some advertisements for filtered brands of cigarettes in the 1960s and 1970s which were produced in response to the scientific findings of the health risks of smoking. These advertisements used scientific imagery, typically in the form of a dissected cigarette in the style of the scientific diagram: a simple line drawing with textbook-style annotations. In this way the scientific criticism of cigarettes is turned back on itself: the problem is scientific and so, apparently, is the solution.

This suggests that a naive, Rumpelstiltskin-style approach is inadequate: it is not sufficient merely to name the myth. The simple act of naming a myth, however, is not without its critical value. Naming denaturalizes the myth, making it more tangible: it becomes a 'thing' to be manipulated and criticized (whose interests does it serve?). That is, naming is an essential first step in the process of criticism, but it is not sufficient in itself. Sontag addresses a similar problem in her analysis of the metaphors of illness. She argues that 'metaphors cannot be distanced just by abstaining from them. They have to be exposed, criticised, belaboured, used up' (1991: 179). In addition, Sontag proposes that the process of identifying and criticizing metaphors should be guided by the effects of the metaphors: 'Not all metaphors applied to illnesses and their treatments are equally unsavoury and distorting' (1991: 179). However, this simply postpones the critical question: which metaphors or myths? And, who should decide?

Perhaps even more important than providing semiological accounts of images is the cultivation of a critical approach: the communication of the means to criticism and an understanding of the means by which propagandists of all complexions contest mythological space. While it may be argued that this in itself is propaganda on behalf of a critical academic discipline with vested interests, it might just as readily be contended that if such an approach were realized, the academic discipline would become redundant. This is not to deny the value of 'off-the-peg' critiques: people's time for such critical reflection is limited in comparison with the infinite possibilities of semiological analyses.

Hybridizing semiology

This final section provides a brief discussion of two potential ways of addressing some of the problems identified above. The integration of semiology with interactive data gathering techniques offers one means of addressing the problem of subjectivity by reinstating the lay reader. The potential for a *rapprochement* with content analytic techniques addresses a different aspect of the problem of subjectivity by emphasizing a systematic approach to sampling and analysis.

Communicative validation: interviews and focus groups

In order to assess the extent and use of socially shared cultural knowledges within a given group of people, semiology may be combined with some form of interactive data gathering. Focus groups or interviews are the obvious choice, and the interviewer's job will be to focus participants' attention on the material without leading their responses. This is best done by asking general questions such as 'What do you think this picture is about?', and requiring participants to be precise about the aspects of the material that give them a particular impression. The subjective nature of reading should be stressed to help participants relax: the exercise is not a test or guessing game. The researcher can also ask about specific aspects of the material: 'Why do you think they've used this colour here? What impression does it create?'

As usual, interviews should be recorded and the researcher should ensure that references to parts of the material are explicit for later reference. This is made easier if a video recording of the material is made, and participants are encouraged to point to the relevant part of the material as they speak. The transcript would then be coded thematically, perhaps with reference to a prior semiological account.

Content analysis

Semiology and content analysis are often held to be radically different analytic tools, but, as both Leiss et al. (1997) and Curran (1976) argue, there is plenty of scope for a *rapprochement*. Semiologists may import the systematic sampling procedures of content analysis. This will go some way towards addressing the criticisms that the approach manufactures self-confirming results and that it is not legitimate to generalize the conclusions of a semiological analysis to other material. The sharper systematization of analysis that content analysis advocates may also help the semiologist to combat charges of selectivity (for example in generating denotational inventories and matrices of potential syntagms). The resulting analyses should be more reliable (replicable) and less prone to the idiosyncrasies and skill of a given analyst.

In addition, the inclusion of more interpretive codes (based on connotation rather than denotation) in content analyses is evidence of the reciprocal influence of semiology. However, such analyses lose the structural aspects of a purely semiological approach: how meaning is created in the spatial relationships among elements within the individual image. However, this manner of exposition, even in the hands of the most adept and laconic of researchers, requires a vast amount of space if the analysis is to cover even a fraction of the standard sample size routinely entertained by the content analyst. The major obstacle to a complete integration of the two approaches is thus logistical. The solution might be to employ the two approaches side-by-side. A semiological account of a small sample of images may exemplify different content analytic codes. For example, a content analytic code relating to, say, 'myths of beauty', applied quantitatively to a large sample of advertisements, might be illustrated qualitatively by a semiological account of the present advertisement. This account would be partial in that it would focus on relevant aspects of the image rather than analyse the entire advertisement. It would enhance the transparency of the content analytic procedure by making the method and criteria of coding explicit and open to examination by the reader.

STEPS IN SEMIOLOGICAL ANALYSIS

1   Choose the images to be analysed. Identify appropriate sources of material. What kind of material is most suitable for addressing the research question? How can it be accessed? Contemporary or historical? For example, media archives, commercially available material, download from the Internet? Select the sample: how much material? Account for constraints of time and available reporting space. What are appropriate selection criteria? Are findings to be generalized beyond the sample; if so, to what? Make criteria for non-random sampling explicit and comment on how the resulting sample is unrepresentative, e.g. seasonal effects.

2   Compile a denotational inventory – a systematic survey of the literal contents of the material. Include all text (linguistics and typography) and images. Create a list or annotate the material. This helps the analyst familiarize himself/herself with the material and combats the selectivity problem. It also highlights the process of construction of the image. Add detail: while it is not possible to provide an exhaustive account, it is important to be as precise and comprehensive as possible. The process of translation into language can help identify less obvious aspects of composition and content that contribute to overall signification. Note size, colour, location, etc. of all elements. Paradigmatic reconstruction: what are the unchosen alternatives for each identified element? Absent alternatives contribute to signification by delimiting the meaning of the chosen elements.

3   Examine higher levels of signification: connotation, myth and referent systems. What do the elements connote? Which constituent elements contribute to each identified higher-order sign? Identify the cultural knowledges to which the images refer and by which they are interpreted. Different elements may be polysemic, and may contribute to more than one higher-order sign. The cultural knowledge and values that are assumed in the reader may be used to 'reconstruct' the 'ideal' reader or identify social indices. Syntagm: how do the elements relate to each other? Correspondences, contrasts? Cues to emphasis and relationships, e.g. colour, size, positioning? How does the text relate to the image? Anchorage, relay? Redundancy?

4   Decide when to stop. Has the analysis addressed the research question? Check that all elements of the denotational index are included and that their interrelationships have been considered, e.g. matrix, mindmap.

5   Select reporting forms. Choose presentation format, e.g. table, text and structure. Include references to each level of signification: denotation, connotation, myth and the referent systems required to grasp higher levels of signification. Note how elements are related. When several analyses are presented, especially for comparative purposes, it may be helpful to indicate their relationship, e.g. by employing the same structure for each analysis.

References

Barthes, R. (1957) *Mythologies* (trans. A. Lavers, 1973). London: Paladin.

Barthes, R. (1964a) *Elements of Semiology* (trans. A. Lavers and C. Smith, 1967). New York: Hill and Wang.

Barthes, R. (1964b) *The Rhetoric of the Image: Image, Music, Text* (trans. S. Heath, 1977). London: Fontana.

Cook, G. (1992) *The Discourse of Advertising*. London and New York: Routledge.

Curran, J. (1976) 'Content and structuralist analysis of mass communication'. Social Psychology project, Open University.

George, R.T. de and George, F.M. de (1972) *The Structuralists: from Marx to Lévi-Strauss*. New York: Anchor.

Hawkes, T. (1977) *Structuralism and Semiotics*. London: Routledge.

Leach, E. (1970) *Lévi-Strauss*. London: Fontana.

Leiss, W., Kline, S. and Jhally, S. (1997) *Social Communication in Advertising: Persons, Products and Images of Well-Being*, 2nd edn. New York: Routledge.

Peirce, C.S. (1934) *Collected Papers, Volume 5*. Cambridge, MA: Harvard University Press.

Saussure, F. de (1915) *Course in General Linguistics* (trans. W. Baskin). New York: The Philosophical Library, 1959; New York: McGraw-Hill, 1966.

Sontag, S. (1991) *Illness as Metaphor and AIDS and its Metaphors*. London: Penguin.

Williamson, J. (1978) *Decoding Advertisements: Ideology and Meaning in Advertising*. London: Marion Boyars.

14

Analysis of Moving Images

Diana Rose

KEYWORDS

coding
narrative

representation
translation

In this chapter, I will discuss a method for analysing television and other audiovisual material. The method was developed specifically to look at representations of madness on television and, inevitably, some of what I have to say will be specific to that topic. However, much of it has a more general application in that it consists of a set of concepts and techniques that can guide the analysis of many social representations in the audio-visual world.

Part of the general applicability of the method derives from its theoretical foundation. Indeed, conceptual argument is critical at each point in the development of the technique. I shall begin, therefore, by saying something about the theoretical foundations of this method, confining myself at this point to the most general level.

What precisely are audiovisual media like television? Is television like radio with pictures? I would argue not. Apart from the fact that radio itself is not simple, audiovisual media are a complex amalgam of meanings, images, techniques, shot framing, shot sequence and much more. It is therefore imperative to take this complexity into account when carrying out an analysis of its content and structure.

Every step in the process of analysing audiovisual materials involves translation. And every translation involves decisions and choices. There will always be viable alternatives to the positive choices made, and what is left out is as important as what is present. Choice in a multiple field is especially important when analysing a complex medium where translation will usually take the form of simplification.

There can never be an analysis that captures a single truth of the text. For instance, in transcribing televisual material, decisions have to be made about how to describe the visuals, whether to include pauses and hesitations in speech, and how to describe special effects such as music or changes in lighting. Different theoretical orientations will lead to different choices about what to select for transcription, as I shall show below.

As already argued, there is no way to collect, transcribe and code a data set that will be 'true' to the original text. The question then is to be as explicit as possible about the means that have been used for the various modes of translation and simplification. Bernstein (1995) has suggested that we call the text 'L1' (the L standing for language) and the coding frame 'L2'. The resultant analysis is then an interaction between L1 and L2. It is a translation from one language to another and, for Bernstein, it has rules or procedures. The problem with this model is that it assumes only two steps. Or, perhaps, it assumes that processes of selecting, transcribing and coding data can be seen as a single language. However, the distinction does make clear that there can be no simple reflection of the data set in the final analysis. Processes of translation do not produce simple copies but proceed interactively to a new outcome.

Let us take an example, again from the field of transcription. Potter and Wetherell (1987) have proposed a method for transcribing speech. They make much of the importance of describing pauses and hesitations and the length of these silences in their description. Is this 'truer' than a simple word-for-word transcription? I would argue not. What about inflection and cadence (see, for example, Crystal and Quirk, 1964)? And more important for present purposes, what about the visual aspects of communication? Kinesics is an approach described by Birdwhistell (1970) but rarely used. It describes the non-verbal dimensions of communication. An emphasis on speech or discourse can never include these features. Saussure recognized this long ago when he said that semiotics is the science of signs, and signs are not limited to the realms of speech and writing.

To turn to the analysis of media, Wearing (1993), following Potter and Wetherell, analysed press reports of a murderer deemed to be insane. The analysis stayed wholly at the level of the text, ignoring layout, headlines, photographs and positioning in relation to other stories. Wearing insisted that a new portrayal had been produced by the intertwining of two discourses – the journalistic and the psychiatric. We have to say that media representations are more than discourses. They are a complex amalgam of text, written or spoken, visual images and various techniques for inflecting and sequencing the speech, the pictures and the positioning of these two.

The point is not that there is a way of capturing all these nuances to produce a truer representation. It is rather that some information will always be lost, other information may be added, and so the process of analysing speech and pictures is like a translation from one language to another. At the same time, it will usually entail a simplification when the immediate text is as complex as television. The end product will usually be a simplification as well – a set of illustrative extracts, a table of frequencies.

There are cases where analysis exceeds the text, in both length and complexity. Many works of literary criticism take this form, Barthes's (1975) *S/Z* being a case in point. In the work of Birdwhistell (1970), mentioned above, it took two years and a whole book to analyse a two-minute sequence of a person lighting and smoking a cigarette. Perhaps this shows the absurdity of trying to capture everything intrinsic to the immediate text in the analytic work.

Further, and as already argued, televisual materials are not defined by text alone. The visual dimension involves techniques of camera and direction that are only secondarily textual. They produce meanings, to be sure, but these meanings are generated by specialist techniques.

Rather than aim for an impossible perfection, we need to be very explicit about the techniques we use to select, transcribe and analyse data. If these techniques are made explicit, then the reader has a better opportunity of judging the analysis that has been undertaken. Because of the nature of translation, there will always be space for opposition and conflict. An explicit method provides an intellectual and practical open space where analyses can be debated.

For the rest of this chapter, I will describe a method for analysing television and endeavour to make this description as explicit as possible. This method was devised specifically for analysing representations of madness on British television. Whilst the method is not confined to this subject area, madness is the topic I shall use for my examples. In the course of this, a few theoretical points, which I believe are general, will be addressed.

Selecting the programmes

The first task is sampling and selecting material for recording off air. Which programmes are selected will depend on the topic area and the theoretical orientation. For instance, a researcher may be particularly interested in a topic covered mostly by documentary programmes. S/he may even have advance knowledge of broadcasts to do with the topic. Even with this level of knowledge, the selection process is not transparent. What to leave out is just as important as what to include and will affect the resultant analysis. The questions of omission and absence were central to the early semioticians (Barthes, 1972). Theoretical and empirical choices influence the selection of programmes or stories which are not self-evident examples of the topic being considered.

A common way of selecting programmes is to do a broad sweep of prime time coverage and then pick out coverage of the topic of interest. This, of course, means viewing the entire data set which can be a very lengthy process. With prime time coverage the number of hours to watch is in the hundreds. Gerbner and his team (Signorelli, 1989) have used this method to study representations of violence on prime time over a 20-year period in the

United States. This is also the route I chose to look at representations of madness on television.

Within the process of recording there are at least two steps. The first is when and how much prime time to record. I selected an eight-week period in early summer of 1992 and recorded prime time on BBC1 and ITV, these being the popular channels. The news was routinely recorded as were two soap operas, two drama serials and two situation comedies from each channel. Documentaries were also included.

The choice of dates was pragmatic. Different results may have been revealed had the recording taken place in autumn or winter. Televisual media are affected by the annual cycle. This would have been more important if the object of analysis had been political stories. It should be noted that random sampling would not overcome this problem since the 'population' is not homogeneous.

The next problem was the selection of extracts depicting madness. When is a representation a representation of madness? For instance, the Glasgow Media Group (Philo, 1996) included agony columns and chat shows in their analysis of media coverage of madness. I used a much tighter definition, following Wahl:

> I would favour, for example, the presence, *within the media presentation*, of a specific psychiatric label (including slang designations such as 'crazy', 'madman' etc., as well as formal diagnoses such as schizophrenia or depression) or indication of receipt of psychiatric treatment as the appropriate criteria. (1992: 350)

It is important to be explicit about the reasons for choosing a definition such as Wahl's. The choice to take definite mental illness as the focus of the work has an ethical basis. Such is the scope of the net of psychiatry today that almost any human problem can become its subject. But it is those with the most severe problems who are outcast and excluded and this may be affected by how they are represented in the media. Hence there is an ethical concern to focus on mental distress serious enough to come to the attention of a psychiatrist. Such ethical concerns, particularly when they are also to do with social exclusion, may well apply to other excluded groups also.

The final problem with selecting the data set concerns metaphors. Mental illness terminology is routinely used as tease and insult: 'You're a raving nutter'; 'Who is this loony schizo?'; 'She's mad about the boy.' These uses of mental illness terminology are important for the overall representation of madness on television. They were noted in the analysis to be described here.

Metaphoric use of mental illness terminology can be more tightly or more lightly connected with other representations of madness. There remains the question of what metaphoric uses to include. However, if language is a system, then signs belonging to one context appearing in a completely different one will still carry some of the weight of the initial meaning. At first sight, the famous phrase 'She's mad about the boy' seems to have little to do with psychiatric disorder. But the term 'mad', generic for centuries, is still tinged with notions of extreme and excess, and even emotional danger, when located in its new context.

The question of definition would have to be decided for any analysis of prime time television and there are certainly other topics (such as physical disability) where metaphor would be an issue. Defining what counts as a representation of the topic of interest will involve theoretical choices but also ethical choices, as has been discussed.

Transcription

The purpose of transcription is to generate a data set that is amenable to careful analysis and coding. It translates and simplifies the complex image on the screen. Early researchers did not have video recorders (Nunnally, 1961) and coded straight from air. It would be possible to do this with a coding frame of only two or three dimensions but anything more detailed requires the capture of the medium in the written word. This, as has been said repeatedly, is a form of translation.

It is important to decide on the unit of analysis. This is a point made strongly by conversation analysts (Silverman, 1993) and those who have produced computer techniques for analysing qualitative data, such as ETHNOGRAPH and NUD*IST. In the study I am using for purposes of illustration, the unit of analysis was taken to be the camera shot. When a camera switched content, a new unit of analysis began. The definition of the unit of analysis was therefore basically visual.

Conversation analysts or discourse theorists typically take the unit of analysis to be a line, sentence or paragraph. Thus the unit is speech-based. Mindful of the importance of non-verbal aspects of audiovisual texts, I chose the unit of analysis on the basis of visuals but also, pragmatically, because in the vast majority of cases these are relatively simple to work with. There is a place for pragmatism in complex analyses.

Television is an audiovisual medium and there must be some way of describing the visual as well as the verbal dimension. I have emphasized the visual dimension and it is now time to look at this in a little more detail. It is impossible to describe everything on the screen and I would argue that the transcription decisions should be theory driven. In the study on madness, it was proposed theoretically that mental illness was stigmatized, seen as different and excluded. It was further proposed that the televisual representation of this would often take the form of single, isolating shots and scrutinizing close-ups. Therefore, it was decided to code the camera angle for each unit of analysis (each camera shot), and also to code how many people appeared in each shot. This was to test the idea that mentally distressed people are photographed differently from those not so diagnosed. In this case, the procedure can indeed be seen as a form of hypothesis testing (Kidder and Judge, 1986).

Different theoretical orientations would lead to different choices about how to select and transcribe. For instance, the structuralist/psychoanalytic tradition represented by the journal *Screen* would tell a different story (Cowie, 1979; MacCabe, 1976). *Screen* theorists focus on the level of symbols, especially those to do with gender and sexuality, and unconscious relationships. So, they have done detailed work on shot–reverse–shot sequences which work to establish relationships between characters. The camera 'sets the scene' for the relationship by filming first one character, then the second from the first's point of view, and then the first from the second's point of view. The study on madness did not look at individual shot sequences because there was nothing in the theory to suggest this would be important. It is open, nonetheless, to question the choices made from a different theoretical orientation. There may have been occasions where shot–reverse–shot sequences signalled difficulty and closeness but my decision was to focus the visual part of the analysis on camera angle.

Mood and the expression of difference can also be represented through lighting and music and other effects. Shadowy photography implies something dangerous that should be hidden, and eerie music contrasts with the light-heartedness of most music on television. Should people with mental distress be filmed in shadowy shots, or with a background of haunting music, this again emphasizes difference.

Camera angle, single versus group shots, lighting and music are all conventions of film and television. Indeed, haunting music can be referring directly to the filmic conventions of horror movies. There is a diagetic space with its own conventions. A structuralist analysis would focus on this space in its specificity. However, the method I propose is one of *contrasts*. We want to investigate whether a certain group in society and a certain condition – mentally ill people and their associated illness – is represented differently from 'ordinary' folk who appear on television at the same time.

Gilman (1982) has carried out very detailed work on visual representations of the mad person since the middle ages. He focuses on art and sculpture rather than moving images. Posture, demeanour, gesture, size and much more were important to this endeavour. The analysis has some similarities with the *Screen* theorists mentioned above.

There are yet other aspects of the visual dimension of television which could have been coded: for example, the colours of clothes, with dark colours implying depression, and even the relative position of characters in two-shots and group shots. For instance, it became evident with one depressed character that she was always in a 'lower' position than one of the other key characters in the story. If he was standing, she was sitting; if he was sitting, she was reclining. These aspects were not systematically noted in the transcription, but they could have been.

Other topics, other theoretical positions will require the selection of different aspects of the visual text for transcription. What is important is that the criteria for selection should be explicit and have a conceptual grounding. It should be conceptually and empirically explicit as to why certain choices were made and not others.

In the light of these choices, material was selected, recorded and transcribed. The transcription is in two columns and camera shots are signalled by paragraph breaks. The left-hand column describes the visual aspect of the story, in the terms proposed above, and on the right is a verbatim transcription of the verbal material.

What do we mean by 'verbatim'? Not that every pause, hesitation, false start and silence should be noted. There would be times when these things are important. Even with representations of madness, it could be hypothesized that mentally ill people are marked off by different rates, inflections and tone of their discourse. These supra-linguistic features are significant from some theoretical points of view, and are significant on some occasions from nearly all theoretical points of view. In cases other than madness, it might be of the first importance to include these factors. It was decided, however, that what was paramount was the *semantic content* of television's discourse on madness, and therefore the transcription was verbatim but omitted the kinds of phenomena stressed by conversation analysts.

The content does not stand alone, nonetheless. We shall see in the next section that each story was analysed as to its narrative structure. Whilst this is strictly a matter of coding and not transcription, it is important to point out that structure was not ignored.

Two examples of transcripts from the data on representations of madness on television are given as follows. The first is fairly straightforward: it was easy to transcribe. The second is an extract from the most difficult story in the entire data set. It is theoretically important that the story was difficult to transcribe, since it embodied ideas of chaos, transgression and difference. This locks into the theory that guided the coding frame, as we shall see in the next section. The camera codes are discussed later and given in Table 14.1.

'The Bill', ITV, 28 May 1992

Visual	Verbal
Front of hotel, forensics, PO, DI comes out, another DI enters frame, both MW	DI1: Ian.
	DI2: Hello, Jack, how are you? Fill me in.
	DI1: Morgan's at the hospital now. He looks fit for all three killings. He's an alcoholic with a history of psychiatric disorder, no previous for violent offences.
	DI2: How did you get onto him?
	DI1: Your Sergeant R found personal possessions belonging to the victim, PH. I suppose he could have found her body by the railway line and then robbed it. Much more likely he killed her before dumping her there.
	DI2: And our girl AA is very nearly his latest victim.
	DI1: Yeah. Must have put up one heck of a fight. Otherwise.

'Casualty', BBC1, 4 July 1992

Visual	Verbal
Woman with arm in sling sitting MCU, man pacing, leaps on her, man CU then ECU, attacks her, she struggles	Man: . . . evil, fixes darling, ebony black devils. You know what I'd like to do with them? I'd like to bite the bastards' heads off and put them
Woman rises, man grabs her, bites her, ECU, attacks	between my
	Wo1: Get away from me.
Staff come running, WA	Man: Growls. Screams.
Nurse in cubicle with 2nd Wo, second nurse enters, exit both nurses	Nurse: Ash, quick, there's a bloke gone berserk out here. Come on.
Staff struggling with man, WA, Wo1 led away, distressed, everyone screaming	Wo1: Oh my arm, my arm, oh, oh, oh, my God, oh.
Camera tracking scene	
Wo1 and two nurses pass cubicle occupied by Wo2, MCU, she exits, moves across corridor and picks up bottle sitting on trolley. She walks past scene with man who now has a blanket over his head	Charge nurse (Charlie): Calm down, calm down.
	Nurse: Easy.
	Charlie: Don't just stand there.
Other people come to control man, WA	Man: I'm choking.
	Charlie: Alright, alright. Take it easy. Alright, alright.
Charlie starts to remove blanket from man's head	Porter: No, I, I wouldn't.
	Man: I'm going to faint.
Blanket removed, man lying on ground, WA	Charlie: Alright. Alright. I'm going to take it off now. Now you behave yourself.
	Man: Alright . . . (inaudible) . . . lovely.
Man punches Charlie in the face, WA	
Aerial shot chaos	Charlie: Oh!
	Man: Oh!
Wo2 exiting hospital, police officers pass her and enter MW	(No speech)

Devising a coding frame

The full coding frame is given in Figure 14.1. It has a hierarchical structure in line with the proposition that representations of madness on television will signify at more than one level. This section will concentrate, however,

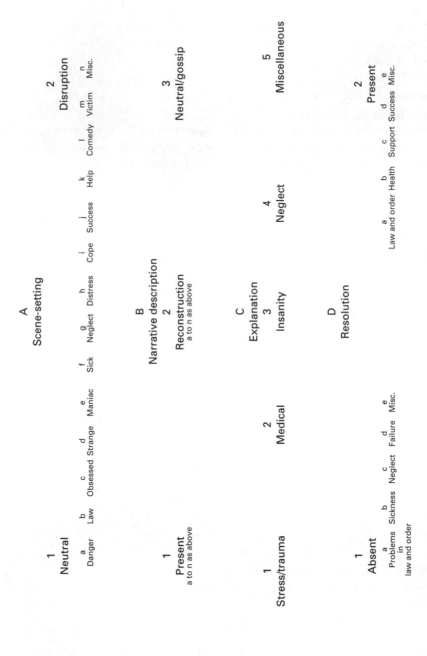

Figure 14.1   *Coding frame with four narrative elements: scene-setting, narrative description, explanation and resolution*

on the theory underlying the coding frame and its epistemological status. I shall make no attempt to spell out in words what exists in diagrammatic form.

Bernstein's L2 is the coding frame proper or the language of description. The coding frame used in the study of representations of madness on television was very complex and I would like to make two main points. First, this instrument is theoretically grounded. Secondly, it is designed so that theoretical derivations can be refuted. Let us take these two points in sequence.

The theory used, and modified, was Moscovici's (1984; 1994) work on social representations. One of the central tenets of the theory is that social representations function to make the unfamiliar more familiar. This point has also been made about televisual representations by Roger Silverstone (1981). My argument is that, from this point of view, madness is a special case. For social and psychological reasons, representations of mental ill-health, be they in the media or as everyday conversation, *maintain madness in an unfamiliar position*. Familiarization, social or psychological, does not structure the representational field of madness. There are two reasons for this. First, the content of many representations emphasizes danger, menace and threat. The mad killer or psychotic murderer is a distinguishable theme in the British media. But more than this, the structure of the representations around madness is unstable. There are myriad meanings of madness that resist fixity and threaten in a semiotic sense. Meaning is ruptured by chaos and transgression.

Moscovici has a concept of anchoring. A new, and unfamiliar, social object will be made more familiar by being assimilated to one that is already familiar. My argument is that madness either is not assimilated at all and stands excluded, or is assimilated to other objects that are never quite made familiar, such as people with learning disabilities, people with physical disabilities, people or things who take part in the monstrous.

What does this mean for a coding frame? The coding frame was derived from two sources: the theory referred to above, and also preliminary reading of the data. In 157 hours of prime time, there were six hours of material relevant to mental health. These are the six hours that were transcribed and influenced the design of the coding frame.

So far, we have conceptualized the coding of content. But many forms of text and textual practice have a discernible structure. This is often referred to as narrative form (Todorov, 1977; Chatman, 1978). Narrative structure refers to the form of a story in that it has an identifiable beginning where the state of play changes, a middle where the different forces play out their roles, and an end where outstanding issues are tied up. This end of the story is often referred to as 'narrative closure'. There is also an issue around 'voice' in narrative and the identity of the narrator. This issue was not included as it seems less relevant to the television text than to, for instance, the novel.

Television stories partake of narrative structure. In line with the theory of semiotic instability outlined above, I was interested to know whether stories about madness were narratively distinguishable from those which were about other topics. For example, do they exhibit narrative closure?

The coding frame, then, had a hierarchical structure with the top of each hierarchy being a narrative element (see Figure 14.1). The body of the story was coded according to 14 content categories, a large number being required to capture the multiple, shifting meanings of madness. Presence or absence of resolution, and type of resolution, were also coded.

I have put forward the idea that madness, and other objects of difference and exclusion, disrupt semiotic certainty by being made up of multiple, conflicting, shifting meanings. At the same time they threaten because some of these meanings are dangerous. What if this theory were wrong? Qualitative research is often criticized for seeing only what it wants to see. But the theory can be disconfirmed. For instance, it would be open to a critic to argue that surely the dominant meaning of mental illness, in our culture if not in the media, is precisely 'illness'. In this case, the present analysis would reveal a high proportion of units in the 'sickness' category and very few units allocated to other codes. Medicine would be the dominant discourse around mental illness on television, and this meaning would be general and would anchor the 'mental' half of 'mental illness'. This is not what was found. However, the structure of the coding frame makes it possible to find an overarching discourse and thus to disconfirm the theory that difference is also made up out of semiotic slippage and, sometimes, a chaos of meanings (see the 'Casualty' extract).

The method of contrasts, used with the visual material, also holds the possibility of disconfirming the conceptualization. It would, for example, be possible to find that there was no difference whatsoever in the camera angles used to film people designated mentally ill when compared with those without the designation. So, the proposal that filming techniques mark off the mad person as different, isolated and excluded, would have to be rejected.

The mechanics of coding

I shall begin with the verbal dimension of the text. The coding frame described above has basically three levels and it is highly likely that other coding frames designed for use with audiovisual material will have more than one level. I have labelled the first level with a capital letter, the second with a number, and the third with a lower-case letter. Codes look like this:

A2a   scene-setting, disruption, danger
B2f   narrative description, reconstruction, illness
C1   explanation, stress (the 'explanation' codes have only two levels)
D1c   resolution, absence, neglect

Each unit of analysis (camera shot) is allocated a code. There will be occasions when a single code does not fully capture the density of meaning in the unit, and in these cases two or even three codes need to be allocated.

There is an issue here of reliability. As we have said, the process of coding is a process of translation. The researcher is interpreting the meaning of each unit of analysis. Although the interpretations are constrained by both theory and the coding frame, it does make sense to ask whether other coders would have come to the same conclusion.

An exercise was then undertaken to see what the degree of commonality might be when eight separate people coded three selected stories. The level of agreement ranged from 0.6 to 0.78. The level of agreement was directly related to how familiar the coder was with the theory and the coding frame. Whilst this touches on one of the thorniest problems with assessing reliability, it shows that the coding procedure is at least replicable. From the epistemological point of view which I have been using, the coders were using a common set of translation procedures to turn the transcript into a series of codes. The crucial point is that this set of translation procedures is made explicit and available to inspection in the diagram of the coding frame (see Figure 14.1).

To turn now to the visual dimension. Here things are simpler as, once the selection choices were made, the transcription and coding were more straightforward. First, the camera angle of each shot in the data set is coded. Secondly, a note is made of whether the shot is a single shot, a two-shot (two people in frame) or a group shot. Finally, a count is made of the number of shots that use shadowy lighting and the number of times music is used and its nature.

The codes for visual analysis can be seen at work in the extracts. They are, in fact, transcribed and coded in one movement. While there are infinite gradations in filming characters, television does make use of some conventions in photography. This is to our benefit since it is known that, for instance, the close-up is an emotional and scrutinizing shot. On the other hand, the medium close-up and medium wide shots often signify authority (as with newscasters and experts). The full set of visual codes can be found in Table 14.1.

The method of contrasts entails a comparison between the camera angles typically used to film those designated mad and to film those not so designated. Since the conventions of the shots are partially known, this allows an inference as to whether mentally distressed people are being signified differently to others in the visual code.

Table 14.1   *Visual analysis: camera angle codes*

ECU	Extreme close-up
CU	Close-up
MCU	Medium close-up
MW	Medium wide
WA	Wide angle
Tracking	Camera follows action
Environment	Shot other than a person

Usually, the two modes of visual and verbal will tell the same story, since this is a convention of television. However, there is the possibility of conflict or contradiction (or irony and sarcasm) between the two: for instance, a picture of a homely grandmother with a child on her lap as the reporter's voice-over describes her double murder of her neighbour's children. It will normally be clear which of the modes carries the weight of the meaning but, where there is evenly balanced conflict, this should be noted.

Tabulating the results: the question of numbers

The outcome of the processes described above will be tables of frequencies. To this extent, the procedure is a form of content analysis dating back to the seminal paper of Berelson (1952) and described in various collections throughout the 1950s and 1960s (for a relatively recent example see Krippendorff, 1980).

Content analysis has been criticized by media theorists such as Allen (1985) and only partially accepted by researchers such as Leiss et al. (1986). This critique derives from semiological approaches to texts. It is said that numbers cannot be meaningfully applied to significations and that simple counts of appearances of a word or theme in the text ignore structure and context. The detail which can be extended to a semiotic reading of a text is well illustrated by Barthes's *S/Z* (1975). Here is an instance where the translation does not constitute a simplification but is a book-length exegesis on a short story.

Let us take the criticisms in turn. The first is the proposition that meanings cannot be counted. That is to say, that meanings are always context-specific and allocating a number to semantic units suggests a spurious equivalence of different instances. Meanings are not discrete and even values are too ineffable to be measured.

Osgood (1957) was one of the first to count meanings. It is noteworthy that Osgood developed a theory of meaning that was neo-behaviourist in orientation so that, while focusing on the text, he could claim that his analysis was theoretically grounded. The most important tool that was produced by this approach was the semantic differential (Osgood et al., 1957). This is eschewed by more literary-based forms of analysis.

While the theory today looks absurd, this is a first example of the attempt at quantitative semantics within a defined theoretical framework.

Osgood had a neo-behaviourist theory of meaning. The method described above has its theoretical roots in notions of social representation (Moscovici, 1984; Jodelet, 1991). Numbers in tables, then, are not free-floating but are anchored to a conceptual perspective. What a number signifies depends upon the nature of the empirical material and the nature, too, of the language of description. There is nothing unusual in this. Mathematics uses theories, including theories that deal with chance, randomness and probability.

So, what exactly does it mean to count representations, meanings or other techniques of imaging? Table 14.2 shows the outcome of the analysis of

Table 14.2 *Examples of results of content analysis in tabular form: distribution of frequencies of semantic elements in scene-setting and description shots on the news*

	Danger	Law	Obsessed	Strange	Maniac	Sick	Neglect
No. of units	168	60	9	1	3	84	63
% total ($N = 697$)	24.1	8.6	1.3			12.1	9.0

	Distress	Cope	Success	Help	Comic	Victim	Misc.
No. of units	28	8	9	25	0	7	67
% total ($N = 697$)	4.0	1.2	1.3	3.6		1.0	9.6

representations of madness for the first two narrative elements (scene-setting and narrative description) for the news. The table should be read like a map. It shows the points of emphasis and stress and the points of lack and absence in the news data. It would not be sensible to say there was 'twice as much danger as sickness' although a metric reading of the figures would come to that conclusion. It makes more sense to say that danger dominated themes of sickness, and that the lack of themes of success and coping say something significant about how mental health problems are represented on the news. What is absent is just as important as what is present, as semioticians have taught us.

I have said before that it was possible, with the visual material, to employ a method of contrasts. Since both mentally ill and mentally well people appear in the programming, their visual depiction can be compared. Table 14.3 shows such a comparison. It will be noted that the chi-squared statistic is employed, which seems to say that the numericization of the data amounts to more than maps. It is easier to assign true numbers to visual data because of the conventions discussed above. Even here, the view holds that numbers are not rigid indicators but species of signs. Nonetheless, high significance levels are telling.

Now to the criticism that content analysis ignores structure. This criticism stands. If we have learned anything from Chomsky, it is that structure carries meaning. And this has been accepted in the above analyses. Since

Table 14.3 *Example of tabular results of visual analysis: type of shot and character in the soap opera Coronation Street*

Type of shot	Mrs Bishop*	Mr Sugden**	Others	Total
ECU/CU	45	8	9	62
MCU	42	33	41	116
MW	22	36	16	74
Other	22	9	3	34
Total	131	86	69	286

Chi-Square = 45.6; d.f. = 6; $p < 0.001$.
* suffering a mental breakdown
** a friend who tries to help.

Table 14.4   *Narrative structure: frequency distribution of types of narrative sequence in television drama*

As can be seen from the coding frame, stories were coded according to their structure. Each unit was assigned a code, and then the story structure was summarized. This table presents the codes and results for drama.

A1   scene-setting, neutral
A2   scene-setting, disruptive
B1   narrative description in the present
B2   narrative description in the form of reconstruction of events
B3   neutral facts (news) or gossip (drama)
C   explanation
D1   resolution with absence of social harmony
D2   social harmony restored.

Narrative sequence	No
A2/B1/D1	29
A2/B1/D2	4
A2/B1	12
B1/D1	19
B1/D2	7
B1 only or B3 only	28
A2 only	8
D1 only	3
D2 only	4
Other	7
Total	121

we are dealing with audiovisual material, structure has been conceptualized in terms of narrative form. Indeed, many semioticians have used this concept, deriving as it does from the work of Propp (1969) and Lévi-Strauss (1968). Narrative structure on television is often open – for example, in soap operas, to keep up the suspense. But the analysis of narrative structure in the representation of people designated mad showed that lack of narrative closure was the norm. This, of course, adds weight to the idea that representations of madness on television are chaotic and resist the fixity of anchors. Here we see representations as often structureless. Table 14.4 shows the results of the analysis of narrative structure in drama programmes. The majority of sequences have either no ending at all or no restoration of social harmony.

The other method of presenting data is to use illustrative quotations. In an analysis where the method is theoretically grounded and where data are also presented numerically, it is arguable that exemplary quotations can be used to illustrate and confirm or disconfirm the theoretical and methodological propositions. In other words, rules for the selection of illustrative quotations can be themselves conceptually grounded. This means that it is not necessary to choose illustrative quotations randomly. Rather, they should be selected to both verify and disconfirm the conceptual principles and the numerically presented aspect of the empirical data.

Conclusion

This chapter has tried to do two things. First, I have tentatively proposed some methods for analysing television and other audiovisual material. Some of the techniques put forward should be adapted for contents other than madness. But secondly, I have tried to draw out the epistemological pitfalls and ethical consequences of this type of analysis.

At risk of repetition, I will say that each step in the analysis of audio-visual material is a translation and, usually, a simplification. There can be no perfect reading of the text. The point, then, is to be explicit about the theoretical, ethical and practical grounds of the technique and open up a space where the work itself can be debated and judged.

STEPS IN THE ANALYSIS OF AUDIOVISUAL TEXTS

1 Choose a theoretical framework and apply it to the empirical object.
2 Select a sampling frame – time or content based.
3 Select a means of identifying the empirical object in the sampling frame.
4 Construct rules for the transcription of the data set – visual and verbal.
5 Develop a coding frame based on the conceptual analysis and preliminary reading of the data set: to include rules for the analysis of both visual and verbal material; to contain the possibility of disconfirming the theory; to include analysis of narrative structure and context as well as semantic categories.
6 Apply the coding frame to the data, transcribed in a form amenable to numerical translation.
7 Construct tables of frequencies for units of analysis, visual and verbal.
8 Apply simple statistics where appropriate.
9 Select illustrative quotations to complement numerical analysis.

References

Allen, R. (1985) *Speaking of Soap Operas*. Chapel Hill, NC: North Carolina Press.
Barthes, R. (1972) *Critical Essays*. Evanston, IL: North Western University Press.
Barthes, R. (1975) *S/Z*. London: Cape.
Berelson, B. (1952) *Content Analysis in Communication Research*. Chicago, IL: Glencoe Free Press.
Bernstein, B. (1995) *Pedagogy, Symbolic Control and Identity*. London: Taylor and Francis.
Birdwhistell, R.L. (1970) *Kinesics in Context: Essays on Body – Motion Communication*. Harmondsworth: Penguin.

Chatman, S. (1978) *Story and Discourse: Narrative Structure in Fiction and Film*. Ithaca, NY and London: Cornell University Press.

Cowie, E. (1979) 'The popular film as a progressive text', *m/f*, 3: 59–82.

Crystal, D. and Quirk, R. (1964) *Systems of Prosodic and Paralinguistic Features in English*. London: Mouton.

Gilman, S. (1982) *Seeing the Insane*. New York: Wiley.

Jodelet, D. (1991) *Madness and Social Representations*. Hemel Hempstead: Harvester Wheatsheaf.

Kidder, L. and Judge, C. (1986) *Research Methods in Social Relations*, 5th edn. New York: CBS.

Krippendorff, K. (1980) *Content Analysis: an Introduction to its Methodology*. London: Sage.

Leiss, W., Kline, S. and Jhally, S. (1986) *Social Communication in Advertising*. Toronto: Methuen.

Lévi-Strauss, C. (1968) *Structural Anthropology*. Harmondsworth: Allen Lane.

MacCabe, C. (1976) 'Theory and film: principles of realism and pleasure', *Screen*, 17: 7–27.

Moscovici, S. (1984) 'The phenomenon of social representations', in R.M. Farr and S. Moscovici (eds), *Social Representations*. Cambridge: Cambridge University Press. pp. 3–69.

Moscovici, S. (1994) 'Social representations and pragmatic communication', *Social Science Information*, 33 (2): 163–77.

Nunnally, J. (1961) *Popular Conceptions of Mental Health*. New York: Holt, Rinehart and Winston.

Osgood, C. (1957) 'The representational model and relevant research methods', in I. de S. Pool (ed.), *Trends in Content Analysis*. Urbana, IL: University of Illinois Press. pp. 33–88.

Osgood, C., Suci, G. and Tannenbaum, P.H. (1957) *The Measurement of Meaning*. Urbana, IL: University of Illinois Press.

Philo, G. (ed.) (1996) *Media and Mental Distress*. London: Longman.

Potter, J. and Wetherell, M. (1987) *Discourse and Social Psychology*. London: Sage.

Propp, V. (1969) *The Morphology of the Folktale*. Austin, TX: University of Texas Press.

Signorelli, N. (1989) 'The stigma of mental illness on television', *Journal of Broadcasting and Electronic Media*, 33 (3): 325–31.

Silverman, D. (1993) *Interpreting Qualitative Data: Methods for Analysing Talk, Text and Interaction*. London: Sage.

Silverstone, R. (1981) *The Message of Television: Myth and Narrative in Contemporary Culture*. London: Heinemann.

Todorov, T. (1977) *The Poetics of Prose*. Oxford: Blackwell.

Wahl, O. (1992) 'Mass media images of mental illness: a review of the literature', *Journal of Community Psychology*, 20: 343–52.

Wearing, M. (1993) 'Professional discourse and sensational journalism: media constructions of violent insanity', *Australian Journal of Communication*, 20 (1): 84–98.

15

Analysing Noise and Music as Social Data

Martin W. Bauer

KEYWORDS

cantometrics	musical tastes
cultural indicators	noise
melodic complexity: frequency,	notation and transcription
magnitude, progression,	sound
music	soundscape
musical meaning	total musical event

A passion for music is a confession. We know more about an unknown but musical person than about an unmusical person with whom we spend all our days. (E.M. Cioran)

If you want to know about the sixties, play the music of the Beatles. (Aaron Copland)

The music of a well-ordered age is calm and cheerful, and so is its government. The music of a decaying state is sentimental and sad, and its government is imperilled. (Hermann Hesse, *Glasperlenspiel*)

Rarely has there been a movement in art that showed so clearly as bop the lineaments of the social forces behind it . . . the shape of the music itself – the actual length and pitches of the notes – to a large degree was determined by shifts in the structure of society. (J.L. Collier)

These quotations hint at the potential of music to mirror the social world, present or historical, that produces and consumes it. For Aaron Copland, the Beatles express the culture of the 1960s (see Macdonald, 1995); for Hermann Hesse, the character of music is correlated with the state of an age and its government; and for J.L. Collier the bebop style of jazz reflects the social forces that changed American society during the 1940s.

In this chapter I introduce some of the methodological approaches to construct 'cultural indicators' from the music and noise that people produce and to which they are exposed. Cultural indicators measure elements of cultural life that reflect our values and our life world; these change slowly over long periods, and are only to a limited extent subject to social engineering (Bauer, 2000).

Attempts to consider music and noise as social data must assume a systematic relation between sounds and the social context that produces and receives them. Three steps of analysis are required to pursue the construction of cultural indicators from musical or sound materials:

1 We need to record and transcribe the sound event for the purpose of analysis.
2 This transcription may depict sound and music in a similar form as speech, with an order of elements (paradigm, language) from which sequences are generated according to rules of production (syntagm, speech/grammar). Elements of sound are linked in more or less complex sequences. In music we describe these with, for example, the dimensions of rhythm, melody and harmony; for noises we recognize cycles, loudness and character.
3 A particular structure of sounds is associated with a social group that produces it, is exposed to it, and listens to it.

This latter correlation is a much-debated theoretical problem (Martin, 1995). A weak version claims that empirical correlation between sound variables and social variables can be expected because of the functional character of music and noise in many social contexts (indicators). A stronger version of this dependency claims that structural similarities are to be expected: the order of the social world is mirrored in the order of musical elements (homologies). The strongest and at the same time the weakest version claims that musical activities, as they are independent of the present social field, have the utopian power to anticipate the imminent social order: by paying attention to certain kinds of musical expression, we can see the future (prophetic function).

I do not want to focus on the ethnomusicological, sociological, social psychological or philosophical evidence for the relationship between music and society. My concern is with the methodological fallout of such arguments: how to demonstrate or to disprove that sounds mirror or anticipate the social context that appreciates them. Sounds are constrained by their social contexts, and therefore imprinted by the contexts. In this sense we can consider sounds as a medium of representation.

Tagg (1982) distinguishes four instances of musical sound (see Table 15.1): the sound as conceived by a composer (M1); the sound object as it is

Table 15.1   *A system of sound analysis*

Activities	Traces, fixations	Contexts
Poiesis, production (M1)	Sound recording (M2)	Historical context
	Transcription (M3)	Social system
Aesthesis, reception (M4)	Secondary coding (M3)	

performed and possibly recorded (M2); the sound as it is transcribed into notation (M3); and finally the sound as it is appreciated (M4). Sounds are produced by somebody and received by others, either purposefully or involuntarily. The production of sound events is often called 'poiesis'; while their reception and appreciation is called 'aesthesis'. This production may be purposeful as in the case of music, or unintentional in the case of the fallout noises from daily activities such as driving a car. Sounds are appreciated wilfully, for example at a rock concert, or unwillingly as noise emanating from passing traffic or the 'musical taste' of the neighbours. The appreciation of sounds in these two contexts is likely to be very different.

Sounds are recorded to obtain a material trace. In order to facilitate analysis this recording needs to be transcribed in a system of symbols that highlights certain features of the events, while neglecting others. Ultimately, these sound events take place in the context of a social system whose workings we want to understand by examining its sound production and reception. The problem of 'cultural indicator' is defined by the search for systematic correlation between the production/reception and the traces of sound, and between the traces and the context of the social system. By 'correlation' I do not necessarily mean a strict statistical correlation of values on an ordinal or interval scale, but the simple co-occurrences of features or the similarities of structures.

Recording and transcriptions

Music is primarily a sound event in time, so we need to keep a memory of it if we are to analyse it. This record can be made in many ways: with a phonograph recording acoustical signals, as a tonal film recording of the events, or by transcribing it in a conventional musical notation.

Acoustic recording has developed considerably in the twentieth century, but all recordings basically consist of two elements: the microphone and the recorder. In recording, we have to consider the number of sources that are involved in producing the music or the sound. An analytic approach would want to consider the different sources both independently and in their coming together in a coherent sound. A multi-channel recording machine with various microphones is necessary for recording the complex sound events of an orchestra, while a small tape recorder with a single microphone may be sufficient to record a melody sung by a single singer. In recording a small jazz combo, a rock band or large orchestra, we need to consider where to place the microphones so that the various sources of sound are recorded with sufficient clarity (see, for example, Nisbett, 1983). In order to distinguish different street noises, or to analyse the bass line or the contributions from the piano and the guitar in a jazz or rock concert, these need to be recorded with a sufficient degree of quality. The quality of recordings for research purposes is located somewhere between the unreliable memory of the live listener and the perfect hi-fi recordings of the music industry: it must be adequate to the level of resolution that is intended in the analysis.

Separating music from its visual performance by making an acoustic recording of it already constitutes a selection. Lomax's (1959) definition of a 'total musical event' includes the musician, the audience and the occasion – a complex of activity that is not only acoustic but also visual, and which involves many kinds of movement. For recording some sound events, therefore, film or video will be the most appropriate medium, depending on the genre and the purpose of the research. So, for example, sheet music of a pop song or a jazz standard is only a very limited record of the actual performance in the context of a club (Tagg, 1982).

Many musical cultures have developed standard notation for memorizing music, to coordinate its performance, and to teach the novice. Such notation becomes an additional cultural force in the development of music (Sloboda, 1985: 242ff). In social science, one uses musical notation for analytic purposes. This notation aims to capture certain features of sound that are indicative of the context that produces it. Thus social research may use live recordings and their transcriptions, or existing recordings or notations, and develop secondary notation for particular purposes.

Primary notation represents the original sound event in a particular manner, and in principle can be achieved in various ways. For example, the sound that emanates from pressing the key A in the fourth octave of the piano keyboard can be represented as a dot in the second space of the Western notation system, which represents its pitch and length. Or it can be represented as

P57   u200   190

where P57 stands for pitch, u200 for duration in hundredths of a second, and 190 for loudness. The same tonal sound can be represented for computing purposes as a function with arguments (see Leman, 1993: 125):

pitch_event [pitch (a4), duration (q), loudness (mf)]

These descriptions abstract some features of sound while neglecting others such as the vibration, the attack or the continuous fading of the tone. The conventional Western notation system (Read, 1969) consists of five lines; a clef symbol describes the pitch level of reference ($\oint$ for treble and $\mathcal{P}$ for bass), conveniently oriented in the middle of the piano keyboard; several kinds of flagged dots represent the length of a tonal event, and their positions on or between the lines represent its pitch. A multitude of additional symbols complement this Western notation, for pauses, linkages, loudness, alterations and tonalities. Rhythm, harmony and melody are easily represented in this system, but it fails to represent tonal changes smaller than the minimal half-tone (semi-tone) step. Many singing cultures of the world, for example blues singing, entertain melodic fluctuations that are smaller than the half-tone step. To transcribe such changes more precisely, ethnomusicologists have developed the melograph (see Merriam, 1964). For social research purposes it is often necessary to develop purpose-related transcriptions systems, as for example in cantometrics to compare singing events across cultures, or to analyse music videos (see below). Secondary notation takes the primary notation as its base data.

The traditions of academic musical analysis take the musical score, mostly written in the conventional Western system of notation, as the raw material for unravelling the laws of musical construction that order the elements (Bent and Drabkin, 1987). Musicological analysis focuses on the internal structure of music; by contrast social scientific analysis takes these internal features of music and correlates them with external patterns of reception and production. The problem is to decide which features are meaningful, that is, are in a non-random relationship with external characteristics of production and reception. Here, we want to consider Dowd's (1992) and Cerullo's (1992) indexes of melodic features or Alexander's (1996) measure of the diversity in popular music production.

Musical meaning: internal and external references

If music or sound has linguistic qualities, the analogy is strong on syntax and pragmatic functions but controversial on semantics (Reitan, 1991). In other words, musical elements may make different degrees of sense, but do not have the meaning of a single referent. Music is rich in connotations, but its units are less defined in its denotation. For example, Beethoven's Ninth Symphony is rich in musical order *and* in social function, for example for celebrating the fall of the Berlin Wall in 1989 and the impending German reunification, or the launch of the Euro in January 1999. Its semantic meaning outside the social usage of its performance is, however, uncertain.

We can distinguish internal from external references of music (Mayer, 1956: 256ff). Internally, a piece of music may refer to previous music by 'citing' a melody or a harmonic pattern. This is an obvious practice in the genre 'theme and variations' in classical and jazz music. A musical idea is taken up from somebody else, and new music is developed around it. External references are either mimetic or connotative; the connotative is distinguished into idiosyncratic or symbolic. Mimetic are those references where the musical event imitates world events by similarity of noise or movement, or emotions by a succession of tension building and releasing. For example, the slow walking pace of an elephant may be musically represented by a slow series of low-pitched notes from a tuba, while running upstairs may be represented by a scale of rising tones from a clarinet. In the theory of musical form, mimetic attempts are called programmatic music: well-known examples are Mussorgsky's *Pictures at an Exhibition* (1874), Berlioz's *Symphonie fantastique* (1830) or even Gil Evans and Miles Davies's *Sketches of Spain* (1960). Secondly, connotative meaning of music stems from elicited images and associations that are idiosyncratic. Meaning may arise spontaneously, or may relate to images and feelings that are associated with the memory of its first encounter. There is no particular relation to the musical material: associations are entirely contingent on the particular listener. Finally, connotations of music may be shared by a social group: a song, a piece of orchestral music, or a pop group comes to stand for the group's history and their struggles. The elicited associations are cultivated collectively, often reinforced by a discourse about this music and its supposed meaning. We find the music expressing a particular national character. Other forms of symbolic conventions are the compositional codes of eighteenth-century France: certain tonalities always express certain feelings and moods – for example, C major stands for common rejoicing, while F minor stands for lamentation or sorrow (Nattiez, 1990: 125).

The functional analysis of music considers another type of meaning: what are the effects of musical activities in a particular setting. Is music used to speed up work (Lonza, 1995) to encourage pleasure (Frith, 1988) to support religious events (Leonard, 1987) to foster social protest (Pratt, 1994) or to exclude by demonstrating taste and social distinction (Adorno, 1976)? These questions address the pragmatics of music.

Noise and soundscapes

Sound is a physical event that impinges on the human auditory system and is perceived as having loudness, pitch, volume, density and complexity. The world of music selects from a spectrum of sounds and thus distinguishes music, the intended sound, from noise, the unintended sound. We also distinguish between natural sounds such as wind or birdsong, and artificial sounds such as music purposefully produced or noise that is the often annoying fallout of human activities. The effect of prolonged exposure to annoying noise is so strong that it amounts to a form of torture. Noise is the subject of intensive study because of its potential detrimental effects on human well-being at work or at home (Jansen, 1991).

Musical history can be described as shifting the boundaries between music and noise: noises of past times may become the music of the present. For Nattiez (1990), noise is a semiological problem subject to shifting definitions. It is subjectively defined as something 'disagreeable' and 'disturbing', depending on conventional criteria such as too high a volume, an absence of defined pitch, or disorder. This social change is due to the fact that the boundaries between music and sound are not identical in the spheres of production, physical description and aesthesic judgement (see Table 15.2). What composers choose to call music may be physically harmonic, and agreeable to the listener (line 1 in Table 15.2). On the other hand, the musician's music may be physically beyond the harmonic spectrum, but still within the boundary of agreeable sound (line 3). Further down the table, the musician's sounds are beyond physical harmony, and are also rejected by listeners (line 4). This constitutes a challenge to the

Table 15.2   *The mapping of the music/noise distinction*

Poietic level: composer's choice	Neutral level: physical description	Aesthesic level: perception, judgement
1 Music	Harmonic spectrum	Agreeable sound
2 Music	Harmonic spectrum	Agreeable sound
3 Music	Complex noise	Agreeable sound
4 Music	Complex noise	Disagreeable noise
5 Noise	Complex noise	Disagreeable noise

conventional listener that is common in musical history. Consider the highly complex sounds of 12-tone music which, for many people, is still disagreeable after nearly a century, or the guitar sounds emanating from Jimi Hendrix, or John Coltrane's saxophonic 'sound sheets' in the free jazz of the early 1960s – all of which, after having stirred much (and persistent) rejection, have become classical forms of musical expression. Line 5 presents those noises that not even the musician would choose.

This disjunction between musical expectations and musical production is socially significant to the extent that it qualifies as a social indicator. Attali (1985) has made it the theme of a book to explore the 'prophetic power' of noise over the centuries. For him, music is a very sensitive way of perceiving the world. He formulates a programme of observing music-making in order to anticipate the evolution of society: 'music is prophetic and . . . social organization echoes [it]; . . . change is inscribed in noise faster than it transforms society' (1985: 5); 'can we hear the crisis of society in the crisis of music?' (1985: 6); 'it makes audible the new world that will gradually become visible' (1985: 11). Not only does music represent the current state of affairs in conventional order, but in breaking conventions the 'noise' anticipates a social crisis, and indicates the direction of change in its new order. Today's noisy music announces the new political and cultural order: 'music is ushering the new age' (1985: 141).

In studying noise as a cultural indicator, Attali focuses on artificial sounds that are produced purposefully for musical expression. Sound as comprising both natural and artificial noise is the concern of the Canadian composer R.M. Schafer's analyses of 'soundscape' (Schafer, 1973; 1977). The soundscape is described by a vocabulary that is analogous to that of the landscape (see Table 15.3). Schafer notes that the soundscape of the world is changing: new sounds that differ in quality and intensity are created, while old sounds disappear. We have learnt to ignore most of this soundscape that surrounds us daily, even while we are being affected by it. The world soundscape is a 'vast musical composition' that should not be left to chance. With his World Soundscape Project Schafer instigated a social movement (The World Forum for Acoustic Ecology: http://interact.uoregon.edu/ MediaLit/WFAEHomePage) of recording, analysing, evaluating, documenting and redesigning the world's acoustic ecology. This programme is motivated by a curious mixture of outrage about levels of 'noise pollution'; a curatorial care for sounds that face extinction, such as the sounds of

Table 15.3   *Landscape and soundscape vocabulary*

Visual landscape	Audible soundscape
Eye witness	Ear witness
Design versus nature	Ratio of natural to artificial sounds
Clair voyance	Clair audience
Figure–ground	Signal–noise, hi-fi, lo-fi
Telescope	Recording
Microscope	Distribution
Photograph	Sonograph
Schizophrenia	Schizophonia
Dominance = height, size	Dominance = loudness
Coniferous gardens	Soniferous gardens

horse-drawn carriages, which are to be preserved for future memory; a sense that enhancing our auditive sensitivity for otherwise ignored sounds has therapeutic effects improving our listening capabilities; the collecting of recorded noises to make into music; and a re-engineering mission of noise abatement and improvement of our sound environment in a 'search for the harmonizing influence of sounds in the world about us' (Schafer, 1973; Adams, 1983).

Musical notation is inadequate for noises (it stands helpless before the Harley-Davidson: Schafer, 1973), and physical measurements are technically too cumbersome to make for a great variety of everyday noises. Because of these difficulties, Schafer has suggested the development of various research techniques.

Sound can be recorded by positioning microphones at different locations for 24 hours or longer. The loudness of the noises is measured continuously to obtain a 'loudness profile'. These profiles are compared in order to measure the rhythms of collective life and the significance of certain noises in different communities – for example, comparing a rural and an urban environment. Exploring these profiles in conversation with local people reveals, for example, that in a rural Swiss village the sound of the church bell is not only a time signal, but is also used to forecast the weather: the distant sound of the bell varies with the pressure conditions of the air. The weather has a sound quality in rural life, but not in urban environments.

The 'listening walk' includes promenading in a particular locality, a landscape, a street or a building while consciously focusing on those noises that normal activity would relegate to irrelevant background. This technique reactivates hearing and heightens awareness, and is used to prepare informants in a soundscape study for talking about the sound environment that is normally ignored and is difficult to verbalize (Winkler, 1995a; 1995b).

The 'sound diary' is a technique where informants are asked to time-sample a day or a longer period, and to record and/or to describe at predefined intervals, for example every 30 minutes, the noises that are instantaneously audible. Besides the effect of raising awareness of the audible environment, the problem of systematic recording arises: what is the language used to describe sounds? Do we describe solely in terms of sound characteristics such as loudness and duration, cracking, squeaking, hammering, etc., or do we describe directly in terms of sources, for example a car passes by, a clock is ticking, etc., or in terms of instantaneous emotional experience and meaning? A sound diary will therefore distinguish three types of information – sound characteristics, source and significance – for example, in several columns of a sampling record, while other columns record the time, the place and the activity of the observer. The collection and comparison of sound diaries amounts to a description of a 'normal soundscape' for a group of people, and as such is a cultural indicator, the changes of which can be mapped out across both contexts and time.

Schafer (1973) has suggested a number of analytic concepts for characterizing different soundscapes. Is the sound hi-fi or lo-fi? High-fidelity sound, which we expect from our CD player, has clear and discrete signals against little ambient noise. In low-fidelity sounds, distinct signals are less audible because of the strong ambient, indistinguishable noise. The countryside is more hi-fi; the cities are more lo-fi. Furthermore the ratio of technological to natural noises is changing: Schafer's estimates, derived from literary and anthropological sources, are that the ratio of technical and artificial noises to natural and human noises has changed from 'primitive cultures' at 5:95, to pre-industrial society at 14:86, to post-industrial cultures at 66:34.

Cantometrics: singing as a cultural index

Alan Lomax (1959; 1968; 1970), a pioneer in the study of folk music, has developed musical analysis into a diagnostic instrument of cultural practices: show me how you sing, and I will tell you how you grew up. Traditional folk-singing is transmitted orally without formal notation, is performed by non-professional musicians, and is associated with particular social events, such as work, religious ceremonies, child-rearing or social protest. Lomax's inspiration for his project came from observing differences between American white and black folk-singing, and from travelling across Spain and Italy in the 1950s, where he noticed a north–south divide in styles of singing: in the north he found open deep-voiced choral singing as in Alpine choirs; and in the south he found individual closed high-pitched singing, as in the Italian serenade or the Andalusian flamenco. His observations are confirmed by traditional Italian musical prejudice, according to which the 'southerners can't sing together'. From these observations he developed hypotheses on the correlation between singing and social factors, in particular the social position of women, permissiveness on pre-marital sex and the treatment of children. Repression and cruelty arising from a local history of domination and exploitation correlate with high-pitched closed and individual singing styles.

A song is 'a complex human action – music plus speech, relating performers to a larger group in a special situation by means of certain behaviour patterns, and giving rise to a common emotional experience' (Lomax, 1959: 928). This music has a social function: 'the primary effect of music is to give the listener the feeling of security, for it symbolizes the place where he was born, his earliest childhood satisfaction, his religious experience, his pleasure in community doings, his courtship and his work – any or all of these personality-shaping experiences' (1959: 929). Lomax infers that folk-singing is the most conservative of cultural traits, with a longer cycle of change than other art forms; and hence it is privileged as an indicator of culture and of cultural change. Folk music is a 'total musical event', which is music in context, and as such it is diagnostic to the listener/ observer; oral traditional folk-singing is woven into the local context and takes its form, energy and appreciation from the situation within which it arises, and so reflects these conditions very closely. Authentic folk-singing is an index, a sign that gains its meaning from a correlation with its conditions of production.

Between 1962 and 1970 Lomax and his colleagues analysed a corpus of 3525 tape-recorded folk-songs sampled from 233 different localities, which resulted in an atlas of world folk-music styles. They proposed the analytic system of 'cantometrics' – a set of musical 'phonemes' taking different meanings in different contexts, but within which the differences of the world's folk styles are represented. Thirty-seven characteristics of folk-singing – among them group activity, rhythm, melody, phrasing, tempo, and textual and vocalization characteristics – are coded on scales that are defined in detail (Lomax, 1968: 34–74). This system is an 'intentionally coarse grid . . . [not] to describe musical idiolects or dialects or any one musical statement, but to point to differences in style at the regional or areal level' (1968: 35). Each musical recording is coded by a trained coder, and the data are computerized and checked for reliability to allow for further analysis. The musical variables are statistically related to socio-cultural variables of the locality, such as forms of agricultural production, complexity of social stratification, severity of sexual mores, male dominance and social cohesion.

The outcomes of these studies were several. First, the researchers proposed a ninefold classification of world folk styles into Amerindian, Pygmoid, African, Melanesian, Polynesian, Malayan, Eurasian, Old European and Modern European. Secondly, they identified two principal types of singing within the individual–cohesiveness dimension (models A and B). Thirdly, they offered a test of hypotheses relating singing styles to the emotional economy of the local culture:

> the conditions which work most strongly against solidarity of the singing group are two varieties of masculine dominance: direct assertiveness and control of feminine sexuality, both symbolized by the introduction of disturbing and idiosyncratic noise into vocalization. (1968: 198)

Female/male complementarity in subsistence work correlates with cohesive, polyphone and relaxed singing styles. The degree of stress applied to infants (such as circumcision) relates to the range of voice used in singing.

The probability of coordinated choral singing is reduced by male aggressiveness, diffuse organization of subsistence work, rigid stratification, masculine dominance in production, or repressive control over female sexuality.

Lomax's cantometrics has been criticized by Nettl (1990, 48), as it is based on limited samples of native music. The analytic language is Western, and uses in many cases inadequate categories, while 'real understanding' would require the use of indigenous distinctions. The small local samples of around 10 songs brush over much local variety of song styles, and so the resulting classification is rough and shows many anomalies. And finally, the restriction to songs excludes instrumental folk music from Lomax's characterization of local musical culture. Despite these shortcomings, his data provide a baseline for monitoring the loss of variety of world musical culture, and allow us to test predictions of what happens when social groups migrate, evolve their social relations and develop hybrid forms of musical expression.

Musical feature analysis: embellishment, complexity and diversity

Most musical events, from a Western point of view, can be characterized by several dimensions: the melody, which is the sequence of tones that we can easily remember; the harmony, which is the system that orders the melody; the rhythm, which is the timing of musical progression; the phrasing, which is the linking and the separation of notes into larger units; the dynamics, which is the variations in loudness and speed; the form, which is the larger patterns of repetitions; and the orchestration, which is the assignment of instruments to particular roles. Each of them has their own conventions, which, separate and in combination, can serve as cultural indicators.

Melodic embellishment as deviation from expectation

Cerullo (1992) has developed a measure of the progression of a melody in vocal/instrumental music such as national anthems. Her theoretical inspiration is the relationship between symbolic conventions, their violation and the resulting attention. The hypothesis is that deviations from conventional melodic progressions raise the attention of the listener, and move them from a passive to an active mode of exploring meaning. In order to explore this stimulating power of music, Cerullo developed a measure of melodic syntax. A melody is a progression of notes that form a recognizable Gestalt – something that we easily remember, hum or sing. The structure of a melody is the relation between notes. A single note is meaningless: it gains its significance from a relationship with other notes, which can be the same, or higher or lower. Melodic lines or progressions are characterized on a continuum from a line that is basically conventional, highly stable, constant and fixed with minimal movement on the tonal scale, to a line that

Table 15.4   *Pitch–time matrix of the first two
melodic phrases of 'God Save the Queen'*

Note	Time, beat	Pitch ranking
G	1	0
G	2	0
A	3	2
F#	4	−1
G	5.5	0
A	6	2
B	7	4
B	8	4
C	9	5
B	10	4
A	11.5	2
G	12	0
etc.	etc.	etc.

is embellished or distorted, embodies opposites, is erratic in its progression and unpredictable, and uses a wider range of sounds by breaking new ground. Four variables are constructed to represent this continuum: frequency of melodic motion, magnitude of motion, methods of line construction, and ornamentation of central notes.

The tool developed for this analysis is the pitch–time matrix (see Table 15.4). This method presents two features of the musical event: the musical time or beat, and the pitch ranking, which is the relative deviation from the tonal centre of diatonic melodies in half-tones. If the tonal centre of a song is G, that is, the tonality of the song is G major or G minor, an A following the G will get the value +2 as the A is two half-tones above the G, and an E following the A will get the value −3, as the E is three half-tones below the G. The pitch-time graph of the first two melodic phrases of 'God Save the Queen' is shown in Figure 15.1. The standardization to the tonal centre (tonica = 0) allows comparison of different melodies in the same graphical representation. On this melodic transcription the indicators are defined as follows. *Frequency* refers to the number of directional changes in the melody – how many times a movement upwards changes into a movement downwards. *Magnitude* indicates how drastic the changes in the melodic progression are by relating the average size of melodic steps. *Disjunctness* represents the intervals in a melody. Conjunct motion is smooth: notes progress in nearly successive degrees up and down the scale. Disjunct motion is jagged: the notes of the melody are separated by large intervals. *Ornamentation* looks at the relation between music and text. Sometimes a single syllable of text extends over several different notes, therefore ornamenting and stressing the text. Decoration is present when we have more notes than syllables in the text, and it considers the frequency of such instances. Each of these measures has a precise mathematical definition derived from the pitch–time matrix (Cerullo, 1989: 212ff), giving scores for each song that is analysed.

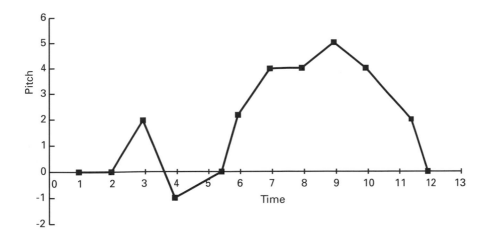

Figure 15.1 *Pitch–time graph of the first two melodic phrases of 'God Save the Queen'*

Using these four indicators of melodic progression, analysis of 154 national anthems found that the more frequent directional changes are, the larger is their magnitude, and the more disjunct are interval progressions, and the more ornamentation will be used. They therefore are likely to represent an underlying continuum of 'overall musical embellishment'. The criterion of internal consistency is satisfied. The validity of the measures is demonstrated by showing how national anthems vary consistently across geographical regions, and across the periods and political circumstances of their adoption.

An obvious limitation of the method is its assumption of Western-style music: the pitch–time matrix assumes musical materials that are based on 12 half-tones and a central tonality, an assumption that is wrong for the music of many other cultures.

Changing complexity in popular music

Dowd (1992) analysed the 'Number One' songs of the Anglo-American pop charts between 1955 and 1988. Music is like language in that it can be used in a 'restricted' or an 'elaborate' manner, and the key problem was to measure the changing complexity of songs over time. Three variables of pop songs were constructed following Cerullo (1992): melodic ornamentation (ornamentation); melodic form (frequency, direction, disjunctness); and chordal structure (the proportion of minor, major, I, V and IV chords). For each variable a score was developed on a continuum from low to high and elaborate complexity. Songs were further coded in tempo (beats per minute), duration (minutes) and whether they are instrumental or singing plus instrumental. This set of dependent and control variables was related year by year to a set of independent variables characterizing the music industry in order to test the concentration hypothesis: the smaller the number of labels in the Top 10 market, the more restricted is the musical code of Top 10 songs – a characteristic that has been described as 'musical entropy' (Peterson and Berger, 1975). Time-series regression analysis does not confirm the concentration hypothesis in relation to melodic form, but it shows a relation to harmonic features: a larger number of record companies in the Top 10 in the preceding year increases the harmonic complexity of the current year's Top 10 songs, while a faster turnover of songs per year restricts the chordal structure. The fewer Top 10 songs there are in any one year, the more likely is more elaborate music. Furthermore, it was found that black musicians and performers who sing their own material generally used a more elaborate musical code, both in melody and in harmony. Equally, longer songs and purely instrumental music use more elaborate codes. The absence of a keyboard, the use of acoustic guitars, performers singing somebody else's composition, and larger turnover per year lead to more restricted musical expression.

Using a simple numerical coding of melodic and harmonic features of pop music, Dowd and others (for example, Alexander, 1996; Peterson and Berger, 1996) have constructed indicators. They determined the influence of the external conditions of production on the internal structure of music itself, thus demonstrating in detail how the autonomy of musical expression in pop culture is constrained by conditions of market supply. The more we know about these constraints, the more we can confidently reverse the analysis of this musical genre as a proxy indicator of the production context, which may be a cheap and quick way of establishing information about business trends and developments.

Towards an analysis of musical multimedia

Cook (1998) presents a methodology for the study of video clips in popular music. The challenge here was to identify the contribution of music to the construction of meaning where moving images, song text and sounds are interwoven. What we perceive as this interwoven texture is different from what we would perceive if we were to look at the three modes – images, text and sound – in isolation. While each of the three modes interprets the others, it seems to be a characteristic of music in film that it becomes background, and is unnoticed even by the analyst: 'the best writing on music videos . . . is undermined by the relative crudeness of its categories for the description and analysis of musical structures' (1998: 150).

To fill this analytic lacuna, Cook suggested a graphical analysis which he exemplified with Madonna's video *Material Girl* (1985). First, the text and musical features are juxtaposed. The text consists of four-line verses and refrains; and the musical structure supports this duality with characteristic sequences for both elements. The music also provides a repeated introduction and a coda. The musical events are depicted in a line showing the distribution of materials in units of four or eight bars from bar 1 to bar 137, marked as introduction, verse, refrain and coda. This reveals that the song consists of three larger units of partial repetition and extension.

Secondly, music and images are juxtaposed in a second graph. This is a more complicated picture with 11 lines: the musical material in eight-bar units (line 1) against which all other elements are synchronized, the continuous basic groove (line 2), the introductions 1 (line 3) and 2 (line 4), the verses (line 5), the refrains (line 6) and the coda (line 7). The image materials are depicted by the enumeration of the shots (line 8), camera 1 (line 9) and camera 2 (line 10), which shows the cuts in relation to the eight-bar units, and finally the duration of shots (line 11). This graph shows how the different elements change in conjunction or disjunction with musical units – how introduction, verse or refrain gets a repetitive or evolving visual treatment.

This is an elaborate and detailed analysis for a music video of a few minutes. Going beyond Cook – who intends to show that music only has potential meaning, while the actual meaning arises from its encounter with text and images – one could imagine taking his analytic notations as raw material for, in a similar fashion to Cerullo or Dowd, a secondary notation to construct cultural indicators. What about an index for the synchronicity of changes between music elements and film shots? There is room for further development.

Musical taste: an index of social position

One last area where musical materials are used as social indicators is in large-scale studies of musical taste and appreciation: tell me what you are listening to, and I will tell you who you are. Adorno (1976) has suggested a sevenfold typology of musical reception: expert, good listener, cultural consumer, emotional listener, resentment listener, entertainment listener and musically indifferent. These types characterize listeners of music in contemporary industrial societies; they represent discontinuities in behaviour that reflect the 'degree of adequacy' between the music and the act of listening and the capacity to verbalize what is heard. The typology has attracted criticism (see Martin, 1995) for lacking empirical foundation (the sources of Adorno's percentage figures for each type are not documented), and for its musical elitism which reserves 'adequacy of listening' for professionals and relics of a leisurely European aristocracy, relegates the jazz fan to 'resentment', and disregards popular music altogether.

Bourdieu's (1984) analysis of French tastes of the 1960s has a more empirical flavour. Musical tastes are, among other tastes, part of a 'habitus' or 'lifestyle' that informs a taken-for-granted judgement of likes and dislikes that is collectively shared by social groups. In a pioneering application of statistical correspondence analysis to questionnaire data, people identified whether they liked Gershwin's *Rhapsody in Blue*, Strauss's *The Blue Danube* or Bach's *Well-Tempered Clavier*, in conjunction with other art or everyday tastes and socio-economic indicators. This analysis depicts a two-dimensional social space of high or low economic capital and high or low cultural capital. It shows the concordance of characteristics such as driving a Citroen 2CV, liking jazz music, and being a school teacher. Such maps of tastes are the basis of much current consumer research, where musical taste may indeed be a salient marker of a certain 'lifestyle' or, more traditionally, of a certain social position. Buchhofer et al. (1974) have compiled 25 different research designs for such investigations. Beyond the strategic usage for music marketing, such studies demonstrate that the appreciation of a particular music is functional less with regard to universal dispositions, and more with regard to socially cultivated stereotypes.

Conclusions: so what?

The status of musical meaning is controversial: can music carry meaning on its own, or only in conjunction with images or language? For the purpose of social science we can leave this issue unresolved, as we are using music as an indicator for social structures, and so by definition its meaning arises from this correlation. Music is an event in time: it is only available for analysis and as a cultural indicator through recording and transcription. Various attempts to construct indicators of social affairs on the basis of musical material have been briefly introduced: Lomax's universal rating system of singing styles; Cerullo's and Dowd's attempts to relate melodies to social forces; Peterson and Berger's measure of pop music as an indicator of the concentration in the music industry; Schafer's soundscapes both to enhance our awareness of sound pollution, and to keep a record of a sound environment that is historically changing and for which we don't have a memory; Attali's suggestion that noise in any historical period is fore-shadowing the social order of the future; and finally Cook's suggestion for a complex analysis of music videos which could be the basis of social indicators as yet undefined. Most of these suggestions are undertakings of individuals or small networks of researchers. None of these methodologies has reached the critical mass that would give rise to a discourse of good or bad practice; the main issue seems to be to prove their significance for the social sciences in the first place.

The dominance of verbal data in the social sciences leaves sound and music as generally underexploited resources for social research. The current pervasiveness and universal emotional power of sounds, and of music as a medium of symbolic representation, would suggest they could be a useful source of social data. This potential is, however, not matched as yet by an efficient methodology and a critical mass of research. It remains unclear to me whether this undervaluation as a source of data is due to intrinsic characteristics of the medium, or to a historical accident. As is often the case in a market-place, with limited resources and deadlines, what is needed are efficient ways of collecting and analysing sound events in order to compete with the efficiency of the opinion polls and the focus group, or of the content analysis of textual materials. This efficiency has not fallen from the skies, but is the outcome of years of rationalization and industrialization.

As yet, sound materials are an untrodden field for methodological cultivation in the social sciences.

STEPS TOWARDS A CONSTRUCTION OF MUSICAL INDICATORS

1 Decide on the kind of musical activity that may be indicative of and comparable across different social groups, or across time for one particular group.
2 Record relevant sound materials produced and appreciated by particular groups of people.
3 Establish a transcription for relevant musical features (melody, rhythm, harmony, etc.).
4 Define indicators on the basis of the transcription.
5 Relate these indicators to other characteristics of the group (validation).
6 Compare the indicators across different social groups, or for the same group over time.

STEPS TOWARDS A SOUNDSCAPE

1 Decide on locations for the recording of a soundscape.
2 Decide on a manageable time sampling frame: for example, record an entire day, or five minutes every half-hour.
3 Make recordings and measure the loudness, either continuously or on average for a particular time interval. Obtain a loudness diagram.
4 Verbalize the sounds that are being recorded. Elicit comments of people living at the location by qualitative interviewing from the record, or verbalize the sounds yourself.
5 Alternatively, obtain standards ratings or sound diaries in parallel with the recordings, where informants make a diary entry at predefined time intervals.
6 Tabulate the sounds by distinguishing onomatopoeic characteristics such as squeaking or cracking, the sources of sound, the loudness, and ongoing human activity, in relation to location and time.
7 Condense these tabulations to establish characteristic sound patterns by location and time.
8 Establish hi-fi and lo-fi estimates and natural/artificial sound ratios, and compare these across time and space..

References

Adorno, T.W. (1976) *Introduction to the Sociology of Music*. New York: Seadbury.
Adams, S. (1983) *R. Murray Schafer*. Toronto: University of Toronto Press.

Alexander, P.J. (1996) 'Entropy and popular culture: product diversity in the popular music recording industry', *American Sociological Review*, 61: 171–4.

Attali, J. (1985) *Noise: the Political Economy of Music*. Manchester: Manchester University Press (first published Paris, 1977).

Bauer, M. (2000) ' "Science in the media" as cultural indicator: contexualising surveys with media analysis', in M. Dierkes and C. von Grote (eds) *Between Understanding and Trust: the public, science and technology*. Reading: Harwood. pp. 157–178.

Bent, I. and Drabkin, W. (1987) *The New Grove Handbook in Music Analysis*. London: Macmillan.

Bourdieu, P. (1984) *Distinction: a Social Critique of the Judgement of Taste*. London: Routledge.

Buchhofer, B., Friedrichs, J. and Ludtke, H. (1974) *Musik und Sozialstruktur. Theoretische Rahmenstudie und Forschungspläne*. Cologne: Arno Volk.

Cerullo, K.A. (1989) 'Variations in musical syntax', *Communications Research*, 16: 204–35.

Cerullo, K.A. (1992) 'Putting it together: measuring the syntax of aural and visual symbols', in R. Wuthnow (ed.), *Vocabularies of Public Life: Empirical Essays in Symbolic Structure*. London: Routledge. pp. 111–29.

Cook, N. (1998) *Analysing Musical Multimedia*. Oxford: Clarendon.

Dowd, T.J. (1992) 'The musical structure and social context of Number One songs, 1955–1988: an exploratory analysis', in R. Wuthnow (ed.), *Vocabularies of Public Life: Empirical Essays in Symbolic Structure*. London: Routledge. pp. 130–57.

Frith, S. (1988) *Music for Pleasure: Essays in the Sociology of Pop*. Cambridge: Polity.

Jansen, G. (1991) 'Physiological effects of noise' in C.M. Harris (ed.) *Handbook of Acoustical Measurements and Noise Control*. New York: McGraw-Hill.

Leman, M. (1993) 'Symbolic and subsymbolic description of music', in G. Haus (ed.) *Music Processing*. Oxford: Oxford University Press. pp. 119–239.

Leonard, N. (1987) *Jazz-myth and religion*. Oxford: Oxford University Press.

Lomax, A. (1959) 'Folksong style', *American Anthropologist*, 61: 927–54.

Lomax, A. (1968) *Folk Song Style and Culture*. Washington, DC: AAAS.

Lomax, A. (1970) 'Song structure and social structure', in M.C. Albrecht, J.H. Barnett and M. Griff (eds), *The Sociology of Art and Literature*. London: Duckworth. pp. 55–71.

Lonza, J. (1995) *Elevator music: a Surreal History of Muzak, Easy Listening and other Moodsongs*. London: Quartet Books.

Macdonald, I. (1995) *Revolution in the Head – the Beatles' Records and the Sixties*. London: Pimlico.

Martin, P.J. (1995) *Sounds and Society: Themes in the Sociology of Music*. Manchester: Manchester University Press.

Mayer, L.B. (1956) *Emotion and Meaning in Music*. Chicago, IL: University of Chicago Press.

Merriam, A.P. (1964) *The Anthropology of Music*. Chicago, IL: Northwestern University Press.

Nattiez, J.J. (1990) *Music and Discourse – towards a Semiology of Music*. Princeton, NJ: Princeton University Press.

Nettl, B. (1990) *Folk and Traditional Music of the Western Continents*, 3rd edn. Englewood Cliffs, NJ: Prentice-Hall.

Nisbett, A. (1983) *The Use of Microphones*. London: Focal Press.

Peterson, R.A. and Berger, D.G. (1975) 'Cycles of symbol production: the case of popular music', *American Journal of Sociology*, 40: 158–73.

Peterson, R.A. and Berger, D.G. (1996) 'Measuring industry concentration, diversity and innovation in popular music', *American Popular Music*, 61: 175–8.

Pratt, R. (1994) *Rhythm and Resistance: the Political Uses of American Popular Music*. Washington, DC: Smithsonian Institution Press.

Read, G. (1969) *Music Notation – a Manual of Modern Practice*. Boston, MA: Crescendo.

Reitan, L. (1991) 'Does it really mean anything: some aspects of meaning', in J. Paynter, T. Howell, R. Orton and P. Seymour (eds), *Contemporary Musical Thought*, *vol. 1*, 625–633. London: Routledge.

Schafer, R.M. (1973) 'The music of the environment', *Occasional Journal Devoted to Soundscape Studies*, 1: 3–35.

Schafer, R.M. (1977) *The Tuning of the World*. Toronto: Knopf.

Sloboda, J. (1985) *The Musical Mind: the cognitive psychology of music*. Oxford: Clarendon Press.

Tagg, P. (1982) 'Analyzing popular music: theory, method and practice', *Popular Music*, 2: 37–68.

Winkler, J. (1995a) 'Das Hören wecken: Erfahrungen mit dem Aktivieren des Hörens in Befragungen über die Klanglandschaft'. Paper presented at Kongressbeitrag Hören – eine vernachlaessigte Kunst?, Basel, June.

Winkler, J. (1995b) 'Klanglandschaften als Räume der hörenden Existenz'. Paper delivered at Berlin Academy of Arts, KlangumWelten, May.

Part III

Computer Assistance

16

Computer-Assisted Analysis: Coding and Indexing

Udo Kelle

KEYWORDS	
coding	interpretive analysis
complex retrieval	ordinary retrieval
computer-assisted analysis	qualitative data
hypothesis examination	theory building

Although software for handling textual data has been available since the mid 1960s, it was not until the early 1980s that qualitative researchers discovered that the computer could assist them in working with their data (Kelle, 1995: 1f). Before that, programs for textual analysis, such as the General Inquirer, had attracted only a limited group of experts in the field of quantitative content analysis. This reluctance of most qualitative researchers to use computers certainly set them apart from the methodological mainstream of quantitative survey and experimental research, where, during the 1960s and 1970s, the computer became an indispensable aid. At that time, electronic data processing devices were seen by many social scientists as tools for nothing more than the statistical analysis of numerical data (or the quantitative content analysis of textual data). The idea that computers could one day become an indispensable tool for the storage, retrieval and manipulation of text was far away.

This situation was radically changed by the advent of the personal computer. Like other *hommes de lettres*, qualitative researchers discovered rather quickly the enormous possibilities for text manipulation that were offered by the new technology. In the mid 1980s, several qualitative researchers with advanced computer knowledge and expertise started, independently of each other, to develop software that could support the analysis of qualitative data. While most of these programs were designed only for the purposes of one specific research project, some packages were put on the market by their developers: programs like THE ETHNOGRAPH, QUALPRO and TAP started a train of development in the field of computing in qualitative social research. A number of additional software packages, NUD*IST, MAX and WINMAX, ATLAS/ti, HYPERRESEARCH, HYPERSOFT (to name only a few), appeared in subsequent years. Nowadays, more than 20 different software packages are available that can assist qualitative researchers in their work with textual data, and some of these programs (especially THE ETHNOGRAPH and NUD*IST) are widely applied in the qualitative community. Their first, sometimes rather awkward and user-unfriendly, versions were rapidly improved, and more and complex functions were added. These developments culminated in a race between developers to include as many features as possible in the latest versions of their programs. Nowadays the field of computer-assisted qualitative data analysis can be seen as the most rapidly developing field in the domain of qualitative methodology, with its own 'networking projects', conferences and discussion lists on the Internet.

Given the fact that the literature describing these software packages in detail (for example Tesch, 1990; Weitzman and Miles, 1995) is always in danger of rapidly becoming out-of-date, this chapter will not concentrate on particular programs, but will discuss more generally those techniques of qualitative data administration and data analysis that can be supported by computer programs. Strong emphasis will be placed on the methodological aspects of computer use in qualitative research.

Conceptual issues

The 'operation called *Verstehen*' (Abel, 1948), the understanding of the meaning of text, can certainly not be performed with the help of an information processing machine, since it cannot easily be formalized (Kelle, 1995: 2). However, there is still a variety of mechanical tasks involved in the analysis of textual data. The qualitative research process often generates huge amounts of interview transcripts, protocols, field notes and personal documents, which, if not managed properly, can result in 'data overload' (Miles and Huberman, 1994). Since data analysis and theory construction are closely interlinked in qualitative research, the researcher generates many theoretical concepts in this ongoing process which are often recorded across numerous notebooks, manuscript pages and index cards. Keeping track of the emerging ideas, arguments and theoretical concepts can be a mammoth organizational task.

These problems have been well known for centuries among scholars who have to work with great amounts of texts. A variety of methods for coping with them have been developed, most of them based either on the construction of indexes (or 'registers' or 'concordances') of various kinds, or on the inclusion of cross-references in the text. Both these techniques can help with an important task of data management: the drawing together of all the text passages that have something in common. Before the advent of computers, 'cut-and-paste' techniques were the most widely used methods in qualitative research of organizing data material in this way: researchers were obliged to 'cut up field notes, transcripts and other materials and place data relating to each coding category in a separate file folder or manila envelope' (Taylor and Bogdan, 1984: 136; see also Lofland and Lofland, 1984: 134).

To computerize such tasks, a non-formatted textual database has to be built up. Unfortunately, standard software like word processors or standard database systems are usually of only limited use for the construction of non-formatted textual databases, since they do not support the techniques of data management that are needed to structure them, such as:

- the definition of pointers containing index words together with the 'addresses' of text passages which can be used to retrieve indexed text segments
- the construction of electronic cross-references with the help of so-called 'hyperlinks', which can be used to 'jump' between text passages which are linked together.

All software packages developed especially for qualitative research are based on one or both of these techniques. Furthermore, current versions of programs like THE ETHNOGRAPH, HYPERRESEARCH, HYPERSOFT, MAX, NUD*IST or ATLAS/ti contain a variety of additional features:

- Facilities for the storing of the researchers' comments ('memos'), which can be linked to index words or text segments.
- Features for defining linkages between index words.
- The use of variables and filters so that the search for text segments can be restricted by certain limitations.
- Facilities for the retrieval of text segments with specified formal relations to each other (e.g. text segments that appear within a certain specified maximum distance of each other).
- Facilities for the retrieval of quantitative attributes of the database.

Techniques of computer-aided qualitative analysis

Examples from research practice show how these techniques can be used to support the analysis of qualitative data.

The use of computers in qualitative research cannot be regarded as one single method, which can be followed step-by-step: it comprises a variety of different – both straightforward and very complex – techniques. Certainly the right choice of one of these techniques can only be made with reference to the researcher's methodological background, his or her research questions, and the research objectives.

A terminological caveat has to be made here: 'computer-aided (or computer-assisted) qualitative data analysis' is certainly misunderstood if one sees software packages like THE ETHNOGRAPH, ATLAS/ti or NUD*IST as capable of performing 'qualitative analyses' in the same way as SPSS can perform analyses of variance. These software packages are tools to mechanize tasks of ordering and archiving texts, and represent software for 'data administration and archiving' rather than tools for 'data analysis'. So the term 'computer-aided qualitative data analysis' as it is used in this chapter refers to the interpretive analysis of textual data where software is used for the organization and management of the data.

Discovering differences, commonalities and relations between text segments

After having collected unstructured textual data through fieldwork or open interviewing, the qualitative researcher may want to construct 'meaningful patterns of facts' (Jorgenson, 1989: 107) by looking for structures in the data. This is often conducted by comparing different pieces of data in order to find commonalities, differences or linkages between them. To some degree this process is similar to solving a jigsaw puzzle. The analyst will start by collecting certain pieces of the textual data that are similar in a certain respect. He or she will analyse several parts and their connections, that is the specific way they could be linked or connected to form a meaningful picture. In their famous monograph *The Discovery of Grounded Theory* (1967), Glaser and Strauss coined the term 'constant comparative method' for this process, whereby 'underlying patterns' are discovered through careful and intensive comparison. The central prerequisite for this is 'coding', that is relating text passages to categories that the researcher either had previously developed or develops ad hoc:

> The analyst starts by coding each incident in his data into as many categories of analysis as possible, as categories emerge or as data emerge that fit in an existing category. (1967: 105)

In practical terms this means

> noting categories on margins, but [it] can be done more elaborately (e.g. on cards). It should keep track of the comparison group in which the incident occurs. (1967: 106)

Most of the software programs for qualitative analysis support this process of categorizing and comparing text segments by offering 'code-and-retrieve' facilities (Kelle, 1995: 4ff; Richards and Richards, 1995), which allow for the attachment of 'codes' (index words) to text segments, and the

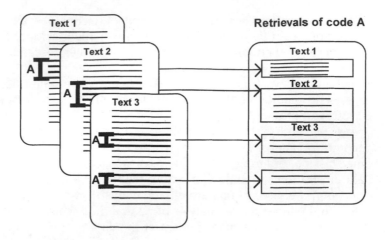

Figure 16.1 *Coding and retrieval*

retrieval of all segments from a defined set of documents to which the same code had been assigned (see Figure 16.1).

The comparison of text passages can be aided by attaching to whole documents particular variables that can be used for selective retrievals where the search for text segments is restricted by certain limitations, permitting, for example, the retrieval of statements about certain topics from only those interview participants who have a certain characteristic in common. For example, a qualitative researcher investigating the division of household labour among married couples could first of all retrieve all the text segments in which wives talk about housework, and then contrast them with text segments on the same topic from interviews with husbands.

The majority of computer programs for qualitative analysis are based on 'code-and-retrieve' facilities. In an article about methodological aspects of computer use in qualitative research, Coffey et al. (1996) warned that the one-sided emphasis on code-and-retrieve operations may lead to a neglect of other computer-aided techniques, especially techniques offered by hypertext systems. Looking at other hermeneutic sciences (especially historical and critical biblical exegesis), one can see indeed that indexing (coding and retrieval) is not always the best tool to support the comparison of text segments (or 'synopsis' as it is called in biblical exegesis). The use of cross-references (hyperlinks) is another important strategy for data administration that would be useful here. Unfortunately, there have as yet been only a few software packages, namely ATLAS/ti and HYPERSOFT, that support the construction of hyperlinks.

Developing typologies and theories

In many qualitative research projects, the comparison of text segments leads to the construction of descriptive typologies and to the development of theories. Since qualitative research often starts with the collection of empirical data and then theories are developed on this basis, qualitative methodologists have sometimes adopted a naive inductivist model of the research process, assuming that theoretical categories will simply emerge from the empirical material if the researchers free their minds of theoretical preconceptions. This approach, which is often influenced by the early methodological writings of Glaser and Strauss (see, for example, Glaser and Strauss, 1967: 37), means that qualitative researchers enter their empirical field with no theoretical concepts whatsoever.

However, one of the most crucial insights of modern philosophy of science and cognitive psychology is the fact that 'there are and can be no sensations unimpregnated by expectations' (Lakatos, 1982: 15). In his later methodological writings, Strauss took this 'theory-ladenness' of empirical observation into account by proposing a 'paradigm model' (Strauss and Corbin, 1990: 99ff). According to Strauss and Corbin, a 'coding paradigm' represents a general theory of action that can be used to build a skeleton or 'axis' of the developing grounded theory. Glaser, although he fully repudiated Strauss and Corbin's concepts in a later book (Glaser, 1992), proposed a similar idea: 'theoretical codes' represent those theoretical concepts that the researcher has at his or her disposal independently from data collection and data analysis (Glaser, 1978).

Such coding paradigms and theoretical codes (which are often implicit at the beginning of an empirical study) can be made explicit by constructing a coding scheme. The following example shows a code scheme from a research project that studies the transition from school to the labour market (Heinz, 1996; Heinz et al., 1998). Open interviews were conducted in order to reconstruct the decision processes of school graduates who entered vocational training courses. In our project the decision processes described by the interviewees were structured according to the following three categories:

1 aspirations, which represent the respondents' preferences that were used to account for occupational options
2 realizations, which consist of the actual steps of action that were taken to fulfil aspirations
3 evaluations, which were the respondents' assessments of the relations between aspirations, conditions and consequences of action.

These categories represent the subcodes (1.1–1.3; 5.1–5.3, 8.1–8.3) shown in Table 16.1.

The second type of code categories frequently used for qualitative coding are codes derived from common-sense knowledge. In the interviews with school graduates, all text passages were coded where the interviewee talked, for example, about experiences in their job, about relevant institutions, about their family and so on. The main categories (1, 5, 8) shown in Table 16.1 represent examples of categories that are drawn from common-sense knowledge.

Table 16.1   *An extract from a coding scheme*

1	*Job and profession*
1.1	Job and profession/aspirations
1.2	Job and profession/realizations
1.3	Job and profession/evaluations
5	*Cohabitation*
5.1	Cohabitation/aspirations
5.2	Cohabitation/realizations
5.3	Cohabitation/evaluations
8	*Children*
8.1	Children/aspirations
8.2	Children/realizations
8.3	Children/evaluations

Both the kinds of codes (derived either from common-sense knowledge or from abstract theoretical concepts) that play the most important roles at the start of the qualitative research process are either rather trivial or highly abstract. Thus they have something in common: they do not denote well-defined empirical events, but serve heuristic purposes. They represent some kind of theoretical axis or 'skeleton' to which the flesh of empirically contentful information is added (Strauss and Corbin, 1990; Kelle, 1994). The research project mentioned above, which started with structuring the material according to the general categories 'aspirations', 'realizations' and 'evaluations', ended up discovering eight different types of biographical aspirations, for example the type 'delegation': some young adults try to delegate the responsibility for their occupational career to the managers of their companies or to the officials at the employment office.

To develop such typologies or theoretical concepts, a fine-grained analysis of text segments is necessary in order to find those aspects (or 'dimensions') that can serve as criteria for a comparison in order to develop either subcategories, or subdimensions of the categories already used for coding. This process of 'dimensionalization' (Strauss and Corbin, 1990: 69ff) may be clarified with another example from our research project. There, the respondents' orientations towards marriage were investigated by first coding text segments according to whether the topics 'marriage' or 'family' were mentioned. In a second step, text segments of those respondents who regarded marriage as a crucial goal in life were selectively retrieved. The comparison of these text passages led to the discovery of three different dimensions of this category:

1 Marriage was seen by some respondents as the only acceptable form of cohabitation.
2 Others viewed marriage as the prerequisite for child-centred family formation.
3 Still others regarded marriage as a kind of safeguard. Respondents with this last orientation advanced three different arguments: marriage was seen as (a) offering financial protection, (b) providing a support for the

bonding between the partners, or (c) a means of fulfilling the expectations of their social environment (parents, relatives, etc.).

Through comparison and dimensionalization, three different sets of code categories were developed in the analysis process: first, categories that refer to how important the issue of marriage was for the respondents; secondly, categories that refer to the orientations towards marriage among those who see marriage as a crucial goal in life (as the only acceptable form of cohabitation, as a prerequisite for child-centred family formation, as a safeguard); and thirdly, categories that refer to arguments for why marriage is a safeguard. The hierarchical relation between these sets of categories is shown in Figure 16.2.

In terms of information science, the tree structure displayed in Figure 16.2 can be formally described as a network or graph in which the categories or codes represent the nodes of the graph, and the lines between them the edges. Using this network approach, it is possible to expand the basic principle of non-formatted textual database systems in which codes were connected by pointers to text segments (Muhr, 1991; 1992). Thereby, it is possible to store electronically the whole structure of the hierarchical typology or graph shown in Figure 16.2. Consequently, not only can this graph be used to give an account of the emerging typology or theory, but it also allows for rather complex retrieval procedures that follow a long path from a node at one end of the network or graph, to a node at the other end.

It should be noted here that graphs may be structured in quite diverse ways: ATLAS/ti and HYPERSOFT are programs that allow the researcher to define all possible linkages between the nodes (permitting the researcher to define 'cycles' and 'loops'). Other programs (such as NUD*IST) impose certain restrictions on the researcher: for example, they might limit the

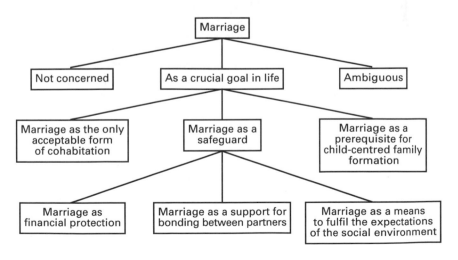

Figure 16.2   *A hierarchical category scheme as a result of dimensionalization*

construction of more tightly structured networks (such as hierarchical trees).

Examining hypotheses

Software for the computer-aided analysis of textual data can also be helpful in refining theoretical concepts and examining hypotheses. However, one must not forget here that qualitative hypothesis examination is a process quite distinct from statistical hypothesis testing. In the qualitative methodological literature, one will find nothing comparable to the precise decision rules that are applied in statistical significance testing. Instead, 'testing and confirming findings' (Miles and Huberman, 1994: 262) or 'verification' (Strauss and Corbin, 1990: 108) mean, in qualitative research, returning to the data (rereading one's transcripts or field notes), or returning to the field (conducting new observations or interviews), in order to find some confirming or disconfirming evidence. Precise rules that are formulated to inform the researcher, with certainty, about when he or she has to reject or abandon a certain hypothesis, are nowhere to be found. Qualitative hypotheses, when they first come into a researcher's mind, are usually not highly specified and definite propositions about certain facts, but tentative, imprecise and sometimes very vague conjectures about possible relationships. Rather than calling them hypotheses, one should call them hypotheses about what *kind* of propositions, descriptions or explanations will be useful in further analysis. They are insights that 'whatever specific claim the successful [hypothesis] will make, it will nonetheless be a hypothesis of one kind rather than another' (Hanson, 1971: 291).

A qualitative researcher investigating gender-specific occupational careers may, for example, develop the hypothesis that there must be a relationship between their interviewees' orientations towards work and family. To examine this hypothesis, complex retrieval facilities can be extremely helpful. Most of the software packages currently available contain such complex retrieval facilities which support the search for co-occurring codes. So co-occurrences can be defined in various ways:

- They are indicated by overlapping or nested text segments to which the codes under investigation are attached, as shown in Figure 16.3.
- They are indicated by text segments that are coded with certain codes (here A and B) that appear within a certain specified maximum distance (proximity) of each other. If this maximum distance is set at, say, eight lines, the program would retrieve all instances where a text segment coded with code B starts within up to eight lines of the start or end of a text segment coded with code A (see Figure 16.4).
- They are indicated by sequential ordering (code A is regularly followed by code B), as shown in Figure 16.4.

Thus the hypothesis of a relationship between work and family orientations may be examined by retrieving all text segments coded with 'work orientation' and 'family orientation'. Of course, the notion of hypothesis testing

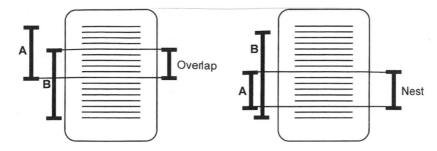

Figure 16.3   *Overlapping and nesting text segments*

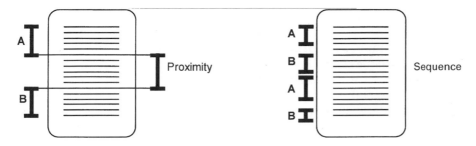

Figure 16.4   *Proximity and sequence of codes*

would be rather misleading here, if one understands it as an attempt to 'verify' or 'falsify' an empirically contentful statement. But this kind of hypothesis examination can lead to the development of falsifiable statements, for example if one finds that the interviewees with specific work orientations also show specific orientations towards the family. Here facilities for co-occurring codes are used as a heuristic device: the objective is to retrieve the original text to which the co-occurring codes were attached. Then the researcher investigates the meaning of a certain co-occurrence by a thorough analysis of the original text. The interpretive analysis of interview texts forms the basis for the clarification and modification of the researcher's initial (general or vague) assumptions.

Developers of two different software packages, HYPERRESEARCH and AQUAD, propose a more formal approach to qualitative hypothesis examination (see Hesse-Biber and Dupuis, 1995; Huber, 1995). When using the hypothesis testing module of HYPERRESEARCH, the researcher formulates his or her hypotheses in the form of 'production rules' in which codes are connected with 'if–then' statements. A researcher who has coded his or her data with codes for 'critical life events' and 'emotional disturbances' may wish to examine the hypothesis that critical life events are always or frequently accompanied by emotional disturbances. He or she could then transform their hypothesis into a query about all co-occurrences of text segments coded as critical life event with segments coded as emotional disturbance. Using HYPERRESEARCH's hypothesis tester, one would formulate the rule:

> *if* 'critical life events' *and* 'emotional disturbances', *then add* 'life event has caused stress'

If the program finds both the code 'critical life events' and the code 'emotional disturbances' in a given document, the hypothesis is confirmed for that document, and the code 'life event has caused stress' is added to it.

HYPERRESEARCH only searches for the presence of certain codes within a given set of documents, and in doing so does not take the precise location of the text segments into account. In contrast, the program AQUAD helps the researcher to use information about the overlapping, nesting, proximity or sequence of text segments for hypothesis examination. Taking our previous example and using AQUAD, one would first code the text segments with the codes *cle* (for 'critical life events') and *emo* (for 'emotional disturbances'). Let us assume that during this process the following hypothesis has come to the researcher's mind: 'Whenever interviewees talk about critical life events, they will also, at the same time, mention emotional disturbances.' One can now operationalize 'at the same time' as 'within a maximum distance of five lines in the interview transcript', and run a retrieval that finds all text segments coded with *cle* where a text segment coded with *emo* also occurs within a maximum distance of five lines. Looking at the result of such a retrieval shown in Table 16.2, one can, for example, see that in the interview 'bioss1', the association of *cle* and *emo* occurs only once (at line 102), while in interview 'bioss2' there are five text passages where text segments coded with these codes are very close to each other.

Thus the co-occurrence of codes (defined as the overlapping, nesting, proximity or sequential ordering of text segments) indicates the presence of critical evidence for or against the hypothesis. Unlike the first example of qualitative hypothesis examination (concerning the relationship between work and family orientations), the primary goal with this more formal approach would be not to retrieve text, but to use the information represented by the codes themselves as a basis for decision-making. Like

Table 16.2   *The result of a co-occuring code search with AQUAD*

Hypothesis 1 / codefile bioss1.cod						
100	102	*cle*	–	102	104	*emo*
Hypothesis 1 / codefile bioss2.cod						
24	28	*cle*	–	26	30	*emo*
65	70	*cle*	–	72	82	*emo*
110	112	*cle*	–	111	115	*emo*
220	228	*cle*	–	212	224	*emo*
450	452	*cle*	–	456	476	*emo*

statistical significance testing, the decision-making process is strictly rule-governed. However, there are certain methodological requirements and limitations to such a strategy:

1   The prerequisite of independent testing requires that a hypothesis is not tested with the same empirical material from which it is developed.
2   The hypotheses must be empirically testable, which means they must be precise enough and have empirical content.
3   The codes that are used for hypothesis testing must denote clearly defined phenomena in a reliable and stable way.

Methodological benefits and problems

Since the advent of the first computer programs that support qualitative research, there has been a lively debate about their potential methodological merits and dangers, with discussants expressing both great optimism (Conrad and Reinarz, 1984; Richards and Richards, 1991) and concern (Agar, 1991; Seidel, 1991; Seidel and Kelle, 1995, Coffey et al., 1996). Concerning the benefits of software for qualitative research, the following three aspects are frequently mentioned in the literature.

First, by mechanizing tedious and cumbersome tasks of data organization, such as searching and copying text segments, a computer can lead to greater efficiency. Thus, software helps to save time, and can assist the management of larger samples (Kelle and Laurie, 1995). However, it is crucial to be aware that a simple increase in sample size alone does not necessarily imply that the research findings will be more valid. In qualitative research, a large sample is usually not regarded as valuable in itself. However, multiple comparisons between purposefully selected cases are crucial for a qualitative study to identify patterns and to develop categories. An increase in sample size may therefore add greater breadth to the scope of the analysis. However, there is also a real danger of software for textual data management being overwhelmed by the sheer volume of information that becomes available when using computer technology. The amount of time and effort required to prepare the data and enter them into the program is not inconsiderable, and increases in tandem with sample size. One should therefore be aware that the potential benefits of a larger sample size may be outweighed by the extra costs in time and effort required for data preparation and data entry.

Secondly, the use of software packages can make the research process more systematic and explicit, and therefore more transparent and rigorous, while systematizing procedures that previously had been unsystematic and enabling researchers to codify exactly how they analyse their data (Conrad and Reinarz, 1984). Thus computers could add trustworthiness to a methodology that has always suffered from the reputation of seducing the researcher into unsystematic, subjective or journalistic styles of inquiry.

Thirdly, by releasing the researcher from boring and cumbersome mechanical tasks, software for textual data management can free up time that can be spent on more creative and analytic tasks. Thus computer programs can enhance the researcher's creativity, by allowing them to experiment and to 'play' with the data, and to explore the relationship between different categories more thoroughly (Lee and Fielding, 1995).

Warnings about the potential methodological dangers of using computers often relate to the possibility that the computer could alienate the researcher from their data, and enforce analytical strategies that go against the methodological and theoretical orientations that qualitative researchers see as the hallmark of their work. In short, the concern is that the use of computer programs may impose a particular methodology on the user. Such worries were especially fuelled by Lonkila's (1995: 46) observation that users' guides, as well as the methodological writings about software for qualitative data management, give the impression of a strong influence of grounded theory. But grounded theory and computer-aided qualitative analysis also share some very problematic aspects, as Lonkila points out: both overemphasize coding, and in doing so neglect other forms of textual analysis, especially the kind of fine-grained analysis employed in discourse analysis. Coffey et al. (1996) have warned that the strong ties between 'code-and-retrieve' software and grounded theory methodology may inspire a new orthodoxy in qualitative research. However, a closer look at the methodological backgrounds of the developers gives the clear impression that different programs have been developed on the basis of rather different theoretical and methodological conceptions. The same holds true for the users: in a meta-analysis of empirical studies, Lee and Fielding (1996: 3.2) have found that 70 per cent of a sample of qualitative studies performed with the help of computers show no explicit relation to grounded theory. Thus, the frequent mentioning of grounded theory can perhaps be explained by the fact that proponents of the grounded theory approach belong to those very few authors who try to describe in detail the analytical procedures applied in qualitative research. Consequently it is not surprising that developers of software that supports qualitative analysis who are in search of a methodological underpinning usually draw on the methodology of grounded theory as one of the best known and most explicit approaches in qualitative analysis.

Lee and Fielding (1991: 8) have linked the fear of the computer taking over the analysis to the famous literary archetype from Mary Shelley's nineteenth-century novel *Frankenstein, or the Modern Prometheus*. Starting from empirical investigations among qualitative researchers who use software for working with textual data, they came to the conclusion that the fear of computer programs as a kind of 'Frankenstein's monster' is often overemphasized: in practice, researchers tend to stop using a certain package rather than submit themselves to the logic of a software program that is totally different from the logic of inquiry they want to employ.

Other concerns mentioned quite frequently in current debates refer to the danger that computers could alienate the researcher from their data (Agar,

1991; Seidel, 1991; Seidel and Kelle, 1995). As with the danger of the computer program taking over analysis, this methodological hazard is also often related to coding. Seidel and Kelle (1995) argue that the distinction between two different modes of coding is crucial for avoiding serious alienation from the data: codes can have a referential function, which means they represent signposts to certain text passages; or they can have a factual function, which means they are used to denote certain facts. The first type of coding is characteristic of an open and inductive style of inquiry employed by an interpretive analysis of textual data in the tradition of hermeneutic and interactionist approaches. The second type relates to a deductive style of textual analysis in the tradition of classical content analysis. By using certain procedures of software for textual data management, analysts can – without realizing – confuse the two modes of coding: they can involuntarily switch from using the referential function of codes (collecting text segments that refer in a broad and general way to a number of somewhat vaguely defined concepts) to treating codes as if they were representations of factual information. Seidel and Kelle note the danger of losing the phenomenon by reifying the codes: the analyst starts to work exclusively on his or her codes and forgets about the raw data, although the necessary prerequisite for doing so has not yet been fulfilled. There is only a loose coupling between a code and a piece of data, instead of a well-defined relation between a code and a phenomenon: the code was not attached to denote a certain discrete event, incident or fact, but only to inform the analyst that there is interesting information, contained in a certain text segment, related to a topic represented by a code. This danger of losing the phenomenon and reifying the codes is especially prevalent with the 'hypothesis testing facilities' described above: by seeking to 'test hypotheses' without having observed the necessary prerequisites, that is by applying strict rules to vague and 'fuzzy' codes, researchers can easily produce artifacts.

Thus, enhanced facilities for coding and retrieval offer fascinating new possibilities for analysts to 'play' with their data, and can thereby help to open up new perspectives and to stimulate new insights. But combining methodologies of theory building and theory testing should not seduce us into simply mixing or even confusing them.

STEPS

From the great variety of different possible strategies two examples are:

1:

Step 1: formatting textual data
Step 2: coding data with ad hoc codes (open coding)
Step 3: writing memos and attaching them to text segments
Step 4: comparing text segments to which the same codes have been attached
Step 5: integrating codes, and attaching memos to codes
Step 6: developing a core category

2:

Step 1:   formatting textual data
Step 2:   defining a code scheme
Step 3:   coding data with the predefined code scheme
Step 4:   linking memos to the codes (not to text segments!) while coding
Step 5:   comparing text segments to which the same codes have been attached
Step 6:   developing subcategories from this comparison
Step 7:   recode the data with these subcategories
Step 8:   producing a numerical data matrix, whereby the rows represent the text documents, the columns the categories (codes) and the values of the categories the subcategories
Step 9:   analysing this data matrix with SPSS

Users who employ other strategies of qualitative analysis (e.g. qualitative hypothesis testing or qualitative comparative analysis) will follow different steps, but will use code and retrieve techniques in one way or another.

References

Abel, T. (1948) 'The Operation called Verstehen', in *American Journal of Sociology*, 54 (5): 211–218.

Agar, M. (1991) 'The right brain strikes back', in N.G. Fielding and R.M. Lee (eds), *Using Computers in Qualitative Research*. Newbury Park, CA: Sage. pp. 181–94.

Coffey, A., Holbrook, B. and Atkinson, P. (1996) 'Qualitative data analysis: technologies and representations', *Sociological Research Online*, 1 (1): <http://www.socresonline.org.uk/socresonline/1/1/4html>.

Conrad, P. and Reinarz, S. (1984) 'Qualitative computing: approaches and issues', *Qualitative Sociology*, 7: 34–60.

Glaser, B.G. (1978) *Theoretical sensitivity: Advances in the methodology of Grounded Theory.* Mill Valley, CA: The Sociology Press.

Glaser, B.G. (1992) *Emergence vs. Forcing: Basics of Grounded Theory Analysis.* Mill Valley, CA: Sociology Press.

Glaser, B.G. and Strauss, A.L. (1967) *The Discovery of Grounded Theory: Strategies for Qualitative Research.* Chicago, IL: Aldine.

Hanson, N. (1971) 'The idea of a logic of discovery', in S. Toulmin (ed.), *What I Do Not Believe and Other Essays.* Dordrecht: Reidel.

Heinz, W. (1996) 'Transitions in youth in a cross cultural perspective: school-to-work in Germany', in B. Galaway and J. Hudson (eds), *Youth in Transition to Adulthood: Research and Policy Implications.* Toronto: Thompson Educational.

Heinz, W., Kelle, U., Witzel, A. and Zinn, J. (1998) 'Vocational training and career development in Germany – results from a longitudinal study', *International Journal for Behavioural Development*, 22 (5): 77–101.

Hesse-Biber, S. and Dupuis, P. (1995) 'Hypothesis testing in computer-aided qualitative data analysis', in U. Kelle (ed.), *Computer-Aided Qualitative Data Analysis: Theory, Methods and Practice.* London: Sage.

Huber, G. (1995) 'Qualitative hypothesis examination and theory building', in U. Kelle (ed.), *Computer-Aided Qualitative Data Analysis: Theory, Methods and Practice*, London: Sage.

Jorgenson, D.L. (1989) *Participant Observation: A Methodology for Human Studies*. Newbury Park, CA: Sage.

Kelle, U. (1994) 'Theories as heuristic tools in qualitative research' in I. Maso, P.A. Atkinson and J.C. Verhoeven (eds.), *Openness in Research: the Tension between Self and Other*. Assen: Van Gorcum.

Kelle, U. (ed.) (1995) *Computer-Aided Qualitative Data Analysis: Theory, Methods and Practice*. London: Sage.

Kelle, U. and Laurie, H. (1995) 'Computer use in qualitative research and issues of validity', in U. Kelle (ed.), *Computer-Aided Qualitative Data Analysis: Theory, Methods and Practice*. London: Sage.

Lakatos, I. (1982) *The Methodology of Scientific Research Programmes. Philosophical Papers*, Vol. 1. Cambridge: Cambridge University Press.

Lee, R.M. and Fielding, N.G. (1991) 'Computing for qualitative research: options, problems and potential', in N.G. Fielding and R.M. Lee (eds), *Using Computers in Qualitative Research*. London: Sage. pp. 1–13.

Lee, R.M. and Fielding, N.G. (1995) 'User Experiences of Qualitative Data Analysis Software', in U. Kelle (ed.) *Computer-Aided Qualitative Data Analysis: Theory, Methods and Practice*. London: Sage.

Lee, R.M. and Fielding, N.G. (1996) 'Qualitative data analysis: representations of a technology. A comment on Coffey, Holbrook and Atkinson', *Sociological Research Online*, 1 (4): <http://www.socresonline.org.uk/socresonline/1/4/lf.html>.

Lofland, J. and Lofland, L.H. (1984) *Analyzing Social Settings: a Guide to Qualitative Observation and Analysis*. Belmont, CA: Wadsworth.

Lonkila, M. (1995) 'Grounded theory as an emerging paradigm for computer-assisted qualitative data analysis', in U. Kelle (ed.), *Computer-Aided Qualitative Data Analysis: Theory, Methods and Practice*. London: Sage.

Miles, M.B. and Huberman, A.M. (1994) *Qualitative Data Analysis: an Expanded Sourcebook*, 2nd edn. Newbury Park, CA: Sage (1st edn, 1984).

Muhr, T. (1991) 'ATLAS/ti: a prototype for the support of text interpretation', *Qualitative Sociology*, 14 (4/2): 349–71.

Muhr, T. (1992) 'Catching bugs and butterflies in networks'. Paper presented at the conference on The Qualitative Research Process and Computing, Bremen.

Richards, L. and Richards, T. (1991) 'The transformation of qualitative method: computational paradigms and research processes', in R.M. Lee and N.G. Fielding (eds), *Using Computers in Qualitative Research*. London: Sage.

Richards, T. and Richards, L. (1995) 'Using computers in qualitative research', in N. Denzin and Y. Lincoln (eds), *Handbook of Qualitative Research*. Thousand Oaks, CA: Sage.

Seidel, J. (1991) 'Method and madness in the application of computer technology to qualitative data analysis', in R.M. Lee and N.G. Fielding (eds), *Using Computers in Qualitative Research*. London: Sage.

Seidel, J. and Kelle, U. (1995) 'Different functions of coding in the analysis of textual data', in U. Kelle (ed.), *Computer-Aided Qualitative Data Analysis: Theory, Methods and Practice*. London: Sage.

Strauss, A. and Corbin, J. (1990) *Basics of Qualitative Research: Grounded Theory Procedures and Techniques*. Thousand Oaks, CA: Sage.

Taylor, St J. and Bogdan, R. (1984) *Introduction to Qualitative Research Methods: the Search for Meanings*. New York: Wiley.

Tesch, R. (1990) *Qualitative Research: Analysis Types and Software Tools*. New York: Falmer.

Weitzman, E. and Miles, M.B. (1995) *Computer Programs for Qualitative Data Analysis*. Thousand Oaks, CA: Sage.

Further reading

Kelle, U. (1997) 'Theory building in qualitative research and computer programs for the management of textual data', *Sociological Research Online*, 2 (2): <http://www.socresonline.org.uk/socresonline/2/2/1.html>.

17

Keywords in Context: Statistical Analysis of Text Features

Nicole Kronberger and Wolfgang Wagner

KEYWORDS

ALCESTE
open-ended question
passive variables

priming
word-association task

Responses to open-ended questions are a useful data source to complement quantitative data obtained from questionnaire studies. Open-ended responses are not restricted by the category choices of the researcher, as are the responses to closed questions. Therefore they give good access to the spontaneous understanding respondents have of a target object. If properly analysed, open-ended responses can be transformed into variables and merged with the set of quantitative data. Also, there are computer programs that allow automatic analysis of such data.

In a certain sense, open-ended questions are a kind of focused 'micro-interview' about a target. However, unlike in extended interviews, responses to open-ended questions can be obtained from a large sample without incurring the workload usually implied by the transcription and analysis of long texts. The obvious advantage of large sample size, however, implies a trade-off between the necessary brevity of responses and the impossibility of asking additional questions as in extended interviews.

Word-association tasks are a variant of open questions. Instead of requiring respondents to give full-sentence answers, in word-association tasks respondents are asked to write down any words they associate with the target object. Associations have the advantage that they do not contain all the different 'filler' words that structure natural languages. Their analysis is more straightforward than open responses.

The design of open questions

Despite the many textbooks concerned with the design of questionnaires, their construction for specific research purposes is still a kind of art. If we are not concerned with commercial survey research, which needs to adhere to a strict standard to ensure comparability, the design of questionnaires for scientific research purposes depends largely on the researcher's creativity and the specific research topic. Standards can only be a rough guide to the basics. The same is true for designing open-ended questions. The rules given in this text are no more than general guidelines, and should motivate the readers to invent their own designs according to the particular research problem. However, three aspects should generally be treated with care: the location of open questions within the questionnaire, the priming and the instruction.

The location of open questions within a questionnaire

An important point in questionnaire design is that questions do not only retrieve information from respondents: they also convey information. Consider the question: 'When did you first learn about genetically modified food?' This sentence makes the respondent aware of the fact that genetically modified food exists, even if he or she has never heard of it before. When you place an open question on, say, biotechnology after this question, your respondent will almost certainly produce ideas about food. It is therefore a good rule to place word associations right at the beginning, or as close to the beginning, of a questionnaire as possible.

A position right at the beginning, however, brings another problem. For open-ended questions, the respondent needs to be in a more spontaneous and trusting mood than for closed questions. A solution to this problem can be an introductory conversation with the respondent, or a set of entirely unrelated questions that serve as a training for the open question to come. To find a balance between these contradictory requirements, some trials with a few respondents, and a subsequent interview about their impressions, should be conducted.

The priming

Priming the respondent, that is focusing his or her attention on the stimulus, is a means of reducing variance in the responses. The priming instruction must be very close to the actual stimulus. If the question is about, say, biotechnology, a good idea is to prime the respondents by asking them to think about the last time they heard somebody speak about biotechnology. Then they should write down who it was, and perhaps also when and where this episode took place. Having completed this priming task, the respondent should be able to concentrate fully upon the stimulus.

Priming may also take other forms. Instead of a verbal instruction to think about the stimulus object, one may present the object in an iconic form. Pictures always produce stronger reactions than purely verbal instructions. Icons should be used cautiously, though. The researcher must be sure that the picture does not convey any specific information that might later bias the response.

The instruction

After the respondent's attention has been focused upon the stimulus object, the instruction should be as direct as possible. An example would be: 'When you think about X (the stimulus object), what comes to mind? Please write down whatever comes to mind about X. You may write up to five sentences.' This instruction contains three messages:

(a)   what the stimulus object is
(b)   what should be written down
(c)   how much should be written down.

Point (a) is straightforward, as is point (b). If a respondent has not heard of the stimulus object before, the interviewer should simply move on to the next question. Point (c) is important: the kind of information the researcher wants to retrieve from open questions and word associations is a pattern of contingencies of words in the sample. This allows the researcher to assess semantic fields related to the stimulus object which are characteristic of sub-groups in the sample. So it is a good idea to motivate the respondent to write down as much as possible.

How many open-ended questions are viable per questionnaire?

Answering open questions is a demanding task for respondents. In order not to overstretch their willingness to fill in questionnaires, probably three open questions per questionnaire are a maximum. The total filling-in time should not exceed, say, half an hour if the researcher does not wish to spoil the respondents' good humour and willingness to collaborate. The researcher should experiment with his or her respondents' willingness, since it also depends to a great extent on their level of schooling and practice in writing.

The sample

Surveys including open questions usually require higher sample sizes than usual. The reason for the higher sampling rates is that open responses always vary much more than answers to closed questions. This variance needs to be taken into account when planning the sample size. Also, constructing contingency tables of words further dilutes the frequency of association contingency patterns.

Research deals with at least three comparisons that afford different sample sizes. If the comparison is (a) between word associations of pre-defined subsamples and social groups, each group should comprise a minimum of 100 respondents if a fairly high consensus is expected within the groups. The sample should increase as the expected consensus decreases. If the study aims (b) to find and compare subgroups with different responses to an open question, it will be difficult to estimate the size of such *a posteriori* groups; however, a good bet is a minimum of 400 respondents. If (c) the subgroups are to be compared according to an experimental design involving open questions or word-association tasks (see the section on experimental design below), then each experimental condition should comprise at least 100 respondents.

It is not unusual to combine such subgrouping for specific research purposes. The researcher might, for example, be interested to see whether his or her experimental design produces different results in *a priori* defined socio-economic groups, thus combining (a) and (c). In this case each condition must contain a reasonable number of respondents. The general rule is: the more the better.

Experimental designs

Despite their being open questions and producing a kind of qualitative database, word-association tasks allow a range of interesting experimental designs. Experimental designs can be variations in the wording or in the order of questions in questionnaires. Technically, such designs are called split-ballot surveys.

An example of an experimental design could be to present subsamples with slightly different wordings of the stimulus object: for example, half of the respondents can be asked to write down ideas about 'biotechnology' and the other half words about 'genetic engineering'. Any difference between the two subsamples would indicate different styles of thinking about these two concepts, even though technically the two terms can be considered equivalent.

Scheduling two open questions about two different but related stimulus objects in a questionnaire allows us to assess the semantic interdependence between them. In everyday thinking, conceptual realms are very often hierarchically related. This means that an object A is inferred or thought about within the context of the object B, but not vice versa. For this purpose, the sequence of open questions about stimulus A and stimulus B is varied, with half of the sample being asked A before B and the other half B before A. If, for example, we wish to know whether the semantic realms of 'peace' and 'war' are related hierarchically or not, we might find that respondents have their associations about 'peace' influenced by having first thought about 'war', but their associations about 'war' less influenced by having first thought about 'peace' (see Wagner et al., 1996, for an example).

Preparing open responses for analysis

There are two ways of handling responses to open questions: one is to categorize the responses according to some theoretically informed categorization scheme, and the other is to take the responses as they are. The first way, categorization, introduces a strong and often undue influence of the researcher's conceptional framework upon the data. Categorization is only acceptable if researchers have a strong justification for their categories. Categorizations can easily be added to a quantitative data file, and their analysis by standard statistical packages is quite straightforward. Therefore the remainder of this chapter concerns only the analysis of the natural language responses.

Open responses and word associations can be analysed either by manual content analysis (see Bauer, Chapter 8 in this volume) or by automatic statistical procedures. Classical content analysis is concerned with the meaning of propositions and sentences in utterances which a culturally informed and competent speaker of the respective language can easily discern. Automatic analysis is done with computer programs which even today are incapable of understanding meaning. Computerized analysis substitutes sentence meaning by analysing local co-occurrences of words. The underlying idea is that the meaning of propositions and sentences can be captured if one finds those words that go together in sentences and that are produced by as many respondents as possible.

Imagine the following example. Suppose we conduct a survey about what people think about biotechnology. An open question is added asking respondents to write down whatever comes to their minds when they think of biotechnology. We may get something like the following series of statements:

0001   . . . Biotechnology produces new food. This will make us ill . . .
0002   . . . People might get all sorts of illnesses from eating engineered vegetables
        . . .
i   . . . We do not know yet if genetically engineered food produces allergies
        . . .
k   . . . etc. . . .

Given that a qualified number of respondents produced such or similar statements that basically express the same meaning, we will be able to observe a high number of co-occurrences between 'biotechnology', 'engineered', 'genetically engineered' and 'food' and 'vegetables' on the one hand, and 'ill', 'illness' and 'allergies' on the other hand. The respective terms co-occur either in the same or in subsequent sentences. The program must just be told that the relevant terms are synonyms with respect to the present research question. For this reason programs either allow us to define synonyms by hand, or already possess a dictionary of their own. The result for our example will be that the program produces a graph that depicts the terms 'biotechnology', 'food' and 'illness' in close proximity. This lets the researcher conclude that a substantial number of respondents think of biotechnologically manipulated food as detrimental to human health.

In general the researcher can do most of the basic analysis by hand and does not need programs like SPAD.t or ALCESTE, although they certainly make life easier. Before we discuss the use of these programs, we shall briefly describe the 'manual' procedure that uses a text editor and SPSS. This will demonstrate the basics of analysing responses to open questions.

The treatment of synonyms

Verbal responses need to be homogenized with respect to synonyms. What counts as a synonym is a tricky question, and depends on the specific research problem. 'Headgear', 'hat', 'cap' and 'bonnet' can be synonyms in some research contexts but not in others. Hence, the researcher must decide which minor semantic variations he or she wishes to retain. If it is acceptable to homogenize these expressions, then we can replace the less frequent expression in the sample by the most frequent one. So, if 'hat' was the most frequent word in the data, any other synonymous expression, such as 'headgear', 'cap' and 'bonnet', can be replaced by 'hat'.

The data often also need to be homogenized with regard to semantically equivalent words across word classes. In a specific research context it might be perfectly correct to equate nouns, adjectives and verbs expressing a related thing, state or activity. One of the two expressions 'to fight' (a verb) and 'battle' (a noun) can be replaced by the other with no loss of relevant detail. The same rule applies to 'beauty' (a noun) and 'beautiful' and 'pretty' (adjectives). Generally the most frequent synonym should replace the less frequent ones.

Synonyms can best be homogenized if the researcher produces two word lists, of which one is ordered alphabetically and the other by word frequency. Both SPAD.t and ALCESTE allow us to produce such lists, but there are a number of other programs on the market that also allow us to read in verbal data and produce word lists. Such lists are too cumbersome to produce by hand, even with small samples.

It is often difficult to decide what to do with negations. Should words like 'no', 'not', 'don't', 'never' and 'against' be connected with the negated word or expression by, for example, a hyphen or other symbol, or not? It is often sufficient to homogenize the different forms of negation existing in the texts, because the negation will then appear jointly with the negated word in the analysis, if they are frequent enough in the data. This certainly depends on the specific research problem.

Selecting the relevant words and preparing the data file

Once homogenized, the data set must be inspected for relevant words using a word list ordered by frequency. An average sample of, say, 200 respondents often produces more than 1000 different words, most of which are very infrequent. The words that produce contingencies are those with a bearing on the stimulus object and with a reasonable frequency in the sample. The number of relevant words used for further analysis will rarely exceed 20, even in large samples. Similar to the scree test in classical factor analysis, the number of relevant words is determined by some significant bend in the distribution of words ordered according to frequency. This technique is fairly reliable in separating relevant shared words from idiosyncratic ones.

As radical as it may seem to reduce a list with 1000 or more words to a mere 20 or so, it is a necessary step if we wish to find fields of co-occurring words. The less frequent a word, the less likely it is that a fair number of contingencies with other words will be observed in the sample.

As a kind of safeguard, it is generally advisable to include up to twice as many words in the data set as turned out to be relevant according to the scree test. That is, the researcher might want to include words with less than the required minimum frequency of occurrence. Although this 'surplus' of words will only rarely be included in the subsequent analysis, it might well be that some unforeseen result makes us want to look at additional words to clarify the specific meaning of word classes. Especially when comparing the semantic structures across different samples, these additional words may turn out to be necessary to ensure complete overlap between the word lists of different samples.

It should be noted that among the most frequent words there will be a high number of auxiliary verbs, fillers and other linguistic forms that are irrelevant for the research. These, of course, will not enter the list of relevant words to be analysed, but will be discarded.

Ideally, the prepared word data will be added to the file containing the quantitative data of the study. This means merging the quantitative data file with a file containing the same number of cases and *n* variables, where *n* is the number of relevant and frequent words plus the 'surplus words', and each of the variables designates a word. This file will be an indicator matrix, where a 1 in column *i* means that the respondent used word *i*, and a 0 means that he or she did not. Note that both files need to be ordered according to a joint criterion before merging. Space prohibits extensive treatment here of how to prepare the data file (see Wagner, 1997, for a recipe), but suffice it to say that search-and-replace procedures in text editors, as well as certain procedures in SPSS, easily allow the conversion of the word data file into an SPSS data file in a few steps.

Statistical analysis of word lists using standard statistical packages

Once the indicator matrix has been produced and/or merged with the quantitative data file, statistical analysis is straightforward. Since the *n* word variables represent categorical data, methods like correspondence analyses (ANACOR in SPSS) are the methods of choice. (Note that HOMALS is not very convenient for analysing indicator matrices, because this program will process the 0 occurrences as well as the 1 occurrences simultaneously, which blurs the resulting graphs considerably.) Alternatively, multidimensional scaling can be applied to a correspondence matrix depicting the pattern of co-occurrences between words.

Correspondence analysis operates on correspondence matrices, and it compares row and column profiles of categories. It calculates the chi-squared distances of row/column profiles from the average row/column profile, and subjects the resulting distance matrix to an eigenvalue decomposition. This results in an $(n-1)$-dimensional space, where n is the number of rows or of columns, whichever is smaller. The rows/columns are then projected into this space and appear closer to each other the more their profiles are similar (see Greenacre, 1993).

This statistical method can operate on symmetrical and square word-by-word matrices, depicting the frequencies of co-occurrences of words, and on asymmetrical matrices where, for example, rows are socio-statistical categories and columns are words. In the case of word-by-word matrices, accordingly, classes in the resulting space are composed of words that appear in similar contexts. In the case of asymmetrical matrices, classes reveal the common or distinct use of words by respondents pertaining to different socio-statistical categories. Because it is applicable to all sorts of matrices, correspondence analysis is frequently used to analyse verbal data.

Whereas correspondence analysis takes distances between profiles into account, multidimensional scaling only analyses square and symmetric correspondence matrices by interpreting them as similarity data. The matrix is then subjected to eigenvalue decomposition, and an n-dimensional space is constructed where objects are closer the more frequently they jointly occur in responses. This method is less commonly used, but deserves attention in certain research designs.

Statistical analysis of natural text using ALCESTE

Overview

ALCESTE is a computerized technique as well as a methodology for text analysis. It was developed by Max Reinert (1983; 1990; 1993; 1998) as a technique for investigating the distribution of vocabulary in a written text and in transcripts of oral text. It is also a methodology, because the program integrates a multitude of highly sophisticated statistical methods into an organic whole that perfectly suits its aim of discourse analysis. Taken together, the program realizes a complex *descending hierarchical classification*, combining elements of different statistical methods like segmentation (Bertier and Bouroche, 1975), hierarchical classification and dichotomization based on reciprocal averaging or correspondence analysis (Benzécri, 1981; Greenacre, 1993; Hayashi, 1950) and the theory of dynamic clouds (Diday et al., 1982).

Like all other methods designed for analysing responses to open questions, ALCESTE is not a technique for *a priori* hypothesis testing, but one for exploration and description. While, unlike manual methods of qualitative analysis, it is insensitive to meaning and context, its advantage is that within a short time the researcher can gain an impression of a voluminous data corpus.

The preconditions for good results with ALCESTE are the following. First, text data which are to be analysed with ALCESTE must show a certain *coherence*. This is normally the case when data such as responses to an open question, interviews, oral accounts, media data, articles or book chapters focus upon one topic. Secondly, the text has to be sufficiently *big*. The program is suitable for text data from a minimum of 10,000 words up to documents as voluminous as 20 copies of *Madame Bovary*.

In ALCESTE, a statement is considered an expression of a point of view, that is, a frame of reference, uttered by a narrating subject. This frame gives order and coherence to the things being talked about. When studying text produced by different individuals, the aim is to understand points of view that are collectively shared by a social group at a given time. When thinking about an object, there always exist different and contrasting points of view. The assumption of ALCESTE is that different points of reference produce different ways of talking, that is, the use of a specific vocabulary is seen as a source for detecting ways of thinking about an object. The aim of an ALCESTE analysis, therefore, is to distinguish word classes that represent differing forms of discourse concerning the topic of interest.

The ALCESTE analysis

PREPARING THE TEXT DATA First, the corpus of texts is set up by the analyst. Each respondent's text or other natural text unit is characterized by relevant attributes, such as age, sex, profession, etc. Secondly, the relevant units of analysis are defined. In natural language a statement is a meaning unit that unites propositional content with a subject's intention, belief, desire and worldview. In contrast to a single word, a statement is about an object *in the view of* a speaking or writing subject. It is this double dimension of subject and object that makes the statement the suitable unit for studying discourse that takes place among individuals and within groups.

Generally speaking, the definition of a statement can be syntactic, pragmatic, semantic or cognitive. To avoid ambiguities, statements are operationalized as 'contextual units' in the ALCESTE nomenclature. The program automatically determines contextual units by considering punctuation on the one hand, and the length of the statement (which can be set by the user) up to a maximum of 250 characters on the other.

In order to eliminate synonyms (see above), different forms of the same word (for example plurals, conjugations and suffixes) are automatically reduced to the root form. Irregular verbs are identified and transformed to the indicative. All this is achieved through the help of a dictionary, and results in a matrix containing the so-called 'reduced forms'. This procedure often considerably increases the number of 1 entries in the data matrix, and makes the method statistically more powerful.

Another point is that not all words convey relevant information. Clearly, in a text, the word 'hunger' is more relevant than the article 'the'. Again based on a dictionary, the corpus is subdivided into a group of 'function words', such as articles, prepositions, conjunctions, pronouns and auxiliary verbs, and a group of 'content words', such as nouns, verbs, adjectives and adverbs. It is this second group of words that carries the sense of discourse, and the final analysis is based on these words. The function words are excluded from the primary analysis, but serve as additional information. It should be noted, however, that ALCESTE also works on text in languages for which no dictionaries exist; in this case no root forms are created or function words identified.

The segmentation into contextual units and the identification of discourse-relevant words concludes the first steps executed by ALCESTE.

CREATING THE DATA MATRICES   The aim of the ALCESTE methodology is to investigate statistical similarities and dissimilarities of words in order to identify repetitive language patterns. Technically such patterns are represented by an indicator matrix relating relevant words in columns, and contextual units (that is the operationalization of statements) in rows. Remember that an indicator matrix is a table with 1 if a given word is present and with 0 if it is absent in a respective statement. Usually this is a rather empty matrix containing up to 98 per cent zeros.

The distribution of entries in this matrix, as well as the consequent result, slightly depend on the size of contextual units used in cutting the text. In order to reduce the ambiguity of possible results and to find a solution that is relatively stable, ALCESTE always calculates matrices and solutions for two slightly different unit sizes. For example, one matrix may be based on units of minimum size 10 words, and the other on 12 words. If the two classifications resulting from the two matrices are reasonably similar, ALCESTE, or the researcher, can assume that the chosen unit sizes are adequate for the present text. If not, the unit sizes can be varied until a relatively stable solution is found. Experimentally varying the size of text units is a kind of empirical test for the stability of a result.

SEARCHING A CLASSIFICATION   The next step consists of identifying word classes. The method is a descending hierarchical classification analysis, which is suitable for large-scale indicator matrices with few entries. (Note that for descending hierarchical classification analysis we use the term 'class' instead of 'cluster', which is used for the more traditional ascending cluster analysis.)

The total set of contextual units in the initial indicator matrix (contextual units by words) constitutes the first class. The aim of the next step is to find a partition of that class into two that maximally separates the resulting classes such that the two classes contain different vocabulary and, in the ideal case, do not contain any overlapping words. Technically this consists

Table 17.1   *Decomposition of the original matrix into two classes*

	Specific vocabulary of class 2			Overlapping vocabulary			Specific vocabulary of class 3		
	food	*fruit*	. . .	*say*	*word j*	. . .	*cure*	*cancer*	
Class 2	45	12	. . .	20	k_{2j}	. . .	0	0	k_2
Class 3	0	0	. . .	21	k_{3j}	. . .	33	20	k_3
	45	12	. . .	41	k_j	. . .	33	20	k

of decomposing the matrix into two classes through optimal scaling and cutting the ordered set of words where a chi-squared criterion reaches a maximum. Table 17.1 shows an idealized example of such a decomposition. The two resulting subsets or classes 2 and 3 are optimally separate in the sense of having as little overlap as possible in terms of words. The numbers in the table (k_{2j}, k_{3j}) indicate the frequency of contextual units for each class containing a specific word j. In our example, class 2 consists of statements containing words like 'food' and 'fruit', while words like 'cancer' and 'cure' are typical for class 3. Of course, it will rarely be possible to separate statements such that words occurring in one class do not appear in the other. There will always be some overlapping vocabulary, like the word 'say' in the example.

As usual, the chi-squared procedure consists of comparing an observed distribution with an expected one. In more technical terms, the procedure finds, out of all possible partitions, those two classes that maximize the following chi-square criterion:

$$\chi^2 = k_2 k_3 \sum_{j \in J} \left[\left(\frac{k_{2j}}{k_2} - \frac{k_{3j}}{k_3} \right)^2 / k_j \right]$$

where

$$k_{2j} = \sum_{i \in I_2} k_{ij}; \quad k_2 = \sum_{i \in I_1} k_{2j}; \quad k_j = k_{2j} + k_{3j}$$

In the present case, the distribution of words in each of the two classes is compared with the average distribution of words. If there exist different forms of discourse employing differing vocabulary, then the observed distribution will deviate systematically from a distribution where the words are independent from each other. In this context, the chi-squared criterion is used not as a test, but as a measure of a relationship existing between words; the procedure searches maximally separate patterns of co-occurrence between the classes. To determine when this chi-squared maximum is reached, ALCESTE uses other statistical procedures.

The descending hierarchical classification method is an iterative procedure. In the following steps, the bigger of the classes 2 and 3 is decomposed next, and so on. The procedure stops if a predetermined number of

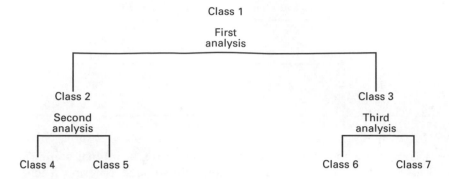

Figure 17.1   *A schematic representation of ALCESTE's descending hierarchical classification*

iterations does not result in further divisions. The final result is a hierarchy of classes (Figure 17.1).

DESCRIBING AND INTERPRETING THE CLASSES   ALCESTE produces a voluminous result file offering various sources for interpretation. Here we describe the most important sections of the output. For illustration, we use a study comparing different texts and interview responses about biotechnology (Allum, 1998). The author analysed, among others, the British sample's response to an open question from the 1996 *Eurobarometer* survey (46.1):

> Now, I would like to ask you what comes to your mind when you think about modern biotechnology in a broad sense, that is including genetic engineering.

The 973 responses were transcribed verbatim and subjected to an ALCESTE analysis.

ALCESTE computes for each class a list of words that are characteristic for that class. The strength of association between each word and its class is expressed by a chi-squared value, and all words exceeding a certain chi-squared value are listed. The larger this value, the more important the word is for the statistical construction of the class. These word lists are the basic source for interpreting the classes.

The ALCESTE output file contains not only content words, but also function words and – if introduced – also attributes of the respondents. Note that function words and attribute variables do not enter the classification analysis, but serve as illustrative variables for class description. They are 'passive' variables.

The ALCESTE analysis of the responses to the open question on biotechnology yields a six-class solution. Table 17.2 lists the most typical words for the classes ordered by strength of association. A closer look at the word lists allows us to name each class. Class D, for example, comprises a discourse relating biotechnology to reproduction and embryology. For each

Table 17.2 *Example of semantical classes stemming from an open question sample (Allum, 1998: 35). The words are ordered by strength of association. A + at the end of a word indicates its root form*

A Interfering with nature	B Don't know	C Unspecific worry	D Reproduction	E Curing disease	F Food
interfer+	hear	engineer	artificial	cancer	grow
mess+	know	genetic	babies	cure	animal
nature	understand	put	inseminat+	disease	food
around	else	abuse	test	improve	fruit
leave	nothing	careful	tube	new	ear
take	real	concern	pregnanc+	find	farm
play+	can_t	tell	sperm	help	down
trying	idea	approve	baby+	develop	bacteria
feel	sure	bean	dead	drug	crop
course	mean	create	spec+	treatment	improving
god	say	end	woman	energy	plant
go	mind	soya	worry	medical	tomatoes
let	opinion	they_ve	cloning	medicine	using
alter	risk	use	organ	prevent	keep
bad	that_s	into	pig	research	rid
happen	comment	to	selection	technolog+	chemical
look	word	get	human	aid	detect
natural	answer	give	manipul+	better	easi+
question	hard	make	stuff	childless	environm+
race	come	think	clue	communic+	eradicate
etc.	etc.	etc.	etc.	etc.	etc.

class, the output file also contains a number of characteristic word combinations:

```
*** classe n°4 (20 SR maximum) ***
3  4  15  test+ tube+ babies
2  4   6  test+ tube+
2  4   6  artificial insemination
2  4   2  I suppose+
2  4   2  I think.
2  4   2  or not
2  4   2  about it
2  4   2  with animal+
2  4   2  a baby+
2  4   2  fertility treatment+
etc.
```

This list shows that statements in class D often contain the words 'test', 'tube' and 'babies' in combination.

A further and important key for naming and interpreting the discourse in each class is the set of original and prototypical statements associated with it. This list is provided by ALCESTE, and allows us to determine the context within which each word is used in the original text. The following are the

most prototypical statements from which class D is derived (note that a #
marks relevant words for the class, a $ indicates the end of a response):

```
6 35 Clé sélectionnée : D

 224 105 0293 #test #tube #babies #artificial #insemination
#cloning #transplanting #pigs #organs into #humans$
 157 47 0400 ranges from #cloning DNA and #test #tube #babies$
 659 47 2028 #test #tube #babies #transplants$
  80 42 0489 makes a #woman have a boy or #girl if she wants it
there could be production of #babies by #test #tube #creation
it_s a-lot-of rubbish to have straight cucumbers vegetables
have #lost their taste$
 679 39 2068 #test #tube #babies issue about women on TV and
#sperm and father #baby$
 750 36 2103 #test #tube #babies messing about with #stuff you
shouldn_t$
0449 they can #manipulate chemistry of the #human #species$
 146 35 0407 #test #tube #babies$
 211 35 0347 #test #tube #babies$
 319 35 0213 the lady having a #baby from her #dead husbands
#sperm$
 769 35 2142 #test #tube #babies$
 592 29 2397 terminating a #pregnancy if foetus has #illness
#selection #artificial #insemination$
. . . . . . . . . . . . . . . . .
```

The results can then be represented graphically in a correspondence
space. For this purpose, a matrix cross-tabulating classes and words in their
reduced (root) form is subjected to a correspondence analysis. This provides
a spatial representation of the relations between the classes, where their
positions reflect their relationship in terms of proximity. Three graphs are
produced: the first represents the relationships between the content words,
the second represents the function words, and the third projects the passive
variables, that is the attributes of the respondents, into the space of the
content words and of the discourse classes. The three graphs can be
superimposed and read in conjunction.

Finally, the results have to be interpreted. This is where the researcher
and his or her knowledge of the field comes into play, to give an empirically
justified theoretical interpretation. In the ideal case, this interpretation
should give semantic content to the purely structural information about the
discursive space produced by ALCESTE, by drawing on other methods of
text and discourse analysis.

As well as the ALCESTE analysis, the response data presented here were
content analysed and categorized by hand in the traditional way. In Figure
17.2, the ALCESTE classes and the evaluative categories derived through
the manual content analysis are projected into a correspondence space. As
can be seen, the statements pertaining to the classes 'interfering with
nature' and 'unspecific worry' are clearly categorized as negative, and the

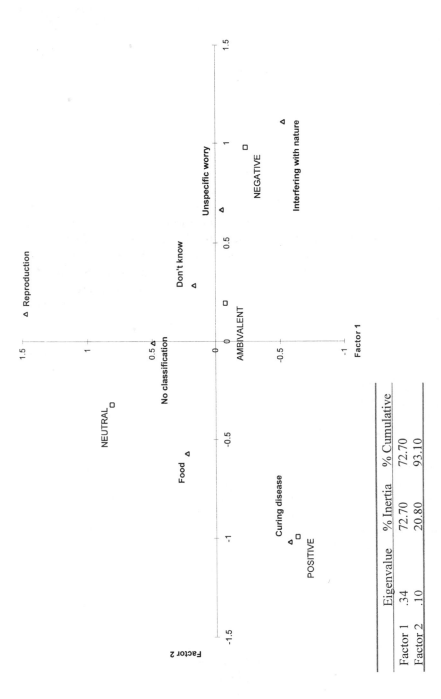

Figure 17.2 *The ALCESTE classes and the evaluative categories derived through the manual content analysis are projected into a correspondence space*

	Eigenvalue	% Inertia	% Cumulative
Factor 1	.34	72.70	72.70
Factor 2	.10	20.80	93.10

class 'curing diseases' at the opposite pole is categorized as positive. The remaining categories of 'neutral' and 'ambivalent' evaluation fall in between, and appear in proximity to those ALCESTE classes that could not be classified, or that contain 'don't know' responses. This high correspondence between automatic and traditional content analysis represents a mutual validation of the different methods.

Problems and examples

Despite its great versatility, ALCESTE has some shortcomings. The principal one is that there exist dictionaries for only a handful of languages: at present, English, French, Italian, Portuguese and Spanish are covered. Unfortunately, not all the dictionaries are complete, and they sometimes fail to identify simple plurals and other forms. Non-Roman languages are not covered at all. However, it is not too difficult to construct a dictionary of function words for any language (how to do that is explained in the manual). Excluding articles, conjunctions and similar words from the analysis improves the ALCESTE result substantially. Another possibility for handling the problem of the lack of dictionaries is to do some content-specific preparation of the text by hand. Preliminary analyses allow us to identify relevant words that can be reduced to their root form with the help of search-and-replace functions, as described above.

ALCESTE is very complex, but nevertheless it is relatively transparent once the user has identified the settings for the most important parameters. In general, the standard form of analysis produces sensible results in about 80 per cent of cases.

There are a number of studies that give an idea of how to use ALCESTE. Reinert (1993) analysed 212 nightmares reported by French adolescents. By comparing and contrasting the vocabulary distributed across three classes, Reinert identified three main topics in the nightmares: separation, which refers to the social world of the dreamer; being enclosed and being threatened by an aggressor, which refers to the perceptible world of the subject; and falling and plunging, which refers to the archaic, proprioceptive world of the individual.

Noel-Jorand et al. (1995) applied the method to oral accounts by 10 physicians who were undertaking a scientific expedition to Mount Sajama (6542 m high). The discourse analysis was carried out to contribute to the understanding of psychological adaptation to extreme environments. The authors differentiated several forms of coping with fear and anxiety.

Lahlou (1996; 1998) applied ALCESTE separately to interviews and entries in an encyclopedia that referred to eating and related activities. He was able to show that the classes appearing from analysing the interviews – with the exception of one class – are virtually identical to the classes derived from the encyclopedia. Similarly, Beaudouin et al. (1993) analysed responses to the open-ended question 'What is an ideal breakfast?' The analysis yielded six classes that can be summarized on a more abstract level as two categories: the name of products associated with breakfast, and the spatial, temporal and social context of breakfast.

Outlook

It has been shown that open verbal responses in questionnaires can be analysed 'by hand' using standard statistical procedures, as well as by fully automated procedures that are specifically designed to work on textual data. Besides ALCESTE, there is an older program, SPAD.t (Système portable pour l'analyse des données textuelles: Lebart et al., 1989; Lebart and Salem, 1988), which lies somewhere between manual analysis and ALCESTE. It is also specifically designed for text data, and allows us to apply a wide variety of statistical procedures, such as different versions of correspondence or cluster analyses. It does not work with dictionaries, and can therefore be used with almost any language that uses Roman letters. The program PROSPERO, which is being developed at the University of Paris, goes a step beyond even ALCESTE's capabilities: it is designed to take account of semantic and grammatical relationships in the French language.

Automatic text analysis is a powerful tool that allows us to tackle corpora of text whose sheer size is beyond the reach of even the most motivated qualitative analyst. Analysing open responses in questionnaires is just a minor example of such tasks, the majority of which will involve extensive media and interview data.

PRACTICAL STEPS OF CONDUCTING AN ALCESTE ANALYSIS

1. *Suitable data*: texts that are produced without or with little structuring by the researcher will be best suited for an ALCESTE analysis (e.g. responses to an open question, narrative interviews, media articles etc.).
2. The data corpus must be coherent and homogeneous, i.e. the texts are produced under similar conditions and focus on the same topic. A minimum of 10,000 words must be assembled as ASCII file with line breaks.
3. *Data preparation*: symbols like the asterisk (*) or the Dollar sign ($) have a special meaning in ALCESTE; therefore must be replaced by other characters. Apostrophes and specific non-universal characters must be replaced by transliterations (e.g. the German Umlaut 'ä' must be replaced by 'ae').
4. Label Text units with 'passive variables', the attributes of the speaker or features of the text.
5. If ALCESTE does not provide dictionaries, a dictionary needs to be constructed to exclude function words (articles, prepositions). The manual explains how to do that. Some data preparation can be done

---

by hand (using find-and-replace as available in text processing programs).

6. *Running the program*: a first ALCESTE analysis can be run by using the default parameters. More experienced users can change the parameters according to research needs.

7. To ensure stable results ALCESTE computes two classifications employing different lengths of text units. An acceptable solution classifies at least 70% of the text units. Stable classes can be increased by manipulating the ALCESTE parameters.

8. *Looking at the results*
   a) The resulting word classes must be interpreted. The ALCESTE output file offers support for interpretation: word lists with the characteristic vocabulary of a class, frequent word combinations, full text of the original statements in a class.
   b) 'Passive variables' and function words associated with a class give further information on the context and dynamics of discourses.

9. Integrate the different outputs into a comprehensive interpretation.

Note

The authors gratefully acknowledge Nicholas C. Allum's permission to use data and results from Allum (1998) as an illustrative example of the ALCESTE procedure.

References

Allum, N.C. (1998) 'A social representations approach to the comparison of three textual corpora using ALCESTE'. Unpublished Thesis, London School of Economics and Political Science.

Beaudouin, V., Lahlou, S. and Yvon, F. (1993) 'Réponse à une question ouverte: incidence du mode de questionnement'. Paper presented at Secondes journées internationales d'analyse statistique de données textuelles, Montpellier.

Benzécri, J.P. (1981) *Pratique de l'analyse des données: linguistique et lexicologie*. Paris: Dunod.

Bertier, P. and Bouroche, J.M. (1975) *Analyse des données multidimensionnelles*. Paris: Presses Universitaires de France.

Diday, E., Lemaire, J., Pouget, J. and Testu, F. (1982) *Eléments d'analyse des données*. Paris: Dunod.

Greenacre, M.J. (1993) *Correspondence Analysis in Practice*. London: Academic Press.

Hayashi, C. (1950) 'On the quantification of qualitative data from the mathematics-statistical point of view', *Annals of the Institute of Statistical Mathematics*, II.

Lahlou, S. (1996) 'A method to extract social representations from linguistic corpora', *Japanese Journal of Experimental Social Psychology*, 35: 278–91.

Lahlou, S. (1998) *Penser manger*. Paris: Presses Universitaires de France.

Lebart, L. and Salem, A. (1988) *Analyse statistique des données textuelles*. Paris: Dunod.

Lebart, L., Morineau, A., Becue, M. and Haeusler, L. (1989) *Système portable pour l'analyse des données textuelles, version 1.1, Manuél de l'utilisateur*. Paris: CISIA (1 Avenue Herbillon, F-94160 Saint-Mandé, France).

Noel-Jorand, M.C., Reinert, M., Bonnon, M. and Therme, P. (1995) 'Discourse analysis and psychological adaptation to high altitude hypoxia', *Stress Medicine*, 11: 27–39.

Reinert, M. (1983) 'Une méthode de classification descendante hiérarchique: application à l'analyse lexicale par contexte', *Les Cahiers de l'Analyse des Données*, 8 (2): 187–98.

Reinert, M. (1990) 'ALCESTE. Une méthodologie d'analyse des données textuelles et une application: Aurélia de Gérard de Nerval', *Bulletin de méthodologie sociologique*, 26: 24–54.

Reinert, M. (1993) 'Les "mondes lexicaux" et leur "logique" à travers l'analyse statistique d'un corpus de récits de cauchemars', *Langage et société*, 66: 5–39.

Reinert, M. (1998) *Manuel du logiciel ALCESTE (version 3.2)* (computer program). Toulouse: IMAGE (CNRS-UMR 5610).

Wagner, W. (1997) 'Word associations in questionnaires – a practical guide to design and analysis', in *Papers in Social Research Methods – Qualitative Series*, Vol. 3. London: London School of Economics, Methodology Institute.

Wagner, W., Valencia, J. and Elejabarrieta, F. (1996) 'Relevance, discourse and the "hot" stable core of social representations: a structural analysis of word associations', *British Journal of Social Psychology*, 35: 331–52.

Part IV

Issues of Good Practice

18

Fallacies in Interpreting Historical and Social Data

Robert W.D. Boyce

KEYWORDS

adversarial fallacy
fallacy of anachronistic narrative
fallacy of disproportionate
  evidence
fallacy of necessary and sufficient
  causes
fallacy of reduction

fallacy of relativized evidence
fallacy of self-validation
fallacy of the furtive fact
fallacy of the mechanistic
  cause
fallacy of the missing middle
fallacy of the superfluous cause

History as an academic subject sits uncomfortably among the social sciences. This is illustrated vividly by the fact that in the UK, economic and social history receives funding from the Economic and Social Research Council, whereas political, intellectual and international or diplomatic history – what, for lack of a better term, might be called traditional history – relies for funding upon the Arts and Humanities Research Board. Functional divisions of this sort obscure the fact that much historical work straddles these somewhat artificial boundaries. How, for instance, should one categorize Keith Thomas's *Religion and the Decline of Magic: Studies in Popular Beliefs in Sixteenth- and Seventeenth-Century England*, or E.P. Thompson's *The Making of the English Working Class*, or Richard Evans's *Death in Hamburg: Society and Politics in the Cholera Years 1830–1910*, three excellent works that contribute to our understanding of intellectual and political as well as social history? Rather than two or three categories in the past 50 years the academic discipline of history has become increasingly divided and subdivided, and now comprises at least a dozen components. But at the risk of gross simplification, it may be said that the division imposed by the public funding bodies reflects a basic difference over methodology which divides the profession. Practitioners of economic and social history, or what has variously been called scientific, quantitative, cliometric or simply new history, with few exceptions deliberately associate themselves with the social sciences. Historians of the traditional sort, on the other hand, remain uneasy if not actually hostile to the idea that their activities are a form of science, and by and large prefer to be linked instead with the humanities. Nevertheless, they would vigorously deny that this implies any less rigour in their use of evidence or tests of validity. They would also observe that their range of subject matter comprehends most of the areas treated by their 'scientific' colleagues, and much more besides. According to Robert Fogel, winner of the Nobel prize for his pioneering work in cliometrics:

> 'Scientific' historians tend to focus on collectivities of people and recurring events, while traditional historians tend to focus on particular individuals and particular events. (Fogel and Elton, 1983: 42)

But the 'scientific' historian, at least one of Fogel's stripe who builds or tests models using mathematical and statistical tools, has seldom ventured beyond economic, social or demographic history, whereas the traditional historian's 'events' include political, intellectual and social developments, revolutions, wars, migrations, political parties, governments, states, customs, beliefs and inventions, childbirth, love, marriage and death, and his 'individuals' include the powerful and the poor, the famous and the infamous, the creative and the destructive, and as often as not groups rather than single persons. The traditional historian's subject field is thus exceptionally wide. Indeed, the only constraint she would recognize is that it should be of some social significance. This being the case, one might be tempted to conclude that history (henceforth meaning traditional history unless otherwise indicated) is a virtual social science or even, because it straddles all the social sciences, the qualitative discipline *par excellence*.

Doing history

Before deciding where history stands in relation to the social sciences and what it has to offer students engaged in qualitative research, it may be useful to describe briefly what historians do when they 'do history'.

The recording of history is as old as written records themselves. As an academic discipline, however, it emerged only in the late eighteenth century or early nineteenth century, along with the secularization of thought and the rise of the modern social sciences. One should perhaps say instead 'the *other* social sciences', since few practitioners at the time thought to distinguish history from the other disciplines. The nineteenth century was the great age of history, when historians engaged in the promotion of liberalism or in some cases anti-liberalism, in the forging of self-conscious nations, and in providing a rationale for new ventures in overseas empire building, and were rewarded with the establishment of history chairs throughout the university system. The great nationalist historians – Treitschke in Germany, Michelet in France, Macaulay in Britain, Koskinen, author of the first important history of Finland, Palacký, the historian of Bohemia – set about implicitly and in some cases explicitly to demonstrate that 'history' had marked out a special place for their particular nation, whose unique experience or character warranted claims for self-government, independence or enhanced status in the world. In this respect, their project bore a distinct resemblance to that of Saint-Simon, Comte, Hegel, Marx, Engels and Spencer, all of whom, whether idealist or materialist, engaged in forms of historicism that assumed that the whole of human existence, past, present and future, was shaped by vast impersonal forces operating on the basis of discoverable laws. Increasingly, scientific history also yielded works whose devotion to manuscript sources made them massive, pedantic and nearly impenetrable to the ordinary reader.

Towards the end of the nineteenth century a marked reaction set in against this form of positivism and the assumption that the course of history is determined by discoverable laws. Influenced by the work of philosophers such as Friedrich Nietzsche, Henri Bergson, Benedetto Croce and later R.G. Collingwood, historians increasingly insisted upon the uniqueness of their activity. The past could be understood not by logical deduction or induction, but through a process of empathy with the subject. Since historians dealt with dynamic processes rather than static situations, they had to do more than observe events from the outside. They had to enter the spirit that informed or guided these processes, to 'get inside' them, a process commonly known by the German term *Verstehen*, to distinguish it from *Wissen* meaning in this case (mere) factual description of outside appearances. But neither at the start of the twentieth century nor today have historians reached a consensus on any one approach. While it is probably fair to say that historians as a group are distinguished by their relative indifference to methodological issues, a lively dispute continues among epistemologists and scholars of historical method as to whether the nature of all historical explanation is essentially similar to that employed in the social (or natural) sciences.

The core of the dispute revolves around what has come to be called covering-law explanations in history. Carl Hempel, Sir Karl Popper, Ernest Nagel, Maurice Mandelbaum and others have argued that the historian, consciously or unconsciously, engages in the application of laws or principles or established regularities formulated in the natural and social sciences (Gardiner, 1974). While she may seek to explain a specific event or the behaviour of a single individual or group of individuals, the event or behaviour is bound to be an instance of a recognizable phenomenon or set of phenomena, governed by social principles and laws, if she is engaged in socially worthwhile research. In Fogel's words:

> historians do not really have a choice of using or not using behavioral models, since all attempts to explain historical behavior . . . whether called *Ideengeschichte*, 'historical imagination', or 'behavioral modelling', involve some sort of model. The real choice is whether these models will be implicit, vague, and internally inconsistent, as cliometricians contend is frequently the case in traditional historical research, or whether the models will be explicit, with all the relevant assumptions clearly stated. (Fogel and Elton, 1983: 25–6)

Proponents of this view have not minimized the difficulty of specifying the covering laws implicit in historical explanation. Popper, in *The Open Society and its Enemies*, admits the difficulty:

> If we explain . . . the first division of Poland in 1772 by pointing out that it could not possibly resist the combined power of Russia, Prussia and Austria, then we are tacitly using some trivial universal law such as: 'If of two armies which are about equally well armed and led, one has a tremendous superiority in men, then the other never wins.' . . . Such a law might be described as a law of the sociology of military power; but it is too trivial ever to raise a serious problem for the students of sociology, or to arouse their attention. (1945: 264)

Nevertheless, Popper could see no other basis for accepting an historical explanation except as an informal exercise in deduction. Hempel similarly accepts that the historian, in seeking to explain complex events, can seldom formulate the laws in question 'with sufficient precision and at the same time in such a way that they are in agreement with all the relevant empirical evidence available'. Like the natural scientist engaged in field-work, the historian merely points towards the relevant laws, or, as Hempel would have it, drafts an 'explanation sketch' comprising an indication of the laws and the requisite initial conditions, then devotes himself or herself to the elaboration of the specific circumstances of the particular event. In so far as concepts such as belief systems, political ideologies, revolution, genocide, education, employment, speculation, prosperity and suchlike are used, however, the historian is dependent upon abstractions of potentially definable regularity. In any case, neither the historian nor her subject, whether one individual, a community or a whole class of people, can exist or think or act outside society and hence outside the regularities or laws identified by social scientists. The historian who imagines that she can understand their behaviour simply by the application of common sense is, to borrow a phrase of the economist J.M. Keynes, almost certain to be the unwitting slave of some outdated social theory.

Few historians working in the traditional subject fields would wholly disagree with the latter claim, since most of them would readily recognize their debt to the social sciences. Nevertheless, most if not all of them would almost certainly reject the main premise of the argument, that their task is essentially one of identifying covering laws or applying them with suitable qualifications to specific events. This dissociation from covering-law theory is due partly, but only partly, to a reluctance to be thought of as the footsoldiers or fieldworkers of the social scientists, gathering the data and compiling the examples for others to build their generalizations upon. Partly it is due, as William Dray and Sir Isaiah Berlin argue (Gardiner, 1974: 87–8, 161–86), to the historian's conviction that the concept of the historical actor as agent, and therefore of the open-endedness of history itself, is incompatible with the deterministic assumptions of the social sciences. But it also follows from the historian's conviction that her explanation of events characteristically employs a different methodology. As Dray puts it, the reference to covering-law theory as a description of her professional activity is foreign to her 'universe of discourse' (Gardiner, 1974: 87). Even when her subject is in the first instance a physical thing such as a country house, a sport, an army or a plague; an abstract thing such as a belief system, an ideology, a marriage ritual or the symbolic representation of war; or a specific event such as a war, a peace conference or an election; the issue requiring explanation is the logic of a specific human endeavour, by an individual or a group of individuals. The findings of the social sciences may be useful in pointing towards potentially fruitful lines of investigation, but they cannot substitute for proof, which derives only from the historical record. The historian's challenge is not to apply or test social theories, but to determine 'what series of connected intentions, decisions, and actions . . . in connection with what series of situations and accidents' can explain her subject's behaviour or the phenomenon in question (Hexter, 1971: 33). She does so by describing the world of her subject, painting it in the round and, as it were, from within. Herbert Butterfield, for many years Professor of Modern History at Cambridge, puts it thus:

> Our traditional historical writing . . . has refused to be satisfied with any merely causal or stand-offish attitude towards the personalities of the past. It does not treat them as mere things, or just measure such features of them as the scientist might measure; and it does not content itself with merely reporting about them in the way an external observer would do. It insists that the story cannot be told correctly unless we see the personalities from the inside, feeling with them as an actor might feel the part he is playing – thinking their thoughts over again and sitting in the position not of the observer but of the doer of the action. If it is argued that this is impossible – as indeed it is – not merely does it still remain the thing to aspire to, but in any case the historian must put himself in the place of the historical personage, must feel his predicament, must think as though he were that man. Without this art not only is it impossible to tell the story correctly but it is impossible to interpret the very documents on which the reconstruction depends . . . We may even say that this is part of the science of history for it produces communicable results – the insight of one historian may be ratified by scholars in general, who then give currency to the interpretation that is produced. (quoted in Dray, 1957: 119–20)

The last point is an important one. Some epistemologists have construed the historian's argument to rest merely upon a 'correspondence' or 'coherence' theory of truth, wherein the historian does no more than ask if the behaviour of her subject or the event in question 'makes sense' to her or is consistent with her own experience (Gardiner, 1974: 155). In fact, the question the historian poses is not whether it makes sense to her but whether it makes sense within the experience of her subject or the other circumstances of the time, so far as these can be known. To answer this requires the historian to explain the system of ideas governing her subject's behaviour, which may be – almost certainly is – substantially different from her own. Precisely how she goes about it may be illustrated by taking one example: East–West relations in the immediate aftermath of Stalin's death in March 1953, when Stalin's successors indicated their willingness for détente and an end to the Cold War.

Here the historian who is interested to know why the West did not seize on Soviet initiatives or signals to end the Cold War would doubtless turn her attention to the leaders of the principal Western powers who had the opportunity to respond to the Soviet moves. She would recognize that leaders even of the most powerful states are not wholly free. Their actions are constrained both by external factors such as alliance commitments, constitutional laws and political structures, and by internal factors such as involuntary beliefs, convictions or fears. What latitude they have is a matter for empirical testing by recourse to the oral and written evidence. The historian does this in the exercise of 'getting inside' the world of his subjects, in this case of the American President, Dwight Eisenhower, her Secretary of State, John Foster Dulles, and other Western statesmen. Directly or indirectly, she then establishes the mental calculations that they might have made in responding to the Soviet signals. She commonly employs empathy, projection, insight, intuition and so forth in the exercise of explaining their actions. But she combines it with an inductive, empirical process of building and modifying her explanation in light of the available evidence. To get inside John Foster Dulles's mind, she does not simply ask, 'What would I have done had I been called upon to judge the Soviet Union's intentions in the mid 1950s?' She engages in a careful reading of the confidential reports from US diplomatic missions and intelligence sources that may have crossed Dulles's desk at this time, and attempts to determine whether Dulles actually read them and was impressed by them. She reads Dulles's telegrams to overseas envoys, his public speeches, his memoranda to President Eisenhower, and if available his private diaries, in order to appreciate how he represented his actions. Since this is contemporary history, she might examine media recordings; and even now she could seek witness interviews. She considers the possible influence upon Dulles's calculations of the intensely religious milieu in which he grew up, his education, his legal training, his age, his health. She considers how Dulles reacted in earlier situations that bear some resemblance to the one in question. She casts her net more widely to examine the contemporary accounts by foreign observers of the East–West scene. And she places this beside similar studies of the behaviour of the other statesmen involved. The historian does not simply let her imagination run wild, but, as Collingwood and Butterfield suggest, attempts to empty her mind of her own prejudices in order to catch her subject's outlook and feelings. In this way she builds up a picture of the influences upon her subject's calculations: the personal and private, the emotional and religious, the political, the official, the international. The more she knows about her subject and his personal world, the more consistent with the evidence her description of her subject's calculations becomes. And while it can never be more than a tentative, provisional explanation, since new facts may always come to light and even wholly new factors bearing upon the calculation may be identified, the historian can hope to produce an account that is plausible and open to examination and refutation.

The historian's work thus bears a close resemblance to the activities of an investigating magistrate or forensic investigator, whose task is also to explain motives, reasons or causes of a specific human action, and which is similarly carried out by building up a detailed picture of the circumstances surrounding the individual or group involved in the event. While this method neither rests upon laws nor seeks to construct new laws, it depends upon rigorous standards of evidence and logical methods of interpretation. It is pragmatic and inductive; it involves the testing of hypotheses and the explicit and careful recording of sources. From time to time it is even well written. And since it possesses all these characteristics, it deserves a place alongside if not within the social sciences.

Historians' fallacies

If the foregoing provides a recognizable picture of how the historian normally proceeds, it also points to the peculiar problems facing historians. For while they commonly deal with very specific events, the exercise of explaining human motives or behaviour is likely to embrace an extremely wide range of evidence and possible interpretations. Thus even while their research topics create the impression of narrow specialism, historians are usually generalists. This confronts them with problems in the framing of questions, the logical construction of arguments and the handling of a wide range of qualitative evidence. Since all social scientists are prone to the same mistakes, the balance of this chapter will be devoted to some of the more egregious ones. Several have been drawn from David Hackett Fischer's *Historians' Fallacies: Towards a Logic of Historical Thought* (1971), which I recommend to anyone seeking a more extensive discussion of methodological problems facing historians. Others, along with the various illustrations, are drawn mainly from my experience as an international historian.

The fallacy of the missing middle

In the first section of his book on fallacies of question framing, Fischer identifies 11 errors of procedure, perhaps the most common being what he calls the fallacy of false dichotomous questions, or what we may call more crudely the fallacy of the missing middle. Examples appear frequently in the daily press, along the lines: 'Swampy, hero or law-breaker?' or 'The

Scott Report: damning indictment or apologia?' Historians seem equally prone to this fallacy, and in America dozens of highly regarded historians have supplemented their incomes by editing student texts with titles such as *The Medieval Mind – Faith or Reason?* or *Jean Monnet – Genius or Manipulator?*

The trouble with all these propositions, of course, is that they suggest a dichotomy between two terms that are in fact neither mutually exclusive nor collectively exhaustive. The Scott Report to the UK House of Commons on the export of defence equipment was probably both an indictment and an apologia, both . . . and . . . and more. Similarly Jean Monnet, a genius and synthesizer, manipulator and idealist, technician and politician, is far too interesting to be reduced to one or two labels of any sort. Hence the question itself inevitably distorts the answer offered. This is probably obvious enough, but it is remarkable how often professional scholars fall into this error.

The adversarial fallacy

The adversarial fallacy bears a resemblance to the fallacy of the missing middle, but reflects a conscious decision on procedure: to assume that the truth will more quickly be reached if each historian adopts an adversarial position. This common strategy can be seen particularly clearly in the history of the Cold War. Most of the books by Western academic historians in the late 1940s and 1950s proceeded on the assumption that the Western powers were innocent of all aggressive intentions and guilty at most of misperception, whereas the Soviet Union sought constantly and aggressively to extend its territorial domination. They were followed by the so-called revisionist historians, by and large American scholars who, influenced by the Vietnam War and conflicts in the Western hemisphere, asserted the opposite view, that the USA was the imperialist power and that the Cold War is to be explained almost exclusively by American efforts to secure global hegemony. Now it should be said that it is just possible that either position *might* be true. The fallacy of the historians is to *assume* that one or the other position is true, without standing back and examining whether it is or not.

The fallacy of the superfluous cause

Fischer discusses a number of fallacies of causation, but a fairly common one that he does not discuss may be called the fallacy of the superfluous cause. Here the mistake is to explain an event by reference to the motive of one or another agent, which can be demonstrated to have existed, but which had little or no actual influence upon the outcome. One particularly good example is the explanation offered by several American historians for the decision of the British government to return to the gold standard in April 1925. These historians have been able to demonstrate that American central bankers strongly wanted Britain to return to gold and encouraged the British authorities to do so. They have also been able to demonstrate that Britain's return was likely to have benefited the USA and did in fact damage the British economy. They have therefore concluded that Britain returned to gold because it was pressured or induced to do so by the USA. What they failed to do, however, was to examine closely the calculations of the British authorities. Had they done so, they would have found that the British authorities had their own reasons for seeking to return to gold and that US pressure did not figure at all in their calculations (see, for example, Costigliola, 1977). Hence it was a wholly superfluous cause.

The fallacy of necessary and sufficient causes

Historians who are uncomfortable with the idea that they are mere tellers of stories and are anxious to instil rigour in their work not infrequently break down their explanations of events into discrete factors, or label them as necessary and sufficient causes or sometimes underlying and immediate causes; and they usually describe their work as analytical rather than (merely) narrative (see Hexter, 1971: 110–18; Elton, 1970: 121–4). The practice is particularly common in school texts, where the motive is partly to show that large events such as the French Revolution or World Wars I and II have complex origins involving economics, culture, technology, demography, climate and so forth. The aim is laudable, but the results are never convincing because the approach is inherently flawed. In the first place, many of the factors will be found to have been present before the event occurred, and thus do nothing to explain why the particular event occurred when it did. Secondly, the assumption, implicit or explicit, is that the factors can be quantified in such a way as to explain the event. But the result is inevitably a circular argument: that event A happened because factors X, Y and Z increased in size or intensity to the point where A happened. Adding a refinement such as the introduction of underlying and immediate causes does not remove the problem. For it omits the one thing necessary for historical explanation, namely the description of how these causes or factors affected the behaviour of the subjects, their thought patterns or beliefs, their calculations and their actions over the period of the event in question. Thus, one way or another, the historian must tell the story (engage in narrative) in order to demonstrate the coherence of his analysis. To pretend otherwise is to commit the fallacy of necessary and sufficient causes.

The fallacy of anachronistic narrative

At least as common but better known is what Fischer calls the fallacy of presentism. We might also call it the fallacy of anachronistic narrative, for the error is to read the past as if it was nothing but a staging ground for the present. In the British context the most notorious example is the Whig interpretation of history, which would have it that the whole of British political history is little more than the story of Whigs or liberals struggling to throw off the tyranny of arbitrary authority and tradition. The inference – a false one – is that all the agents shared the same motives and worked for the same ends; and that all events are to be examined only in so far as they contribute to the elaboration of this story. In recent years one can discern a similar trend among British international historians in their accounts of the inter-war period. It is an extraordinarily important period in British history, which ends with the failure of appeasement, the outbreak of World War II, the near extinction of democracy and freedom in Europe, the Holocaust, the dislocation or shattering of the great colonial empires, and the beginning of 50 years of Cold War. For that reason, historians commonly examine the inter-war period in search of the origins of these calamitous events. There is nothing wrong with this, but the picture thus created is one in which the political leaders of Britain, France and other countries were almost wholly preoccupied with the approach of war. This may well have been true for Hitler, but it was probably not the case for most leaders of the democratic powers. Once the world economic crisis began in 1929 and production slumped, unemployment soared, and the capitalist system itself seemed on the verge of collapse, their main preoccupation was almost certainly the domestic economy and attacks from domestic political opponents; and this probably remained true until at least 1938. Only then did the threat of war rise to the top of their agenda, and even then not all the time. Thus, as in this case, historians may distort the past by taking a particular outcome in history and stripping away everything that happened except the direct antecedents of the event in question. Unless proper allowance is made for this selectivity, it distorts both context and motives, and the historian is then guilty of what we may call the fallacy of anachronistic narrative.

The reductive fallacy

Still on fallacies of causation, we reach the reductive fallacy. As Fischer observes, historians are bound to tell selected truths and hence their causal models must be reductive in some sense, but some causal models are more reductive than others. When a causal model is reductive in such a degree or in such a way that the resultant distortion is dysfunctional to the resolution of the causal problem at hand, then we may say that the historian is guilty of the reductive fallacy. One common form of this fallacy is to identify a single element in the proffered explanation and to claim, for no compelling reason, that it is the key to the whole 'story'. A.J.P. Taylor was a master of this form of the reductive fallacy: he loved to identify the most trivial fact or factor as deserving of special mention, probably just to provoke his readers or listeners. One of the most striking instances in recent years was offered by Jacques Parizeau, leader of the separatist Parti Québecois, premier of Québec and, it might be added, a former Professor of Economics at the Université de Montréal. Upon learning that the second referendum on sovereignty for Québec in October 1995 had been defeated by a single percentage point, Parizeau publicly blamed the outcome on Québec's ethnic minorities and big business. In a sense he was right: minority groups and directors of some of Québec's largest firms (francophone as well as anglophone) had almost certainly voted strongly against sovereignty or independence. But together they amounted to barely 10 per cent of the province's population. Of equal importance in electoral terms was the rejection of the sovereignty option by the francophone Outouais region, where many people depend for work on the Canadian federal capital of Ottawa – Hull. No less importantly, the nearly 100 per cent francophone ridings around Québec City divided almost equally for and against sovereignty. Unlike the ethnic minorities or big businessmen, one might have expected voters of Québec City strongly to support sovereignty, since their town was likely to become the future capital of an independent Québec and to gain much of the resulting increase in employment and prestige. For Parizeau to concentrate only upon one or two small groups of voters whose behaviour was wholly predictable, while ignoring other groups of at least equal importance and greater value for the understanding of the majority's views, was thus a bizarre as well as an obnoxious interpretation of the evidence. In doing so, we may say that he committed a reductive fallacy.

The fallacy of the mechanistic cause

Another common failure of analysis derives from what Fischer calls the fallacy of the mechanistic cause. This is the error that involves breaking down the components of a causal complex and analysing them separately, and even assessing separately their causal influence as if they were discrete elements determined by discrete forces rather than being dynamically related to one another. One striking example forms the core argument of a well-received book by Geoffrey Luebbert, *Liberalism, Fascism or Social Democracy: Social Classes and the Political Origins of Regimes in Interwar Europe* (1991). Luebbert's study purports to explain why some European countries between the wars sustained democratic forms of government while others abandoned democracy in favour of fascist regimes. He breaks down the components of society into classes, treats them as discrete elements, then concludes that the different outcomes are to be explained by the fact that in countries that adopted fascism, the peasant classes sided with the urban middle class, whereas in the countries that remained democracies the peasant classes distributed their support among several groups and political parties. Aside from being extremely reductionist – what, after all, was the urban middle class? and which political parties in Germany, Italy, France, etc. were purely of one class or another? – the trouble with this approach is that in different countries the various causal elements behaved differently on account of different political traditions, different leaders and different contemporary circumstances. To single out one difference as if this were *the* cause is to assume an identity not only of classes, parties and individual agents, but also of causal relations among them as well. This is an example of the final fallacy of causation, the fallacy of the mechanistic cause.

The fallacy of the furtive fact

In his section on fallacies of factual significance, Fischer again lists approximately a dozen common errors, one of which he calls the fallacy of the furtive fact. This seems to be particularly common among international historians. The error is to believe that facts of special significance are those that are particularly obscure, and that if found they should be accorded a special place in explaining the events in question. The prominence in international history is largely the result of recent interest in spying and subversion as factors in the shaping of international affairs. Intelligence history is intensely interesting, of course, and in some instances it has been shown to be of crucial importance to the explanation of major international events. Several striking examples emerge from the history of World War II. One is the use the Allies made of the ENIGMA machine to decrypt German signals, which undoubtedly contributed to winning the campaign in the desert of North Africa and in the Battle of the Atlantic. Another is the application of counter-intelligence to mislead the Germans over the significance of the D-Day landings in 1944 so as to delay a counter-attack by forces held in readiness in France. But there are many other cases where the fact that certain evidence was deeply buried and hard to retrieve has resulted in it being given undue prominence. It is one thing to show that statesmen received revelatory information from intelligence sources. It is another to demonstrate that this information decisively affected their actions. Often, in fact, the very revelatory quality of the information made it hard for statesmen to fit it into their calculations. This evidently was the case in May and June 1941, when Stalin received secret reports of an impending German invasion, and in 1944 and early 1945, when Soviet spies reported America's development of an atomic bomb. Although this was vastly important information, Stalin seems to have been unable to make sense of it because it did not fit into his picture of the world. But the uncovering of these facts has led some historians to give them great prominence in their accounts.

The fallacy of relativized evidence

Along with anthropology, sociology, international relations and certain other social sciences, history has its adherents of postmodernism. Although not a single school or movement, postmodernists are united in regarding texts both as the basis for our understanding of the past, and also as more or less opaque constructions through which no 'real' past can be retrieved, and whose meaning thus depends essentially upon the prejudices of the individual reader. This has led some historians to devote themselves to the study of historians, the real creators of history, and others to set aside large subjects in favour of the incidents or individuals on the margins of great events, and still others to read the documentary evidence 'imaginatively', going well beyond what more conventional historians would be likely to regard as legitimate inference. Despite the extreme shakiness of the theoretical foundations, some of the published results are good and a few are excellent, although it should be said that their merits have little to do with postmodernism (see Evans, 1997: 244–9). But there is a form of relativism fairly common in traditional works of history that deserves our attention, where different subjects, concepts or institutions are conflated without due regard for their distinctive character. Several examples can be found in J.W. Young's *Britain, France and the Unity of Europe, 1945–1951* (1984), one of a handful of works by contemporary British historians that seek to stand the conventional story of post-war British external relations on its head by dismissing the view that the Anglo-American special relationship was the centrepiece of British policy. Instead they claim that, on the contrary, British policy was shaped by the idea of a 'Third Force' and directed towards the formation of a British-led bloc including continental Europe and colonial Africa. Ventures in revisionism of this sort are common enough in modern historiography, and some have proven successful, but their success hangs on the quality of the evidence supporting them. Unfortunately, in Young's case the evidence is slim indeed. It is made to appear stronger, however, by relativizing quite different things. Thus Britain and British foreign policy turn out on closer inspection to be the policy and sometimes merely the ruminations of Ernest Bevin, the Foreign Secretary. The objection to this conflation is that while Bevin may – or may not – have been prepared to contemplate a 'union' or 'bloc' or a customs union with parts of the Continent, he did not ever spell out any such ambitions, commit himself formally to them, or secure the assent of the Cabinet; and, as Young himself acknowledges, such assent was virtually out of the question in view of the firm opposition of other senior ministers. Similarly, the argument that Britain rather than France deserved the label of 'good European' in the post-war period rests upon the conflating of 'cooperation' with 'integration' and limited initiatives with comprehensive schemes. Britain sought cooperation with France and other continental countries and even, in a vague sense, European unity, but it was cooperation of the traditional sort involving treaties of friendship and mutual defence and unity based on little more than goodwill among sovereign states. It manifestly did not address French fears of a recrudescence of German power which seemed inevitable if German industrial strength were allowed to revive, as Britain and the USA – the 'Anglo-Saxon' powers – clearly wanted. Successive French governments pursued policies that addressed the bases of power, either by breaking up Germany or by integrating it into new European structures so as to limit its national sovereignty. To suggest, as Young does, that Britain's reluctant concession of a formal military guarantee to France is evidence of a commitment to European unity, and in some sense comparable to the goals of the European movement expressed at the 1948 Hague Congress, is to commit the fallacy of relativized evidence.

The fallacy of disproportionate evidence

Possibly the most common problem facing the historian arises from the uneven nature of available evidence. Political historians frequently encounter the problem on account of the fact that institutions of state almost invariably generate and preserve far more evidence than the private individuals, groups or organizations who come into contact with them. Sir Geoffrey Elton, the former Regius Professor of Modern History at Cambridge, has described how this problem arose when studying the efforts of Henry VIII's government to enforce the new political and ecclesiastical order produced by the early Reformation in England. He obtained access to an abundance of sources – statutes, proclamations, court records and so forth. All of it was contemporary with the events in question, and was generally of high quality. But practically all of it was produced by the state and its enforcers, not the victims of the enforcement. Aware of the problem, he sought to compensate for the omission as best he could (Fogel and Elton, 1983: 86–7).

Contemporary historians face the same problem and for quite similar reasons. Robert Skidelsky's *Politicians and the Slump: The Labour Government of 1929–1931* (1970) illustrates the distortions that can occur. One of the first historians to gain access to the official papers when they were released in 1968, Skidelsky, in his well-written and widely read account, was able to confirm that the second Labour government became preoccupied with the escalating public expenditure and budget deficit, yet ignored the radical fiscal innovations proposed by Sir Oswald Mosley (a minister in the government) and certain radical liberal economists such as J.M. Keynes. This is thoroughly documented from the official record, but the picture thus presented of British politics during the slump is nevertheless seriously misleading. In fact, the fiscal problem was only a second-order issue: the great controversy, within parties, between parties and nationally, was whether to abandon free trade for some form of imperial protectionism. This is evident from an examination of the political and economic press and other non-official sources, which confirm almost universal ignorance of the potential for Keynesian fiscal innovation and an intense preoccupation with the revived tariff question. But as the government set its face firmly against any departure from free trade, virtually refusing even to discuss it despite pressure from all sides, the official papers leave the misleading impression that the fiscal problem rather than the tariff issue was the great question of the day. By allowing his work to be shaped this way, Skidelsky has yielded to the fallacy of disproportionate evidence.

The fallacy of selective evidence

The final fallacy, which should be of equal interest to historians and social scientists, may be called the fallacy of selective evidence. It is capable of producing distortions similar to the previous fallacy, but arises consciously from the historian's single-minded attempt to apply a model or prove a theory, which leads him to mine the evidence for any facts or data that will serve his purpose. An example of some political importance is the recent reinterpretation of American foreign policy in the 1920s. Until the 1960s, standard historical accounts asserted that the USA was finally shaken out of its traditional commitment to isolationism by World War II; the Spanish–American War of 1898 and World War I had only temporarily forced it into the international arena. Amidst the crisis provoked by the Vietnam War, a younger generation of historians, drawing upon the work of Charles Beard, D.F. Fleming and others, challenged the prevailing view with an ambitious new interpretation of American history according to which the country had been impelled by its internal dynamics towards external expansion from its beginnings in the Thirteen Colonies. The decade of the 1920s was, however, something of a problem for this new interpretation, since three successive administrations seemed to wash their hands of international affairs, refused to join the League of Nations and, as the older generation of historians claimed, retreated into isolationism. Determined to show that this was wrong, the younger historians sought new evidence of expansionism and found it in the expansion of US financial and commercial activity in Latin America and Europe. The state was presented as hovering in the background, relying upon the influence of American business to secure its overseas objectives. The flaws in this argument are, however, palpable. In the first place, the concept of isolationism, in the American context, arose at the time of the War of Independence and meant avoidance of European diplomatic entanglements so as to leave the USA free to get on without interference from the Old World. It did not mean closing America off from overseas trade, and especially not trade with Latin America, which President Monroe and others sought to isolate from European (political) interference as well. Hence pointing to an increase in trade with Europe in the 1920s does nothing to undermine the older view, and evidence of increased involvement in Latin America, if anything, strengthens it.

Some of the younger historians, aware of this problem, have sought to bolster their argument by demonstrating that the state was actively involved behind the scenes, using American trade and finance as an instrument or weapon in order to have its way in international affairs. Leaving no stone unturned, they have succeeded in finding numerous statements by US political leaders that world trade and commerce were vital to America. They are also able to show that on several occasions American diplomats were prepared to warn reluctant European leaders that if they did not resolve their differences over reparations and mutual defence and security, they would find it impossible to raise capital in American markets. None of the statements, however, is capable of supporting the interpretive weight they are made to carry. To find President Hoover telling an association of American exporters that he regarded foreign trade as vital for America is scarcely proof of anything – although it might have been if he had told them that foreign trade was not vital. It is just what one would expect him or any other political guest to say on such an occasion. If one looks hard enough for the evidence, one can associate politicians with almost any position. Some historians describe Hoover as an 'independent internationalist' (see, for example, Wilson, 1975; and for other revisionist histories, Leffler, 1979; Costigliola, 1984; Link, 1970; Gardner, 1964); but to sustain this claim the historian would have to examine, among other things, Hoover's actions. In this case, Hoover's decision to encourage hopes of greater trade protection during the 1929 presidential election, and later to acquiesce in a massive rise in the already protective US tariff, suggests at the very least that his assertions of commitment to world trade were not to be taken seriously. As for the diplomats' warnings, these were reasonable enough, but they could have been made by anyone and amounted merely to a statement of the obvious, that American bankers would be unlikely to lend to countries lacking financial or political stability when excellent investment opportunities existed closer to home. They were scarcely the clever initiatives of a tough-minded internationalist administration, as the historians claim, since abundant evidence exists to show that the diplomats could do nothing to influence the flow of American investments, for that would create a responsibility to investors which the administration was determined to avoid. To suggest that the diplomats' statements amounted to turning on or off the tap of American capital runs directly contrary to US Treasury policy, which was defended against all attempts by the Treasury's alleged allies, the bankers, to change it. None of these failings, however, has halted the integration of this new view into America's school textbooks and presumably now forms the generally accepted view of the nation's past.

Elton, in debate with Fogel, argued that 'Models . . . dictate the terms of reference, define the parameters, direct the research, and thus are very liable to pervert the search for empirical evidence by making it selective' (Fogel and Elton, 1983: 119). Bearing in mind Elton's own profoundly conservative political outlook and the way it appears to have affected his choice of subject and research output (Evans, 1997: 193–5), it seems fair to say that a great deal of excellent historical work has been inspired by models, at least of the political or ideological kind. But in these cases the historians have retained their critical approach, their respect for the evidence, and their willingness to adapt their theories in light of it. As Richard Evans puts it, historical judgement need not be neutral (even if this were possible):

> But it does mean that the historian has to develop a detached mode of cognition, a faculty of self-criticism and an ability to understand another person's point of view. This applies as much to politically committed history as it does to a history that believes itself to be politically neutral. Politically committed history only damages itself if it distorts, manipulates or obscures historical fact in the interests of the cause it claims to represent. (1997: 252)

Conclusion

As this brief discussion suggests, traditional historians are content to remain outside the field of social science and generally reject the suggestion that in examining the past they are applying covering laws or testing social laws or law-like principles. Nevertheless their subject matter, their sources and their concern for rigorous, open-ended analysis place them close to, if not actually in, the social sciences. Moreover, the historian's methodology faces many pitfalls in problem-setting and problem-solving which will be familiar to the social scientist. Whether one approach to socially useful knowledge is of more value than the other must remain an open question, but there is little doubt that each has something to learn from the other.

STEPS IN HISTORICAL ANALYSIS

1   Ensure that in framing your questions you allow for all possible answers.
2   Consider whether the logic of your analysis is open to the charge of arbitrariness or circularity, and if necessary alter it.
3   Review your sources and handling of evidence with a view to removing sources of bias; review the possibility of widening the range and sources of evidence.

References

Costigliola, F.C. (1977) 'Anglo-American financial rivalry in the 1920s', *Journal of Economic History*, 37 (4): 922 and passim.

Costigliola, F. (1984) *Awkward Dominion: American Political, Economic, and Cultural Relations with Europe, 1919–1933*. Ithaca, NY: Cornell University Press.

Dray, W.H. (1957) *Laws and Explanation in History*. Oxford: Clarendon.

Elton, G.R. (1970) *Political History: Principles and Practices*. New York: Basic Books.

Evans, R.J. (1987) *Death in Hamburg: Society and Politics in the Cholera Years, 1830–1910*. Oxford: Clarendon Press.

Evans, R.J. (1997) *In Defence of History*. London: Granta.

Fischer, D.H. (1971) *Historians' Fallacies: Towards a Logic of Historical Thought*. London: Routledge and Kegan Paul.

Fogel, R.W. and Elton, G.R. (1983) *Which Road to the Past? Two Views of History*. New Haven, CT: Yale University Press.

Gardiner, P. (ed.) (1974) *The Philosophy of History*. Oxford: Oxford University Press. Contains essays by R.G. Collingwood, Peter Winch, Maurice Mandelbaum, William Dray, Carl G. Hempel, Quentin Skinner, W.H. Walsh, John Passmore, Sir Isaiah Berlin and Ernest Nagel.

Gardner, L.C. (1964) *Economic Aspects of New Deal Diplomacy*. Madison: University of Wisconsin Press.

Hexter, J.H. (1971) *The History Primer*. New York: Basic.

Hempel, C.G. (1974) 'Reasons and Covering Laws in Historical explanation', in *The Philosophy of History*, P. Gardiner (ed.) Oxford: Oxford University Press.

Leffler, M.P. (1979) *The Elusive Quest: America's Pursuit of European Stability and French Security, 1919–1933*. Chapel Hill: University of North Carolina Press.

Link, W. (1970) *Die amerikanische Stabilisierungspolitik in Deutschland 1921–32*. Düsseldorf: Droste Verlag.

Luebbert, G.M. (1991) *Liberalism, Fascism, or Social Democracy: Social Classes and the Political Origins of Regimes in Interwar Europe.* New York and Oxford: Oxford University Press.

Popper, C. (1945) *The Open Society and its Enemies.* London: Routledge and Kegan Paul.

Skidelsky, R. (1970) *Politicians and the Slump: The Labour Government of 1929–1931.* Harmondsworth: Penguin Books.

Thomas, K. (1971) *Religion and the Decline of Magic: Studies in Popular Beliefs in Sixteenth and Seventeenth Century England.* London: Weidenfeld and Nicolson.

Thompson, E.P. (1963) *The Making of the English Working Class.* London: V. Gollancz.

Wilson, J.H. (1975) *Herbert Hoover, Forgotten Progressive.* Boston: Little Brown.

Young, J.W. (1984) *Britain, France and the Unity of Europe, 1945–1951.* Leicester: Leicester University Press.

Further reading

Appleby. J., Hunt, L. and Jacob, M. (1994) *Telling the Truth about History.* New York: W.W. Norton & Co.

Dalzell, C.F. (ed.) (1977) *The Future of History: Essays in the Vanderbilt University Centennial Symposium.* Nashville, TN: Vanderbilt University Press. See especially Lawrence Stone, 'History and the social sciences in the twentieth century'.

Marwick, A. (1989) *The Nature of History,* 3rd edn. Basingstoke: Macmillan.

Stern, F. (ed.) (1971) *The Varieties of History: Voltaire to the Present,* 2nd edn. Cleveland, OH: World. Contains chapters by practitioners including Charles Beard, Thomas Cochran, Richard Hofstadter, Sir Lewis Namier and Jacques Barzun, as well as a useful introduction by Stern.

Thompson, E.P. (1978) *The Poverty of Theory and other Essays.* London: Merlin.

19

Towards Public Accountability: beyond Sampling, Reliability and Validity

George Gaskell and Martin W. Bauer

KEYWORDS

communicative validation	representative sample
confidence building	sample size
corpus construction	surprise
public accountability	thick description
quality indication	transparency
relevance	triangulation
reliability	validity

In a recent editorial in *Discourse and Society*, van Dijk (1997) asks the question, 'does anything go, are there no shared normative criteria of quality [for discourse analysis] as in most other serious disciplines of the humanities and social sciences? Of course there are.' He goes on to say that what is needed are criteria for good qualitative analysis. It was concerns such as these expressed by van Dijk that, in part, inspired this volume.

In the discussion of qualitative research the issue of clear procedures and standards of practice has taken second place to an endless and polemical demarcation against 'positivist' methodology. Whatever the merit of this epistemological posturing may be, the 'we against the other' rhetoric leads to the construction of a strange straw man. It crudely homogenizes a variety of scientific self-understandings into the enemy 'positivism'. We want to avoid this discussion altogether: it simply does nothing to advance the interests of qualitative research at this stage.

As qualitative research achieves a critical mass, so it develops a received wisdom about various implicit criteria to assess and guide research endeavours. What is now needed are explicit criteria, a public statement about what constitutes 'good practice' and even ideas about quality management in the research process (cf. Altheide and Johnson, 1994; Flick, 1998; Seale,

1999). This will bring both internal and external benefits. Fundamentally it introduces external public accountability to a practice that has hitherto remained rather obscure and esoteric. In competition with other more established forms of social research this will increasingly legitimate qualitative research practices. For the programme of qualitative research there are the internal benefits of setting a frame for constructive discussion and peer review. There are also the didactic benefits, seen in the potential for more efficient training of new researchers. Larger numbers of students naturally necessitate a more didactic approach to research training.

Moving away from 'anything goes', the posture of revolt against 'quantification', there is a difficult path between two equally undesirable positions. On the one side lurks the Scylla of connoisseurism; on the other the Charybdis of bureaucratization. The connoisseur knows quality when he or she sees it, akin to an aesthetic judgement. The problem here is that there is more demand for good research than there are aesthetes available. When aesthetes disagree it often remains obscure on what basis they do so. The status of the aesthete is amongst other things based on an extended apprenticeship. If qualitative research is to go beyond a handful of masters, such an approach to quality assessment is not viable.

For the bureaucrat, criteria are objectified and become an end in themselves. Has the research met its declared sample size, has reflexivity been documented, or is triangulation evident? The assessment is based on procedural rectitude without any reference to content and the relevance of the results. To avoid these extremes in moving away from anything goes, we would like to discuss two ideas: the indication of qualitative methods, and quality of research for each method.

The indication of the method

The first issue confronting the researcher is which method to use to study a particular problem, and how to justify the design, choice of data and analytic procedures. We can think of this problem as akin to the medical issue of 'indication' of a treatment. A paracetamol is well indicated for a migraine: generally it cures the headache. However, paracetamol is not well indicated for an infection: for this problem antibiotics are better indicated. Interestingly both these interventions carry certain counter-indications: in medicine as in social research, any intervention carries both advantages and disadvantages.

A similar logic of indication may apply to choices between qualitative research procedures. To some extent the choice of method is a function of the researcher's theoretical orientation. But in addition to this we may assume that some methods are better suited to tackling a particular problem than are others. For example, if you wanted to know the content of the media outlet, a content analysis would be better indicated than a set of interviews or a conversation analysis. A more difficult choice is, having opted for content analysis, which of the methods available would be better indicated for the problem at hand: rhetorical analysis, discourse analysis or classical content analysis? What is needed is something like a diagnostic decision tree for the choice of different data elicitation and analytic approaches similar to those available for the indication of statistical procedures.

In quantitative research the level of measurement, for example ordinal or interval, together with design characteristics, such as two or more group comparisons, provide a robust diagnostic for the choice of the appropriate statistical procedures. This gives didactically efficient criteria for a decision about whether to use chi-square, Kendall's tau or Pearson's product–moment correlation to study the relationship between two variables. Similar diagnostic procedures are absent in texts on qualitative research.

In this context a first entry point is to consider two design issues common to all research. First, is the research project covering a single point in time, a cross-sectional study? Or is the project extended over several time points, a longitudinal study? Secondly, is the project focusing on individual experience and actions, or on collective experiences and activities? This may be a primary distinction concerning the indication of different qualitative methods for different purposes. Note here that the distinction between cross-sectional and longitudinal concerns the design of the research and not necessarily the content of the inquiry. Many cross-sectional designs – take interviewing for example – are not restricted to the present, but include reconstructions of the past. The narrative and episodic interviewing techniques very specifically aim to bring the past into the present. Table 19.1 categorizes different qualitative methods with respect to their indication within the two design dimensions and provides a basis for making preliminary choices between methods on informed grounds.

What we must avoid is the hammer–nail mentality. It would be possible to complete any piece of household maintenance with a hammer and a few nails. However, the hammer is not well indicated for certain tasks – repairing a water pipe, for example. The skilful person will select the appropriate tool for the particular task. But if the person only knows how to handle the hammer, then all problems of fixing things in the household become a matter of hammer and nail. This implies that proper indication necessitates the awareness of and competence in using different methodological tools. To transform every piece of social research into a set of interviews or a discourse analysis, or for that matter an experiment, is to fall into the trap of methodological monologic.

Having selected a particular method, the researcher then needs some clear guidelines about how to do it and to do it well. Equally others will want to judge whether the method was conducted appropriately. This is the issue of quality indication for the researcher and for the peer group. This means we need an explicit description of 'good practice' whatever method we may apply. With some independence of the problem we should be able to judge whether a researcher is a competent professional, a posturing amateur or a well-intended novice. There is clearly a relationship between quality of research and the method of indication. Only with efforts to

Table 19.1   *The indication of methods by research design and activity focus*

Cross-sectional (one-off)	Longitudinal (several time points)
Individual action	
Text	*Text*
Individual depth interviews	Content analysis of biographical materials, e.g. diaries
Narrative interviews	Repeated interviews for a case study of an individual
Episodic interviews	
Visual image	*Visual image*
Structural observations	Bemetology
Collective action	
Text	*Text*
Narrative interviews	Content analysis of public materials, e.g. newspapers
Conversation analysis	Field notes in participant observation
Discourse analysis	
Rhetorical analysis	
Argumentation analysis	
Focus group interviews	
Image	*Image*
Film and video analysis	Photographs from different periods
Sound	*Sound*
Soundscape	Soundscape changes
Multimedia analysis	Cantometrics
	Melodic complexity analysis
	Changes in musical tastes

develop quality indication for particular methods can researchers collectively arrive at an understanding of the comparative indication of different methods.

Good practice of research: the emergence of quality criteria

Since quantitative research has a well-developed discourse and tradition concerning the assessment of research quality, in particular through the criteria of reliability, validity and representativeness, it is relevant to start with a consideration of these as a background to issues of quality assurance in qualitative research. In this introduction to the quantitative tradition we will also note parallels to qualitative inquiry.

Reliability and validity

Campbell and Stanley (1966) provide a thoughtful treatment of quality issues in quantitative research in the field of education. Their first quality criterion is internal validity. Internal validity asks whether the design of the research and ways of gathering data, the experimental arrangements, are such as to allow conclusions to be drawn with confidence. While they write in the context of experimental and quasi-experimental designs, the ideas lying behind internal validity have a functional equivalence in qualitative inquiry. If a report on a content analysis says nothing about the coding frame, or an interpretation of some interviews omits details of the topic guide, a reader might wonder if these were the products of careful research or a product of the researcher's imagination.

Perhaps the most substantial treatment of quality is found in measurement theory and in particular psychometrics, the measurement of personal characteristics such as intelligence and personality (Cronbach, 1951; Cortina, 1993). Measurement is the assignment of numbers to objects or events according to rules. Numbers may be 1 and 0 to indicate the presence or absence of a property, the counting of instances, or numerical representations of different amounts of the indicator in question. There are different levels of measurement – nominal, ordinal, interval and ratio – which assign numbers to different amounts of an indicator with different degrees of precision. Whatever the level all measurement is subject to error. In general:

observed score = true score + systematic error + random error

In prose, and for example in the context of intelligence testing, this means that the measured intelligence score is made up of the person's actual level of intelligence, plus any systematic biases inherent in the test itself and chance factors. Krippendorff (1980; 1994) extends these principles to the analysis of textual and film materials.

Reliability and validity are the criteria used to assess the extent to which a particular empirical indicator represents a specified theoretical or hypothetical construct. Reliability concerns consistency of measurement – the extent to which the test is internally consistent and yields the same results on repeated trials. There are two main techniques for establishing reliability: measures of inter-item consistency and test–retest procedures. Validity is the extent to which the instrument captures what it is designed to measure. Validity brings in the idea of purpose: it is not a test that is valid but rather an interpretation of data arising from a specified procedure. There are various forms of validity. First, content validity concerns the adequacy of the sampling of the domain in question. Secondly, criterion validity is the extent to which the test accurately distinguishes between groups known to differ on the characteristic or correctly predicts how people who now differ on the characteristic will perform in the future. And finally, construct validity concerns the relations between test results and the theoretical network surrounding the concept. Because validity always relies on some external criterion, often a previous measure of the same concept, there is always an element of tautology in the assessment of validity argument (Bartholomew, 1996).

The reliability–validity dilemma

It is axiomatically acknowledged in psychometrics that the reliability of an instrument sets the upper limits of validity. With an unreliable ruler it would be difficult to make a useful (valid) contribution to cartography. But at the same time high reliability does not automatically confer validity. However, this specific relationship between reliability and validity makes less sense as we move to the interpretation of textual material or interview evidence. In interpretation, validity may be associated with low reliability: this is what is called the reliability–validity dilemma.

Take classical content analysis of a corpus of text. Two coders might have 100 per cent agreement on the occurrence of particular words, thus showing reliability in the use of a coding frame. However, that does not mean that they have a valid interpretation of the text. The connotation of a word may change with the context. Equally, the absence of agreement between coders may be diagnostic in two ways. On the one hand it may indeed demonstrate poor training of the coders, or random coding of the material. But it may also show that the text does not lend itself to a consensual interpretation. It may be an open text that invites a number of different and legitimate understandings. To this extent low reliability is not merely a number, it is a revealing part of the process of research. Also, interpretation cannot be left to the dominance of consensus, as the minority interpretation may be the right one, and time may prove them right. At least for interpretations one must leave this possibility open (Andren, 1981).

Reliability is predicated on some form of coding frame and this is where the concept of validity is of relevance. With some exceptions a coding frame is normally based on some theoretical concepts. The theoretical ideas are made more concrete by the specification of a set of content analytic categories. Presumed associations between the categories and relations with other indicators form a part of the theoretical network. The extent to which the categories capture, or adequately sample, the data to be analysed could be argued to be rather similar to content validity. Furthermore, the observed relations between the categories and the theory approach the idea of construct validity. Bringing these two streams of reliability and validity together, one might talk about levels of 'objectivity' in the sense of saying more about the object than about the observer.

Representativeness

Much social research aims to make general statements that extend beyond the particular set of empirical observations. This brings into focus the issue of generalization, or what Campbell and Stanley (1966) call external validity. The problem faced by the researcher is on what basis he or she can confidently generalize from the particular research findings to some wider context. This context may be other actors, situations or records. Confidence, or lack of it, is based on the extent to which the sample studied is representative of the wider context: in other words, the extent to which the sample reproduces distributional qualities of this context, whether people, situations or records.

How can claims to representativeness be established? Is it largely a matter of sample size? Certainly with very few observed cases one would be hard put to argue for representativeness. Some general statements about teenagers in contemporary Britain based on a small case study in Manchester would not be very convincing. A reader might reasonably ask whether those in the case study were typical or representative of youth in Britain. But, equally large sample sizes do not guarantee representativeness: it all depends on the logic of the procedure for selecting respondents. If the respondents are self-selected, as in a phone-in to a television programme, questions about biases in the sample, which make them untypical of the population, must be taken seriously.

One of the few examples of a systematic form of generalization comes with the random sample survey. With a probability sample of a specified size it is possible to extend the findings to the population from which the sample is drawn within specified confidence limits. For a probability sample of 1000 and for any observation of 50 per cent, the normally accepted confidence limits are plus or minus 3.2 per cent. This holds true for any population, whether it is the size of London or the whole of the United Kingdom.

Essentially what sampling theory offers is a set of elaborate technical procedures for sample selection, and a basis for assessing and quantifying the confidence of generalizations from the sample to the wider population (Kish, 1965). While similar systematic sampling is applicable to some forms of textual materials, for example media coverage or documentary evidence (Lacy and Riffe, 1996), it is not an option for much qualitative research (see Bauer and Aarts, Chapter 2, this volume). However, the problem of establishing evidence to support claims for typicality of the results of qualitative research remains.

Towards alternative functionally equivalent criteria

As we have outlined, at the heart of the quantitative tradition is a set of criteria for assessing the quality of research. Researchers assimilate the issues of reliability, validity and representativeness in designing, analysing and reporting research, just as others can employ these criteria to judge whether they have confidence in the conclusions reached by another researcher. Against this background of a well-established discourse of what constitutes good quality research, we identify various positions regarding criteria for qualitative research (see Kirk and Miller, 1987; Flick, 1998: 257).

First, there is the position of direct mapping of representativeness, reliability and validity from the quantitative tradition to qualitative research. The criteria, it is argued, are and should be applicable to any form of social data. What conclusions can be drawn from unreliable and invalid observations not based on a systematic sampling rationale? The task for the qualitative researcher is simply to explain how their sample is representative of a population under study, and how the research procedures can be seen to be reliable and valid. This solution is rejected by many qualitative researchers on the grounds that it fails to acknowledge the particular character, aims and objectives of qualitative inquiry. Beyond this there are no non-numerical definitions of reliability, validity and representativeness. Measures of correlation and variance are simply irrelevant to much qualitative inquiry, which concerns meanings and interpretations and not numbers.

A second position is that of outright rejection. Sampling, reliability and validity, it is argued, are 'positivist' and expressions of the male gaze operating with a knowledge interest in control. Qualitative researchers reject positivism and the ambition to control, and therefore reliability and validity are to be rejected. All so-called quality criteria are forms of social control of the scientific community over its members, which need to be rejected in principle. For some the revolt against rigid criteria is the very essence of qualitative research. Liberating as such an attitude of total rejection may be at the early stages of an emerging tradition of research, it is probably self-defeating in the long run. The problems become apparent as the shoots of institutionalization start to flourish. Any journal editor will need criteria for selection of papers, as the supply of material comes to exceed the space that is economically available. This takes us back to van Dijk's editorial dilemma mentioned before. He deplores the fact that his request to improve the description of the analytic procedure was rejected by the authors on the basis that this would constitute the imposition of a 'power discourse', the analysis of which has been a key interest of this very journal. The editor, it seemed, found himself defeated by his own attitude (van Dijk, 1997).

A third position supports the idea of quality criteria, but argues for the development of criteria uniquely relevant to the qualitative tradition. Sampling, reliability and validity have served quantitative research well, but are just not appropriate for the evaluation of qualitative inquiry. A number of such *sui generis* criteria have been proposed to capture aspects of good practice in qualitative research, for example persuasiveness, accessibility, authenticity, fidelity, plausibility and trustworthiness (Hatch and Wisniewski, 1995; Seale, 1999). We see this as a constructive way forward, but would like to offer a systematic approach to the problem.

Our position, based on a defence of the scientific ethos in social research, is the search for criteria with functional equivalence to the quantitative tradition. Qualitative research should develop its own standards and rules, not least to demonstrate its autonomy as a research tradition. This involves neither the rigid emulation of existing standards, nor the rejection of any standards at all, but a 'middle way'. This middle way is to be found by asking what are the functions of the traditional standards and rules of method. From these abstracted functions, it may be possible to construct and respecify standards which are different in substance from quantitative research but which are functional equivalents for qualitative methods.

Once a commitment has been made to establish a set of criteria specific to qualitative research, there are two different ways of proceeding. These are top-down philosophical reflection in the form of deduction from principles, or bottom-up empirical observation of 'good practice', for example as evidenced in procedures and standards for publications, in editorial guidelines and in qualitative research (see Medical Sociology Group, 1987, in Seale, 1999). In the following we attempt a mixture of top-down development of criteria and bottom-up observations. The outcome is a set of criteria which we consider to be functionally equivalent to the traditional criteria of quantitative research in respect of gaining the confidence of peers, demonstrating the relevance of research and thus assuring public accountability of the research process.

We consider claims-making and public accountability to be central issues in the research process. Claims based on empirical research of any kind must go beyond mere conjecture or intuition. Evidence is required to warrant claims that are made in a public arena in the name of social science. But what does public accountability mean in the context of social research?

Public accountability is not an accounting issue of costs and benefits, nor is it the idea that good research commands public support for its conclusions. What we want to capture is the idea that science operates in the public domain. It is not a private enterprise. Its claims and warrants, in order to qualify as public knowledge, are 'objectified' and made public, and thereby open to public scrutiny. This is not a distinctive feature of qualitative research, but applies to any form of science, which we understand as methodologically reflected production of knowledge.

In Table 19.2 the functional equivalent criteria for the quantitative and qualitative traditions are suggested. Within public accountability we see two broad categories providing the basis for quality assurance. These are confidence and relevance, which capture the essence of quality assessment and apply equally to the qualitative and quantitative traditions of research.

Confidence indicators allow the reader and receiver of research to be 'confident' that the results of the research represent 'reality' and are more than the product of the vivid imagination of the researcher. In other words, confidence markers indicate that the results are not made up or faked for a purpose outside research. They are the outcome of an empirical encounter, specified by time and space, with the world that was coordinated by the researchers in a transparent way. For qualitative research, confidence is

Table 19.2   *Functional equivalents for quality assessment with reference to public accountability*

Quantitative tradition		Qualitative tradition
		Triangulation and reflexivity (c)
Reliability of measures (c)	Confidence (c)	Transparency and procedural clarity (c)
Internal validity (c)		Corpus construction (c, r)
Sample size (c)		Thick description (c, r)
Representative sampling (r)	Relevance (r)	Local surprise (r)
External validity (r)		Communicative validation (r)
Validity of measures (r)		

indicated by (a) triangulation and reflexive understanding through inconsistencies, (b) procedural clarity, (c) corpus construction and (d) thick description.

Relevance indicators on the other hand refer to the extent to which the research is viable in the sense that it links to theory 'internally' or is a surprise *vis-à-vis* some common sense 'externally'. Relevance incorporates both utility and importance. Not everything that is useful is also important, and important things may not be immediately or ever useful. The unexpected and the surprise must be a criterion for quantitative and qualitative research alike. However, the two traditions may structure the surprise in different ways: hypothesis testing on the one side, novel understanding and representations on the other. Relevance is indicated by (a) corpus construction, (b) thick description, (c) surprise value and (d) in some cases by communicative validation.

In the following paragraphs we describe six quality criteria that in different ways contribute to confidence and relevance of qualitative research.

Triangulation and reflexivity (confidence marker)

Understanding of other people and also of textual materials feeds on the experience of diversity. The social researcher is always in a position of trying to make sense of another person from another social milieu, inevitably from a base of self-knowledge. Understanding ourselves and the other may be an unending quest, but it takes its starting point from the awareness of divergent perspectives which lead to reflexivity, the decentring of one's own position. Reflexivity implies that before and after the event the researcher is no longer the same person. To call for triangulation of theoretical perspectives and methods (Flick, 1992) is a way of institutionalizing the process of reflection in a research project. In other words, the design forces the researcher to address inconsistencies as an ongoing part of the research process. Approaching a problem from two perspectives or with two methods will inevitably lead to inconsistencies and contradictions. These will require the attention of the researcher in the form of pondering on their origin and interpretation. Of course some inconsistencies can be due to methodological limitations, but they may also demonstrate that social phenomena look different as they are approached from different angles. Just as a mountain has a different shape and appearance from the north, the south or the air, it still remains the same mountain. In qualitative research one wants to see evidence of this labour with inconsistencies, as by struggling with inconsistencies, both within oneself and among colleagues, novel understanding is generated through the fusion of horizons, which each depend on a perspective (Gadamer, 1989: 306). The notion of reporting on reflexivity should however not be mistaken as an invitation to write the researcher's autobiography instead of a research report. The focus of research remains the world and not the researcher.

Transparency and procedural clarity (confidence marker)

Needless to say good documentation, transparency and clarity of procedures of data elicitation and data analysis are an essential part of quality research work. The primary function of documentation must be to enable other researchers to reconstruct what was done in order to check it or imitate it or for historical record (Lazarsfeld, 1951). The memory function of documentation is important. Obvious as this may be, there are structural factors that militate against this requirement. Research papers are often too short to include detailed methodological descriptions. The recent trend of some journals to open a website with appendices for current publications is only a partial solution, as it remains unclear how long these websites will be available after the publication date. Even book publishers become increasingly reluctant to publish books that include a large methodological section. The first request from editors is often to cut short the documentation of methods and procedures. It is hard to imagine how a book like the *Authoritarian Personality* could have sparked such secondary analytic attention without having originally documented the research process in considerable detail. What is needed are minimal requirements for documentation in qualitative research as they exist for example for survey research, such as in the journal *Public Opinion Quarterly*. Clarity in the description of procedures is necessary in all forms of social scientific inquiry.

For qualitative research transparency performs functions similar to internal and external validity in quantitative research. It can be judged from a detailed description of, for example, the selection and characteristics of respondents and/or materials; the topic guide of the interviews and/or the coding frame for a content analysis; the method of data collection, the type of interviewing, or the type of content analysis.

Computer-assisted analysis using CAQDAS may be seen as a welcome structure that brings transparency and discipline into qualitative analysis, albeit by technological fiat. Indeed, flexible coding and indexing, logical analysis of text links in the form of Boolean searches, and the tracking of interpretive thoughts by 'memoing' are innovative features of these new developments (see Kelle, Chapter 16 in this volume). However, these are no magical tools; on the contrary, they bring with them dysfunctional pitfalls which are recognized as 'coding pathologies' (Fielding and Lee, 1998; Seidel, 1991). Many students and researchers run into the problem of losing sight of their research topic in an endless game of ordering and reordering hundreds or even thousands of codes which were supposed to provide 'grounded theory'. Furthermore there is a tendency to use these tools as rhetorical markers, where the mere mentioning of such software packages is supposed to guarantee quality as if by technological prowess.

Corpus construction (confidence and relevance marker)

In much social research the option of systematic sampling is simply not available, and as such claims for representativeness or external validity are a matter of argumentation. Corpus construction is functionally equivalent to representative sampling and sample size, but with the different aim of maximizing the variety of unknown representations. Researchers want to map the representations in a population, and not to measure their relative distribution in the population (see Bauer and Aarts, Chapter 2 in this volume). Sample size does not matter in corpus construction as long as there is some evidence of saturation. Corpus construction is an iterative process, where additional strata of people or texts are added to the analysis until saturation is achieved, and further data do not provide novel observations. A good spread of few interviews or texts across a wide range of strata has priority over the absolute number of interviews or texts in the corpus. A few exemplars from each stratum or social function have precedence over random selection of strata or within strata. Both criteria, corpus construction and representative sampling, build confidence as well as provide reassurance of the relevance of the results.

Thick description (confidence and relevance marker)

In general qualitative research should make extensive use of verbatim reporting of sources. This high-fidelity reportage of verbatim text is similar to the historians' use of footnotes: to reference the provenance of a claim. The reader may accept the interpretation offered, or come to a different view. What should be avoided is the practice or appearance of the careful selection and editing of soundbites judged to support the writer's prejudices. Of course a balance needs to be struck here. A collation of 20 transcribed interviews or of 200 press cuttings would not constitute a piece of social science. At the other extreme, a short paragraph claiming to condense such materials into a few points without sourcing would leave the reader wondering how these heroic generalizations and interpretations came about. In this sense the source is a confidence marker.

Carefully indexed reportage is also a relevance marker, in the sense that it provides the reader with insights into the local colour, the language and the life world of the social actors. An effective report, just like good theatre, brings the reader into the milieu of the social actors. They begin to make sense to him or her, and as that sense emerges, so are the claims and generalizations given credence (Geertz, 1983).

Surprise as a contribution to theory and/or common sense (relevance marker)

A marker of the relevance of any research must be its surprise value. Evidence can be surprising in two ways: either with regard to some common-sense view, or with regard to some theoretical expectation. In quantitative research this is formalized in hypothesis testing procedures and falsification.

Qualitative research requires a similar demonstration of surprise value in order to avoid the fallacy of selective evidence in interpretation (see Boyce,

Chapter 18 in this volume). Thus for textual research one might expect to see evidence of revealing insights, of open-mindedness to contrary evidence, or a change of mind that may have occurred during the research process (Gadamer, 1989: 353). In order to avoid the use of qualitative interviewing or text analysis as generators of citations that can be used to support preconceived ideas, any research needs to document the evidence with an account of confirmed and disconfirmed expectations. Solely confirming evidence is likely to raise doubts and suspicion about the quality of the research and analysis.

Communicative validation (relevance marker)

Validating the analysis of interview or text materials by confronting the sources and obtaining their agreement and consent has been proposed as a quality criterion, so-called communicative, member or respondent validation. It is the basic validation procedure of the programme of 'subject theories' by Groeben et al. (1988; see Steinke, 1998). There are similarities between this criterion and survey feedback, which in the organizational literature of the 1960s was considered a lever of planned organizational change in action research (Miles et al., 1969). In many situations consensual validation, and discussions of disagreements on interpretation that arise, can be of value to the researcher and to the participants. It shows respect for the perspective of the social actor and is consistent with the knowledge interest of 'empowerment'.

However, it cannot be a *sine qua non* for the relevance of research. To take an extreme example: facing the misuse of power of a social actor, the qualitative researcher would surely want to avoid communicative validation. It is likely that the interested social actor would refuse to accept the point of view of the researcher. If the researcher gives in to 'censorship' by the social actor, this would threaten the independence of the research. The actor cannot be the ultimate authority on the description and interpretation of his or her own actions. The observer has a different vantage point from the observed, and this may be of intrinsic value, independent of the consent of the observed. For example tacit knowledge, or the blind spots of self-observation, often escape the immediate awareness of the social actor. The observer is privileged in this respect. First, the observer sees what the actor cannot see about themselves such as tacit knowledge or behavioural routines and taken-for-granted cultural practices. Secondly, the observer sees the whole field, which includes the actor in his or her social and physical environment. This extends beyond the habitual gaze of the actor. Thirdly, the observer as social scientist uses abstractions concerning the practices or representations which the observed actor may not endorse or understand. A classic case is the concept of 'false consciousness' or the 'unconscious'. This is not of course to say that the observer necessarily produces objective and valid descriptions, but rather that he or she may have the advantage of a different perspective *vis-à-vis* the actor. To take the actor as ultimate authority on the structure and function of his or her representations is to lose this opportunity for learning and critique from different perspectives.

Summary and conclusion

We have argued that public accountability of qualitative research rests on claims within the two broad criteria, those of confidence and relevance. To warrant such claims the design, methods and procedures, and the analysis and reporting, need to meet, and to be seen to meet, certain standards of quality. We recalled under this heading the classic indicators of reliability, validity and representative sampling in the quantitative tradition. Through the idea of an abstracted functional equivalence, we offer six criteria of good practice to guide qualitative research. These are the triangulation and reflexivity of perspectives, transparent documentation of procedures, details of corpus construction, thick description of results, evidence of local surprise, and in some circumstances communicative validation. In some respects this is a checklist or recipe with two related objectives. It is intended to act as a set of guidelines, as yet unspecified, to inform the design, analysis and reporting of qualitative inquiry. In parallel it is a summary of what any critical reviewer may ask of a piece of research, and a reminder to the researcher that appropriate steps have been taken to provide the necessary reassurance.

To conclude, this volume has attempted to introduce readers both to the concepts underlying various qualitative research procedures, and to the practicalities of using them. But, with our contributors we hope to have achieved a little more than this. The tradition of qualitative research needs to develop a body of experience and documented expertise to inform choices among different methods (the indication of the method) and to assess the adequacy of a study using a particular method (quality criteria). A collective commitment to elaborate such quality criteria is needed for both teaching and research. To ignore or dismiss the challenge will, in the long run, condemn qualitative research to the backwaters of social science. If qualitative research is to compete on the wider stage it must justify its methods and claims and meet the demands of public accountability, confidence and relevance. Our proposals are not intended as the definitive solution to what is essentially a problem of practice. Rather, we hope these suggestions will stimulate a critical and constructive debate on an emerging concern for many in qualitative research.

References

Altheide, D.L. and Johnson, J.M. (1994) 'Criteria for assessing interpretive validity in qualitative research', in N.K. Denzin and Y.S. Lincoln (eds), *Handbook of Qualitative Research*. London: Sage. pp. 485–99.

Andren, G. (1981) 'Reliability and content analysis', in K.E. Rosengren (ed.), *Advances in Content Analysis*. Beverly Hills, CA: Sage. pp. 43–67.

Bartholomew, D.J. (1996) *The Statistical Approach to Social Measurement*. London: Academic Press.

Campbell, D.T. and Stanley, J.C. (1966) *Experimental and Quasi-Experimental Designs for Research*. Chicago: Rand McNally.

Cortina, J.M. (1993) 'What is coefficient alpha? An examination of theory and applications', *Journal of Applied Psychology*, 78: 98–104.

Cronbach, L.J. (1951) 'Coefficient alpha and the internal structure of tests', *Psychometrica*, 16: 297–334.

Fielding, N. and Lee, R. (1998) *Computer Analysis and Qualitative Research*. London: Sage.

Flick, U. (1992) 'Triangulation revisited: strategy of validation or alternative?', *Journal for the Theory of Social Behaviour*, 22 (2): 175–97.

Flick, U. (1998) *An Introduction to Qualitative Research*. London: Sage.

Gadamer, H.G. (1989) *Truth and Method*, 2nd edn. London: Sheed & Ward (German original 1960).

Geertz, C. (1983) *Local Knowledge: Further Essays in Interpretative Anthropology*. New York: Basic Books.

Groeben, N., Scheele, J. and Scheele, B. (1988) *Forschungsprogramme subjektive Theorien. Eine Einfuehrung in die Psychologie des reflexiven Subjekts*. Tuebingen: Franke.

Hatch, J.A. and Wisniewski, R. (1995) 'Life history and narrative: questions, issues, and exemplary works', in J.A. Hatch and R. Wisniewski (eds), *Life History and Narrative*. London: Falmer. pp. 113–36.

Kirk, J. and Miller, M.L. (1987) *Reliability and Validity in Qualitative Research*. London: Sage.

Kish, L. (1965) *Survey Sampling*. New York: Wiley.

Krippendorff, K. (1980) *Content Analysis: an Introduction to its Methodology*. Beverly Hills, CA: Sage.

Krippendorff, K. (1994) 'On the reliability of unitizing continuous data', *Sociological Methodology*, 25: 47–76.

Lacy, S. and Riffe, D. (1996) 'Sampling error and selecting intercoder reliability samples for nominal content categories, *Journalism and Mass Communication Quarterly*, 73: 963–73.

Lazarsfeld, P.F. (1951) 'The obligation of the 1950s pollster to the 1984 historian', *Public Opinion Quarterly*, Winter: 617–38.

Miles, M., Hornstein, H.A., Callahan, D.M., Calder, P.H. and Schiavo, R.S. (1969) 'The consequences of survey feedback: theory and evaluation', in W.G. Bennis, K.D. Benne and R. Chin (eds), *The Planning of Change*, 2nd edn. New York: Holt, Rinehart and Winston. pp. 457–67.

Seale, C. (1999) *The Quality of Qualitative Research*. London: Sage.

Seidel, J. (1991) 'Method and madness in the application of computer technology to qualitative data analysis', in N.G. Fielding and R.M. Lee (eds), *Using Computers in Qualitative Research*. London: Sage. pp. 107–17.

Steinke, I. (1998) 'Validierung: Ansprueche und deren Einloesung im Forschungsprogramme Subjektive Theorien', in E.H. Witte (ed.), *Sozialpsychologie der Kognition: Soziale Repraesentationen, subjektive Theorien, soziale Einstellungen*. Lengerich: Papst. pp. 120–48.

van Dijk, T.A. (1997) 'Editorial: analysing discourse analysis', *Discourse and Society*, 8: 5–6.

Glossary

accommodation   the process of changing a discourse for one community so that it is relevant and understandable by another community. Scientific accommodation is made as a technical paper for a research journal is transformed for a lay audience.

action orientation   in discourse analysis, highlighting the point that discourse is not just about things, it is also involved in doing things.

adjacency pair   in conversations, two turns in which the second is in some way predictable from the first, such as question and answer or invitation and response.

adversarial fallacy   to assume that the truth will more quickly be reached if each historian or social scientist adopts an adversarial position.

aggregation   refers to amassing data, events or processes. Amassing data is called artificial aggregation. Amassing events and processes is called natural aggregation. For example, artificial aggregation is accomplished by computing statistics, i.e. averages; natural aggregation is accomplished by the joint action of huge masses of events or processes. Aggregation – natural as well as artificial – is seen as the basic mechanism for the emergence of laws.

ALCESTE   computer program for qualitative research that distinguishes different kinds of discourse in natural texts by conducting an automatic statistical analysis.

ambiguity   The basic feature of natural language that causes major difficulties for computerized automatic content analysis; also called polysemy. Words mean different things in different contexts. There is no one-to-one relation between words and concepts. For example, homonyms are words with the same sound or the same spelling but with different referential meanings. The same word can have different sense meanings or have different connotations. By metaphorical use we move words between contexts in order to structure a particular understanding of the world. In irony or sarcasm we say one thing but mean the opposite. Ambiguity in language privileges the human coder for content analysis who can handle these interpretive difficulties efficiently.

analogy   in rhetoric, a comparison made to show similarity. Analogy can also be a form of reasoning in which a similarity between two or more things is inferred from a known similarity between them in other respects.

anchorage   in semiology, when an image is accompanied by text which serves to disambiguate the image, the text is said to anchor the image. To be distinguished from relay.

argument   the basic unit of rhetorical analysis. Usually, a practical argument is a point or a series of reasons used to support a particular claim. Basic elements are claim, data, warrant, backing and rebuttal.

argumentation   (a) a verbal or written activity that consists of a series of statements aiming to justify or refute a certain opinion and to persuade an audience. (b) in narrative interviews, those non-narrative elements of text that justify actions with reasons, explain rules, or mention relations between things or concepts.

artificial week   A systematic sampling technique for mass media contents. It avoids the weekly cycles in media production. First, an initial weekday is randomly specified; then further dates are defined by continuously adding a fixed number of days not equal to seven or multiples of seven (i.e. the number of days in the cycles) up to a defined sample size. This will create an equal distribution of weekdays over a fixed period.

assessment   in conversations, a turn involving evaluation, typically followed by a second turn agreeing with or upgrading the assessment.

backing   a premise that supports the warrant in the argument.

bemetology   An acronym which stands for 'behavioural meteorology'. It refers to the methodological demand of continuously gathering behavioural and experiential data as is done in meteorology.

biographical narrative   an individual's life history is recounted: the life as a whole or certain periods of a life, such as in illness narratives or for career moves.

cantometrics   A complex procedure including 37 analytic features developed by Alan Lomax to compare and typify folk-singing across all human cultures.

CAQDAS   Stands for 'computer-assisted qualitative data analysis software', a recent tradition of software developments to assist qualitative data analysis. These software packages support the indexing and linking of units of analysis; allow the memoing of such linkages in the form of *ad hoc* commentaries; support complex search-and-retrieval operations with indexes; provide graphical tools to represent the linkages between texts; and offer numerical interfaces for the statistical analysis of frequencies of codes in a corpus of materials.

cascade predication   In bemetology, a metaphorical expression introduced to designate behavioural or experiential data as a complex sequence of references: object ← predicator ← predicator value ← time value.

claim   in arguments, a statement that contains structure and is presented as the outcome of the argument supported by facts.

codebook   A basic tool of any content analysis that presents the order of the category/coding system and the definitions for each code with examples. It is best practice in any content analysis supporting reliable coding; and documents the coding process in public.

code value   In content analysis, a code is a category with two or more values. Every text unit is classified into categories, thereby linking each unit with only one code value for each category. Classically code values are mutually exclusive, exhaustive, derive from a single concept, and have no logical connection with the values of other codes.

coding the application of a conceptually derived procedure to a set of materials. The attachment of index words (codes) to unit segments of a record (e.g. an interview transcript or field protocol).

coding frame The systematic order of codes in a content analysis. A good coding frame is internally coherent in the sense that each code derives from an overarching analytic conception.

coding pathologies Dysfunctional practices that arise from the use of CAQDAS. For example, it encourages the construction of extended hierarchical index systems for a handful of interview transcripts. This procedure may become an obstacle for the interpretation of the data as the researcher focuses on the index system and loses sight of his or her research question which requires complexity reduction. The result may be a crisis of the research process.

coding sheet In manual content analysis, coders mark their judgements for each text unit on a coding sheet – one coding sheet for each coding unit. The coding sheet translates the text units into a format suitable for statistical analysis – one value for each code for each text unit for each coder. These records are later entered into the computer as numerical raw data. Coding sheets can be implemented directly as a computer shell, thereby avoiding data entry as a source of error in the process. A coding sheet is always supported by an explanatory codebook.

coding unit The unit of text that is linked to a code, either automatically by computer or by a human interpreter. Units can be defined physically, syntactically, propositionally or thematically.

coherence A criterion of good practice in content analysis. A coding frame is coherent if the codes are derived from an overarching conceptual principle, thus introducing complexity in an orderly manner. It may be regarded as an aesthetic criterion: coherent coding frames make for beautiful content analysis.

communicative validation A quality criterion that may sometimes apply for qualitative research. The results are fed back to the respondents who provided the information and they are asked to agree or disagree with it, to ensure that their situation is not misrepresented. However, in investigative research of powerful actors the invitation to 'censor' the researcher's account may not be appropriate.

complex retrieval a search for coded text segments that is restricted by certain limitations, e.g. the retrieval from documents with a common attribute, or the search for the co-occurrence of text segments to which certain codes had been assigned.

computer-assisted analysis the use of computer software for the management of qualitative data to automate mechanical tasks that are involved in the interpretive analysis of these data.

concluding talk   The final phase of a narrative interview. After the tape recorder has been switched off, the conversation is likely to continue, informally and with a sense of release. This 'small-talk' reveals important clues for the contextual interpretation of the recorded narrative. Concluding talk is to be recollected with a memory protocol immediately after the interview.

concordance   A computer-assisted procedure that lists all the co-texts of a keyword within a given text corpus. Normally the size of the co-text can be specified by the number of words before and after a keyword, or as the sentence or the paragraph within which a keyword occurs. Used to be a labour-intensive manual activity, but is now available in a matter of seconds to assess word meanings or to check the quality of an on-line text retrieval.

confidence building   A feature of good quality research. Reliability and sample size in quantitative research, and triangulation, transparency, corpus construction and thick description in qualitative research, are measures to build confidence in the audience about the research results.

connotation   In semiology, a type of higher-order signification. An additional meaning of a sign beyond its denotation: the denotational sign becomes the signifier to the connotational signified. In order to grasp a sign connotation, additional cultural or conventional knowledge is required.

construction   a term that highlights the role that language plays in creating our social worlds as opposed to merely reflecting or depicting them.

co-occurrence   Computer-assisted analysis that assesses the number of times two words occur together within a specified unit of text. The frequency distribution of these co-occurrences is statistically modelled to achieve a graphical representation of the association structure in a given text corpus.

corpus   A finite collection of materials, which is determined in advance by the analyst with some arbitrariness, and on which work is being done. One may distinguish general-purpose corpora, such as linguistic corpora, from topical corpora, such as a set of qualitative interviews in a social research project.

corpus construction   The process of collecting materials in qualitative research. It is not based on random principles, but is nevertheless systematic, considering relevance, homogeneity, synchronicity and saturation. It involves extending functions and strata (external variables) until the range of focal representations (internal variables) of an issue are saturated.

corpus-theoretical paradox   A selected corpus of opinions, attitudes and worldviews represents a universe of such representations if the range of variety is included; however, the corpus is needed before one can determine these subdivisions of variety. The way out of this paradox is to construct corpora stepwise and iteratively.

critical incident technique   an interview technique to explore the circumstances of events in which a crisis or a problem arose in an organization, for example an accident.

cultural indicators   The time-series analysis of text, image or sound materials to map the fluctuations in the use of symbolic features, references and icons in a community. It is assumed that these changes in the use of features and images indicate the changes in cultural values, ideas and representations, much like the smoke indicates the invisible fire. Indicators are often easier to observe than the cultural values which they represent; thus they are efficient measures from the point of view of research.

data   facts or evidence that are at the disposal of the proponent of an argument.

data analysis   Any approach, qualitative or quantitative, to reduce the complexity in the data material, and to come a coherent interpretation of what is and what is not the case.

data elicitation   The generic term for any method of mobilizing data of whatever kind, by talking to people, by observing people or by collecting material records.

denotation   In semiology, the first order of signification. The literal or primary meaning of a sign. Only everyday knowledge is required to grasp this meaning.

dictionary   a tool in computer-assisted content analysis. It defines a list of concepts by a unique list of token words. A token word is assigned to a single concept. The computer identifies token words as strings, and assigns them automatically to the predefined concept. The construction of a dictionary for a particular text corpus constitutes an interpretation by the researcher. The procedure is limited by the ambiguity of isolated words in relation to concepts.

discourse   (a) talk and linguistic texts of all kinds, including naturally occurring conversation, newspaper articles and interview data. (b) In linguistics, any groupings of words in units larger than a sentence.

eigentheory   The analysis of narrative interviews reconstructs the events (what happened and how it happened) as well as the informant's eigentheories of the events (why it happened, why I did or experienced it this way). Eigentheories typify the informant's own explanations, justifications and sense-making of experiences and events.

episode   a short event with a narrative structure, which may be part of a bigger narrative or story.

episodic memory and knowledge   the part of human memory and knowledge in which concrete events are stored embedded in their context with a temporal structure, linked to specific circumstances and persons (for example, 'my first lesson in school').

ethos   one of Aristotle's three proofs (along with pathos and logos). These proofs structure argument. Ethos is the argument which appeals to personal credibility as evidence for a particular position.

exmanent and immanent questions　In the narrative interview one distinguishes two kinds of questions. Exmanent questions are what the interviewer is interested in; however, these are to be translated into the vocabulary and references of the informant, that is the immanent questions. Not all exmanent questions are translatable, as the informant's narrative may not offer an anchoring point for translation.

fallacy of anachronistic narrative　To read the past as if it was nothing but a staging ground for the present. Also known as Whig history. It is the temporal analogy to ethnocentrism: understanding another culture or time in terms of one's own culture or one's own present.

fallacy of disproportionate evidence　Distortions that can occur because different actors leave different amounts of records behind. The available record may give importance to what was of lesser significance.

fallacy of necessary and sufficient causes　An analytical posture of breaking down explanations of events into discrete factors and labelling them as necessary and sufficent causes or sometimes underlying and immediate causes.

fallacy of reduction　Identifying a single element in the proffered explanation and claiming, for no compelling reason, that it is the key to the whole story. The resulting distortion is dysfunctional for the explanation.

fallacy of relativized evidence　Regarding texts both as the basis for our understanding of the past and also as more or less opaque constructions through which no 'real' past can be retrieved, and whose meaning thus depends essentially upon the prejudice of the individual reader. Also known as the fallacy of postmodernism.

fallacy of self-validation, selective evidence　The single-minded attempt to apply a model or prove a theory, which leads to mining the evidence for any facts or data that will serve this purpose.

fallacy of the furtive fact　the belief that obscure facts have particular significance and that if found they should be accorded a special place in explaining the events in question.

fallacy of the mechanistic cause　Breaking down the components of a causal complex and analysing them separately, and even assessing their causal influence separately as if they were discrete elements determined by discrete forces rather than being dynamically related to one another.

fallacy of the missing middle　Suggesting a dichotomy between two terms that are in fact neither mutually exclusive nor collectively exhaustive.

fallacy of the superfluous cause　To explain an event by reference to the motive of one or another agent which can be demonstrated to have existed, but which had little or no actual influence upon the outcome.

focus group interview　A small number of people, normally six to eight, meeting to discuss an issue of common concern led by a moderator, and often followed by one or two observers.

formulation　in conversation, a turn offered as a restatement, in different words, of the gist of what a previous speaker has said.

genre a type of discourse with distinguishing characteristics, e.g. the Western as a film genre or features as a genre of journalism.

group dynamics The emergent properties of a number of persons interacting, for example in the context of a focus group interview.

homogeneity A principle of corpus construction. Texts or other materials are to be of a single constitutive substance and not a mixture of different materials. For example, it is not advisable to mix transcripts of individual interviews with transcripts of focus group interviews, or newspaper texts with interview transcripts, within a single corpus. These materials need to be analysed separately.

hypothesis examination the use of complex retrieval techniques in computer-assisted analysis to find text segments that can be regarded as evidence or counter-evidence for certain (more or less precise) assumptions.

icon In semiotics, a type of sign in which the relationship between the signifier and the signified is one of resemblance, depiction or reproduction, for example a photograph. This is the least arbitrary/conventional type of sign in Peircean semiotics.

ideal research situation An ideal type of research design which combines data from (a) self-observations of actors in the field, (b) observations by naive observers within the same life world, (c) systematic observation of the field of action, and (d) triangulation of all three types of data.

index (a) In semiotics, a type of sign in which the relationship between the signifier and the signified is one of contiguity or causality, for example, smoke signifies fire. Conventional knowledge is more important for an index than for an icon. (b) In computer-assisted analysis, any tag or marker attached to a text unit for retrieval purposes.

indexical and non-indexical text the analysis of narrative interviews distinguishes two types of text in the transcript. Indexical text refers to events, persons, times and locations giving the basis to reconstruct the structure of events. Non-indexical text is the residual which may include descriptions of experiences, attributions of motives, and general claims and legitimizing arguments. The latter are pointers to the informant's eigentheory.

indexical expression an expression such as 'here' or 'now' that changes meaning according to the immediate situation in which it is said. Conversation analysts argue that all expressions are indexical.

indication of a method In research design, the problem of choosing the method of research appropriate to the problem at hand. For example, for different purposes the researcher will prefer observation over interviewing, or a questionnaire-based survey over focus group interviews. Counter-indication refers to the knowledge of when not to use a particular method.

individual depth interview A semi-structured interview with a single respondent, in contrast to the structured survey interview, and the extended conversations of participant observation.

informant The interviewee in a narrative interview.

initial topic   The first phase of a narrative interview includes the formulation of the initial topic by the interviewer. Its function is to stimulate a sustainable narration. Various rules are suggested in order to achieve this.

interpretive analysis   a hermeneutic (and non-algorithmic) process by which a human interpreter tries to find meaning (*Verstehen*) in qualitative data.

keyword in context (KWIC)   a generic term for computer procedures that support the analysis of texts by looking at single words together with their co-text, for example in concordance or co-occurrence analyses.

keyword out of context (KWOC)   a generic term for computer procedures that support the analysis of texts by focusing on the occurrence of isolated words. These include vocabulary listings, word counts and dictionary-based analyses.

knowledge interests   This refers to Habermas's typification of three knowledge traditions – empirical-analytical, hermeneutical, and critical – each associated with a typical knowledge interest: control, consensus building, and emancipation or empowerment. Not to be confused with a particular research method or an individual's personal interests.

law and chance   Law refers to any regularities which allow predictions of any sort. Chance refers to random events or processes which cannot be predicted. Law and chance should not be confused with determinism and indeterminism.

law of instrument   refers to the observation that the human capacity to define and solve problems depends on the skills and tools available; also known as the functional dependency of thinking. In other words: give a child a hammer, and she will see everything as in need of pounding. The law highlights the significance of methodological pluralism for social research.

lemmatization   the preparatory treatment of the text that is required for efficient KWIC and KWOC analyses. These computer-assisted analyses require routines that reduce different grammatical word forms into a single stem meaning. For example, for the purpose of a particular analysis the word forms 'play', 'plays', 'played', 'playing' are equivalent to the stem 'play', which may be a token of the concept 'leisure activity' (KWOC) or in close association with the word 'child' (KWIC).

lexicon   In semiology, a body of conventional cultural knowledge required in order to grasp higher-order signification like connotation or myth (see also referent system).

logos   one of Aristotle's three proofs that structure an argument (along with ethos and pathos: the three musketeers). Logos is the appeal to reason. Each argument follows a certain logic, a certain logos, a particular standard appeal to what is reasonable or rational.

main narration   The second phase of the narrative interview. The main narration must not be interrupted. The interviewer engages in active listening, note-taking if appropriate, and periodic verbal and non-verbal encouragement to continue. The coda marks the end of this phase, by which the informant clearly indicates, after repeated probing, that there is nothing more to be said.

media as a social fact   Implies that we have to treat media presentations as having constraints and agencies in the social world, just like the stock market, the UN or the nuclear industry.

melodic complexity   A series of attempts to construct cultural indicators from the melodic structure of musical pieces, such as national anthems or Number One hit parade songs. These indicators normally take into account the frequency and magnitude of tone changes, the direction of tonal progression, and the matching of music and text.

metaphor   a figure of rhetoric. An implied comparison between two things of unlike nature that yet have something in common.

metonymy   figure of rhetoric. A substitution of some attributive or suggestive word for what is actually meant.

metric   In content analysis, codes have different metric or scalar quality. They can be categorical, ordinal, interval or ratio scales. Categorical scales classify units; ordinal scales rank order them; interval scales in addition establish the distances relative to an equal unit scale; and ratio scales assess distances from a zero point. Depending on the scalar quality, different statistical procedures may apply for data reduction.

mode and medium of representation   In order to distinguish types of data materials, it is helpful to consider two basic dimensions of representing the world. Mode refers to formal or informal behaviour and communication; medium refers to movement, written text, visual image or sound. This schema allows one to distinguish several types of data and to evaluate the adequacy of particular research methods.

moderator   The role of the interviewer in the conduct of a focus group interview.

modularity   A principle of efficiency for the construction of coding frames in content analysis. The same code is used for different functions in the coding process, which increases the complexity of the coding without adding learning effort.

monitoring behaviour or experience continuously   A methodological demand satisfied by bemetology: as behaviour or experience is an incessantly occurring process, it should therefore be gathered continuously too.

music   Purposively organized sounds that constitute an elaborate multifunctional activity in most cultures. Music is produced by the human voice as singing, by specially designed instruments, and by combinations of the two.

musical meaning   The status of musical meaning, as internal or external reference, is controversial. An internal reference points to other music by way of citation, imitation or similarity. External references are mimetic by imitating movement or emotions with musical means as in programmatic music, or symbolic as in arbitrary associations with collective events or private experiences of emotion.

musical tastes   The empirical association between musical preferences and social categories of people. Musical tastes are part of the cultural capital and social distinctions. Tastes can be used as cultural indicators of the position of people in social space.

myth   In semiology, a type of higher-order signification. The process whereby cultural and ideological meaning are rendered natural, invisible, timeless or 'given'. Semiologists attempt to demystify this process by unmasking the construction of the sign and by reinstating its historical and ideological motivation.

narrative   Some texts are narratives. In a narrative a story-teller puts a number of actions and experiences into a sequence. They are the actions and experiences of a number of characters. These characters either act on situations or react to situations. The changes bring to light new elements of the situations and of the characters that previously were implicit. In doing so they call for thinking or for action or for both. All these elements reveal the plot of the narrative.

narrative and representation   The distinction between narrative and representation reminds the researcher of the epistemic uncertainties of narratives. While the technique of narrative interviewing is justified by the strong affinity between experience and story-telling, the link between narration and lived experience is often tenuous: the neurotic story-teller tells us what he thinks we wish to hear and not necessarily his or her experience; the political story-teller tells us what should have happened; and the person under trauma tells us less than there was to experience.

narrative interview   a specific method of interviewing by asking people to recount their life either as a whole or focused on, for example, an illness or their professional biography. The main part of the interview is a longer spontaneous narrative of the individual's life history, during which the interviewer abstains from directive intervention.

noise   The unpleasant sounds that are produced as side-effects of human activity and mostly without intention. The spectrum of sounds can be separated into noise and music, the boundary of which varies historically and culturally. Shifts in this boundary may have value as an early indicator of cultural trends.

notation and transcription   (a) Musical events can be represented in written format as notation or transcription by making use of elaborate sign conventions. Notation mainly serves the memory of the performer; transcriptions support the analysis of musical events. (b) Any translation of materials from any format into a written format based on conventional notation. The conventions define the level of detail to be retained.

number of qualitative interviews   There are two considerations: the amount of text that can be feasibly analysed, and the saturation of meaning in the sense that no new surprises are to be expected from additional interviews. The objective is to maximize the range of opinions and experiences with a small number of interviews.

object   In bemetology, an object may be anything that is referred to by a predicator of observation or experience. As such it is defined by the leftmost position in the scheme of predication: object ← predicator ← predicator value ← time value.

open-ended question question posed in a questionnaire producing a qualitative data base in order to investigate the natural structure of responses concerning a specific topic.

ordinary retrieval the computer-assisted search for all text segments in a given document or in a set of documents to which the same code or index has been assigned.

paradigm or associative set In semiology, the group of alternative signs which can be substituted for the chosen sign. Members of this set are in some respects similar to the chosen sign (for example, types of hats, different colours), but their differences from the chosen sign help to delimit its meaning.

parallel design This idea suggests that the study of the life world of a community is best undertaken by the coordinated longitudinal analysis of both mediated data and immediate interviews. The interpretation of either data profits from the context provided by the other. For example, neither survey nor qualitative interviews are self-explanatory; their interpretation profits from analysing the cultivation of the symbolic environment by the mass media of a community.

participatory video a video in which those filmed have a strong voice in content, style, editing and distribution.

passive variables variables that describe attributes of a speaker or features of a text unit which are linked to the semantic patterns revealed by co-occurrence analysis.

pathos one of Aristotle's three proofs which structure argument (along with ethos and logos: the three musketeers). Pathos is the appeal to the emotion of the audience in order to persuade.

perception, misperception, informed perception In the analysis of visuals, the difference between 'mere seeing' and 'seeing into', that is seeing the detail and meaning within a framed image.

population The complete collection of items or persons who are the target of statistical inference based on random sampling. A population is defined for practical purposes by a sampling frame.

predicator In bemetology, every term that may not be a definitive description or a proper name and which is assigned to an object (physical or non-physical) is called a predicator. For example, in 'John ← aggressive' the term 'aggressive' is a predicator. The whole expression 'John ← aggressive' is called a predication.

predicator value If the predicator itself is handled as an object, the assignment to that object is called a predicator value. In bemetology the term was introduced to characterize behavioural or experiential data as statements. Example: John ← aggressive ← physical ← yesterday. The term 'physical' assigned to 'aggressive' is said to be the predicator value.

preferred turn in conversations, the second part of an adjacency pair that is most predictable, and is typically said directly. A dispreferred turn is typically delivered with some hesitation, preface or modification. The concept does not imply that the speaker psychologically prefers the kind of response given; it is a statement about regularity rather than affect.

priming   focusing the attention of a respondent on the issue (stimulus) of interest by asking an initial background question or presenting an icon.

public accountability   A feature of good social research and the function of quality indication in social research. Explicit criteria of good practice ensure its public nature. Social research is a public knowledge activity. Public accountability is ensured by confidence building and relevance.

qualitative data   unstructured data, e.g. transcripts of open interviews, field notes, photographs, documents or other records.

quality indication   Every research method has its 'good practice' which is indicated by a number of criteria. For quantitative research we tradition-ally check the representativeness of the sample, the sample size, and the reliability and validity of numerical measures. In qualitative research, equivalent criteria are less clearly developed. These may include triangu-lation, transparency, corpus construction, local surprise, thick description and sometimes communicative validation.

questioning phase   The third phase of the narrative interview. After the main narration phase the interviewer asked the immanent questions by freely translating exmanent questions into the references and the vocabu-lary of the informant. Rules of conduct exclude any why-question or pointing to contradictions in the narrative.

random sampling   In content analysis and survey research, this is the key principle for selecting units of analysis. The sampling frame lists every unit of a population and gives to it a known probability of being selected. This allows the researcher to determine a parameter within a known confidence limit. Random sampling replaces unknown bias by known error. By contrast, corpus construction is a principle of selection in situations where a sampling frame is inconceivable. Haphazard or con-venience selection are unsystematic procedures, in contrast to both sampling and corpus construction.

rebuttal   in an argument, a premise that limits the generality of the warrant with further conditions, for example with 'unless'.

recuperation   In semiology, the process by which myth makers react to demystification by assimilating and neutralizing the criticism.

referent system   In semiology, that which is referred to by the signifier of connotations: a socially shared resource that enables an interpreter to interpret.

reflexivity   (a) a feature of research in the critical tradition. The ways in which researchers should reflect upon their own practices. (b) In dis-course analysis, the consideration of reflexivity flows from the simple fact that the analyst's discourse is no less constructive, action oriented and rhetorical than the discourse being analysed.

relay   In semiology, where both image and text contribute reciprocally to the overall meaning, they are said to be in a relationship of relay. To be distinguished from anchorage.

relevance (a) one of the four principles of corpus construction according to which texts and other materials are to be collected for a single purpose. It serves as a reminder to be focused in the selection of materials. (b) A feature of good quality research. The import of the research evidence for the people involved, for the theory or concepts at stake, or for the purposes of the research project. Markers are representativeness and validation in quantitative research; corpus construction, surprise and communicative validation in qualitative research.

reliability A quality indicator of quantitative social research. An instrument measures a phenomenon consistently if applied repeatedly or by different persons. For example, an intelligence test should on repeated application to the same person give the same IQ score.

reliability–validity dilemma The psychometric definition of reliability and validity implies that reliability is the upper limit of validity. This is not the case for interpretive procedures. In the evaluation of good practice of content analysis a dilemma may arise. Validity of a complex analysis is often bought by reducing coder reliability. Valid interpretations are not necessarily consensual; disagreement is informative by itself. The strict mapping of quality criteria between quantitative and qualitative research is inadequate.

repisode an episode that happens repeatedly (for example, 'Every time I go to school I first meet my neighbour and then my friend').

representation (a) a socially constructed and structured set of meanings and techniques embodied in different modes (formal or informal) and media (movement, text, image and sound). (b) A second-order, lower-dimensional model of real-world first-order, three- or four-dimensional events. (c) The range of opinions, attitudes, views, ideas that are to be saturated in the process of corpus construction. Representations are varieties of meaning revealed through qualitative research.

representative sample A random selection of units of analysis from a population, so that estimates of features derived from the sample are equal to that of the population within known limits of confidence. A representative sample is unbiased and the error margin is known.

research design A number of strategies for research that include making trade-offs between the costs of implementing them and the results to be expected. Design principles include the social survey, experimentation, panel studies, case studies, participant observation and ethnography.

resolution Every measuring instrument represents 'reality' in terms of units of resolution, more or less fine grained. In bemetology the level of behavioural or experiential resolution is the set of predicator values, e.g. the coding scheme used for observing behaviour or experience.

rhetoric the three standard definitions of rhetoric are: (a) the act of persuasion; (b) the analysis of the act of persuasion, the study of the technique and rules for using language effectively (especially in public speaking); (c) a worldview about the power of language to structure human action and belief.

rhetorical canons (parts of rhetoric) the five divisions of the study of rhetoric in classical times: invention, disposition, style, memory and delivery.

rhetorical organization   refers to the point that most discourse is constructed to be persuasive, to win endorsement in the face of competing versions of the event, phenomenon, individual or group that is the object of the discourse.

rhetoric of research   Research is considered to be a public activity that involves persuading others of the value of one's observations. In this context the function of methodology is to redistribute the effort of the researcher to strengthen the logos of an argument rather than its pathos and its ethos.

sample size   An indicator of quality of quantitative social research. The power of a statistical inference depends on the sample size among other things. The larger the sample size, the smaller is the sampling error. More precisely: a doubling of the sample reduces the error by the square root of 2; or to halve the error, a fourfold sample size will be necessary. This logic does not apply to corpus construction in qualitative selection.

sampling   Selecting randomly units of analysis from a sampling frame, so that estimates of the population are obtained with known margins of error.

sampling bias   The unknown differences between a sample and its population. Biased samples are not representative owing to non-coverage in the sampling frame or to inadvertent overselection of subgroups of the population.

sampling error   The known error associated with a particular sampling strategy. Sampling error is expressed in the margin of a mean or variance estimate of an observation.

sampling frame   An operationalization of a population of items or persons expressed in a listing. A sampling frame expresses a population imperfectly and may result in non-coverage of parts of the population.

sampling strategy   A procedure to select randomly items or persons from a sampling frame using existing knowledge, such as systematic sampling, stratification or clustering, or complex combinations of it.

sampling unit   The unit of selection for sampling. Ideally units are selected from a comprehensive listing of the population, for example all members of the electoral roll, or all press articles on a particular topic produced by a keyword retrieval. Sampling units are either identical or larger than coding units. The latter case, for example by analysing all relevant articles in any one issue of a newspaper, is a cluster sample.

saturation   A principle of corpus construction used to select interviewees or texts. The process of selection is stopped as it becomes obvious that additional efforts will not produce any more variety. Additional units yield diminishing returns.

sceptical reading   In discourse analysis, a way of reading a text that involves interrogating its organization and assumptions, continually asking what features of the text are causing one to read it this way. The opposite of traditional academic reading for gist.

Scitexing   the electronic manipulation of images.

self-generating schema   the narrative interview makes use of a universal competence for story-telling. Once a narration is initiated it ushers the story-teller into detailing texture, fixing relevances to a particular point of view, and bringing the story to a close. Other terms are 'story schema', 'narrative logic', 'inherent demands', 'narrative convention' and 'story grammar'.

semantic memory   the parts of human memory that consist of concepts, definitions and their interrelations, rules, and schemata of events. These are generalized and decontextualized from concrete circumstances, people or events.

sign   The basic unit of analysis for semiology. The sign is the arbitrary conjunction of a signifier and a signified.

signified   In semiology, the mental component of a sign. The concept or idea to which the signifier refers.

signifier   In semiology, the material component of a sign which refers to a signified. In speech this is the sound-image.

social milieu   A group of people who think and feel in a distinct way. In qualitative research people may be typified by a combination of stratum and social function on the one hand and characteristic representations of an issue on the other.

sound   Generic term for auditory data that are taken as an expression of human activity and as a form of human communication. Sounds are distinguished into noise, mostly unintended, chaotic and unpleasant, and music, mostly intended, organized and pleasant.

soundscape   A term by the Canadian composer Murray Schafer to analyse and improve the human acoustic ecology. A worldwide project reconstructs, records and describes sounds of everyday life, past and present. The project is descriptive as well as prescriptive, with a mission for noise abatement to improve the quality of modern life. Techniques such as loudness profile, listening walk and sound diary were developed to assess the hi-fi/lo-fi quality or the natural/artificial ratio of a particular soundscape.

stationary and touring model   The terms refer to the field approach of bemetology. Instead of applying questionnaires and inventories, bemetology calls for records of naturally occurring data such as actual behaviour as the basis of personality assessment. The stationary model gathers data in situations such as hospitals, schools and kindergartens where many persons stay for a time. The touring model follows the movements or records the experiences of one person through different situations. The stationary and touring models of personality assessment become feasible with technical resources such as portable computers or specially designed event recorders.

stimulus materials   Techniques such as free association, photo montages, card categorizations and role playing tasks designed to elicit ideas that may be difficult to articulate and to promote discussion in focus group interviews.

strata and functions   in corpus construction, the range of external variables that are controllable for the selection of materials or persons. Additional strata and social functions add variety of representations until saturation is reached. Stratum refers to hierarchical differentiation and function to role differentiation between social groups.

subjective definition   the subjective meaning of a certain word, phenomenon or thing used by an interviewee.

surprise   A criterion of quality in qualitative research. To avoid the fallacy of selective evidence, qualitative researchers may want to document their own surprises during a research project. New evidence in the sense of novel insights may only be credible if they are based on local surprises experienced by the researcher.

symbol   In semiotics, a type of sign in which the relationship between the signifier and the signified is purely arbitrary or conventional, for example a red rose signifies love.

synchronicity   A principle of corpus construction according to which texts and other materials are to be selected from within a single cycle of change. Different materials have different 'natural' cycles of change. The period selected should not exceed one such cycle. Diachronic research involves the comparison of two corpora across cycles of change.

synecdoche   a rhetorical figure of speech where the part stands for the whole, e.g. the crown stands for the monarchy.

syntagm   In semiology, the relations between the chosen signs in a text or image. For text, syntagmatic relations are temporal or linear. For images, the syntagmatic relations are spatial.

talk/text as occasioned   In discourse analysis, the basic point that all talk and text are designed for specific contexts.

theory building   in computer-assisted text analysis, the comparison of coded text segments by the means of interpretive analysis in order to develop a complex network of general concepts, categories or types.

thick description   a marker of good practice of qualitative research. Research is often reported with detailed descriptions of situations, events and experiences as revealed in interviews, observations or documents making extensive use of verbatim citations. This increases the relevance of the evidence, and fosters the confidence of the audience in the data.

time codes   on videos, the seconds, minutes and hours of real-time registering as it passes.

topic   conversation analysts question the idea of a single discourse topic, what the talk is about, since different participants may be pursuing different topics. But they can show how participants display the relevance (or irrelevance) of their current contribution to what they take to be the topic.

topic guide   A set of broad questions/themes based on the research aims and objectives and used to structure the conversation in the course of an interview.

total musical event   A conception of music that goes beyond the mere sound event, but includes the behaviour and experience of the musician, those of the audience, the situation in which the music is played, and the discourse about music among the participants.

trajectories, individual and collective The analysis of narrative interviews, in particular in biographical enquiries, reconstructs through a series of analytic steps the individual and collective career trajectories of events and experiences. Through the systematic comparison of individual narratives the analyst typifies collective experiences with characteristic transitions and event sequences.

translation each step in the empirical analysis involves translation of the material from one context to another.

transparency A criterion of good practice in qualitative research. The selection of the data, the time and location of the collection, and the procedures of analysis should be sufficiently documented so that they can be imitated. It fosters public confidence in the data.

triangulation A criterion of good practice in qualitative research using several methods or conceptualizations on the same problem. This often leads to contradictory evidence which reflects back on the research process. The resolution of these contradictions needs to be documented.

turn in conversations, all of a participant's talk between that of the previous speaker and that of the next. This, rather than the clause, is the basic unit of conversation analysis. It is equivalent to an utterance, but emphasizes the way that utterance is situated within interaction.

validity A quality indicator of quantitative social research. An instrument measures the phenomenon that it is constructed to measure. For example, for a test that claims to measure 'intelligence' evidence is required showing that it does as is claimed. There are various types of validity: concurrent, predictive, construct and face validity.

video evidence the sound and image quality as evidential variables; the angle of recording as possibly involving misrepresentation or bias.

video/photo feedback using a video or photographic image to stimulate informants to comment on images, and thus either explain what is going on, or assist elicitation of memories, opinions or value-laden comments.

visual data as indicators of collective psychological dispositions A film, a TV commercial, a popular painting, a famous photograph may have general resonance for large numbers of people. They may tell us something about their tastes, desires, fantasies or opinions.

visual records Any image which conveys data about a past state of the world can be treated as record. These might include printouts, seismic recordings, photographs of buildings, landscapes, identification photos for passports or employment records.

warrant in argumentation, a premise consisting of reasons, guarantees or rules used to assert that the data are legitimately utilized to support the claim.

word-association task variant of open questions that asks respondents to write down any words they associate with the target object.

Index

Page references followed by an asterisk (*) refer to entries in the glossary.